T0246273

# HEAVEN
# and
# EARTH

**Volume 3: Torah, Chagim, Special Days**

# Yerucham Reich (Raymond Reich, MD)

# HEAVEN and EARTH

## A Real-World View of Jewish Life through the *Parashah* and the Holidays

## Volume 3: Torah, Chagim, Special Days

אשר בך ירחם

gefen
publishing house
בית הוצאה לאור גפן
JERUSALEM ◆ NEW YORK
Est. 1981

Cover Design: Azi Creative Visuals LLC
Typesetting: http://www.optumetech.com

ISBN: 978-965-7801-27-7

135798642

c/o Baker & Taylor Publisher Services
30 Amberwood Parkway
Ashland, Ohio 44805
516-593-1234
orders@gefenpublishing.com

Gefen Publishing House Ltd.
6 Hatzvi Street
Jerusalem 9438614, Israel
972-2-538-0247
orders@gefenpublishing.com

www.gefenpublishing.com

Printed in Israel

Library of Congress Control Number: 2023914447

# הרב משה הלוי פלוטשאק
## ק"ק שערי תורה בברוקלין נ.י.

אהובינו חביבי ועד ורחמינו ראש... תלמיד... חכמים מוהרה"ק... צדיק וחסיד ועניו

ראשיתם תורתך חיים... והוא הגאון... כל... ימ-הק

מתקן האזהרואים... הגה הגרא... צדיקי סוחר ואיש... גאון תורה... מלאך

ספרו המפורסם... מתחת כון... פעה ראש וראשון... כל הלכה. ואתחנו דבגוה הה

... אין פוק... דין ההלכה נשאת... על... רבנו... ספרינו הקדשים...

ואני... חורג... ורחשי'ות... הגברא כהק... מצאוויתך... הקר פרס יוסף צה"ה

... עולנא חדשה הרי... כמה וכמה... ראשונינו... כהמלא"ך והרמב"ן

כללם... וזוד... כולם... האזמ... רמבנים... מוהק...

...הקר יריב... הקר... קרן... כולו... מאתק... רוסא ...

... כאצא... ...

הה' הרתן... הרה' הק' ר' יהודה... הק"ק... על... ...

וקהת... כידו... על ... החסיד של ... ...

והנה... ...

...

...

כה דברי ... החביבו כלבבה
משה הלוי פלוטשאק

# הרב אביגדור בורשטיין

## רב בית הכנסת רננים ירושלים

בס"ד, יום השישי לסדר עלה נעלה התשע"ח

הנה באתי בקצירת האומר לברך את רעי וידידי, כאח לי, הרב החסיד ר' ירוחם ברוך רייך שליט"א ביום שמחת לבו ולבנו -אנו לרגל הוצאת ספרו היקר והחשוב *Heaven and Earth* ואכן, יאה השם למחברו , סולם מוצב ארצה וראשו מגיע השמימה. טוב עין הוא יבורך, ומטיב עינים כרופא מומחה יתברך בכפלים.

שנים רבות הקדיש המחבר להעלות על הכתב מאשר רחש לבו הטהור בדברי תורה וחכמה, דרך ארץ ומוסר, סיפורים מרגשים המחברים בין ארץ ושמים, העושים את התורה הקדושה לתורת חיים. בעין בוחנת, בלב הומה ובתבונת הדעת הצליח הרב המחבר לשזור ולארוג מסכת נפלאה של דברי תורה על פרשיות השבוע, חגים ומועדים ומה שביניהם.

זכיתי להמנות עם ידידיו של המחבר, להוקיר מידותיו ויראת השמים שהיא אוצרו, להתפעל ממסכת דרך ארץ שהנחיל למשפחתו ולסביבתו יחד עם רעיתו החשובה שרה מנב"ת. כל אלו ויותר באים לידי ביטוי בספרו רב האיכות. מבין קפלי הספר הכתוב בחן ובחכמת לבב בוקעת האמונה כי "לך שמים, אף לך ארץ".

והנני לברכו שיזכה לראות בטוב ירושלים, להגדיל תורה ולהאדירה, שיפוצו מעיינותיו החוצה מתוך בריאות הגוף וחדוות הנפש יחד עם רעייתו וכל משפחתו.

אשרנו שזכינו!

בהוקרה מרובה ובידידות עוז

*אביגדור בורשטיין*

הרב אביגדור בורשטיין
ירושלים ת"ו

**RABBI DR. TZVI HERSH WEINREB**

*Executive Vice President, Emeritus*

**212.613.8264** *tel*
**212.613.0635** *fax*
**execthw@ou.org** *email*

ELEVEN BROADWAY | NEW YORK, NY 10004-1303
212.563.4000 | info@ou.org | www.ou.org

In times gone by, books written on the weekly Torah portions were limited either to textual commentary, *pshat*, or to stimulating novel interpretations of a phrase or verse, *drash* or a *gut vort*. Often, these books were collections of rabbinic sermons, delivered for specific audiences over long periods of time.

A new trend has developed, however, and it has become increasingly popular. This trend has come about as a response to an urgent need in the Jewish community. I refer to the need to make the *parashah* relevant to the daily lives of the reader.

The book before you, *Heaven and Earth*, is an example of this trend. Its major feature is its remarkable ability to address "real life" contemporary issues from the perspective of traditional texts and commentaries.

The book's subtitle says it all: *A Real-World View of Jewish Life through the Parashah and the Holidays.* The author, Dr. Raymond (Yerucham) Reich, is a prestigious physician whose "real world" credentials are impeccable. His professional training and experience combine with his humanity and erudition to form the context for his writing.

The author is thoroughly familiar with contemporary Jewish culture, its problems, challenges, and very real successes. He draws from his personal experience and from the experiences of his family and friends. There is a wealth of material here about Jewish history, particularly about the Holocaust era and the American Jewish experience. It is apparent that he comes from a pious background and that he has incorporated that piety into his very soul. *Yiras Shamayim*, fear of heaven, is to be found on every page, as is *ahavas Yisrael*, love and respect for every Jew.

*Heaven and Earth* is both inspiring and instructive. It is inspiring because it delivers a practical spiritual message to the reader. It is instructive not only because of its impressive scholarly content, but because of the historical, scientific, and cultural information that it conveys. The author occasionally draws upon his medical expertise, but also introduces us to men such as Alexander Rubowitz, a long-forgotten hero who deserves to be remembered.

This book will lend itself to multiple uses. The reader may peruse it for his or her own edification. The teacher can use it in the classroom. It will be a wonderful basis for talk at the Shabbos table, particularly if that table is graced by individuals of diverse backgrounds.

This is not just another book on the *parashah*. This is a book to which one can turn as a "workbook" for the integration of day-to-day routine with authentic and uplifting religious teachings.

I especially recommend this book to the many who struggle with "real world" challenges and need an intelligent but practical framework within which to deal with them.

As a fellow author of a book on the weekly *parashah*, I congratulate Dr. Reich for his contribution to the growing literature of edifying and intellectually satisfying English language Torah works.

Tzvi Hersh Weinreb
Jerusalem, Israel
July 4, 2018

*Founded in 1898 as the Union of Orthodox Jewish Congregations of America*
איחוד קהילות האורתודוקסים באמריקה

# הרב אברהם חיים פייער

## Rabbi Avrohom Chaim Feuer

# שערי חסד ירושלים

A breath of fresh air! Those are the words that rise in my heart when I read the lines of this masterpiece, *Heaven and Earth*, authored by my old friend, Dr. Yerucham Reich, who blends the roles of a serious *ben Torah* and an accomplished eye doctor who trained his vision to see Hashem's world through "Torah spectacles."

Somehow every line of this splendid *sefer* refreshes my soul and fills it with a new appreciation for the glory of God and the majesty of His creation. This work speaks for itself. Just open it and read any section, and you will find your mind filled with original insights and a yearning to delve even deeper.

*Yasher koach*, Reb Yerucham!

Rabbi Avrohom Chaim Feuer
Shaarei Chesed, Yerushalayim
July 2018

Rabbi Yehudah Yonah Rubinstein
Inwood, NY

It is interesting that Dr Yerucham (Raymond) Reich chose to call his book, "Heaven and Earth". Open it and start reading and you will soon find that he offers profound insights into both.

As he steers you towards an intriguing or exciting Torah idea, he uses his knowledge of science and human nature to set the stage for a Jewish concept which unfailingly pleases and delights.

He may introduce you to the intricacies of the structure of the Human eye. He may invite you to use your eye to look up at a cluster of stars in the constellation called Taurus and then see those wonders mirrored in the pages of the Chumash.

But don't think that this author is offering his readers heavy intellectual material that you will have to push yourself to read. Dr Reich knows precisely how to inject fascinating stories to bring his chapters to life. He also knows how to use his well known sense of humor to complement his Torah wisdom (wait until you read about the confrontation between the Rabbi and the Goat and you'll see for yourself).

In short he has penned a charming book that will enhance your understanding of the Torah's weekly Parshas as well as the Yomim Tovim. It is also guaranteed to delight the guests at your Shabbos table.

I have to admit that Dr Reich and I have been close friends for a long time. That of course would have to put my role as an unbiased voice attesting to the quality and value of his book somewhat in doubt.

But I am going to insist nevertheless that this is a really excellent work. I am also able to state that if this level of Torah Scholarship can be combined so seamlessly with insights into human nature and science as it has been here, then "Heaven and Earth" will delight you, as it did me.

Rabbi Y Y Rubinstein, Inwood, New York, 11096 yy@rabbiyy.com

# Contents

# Preface

I was supposed to be a Palestinian.

Until fairly recent times, the term *Palestinian* typically referred to the Jews who lived in this land before *hakamas hamedinah*. The Arab residents, town dwellers, farmers, and nomads were "Arabs." Sure, they were in Palestine, and they might have also been referred to as "Palestinian Arabs," but the word *Palestinian* usually meant a Jew.

My parents decided that I would be a Palestinian – they hoped an Israeli – even before I was conceived.

It didn't turn out that way.

The same God Who saved them from murder in the Holocaust – from the Gestapo; from likely death by freezing, starvation, typhus and other diseases; from slave labor and imprisonment; from murder by Poles of returning Jews; Who got them somehow across many hostile guarded borders until they reached the safety of the American zone in Berlin – decided otherwise for me.

They sat in the DP camp, signed up to go to Eretz Yisrael, and waited. The British occupying power in the land had other ideas. Jews were not welcome. And so they waited, with no clear prospect to go anywhere. Even for America, they would have to wait. Many did, languishing in the camps for years.

My mother, *a"h*, whose yahrzeit is this week, was a very clever person, with a good eye and a sharp instinct – a not-uncommon trait among those who managed to survive. But she stood out in that regard.

The American commandant of the camp, Harold Fishbein, struck her as somehow familiar. She asked him if he was from Reishe (Rzeszow), my father's hometown. Apparently annoyed at the question, he responded, "Lady, I'm from Chicago!" and stalked off.

The next day, he approached her and asked how she knew he was, in fact, born in Reishe and brought as a year-old baby to Chicago. Well, if she could fool the Gestapo into thinking she was someone she was not, which she did, this guy was no match for her.

She had lived in Reishe for just a year and a half, after marrying my father, and that had been seven years previously. But she had casually known a family there whom the commandant, she thought, resembled, and she concluded that he was a relative. He was.

He was so impressed that he listed my parents as his relatives; as the relatives of an American officer and camp commandant, they got an early visa to America. And so I was conceived and born in America, raised and educated in America, with an American mindset, a factor that permeates my writing.

I think it likely that everyone in Israel who came from America knows exactly what I mean.

I am both thoroughly American and Jewish in my thinking, the son of Polish Jews from Galitzia, who were raised in Chassidic homes, who survived the Holocaust and built new lives in that blessed land, America. They did not make it to Palestine, they did not become Israelis, but they loved this land, this Eretz Yisrael, certainly as much as – and spiritually more than – they loved and appreciated (and they very much did) the land that took them in, gave them refuge, and allowed them to build, in freedom, new lives in a place where they could raise their children without fear. And my brother and I grew up in an America where we could be fully and freely Jewish as well as fully American.

All these factors – my life as a Jew, as an American Jew, and certainly my life as a physician, as a husband and a father – formed the person and the mindset that resulted in this book, which is an extension of its two-volume predecessor. I did not, in fact, set out to write a book, and it wasn't originally written as a book. It is comprised of things I have thought about, written, and shared with family and community over the years. It was my children who urged me to let it be published, as a legacy to their own children and to anyone who might gain from it.

It is organized according to the *parashiyos* of the Torah and the *chagim* and certainly relates to and derives from the *parashiyos* and the *chagim*, but really it is a real-life, real-world view of our lives as Jews, as human beings, wherever we come from and wherever we live.

It is, I believe, independent-minded. It's not always entirely PC, it's sometimes a *bit* irreverent (in a decent kind of way), but it's quite real, and, I submit, quite true.

Particularly gratifying is that many readers of the first two volumes have told me that they are inspired by my words, that they recognize the important truths therein, and – I really love and appreciate this – that they read from the book out loud to the family at the Friday-night Shabbos table. What could be better for an unconventional scribbler to hear?

And so, dear reader, thank you for taking the plunge and joining me. I pray that we have a long and spiritually uplifting way to go together.

*Yerucham Baruch Reich*
*26 Menachem Av 5782*
*Yerushalayim Ir Hakodesh*

# ספר בראשית

# Bereishis

## Nishmas Chaim: Assessing a Soul

How do you love someone who acts badly? Not your child, not a close relative gone astray, but a stranger, another person, another Jew. How do you love another person, another Jew, whom you do not know at all? Maybe he's not a good person, maybe he's a sinner – you don't even know that. Or maybe it's harder still because you *do* know him or her.

Chapter 32 of *Sefer Tanya*, famously referred to as the chapter of *lev*, the heart (לב = ל"ב = 32), helps us understand that a major hindrance to loving another person, another *neshamah*, is the corporeal burden that our *neshamos* must carry in order to exist in this world, a heavy shell by its very nature prone to decadence, sometimes severe rot. The *nefesh habehamis* covers and hides the divine soul that the Creator infused into us at creation, a part of Him, *k'v'yachol*, within each one of us. Stripping away that burden, that impediment, makes it possible to love another *neshamah* as we do our own – *v'ahavta l'reacha ka'mocha* – for we are all equal in this regard. We are all part of the same divine Source; we have no way of judging, at this level, the greatness of any one *neshamah* relative to another, even as we can strive for spiritual excellence by minimizing and downplaying the physical through dedication to Torah and mitzvos.

God breathed life into Man in a way that was fundamentally different from the way life was conferred on the animal world. The life humans were given is also by its nature fundamentally different from animal life.

Each species was fashioned in the way it, by its nature, would want to be fashioned: *l'daatam* (see *Chulin* 60a, *Rosh Hashanah* 11a). Rashi explains that each entity "agreed" to be created according to the way it wanted its nature to be. Not so man: *al korchacho ata notzar* (*Avos* 4):

> Rabbi Elazar Hakapor says: There is a reckoning for everything; let your *yetzer hara* not fool you into thinking that the grave will be an escape for you [from

3

your bad deeds], for not by your will [whether you like it or not, whether you
agree or not] were you created, not by your will were you born, not by your will
do you live, whether you agree or not you will die, and whether you agree or not
you will have to give an account of your life before Melech Malchei Hamelachim,
Hakadosh Baruch Hu.

Man was created the way God decided, without, *k'v'yachol*, "consultation": the
human being exists and acts not by instinct but by reason and free will. The other
species are described as having sprung from the seas or the earth. Man was fashioned by God utilizing dust from the earth and then infusing him with a Godly
soul (see Avraham Korman's *Habriah v'Hamabul*).

And so Rav Korman, citing the Gemara (*Eruvin* 13b) in which Beis Hillel and
Beis Shammai debate for two and a half years whether it is better that man was created or whether it would have been better for him not to have been created, notes
how odd it is that the conclusion – *noach lo l'adam she'lo nivra*, it would have been
better or *easier* for man if he had not been created – seems to be a complaint against
God for creating us. Philosophers of other nations have contemplated this existential
question as well. Chazal are telling us, says Korman, that this is a reflection of the
reality that we are not here by choice but by obligation, as described in *Avos*, and
once here, we should utilize this life to do God's will and to earn merit before Him.

God has not revealed to us His purpose in creation. But He has made it quite
clear to us that it is entirely for the good, we are blessed to have this opportunity,
and we would be fools to waste it. God put us here. Now it is up to us to use the
powers He breathed into us at creation to strive for that good.

And so we live our lives, hopefully directed for the good. Some of us achieve
the status of tzaddik. We all start out with an equal bit of Godliness within us, but
then we are strapped with baggage, some of which comes naturally to a given
individual and some of which is one's own making. Each of us must strive to make
as little of that baggage as we can, even as that task may not be equally challenging
or difficult for everybody. But we do know that everyone can. And clearly, some
people do it so well that they stand out, above and beyond most others, achieving
an exalted spiritual status while yet in this world.

And we also know, or should know, that only God Almighty Himself knows
what is inside every person. Only He knows our hearts, and only He knows the
full truth about anyone. Society sometimes labels individuals as great or otherwise, and this is natural. It can be quite obvious. But we should not, as individuals
or as a society, arrogate unto ourselves judgments about individuals concerning
matters that are known only to God.

And so it was with some amused distaste that I noted again this year (they've done it in the past and, no surprise, totally blew off my comments to them – after all, I'm not a big rabbi or a member of the to-be-taken-seriously-in-matters-of-religion club) that a popular English-language Orthodox Jewish publication (not the *Jewish Press!*) published its year-end tribute to prominent people in the Torah world who passed on during the year.

About twenty or twenty-five names, some with pictures, appeared tastefully laid out on the memorial page. The editors, the elect cognoscenti, it seems, have God Himself sitting on their shoulders, whispering in their ears, identifying exactly which of those departed were tzaddikim and which *were not*. Because the editors then proceeded to award the designation of tzaddik to some of the departed and to *withhold it* from others, thus clearly stating what was known to Heaven – and on earth, only to them. They must be such insiders with the Ribbono shel Olam that we shouldn't refer to them as insiders, but *Insiders*. They know to whom to award a זצ"ל, whom to give a ז"ל, and whom to apparently downgrade to an ע"ה (the women, by some coincidence). *All on the same page*, making the distinctions very obvious and obviously intentional.

It must not have occurred to them (despite it having been pointed out to them in the past), even if they *are* privy to God's mind, even if Heaven's judgment *was* indeed somehow, perhaps prophetically, revealed to them, that this is not a particularly nice thing to do. And they must have forgotten altogether that Moshe Rabbeinu, who I believe would undoubtedly *not* have done what they did, himself always gets just a plain ע"ה (just like the women on that memorial page). For Moshe Rabbeinu, *alav hashalom* is good enough. I think it should be good enough for everyone, all outstanding Jews, *listed together on the same page*.

Of course the editors meant no harm. But meaning no harm is not the same as doing no harm.

"All of Israel has a portion in *olam haba*, the world to come" (*Sanhedrin* 90a). But that doesn't mean that each person's reward is equal. That depends on how much each of us can negate the influence of the physical and the this-worldly that drag our pure, God-infused *neshamos* down. Different life stories have such different influences on people. The challenge for some is so much greater than for others. We mortals cannot know someone else's entire story. And while we admire some who certainly deserve to be admired and emulated, who deserve our most reverential respect and acclaim, it is only the Bochen Klayos, the Creator Himself, Who knows the true and full story, the true value of each individual. Who is a tzaddik, and *who is not*.

*Va'yitzer* [וייצר] *Hashem Elokim es ha'adam* (Bereishis 2:7) is spelled with two *yuds* (as opposed to the word's spelling when it describes the creation of other living beings, with one *yud*) to denote the special nature of Man, fashioned to be both physical and spiritual, of this world and of the next. *Afar min ha'adamah* (built from the dust of the earth); *va'yipach b'apav nishmas chaim* (He breathed into him the Godly spirit of life), a body derived from below and a spirit derived from Above; *va'yehi ha'adam l'nefesh chayah* (Man became a unique creation among all the rest): he reasons and he speaks (see Onkelos).

The power to reason and to speak, that unique infusion from God, not only sets us apart in creation, but places us in the unique position, based upon our words and our actions, of choosing whether to be primarily of the *adamah*, the dust of the earth, or *adameh l'Elyon*, aspiring to be like the Most High.

How very careful we have to be with our use of those powers God gave us, for with them we define who we are and where we are going. What we do, what we say, what we write, how we act, how we respect and act kindly to others, how scrupulous we are with what God wants of us, how we keep ourselves aware of His Presence, how we subordinate the corporeal part of our existence to the spiritual all allow us to use that very earthiness of which we are built to build, in turn, each of us, that staircase to Heaven that is the ultimate purpose for which we were given that earthiness, that we might, in the end, leave it behind, leave the *adamah* below, as we ascend and fulfill our purpose in creation, to be *adameh l'Elyon*.

*Parashas Bereishis 5780*

## A Special Kind of Noise: Music to Pray By

The mother held the small bundle close to her chest as she sat on the train nursing her child. Threadbare, ragged, alone with the child, she traveled from who knows where to who knows where. Where she had been, one could only guess, but such a guess, at such a time, in a general sense, would not have been much of a guess. It was shortly after World War II, in the ravaged hellhole that was Europe.

My mother was sitting nearby and witnessed this event. The conductor asked the woman where she was headed. Without hesitation, the suckling child disengaged its mouth from nursing and told the conductor which town they were headed for and where they had embarked. And then went back to its labors. The mother turned to my mom and told her that the child, small enough to fit in the small bundle at her breast, was actually four years old. He was her only surviving child. She had nothing else to feed him.

And how many children, in that terrible time, were there no longer among the living, no longer requiring feeding? And how many, the countless many, in that terrible time, were condemned by history never even to be conceived?

In these *parashiyos* of Bereishis and Noach, we read first of the world being populated, then violently depopulated, and then repopulated. High, high drama. The foundation and the continuation of the world. Our children.

And so I am thinking of the Yom Kippur davening, especially Ne'ilah. Especially this year. In our makeshift minyan in the rented smorgasbord room, the children, God bless them, had plenty of room to run around and call out away from the davening area, but that didn't stop them from running noisily through, up and down that spiral staircase, back and forth in the large hall immediately adjacent to where we were davening, by and large uninhibited in their joyous noise.

There we were, trying to concentrate on the most serious day of prayer there is – our one special chance for the year. The chazan needs to be heard; we really don't want to be distracted, *not this day*.

The proper place of small children who make noise in shul and distract the davening is an old question. Objectively, of course, they shouldn't be doing that. That's why many shuls have some kind of childcare provision: have them in shul, let them feel that it is their welcome place, but have it in some manner controlled, so the rest of us can concentrate, even hear. And yet…

And yet. If you listen hard enough, when we daven and there is no sound of children, the sound of that silence can be deafening. The sound of that silence is the sound of dying communities, of shuls in decline. The sound of that silence can be depressing, soul crushing. After Auschwitz, that silence is unbearable.

There is a reason that the chazan on Rosh Hashanah and Yom Kippur should be a man with children. He is best equipped – naturally, intellectually, emotionally, and instinctively – to cry out to the Ribbono shel Olam in the way we must on these holy days of judgment.

And as we stood there during Ne'ilah, during that *this is it* moment, when all hangs in the balance – everything in our lives, our very lives and those of our most beloved ones – there was, I think, no finer music to pray by, no cantorial chant and no choir, no communal singing, nothing more inspirational, no greater incentive, nothing more euphonic, nothing sweeter than the sweet, raucous cacophony of our children, by the grace of Almighty God our living children, the children Hashem has blessed us with, the children whom, in our personal and national hearts, all this high drama is really about.

*Shabbos Bereishis 5782*

# Noach

## Striving for the Light

I used to see him, a quiet elderly gentleman with a mustache, walking his little dog on Hampton Avenue in Manhattan Beach.

I learned that he was Judge Samuel Leibowitz, who many years before had distinguished himself with his brave and dedicated defense of the Scottsboro Boys in Alabama. Nine young black men had been convicted, in 1931, of the worst and most horrifying assault on two white women, upon whose testimony they were found guilty and eight of them sentenced to death. The ninth, aged thirteen, was sentenced to life in prison, because one single holdout on the jury would not agree to have a thirteen-year-old boy hanged.

The boys were innocent. The two women had been pressured by the police, driven by their own sociological imperative, to accuse them falsely of this capital crime. One of the women later recanted and revealed the truth.

A few years later, in Mississippi, a fourteen-year-old boy from Chicago was visiting relatives when he entered a grocery to buy some candy. The twenty-one-year-old white woman minding the store did not like how this uppity black boy did not show her proper deferential respect, and she told her husband a tale. The husband and his brother abducted young Emmett Till from his uncle's house, tortured and mutilated him, gouged out an eye, and finally shot him and threw him in the Tallahatchie River. At their trial, Carolyn Bryant testified that Emmett had physically assaulted her and touched her in a lewd way. The murderers were acquitted based on her testimony. A young white woman, deemed utterly credible by the biased jury, accused him of what, in those days and in that place, was a crime society thought a black man, even a boy of fourteen, *should be* lynched for. Years later, she recanted. It had never happened.

The sad and horrible fact is that the history of cruel and vicious men horribly violating women is as old as mankind itself. Untold numbers of women and girls have had their lives utterly ruined, if they survived at all, by utterly uncaring men for their own amusement or perverse pleasure, as an instrument of hatred or warfare, as a violent expression of utterly self-centered sociopathy. Some societies did not even look down upon it, in history, as long as this violence was visited upon an enemy. Thus, the mother of Sisera was hoping that her by then slain son's tardiness in returning from battle with Israel was because he and his men were busy with this type of endeavor, two or three Jewish women victims to each man.

It used to be a capital crime in most societies, and rightly so. With the breakdown of general morality in some Western societies, that is no longer the case, even if it is severely punished. And proving it can be extremely difficult, adding to the outrage.

But horrible as this crime is, history is also filled with cases of men falsely accused, whose lives were thereby upended and often ruined. In our own time, to mention just a few famous cases, the Tawana Brawley affair was a fabrication manipulated by race hustlers for political purposes ("It doesn't matter if it really happened, it *could* have happened!"), and then there was the Duke Lacrosse team story and many others. False accusations by nefarious women wielding the weapons of tender victimhood and political motivation cannot be justified by the fact that women have historically been so hurt. Believing all women's accusations just because they are women is not justice.

Our nation was roiled, indeed thrown into terrible turmoil, by the Kavanaugh affair in Washington. We cannot know exactly what happened thirty-six years earlier. But it is clear that while no one can prove anything, a large and loud segment of society apparently believes that it is no longer necessary to prove an accusation for it to be believed and acted upon, as long as the end result of that action serves a desired political purpose, regardless of the consequences or the damage caused to individuals, to society, to fairness, to the possibility of a normal functioning society.

On the first day of creation, God declared, "Let there be light!" and there was light. And God saw that the light was good, and He separated between the light and the darkness. It was so good, so clear, so true, so beyond the evildoers that would come to fill this world that God hid a major portion of that light away, reserved for the righteous tzaddikim of *asid lavo*, the distant future end of time. For this world as it is, He also made a distinction within the remaining light. There is the light of this world, truth and justice and goodness, and there is the darkness, where evil dwells. And between them there is dawn and there is twilight, where what is right cannot always be easily distinguished from what is more right, and what is wrong may not be readily distinguished from what is more wrong. Making those distinctions is a key challenge in life, and it is through God's word that we essay to gain the wisdom and the character to do so.

And it came to pass, after ten generations, that mankind filled the land, and the powerful did as they pleased and took what they pleased. *Va'timaleh ha'aretz chamas*: they stole, they took by force what was not theirs. They took women by force, against their will. They invented this most wicked and vile violence against the helpless. The moral destruction they brought to the world caused its physical destruction, for they had negated the very reason for creation – except for the presence of Noach and the possible redeeming future he represented. Noach (נח) found favor, *chen* (חן), in the eyes of God. And that saved the world.

How interesting that we are immediately introduced to the question of whether Noach's righteousness was very great or not so great. Perhaps that itself is part of the metaphor of the twilight and the dawn, when the light and the dark are mixed, and we need God's wisdom to teach us what is light and what is dark, what is right and what is wrong, and also to direct us and help us cope with the many ambiguities of life, when the way is not always so clear.

That God may have saved the whole world for a tzaddik who, although described as a *tzaddik tamim*, may have been such a tzaddik only relative to his wicked generation, who *may not* have been such a great tzaddik in absolute terms, is for us sinners a source of great hope.

God destroyed the world in the Flood for its lack of justice. The doers of violence and mayhem destroy the world. That violence and mayhem may take the form of physical violence – and it may, in fact, take the form of violence against truth, justice, and innocence.

And we have also come to understand that while the light and the darkness may be completely separate and distinct before God, as He separated them in creation, part of *Va'yehi erev, va'yehi boker* is that for us in this world, there is also the mix of the two that it is our mandate to distinguish, to work our way through, and that will always be a part of life – sometimes its greatest challenge.

The Creator knows what will be. *Hakol tzafuy.* Clearly His plan for Klal Yisrael required, for reasons known only to Him, a failed kingship to precede the eternal *malchus* of Beis David as an apparent condition for the rest of history to run its course, including the long picture of *asid lavo*. But what sort of king would that be, in order to make the rest happen as it was supposed to?

So let's note the language of Hashem's message to Shmuel Hanavi about King Shaul when he sinned regarding Amalek, which cost him his kingship. The word used, the concept expressed, is *not charatah* (חרטה), regret, but *nechamah* (נחמה), consolation. The Ribbono shel Olam consoled Himself, *k'v'yachol*, that at least the first king of Israel was the fine and noble if ultimately tragic Shaul, who stood *mi'shichmo va'maalah*, head and shoulders above everyone else in Israel. In the end, he failed, but he paved the way for Malchus Beis David.

And thus, Hashem says in Bereishis, as He decrees the coming *mabbul*, *not* that He has *charatah* over creation, but that He is consoled, using that word twice, in 6:6 and 6:7: *va'yinachem* (וינחם), *nichamti* (נחמתי). Chazal, in *Midrash Rabbah*, offer various explanations of the use of that word here, as to just what Hashem was consoling Himself, *k'v'yachol*, about. I offer an alternate explanation.

The Creator knows what will be. *Hakol tzafuy.* Clearly His plan for the world required, for reasons known only to Him, a failed world to precede the eternal one, apparently as a condition for the rest of history to run its course. There are midrashim that other worlds preceded ours as part of the process. And the world that ultimately made it also needed to start with a civilization that would fail and be destroyed. It was filled with violence, theft, and falsehood. But Hashem consoled Himself that even the world that needed to be destroyed also produced a Noach, a *tzaddik tamim*, who *matza chen b'Einei Hashem*, a very good man who resisted the evil that brought down everyone else in his generation, teaching us that we can indeed resist temptation, no matter how powerful, but with just enough ambiguity about him to teach us that as human beings, even if we think we are mired in twilight or outright darkness, the dawn beckons to us, it *is* reachable, and beyond it, the brightness of the day.

*Parashas Noach 5779*

# Swept Away

God could easily have made the wicked generation of the Flood disappear with a proverbial snap of His celestial fingers, so to speak. Why did He use a flood? Perhaps there was something about a flood that fit the spiritually therapeutic bill: that was what those sinners needed to mitigate, to remediate, to the extent possible, their sullied souls.

And that raises the companion question: Why did God make Noach build an ark rather than just have him magically hover over the waters or sit safely in a gap in the waters, together with his family and all those animals, until the floodwaters abated? The God Who would years later make the Yam Suf split, utterly against the laws of nature, surely could have done that. And why did He make Noach labor at building the ark himself, rather than just *poof!* making one appear. The

God Who had made all the world appear, *poof! just like that!* surely could have done that as well.

God is not capricious, even as He is not in any way limited. There is a divine purpose in everything He does, and a lesson for us, a message, in all that He reveals to us.

Rashi, paraphrasing *Midrash Tanchuma*, explains that Noach spent 120 years building his ark in full view of everyone. People would ask him what he was doing. He told them what was coming. They had their chance – God designed it that they should have their chance, that they be warned to mend their wicked ways and be saved – but they just scoffed and were doomed to be swept away.

God was sending them a message. Sometimes such a message can be open and obvious – such as Noach building the ark and telling those who asked why he was doing so. And sometimes – most often – the message may be quite loud but require significant insight to recognize for what it is.

I was a young boy when the Cuban missile crisis brought us to the brink of nuclear war. We functioned but felt potential doom hanging over us. I remember hesitating, on a particular fateful Shabbos afternoon, about walking over to visit with a friend, lest an atomic bomb hit us while I was apart from my parents. It was that fraught. And then my rebbe told us, "Cuba means *YOU*." It suddenly made sense of the whole thing. What was happening between the USA and Russia had a parallel and thoroughly interconnected encounter between the Ribbono shel Olam and Klal Yisrael. On one level, it was a message to the world; on another level, it was a message to the Jewish People that what *we* do affects the whole world as well as us.

God's messages are everywhere. But we need to be attuned to them in order to hear them.

Noach is credited with *chesed* for caring for and feeding all those animals during their time on the ark. He also spent 120 years building that ark, answering the questions of anyone who inquired, but we are not given to understand that he went one bit out of his way to actively reach out to all those people, all of humanity, to call out to them, to try to convince them to repent and to save themselves. They were swept away. And so he was a *tzaddik tamim b'dorosav*, but his *chesed* utterly pales next to that of Avraham, who, together with Sarah, spent his life completely dedicated to *chesed*, the antidote to what was ailing the world, bringing people *tachas kanfei haShechinah*. What we understand today as *chesed* was essentially their invention, their innovation in the world.

The building of the ark was a message that went unheeded. In the long and often tortured history of humanity, there have been many messages, some heeded and some not, often to the nations of the world, *but always to us.* Always.

In the terrible catastrophe of the COVID pandemic, so many were swept away, *lo aleinu*, and so many laid low. The story behind the story is the *chesed*, the sheer selfless heroism of so many health-care workers, nurses and doctors, aides and orderlies, EMTs and ambulance workers, support staff, respiratory therapists and nurse's aides, including pregnant women, people with families, with young children, who daily, for long hours, put their lives on the line virtually every minute of the day in the most frightening of circumstances, because their inherent kindness and their conscience, their sense of duty and their dedication didn't let them stop.

Like those soldiers who stormed the beaches at Normandy and at Iwo Jima, they marched into a hail of lethal microbes instead of bullets, better protected but still so vulnerable. The soldiers, brave as they were, had no choice. These heroes did have a choice, and they chose selfless *chesed*. It is inspiring and humbling that there are such people in the world, from every walk of life. May Hashem bless them and protect them.

*Chesed* takes many forms, and opportunities to practice *chesed* are many, various, and different for different people and circumstances in life. I would suggest that even as the pandemic was a loud message to us and to all of humanity that we improve our ways, each according to his situation in life, there was also a pointed message to us in the dedication of those heroes – an integral part of the message of COVID – about that divinely appreciated antidote to what ails the world, the redemptive and life-giving power of *chesed*.

*Parashas Noach 5781*

## Ana

Years ago, when I was just starting out in medical practice, an older colleague, a savvy fellow with lots of practical street smarts, advised me which demographic made the best employees and which were the most problematic, from a management point of view. I won't go into specifics, but I understood that while there are all types of individuals, even within specific groups, even so, there are definitely general characteristics of groups that are identifiable as common to the group at large. Common traits, often predictable.

There is no question that individual variations aside, some nations or sociological groups are noted for resistance to imposed regimentation (*don't tread on me; live free or die*), and others, such as the Germans, notoriously crave it.

It is well documented in Scripture and in later history that our ancestors in the *midbar* and their descendants were not easy customers. They drove Moshe – and later other leaders and prophets – "crazy" with their stubborn recalcitrance. They didn't (and many of us today don't) like to be told what to do. (*No! I know better than you!* Recognize that attitude?)

I once hired a fellow from a certain demographic well known to us to do a specific project at the exterior of my house. The project was well researched, professionally advised, well reasoned, and carefully laid out for him. He just needed to do what I asked of him. I mentioned to a friend of that same background that I hired this fellow, whom he did not know, to do such and such. My friend predicted, exactly correctly, that the worker/contractor would tell me I'm crazy, I have it all wrong, he knows better how it should be done. I told him he will do it my way or no way. With no choice and with me standing over him, he did it my way, he did it well, and it was perfect (*phew!*).

Sometimes patients (usually not patients at random but quite typically people we identify with) think they know better than the doctor how to manage their cases. That can, in some instances, be to some degree true, and listening carefully to the patient is critical, but in general, when people try to manage the doctor, usually based on their insufficient knowledge but abundant attitude, it doesn't go well.

And so there is a long history of our people, precious as they are, having a tendency to be difficult at times. No secret. *Am k'shei oref* is a double-edged sword. That stubbornness has gotten us into great trouble but also is a great strength, explaining, in part, why we are still here and why we continue to exist and to thrive as a nation.

And that same *am k'shei oref* who chafed so badly at being given direction was also the same nation that bought itself immortality with its utterly submissive *naaseh v'nishma*, with its utterly loyal *chesed, lechtech acharei bamidbar b'eretz lo zaruah* (Yirmiyahu 2:2), betting their lives and those of their children that the God of their fathers would keep them alive in the wilderness and deliver them to the Promised Land. This duality has been our bane and our salvation.

Two *yerei Shamayim* are having a conversation, as the story goes, and one remarks on the great power of *Ana*. Yes, the other replies, "*Ana Hashem, hoshia na!*" in Hallel is a powerfully stated declaration of faith and request, that request itself a declaration that He is the all-powerful Provider of life and its necessities.

We are all very well aware of that dramatic moment, repeated daily throughout Sukkos and Simchas Torah. The chazan calls out, "*Ana Hashem, hoshia na!*" and the congregation responds with its own thunderous call: Ribbono shel Olam! Save us! Ribbono shel Olam! Grant us success!

"It is," his friend replies, "but that's not what I had in mind. I was thinking of a different *Ana*, something even more powerful: '*Anah Hashem, ki ani avdecha!*' I am Your servant, Hashem. I am utterly yours."

*Ana.* Please. The use of that word in various places in Tanach, including several in Tehillim, is interesting, because it is spelled in different ways. *Ana* with an *aleph* (אנא) and with a *heh* (אנה). The first reference above is with an *aleph* and the second with a *heh*. *Ana* with an *aleph* means "please," a cry: Please, Hashem! *Anah* with a *heh* is most often, in these *pesukim*, also translated as "please." See, for example Artscroll's rendition of *Anah* (with a *heh*), *Hashem, ki ani avdecha,* based on classic *meforshim*: "Please, Hashem, for I am Your servant." So too in multiple other places. *Anah* with a *heh* is thus translated as "please," the same as *ana* with an *aleph*.

But it doesn't have to be. *Anah* with a *heh* is also "Where to?" When Reuven returned to the pit where his brothers had cast Yosef and found him gone, he lamented, "*V'ani anah ani ba*" – *anah* with a *heh*: *To where* will I flee from my father's sorrow? What will become of me?

When King Chizkiyahu is told by the prophet Yeshayahu that he is about to die (in his thirties), he pours out his heart to God. *Anah, Hashem*, he cries out, remember that I have walked faithfully and wholeheartedly before You! *Anah* with a *heh*. *Metzudas Tzion* and others: This means "Please." Rashi: It means "Where?" Where is Your mercy?

So let's revisit "*Anah, Hashem, ki ani avdecha; ani avdecha ben amosecha; pitachta l'moserai*" (I beseech You, Hashem, for I am Your servant; I am Your servant the son of Your handmaid; You have loosed my bonds; Tehillim 116:16).

Hashem! I am Your servant! But not just like any servant. A person who is captured and enslaved will serve his master because he has to, but he dreams of freedom and escape. He does what he has to do to get by. Someone who was born into a life of service, the child of those in perpetual service, knows no other life and seeks no other life. Service is their fulfillment. *I am Your servant, the child of Your servant.* I am utterly at Your service. *Pitachta l'moserai:* Serving You *unshackles* me, it frees me. Serving You, free from any distraction of concentration, is my ultimate fulfillment. (There is no freer person than someone who binds himself to the halachah.)

And so, *Anah, Hashem!* Ribbono shel Olam, where to? Where do You want me to go in life? What do You want me to do? I am yours! I am utterly Yours. And in this, my soul finds its freedom.

We are a nation of seekers. In our souls, we are driven. In our relationship with our God, we look to Him to lead us where we need to go in life. *Ana.* But we live in an age when, sadly, so many of our brothers and sisters are lost, at the far fringes of Jewishness, and some, it seems, even beyond that. And yet, there is something, always, lurking within. Chazal tell us that "*Afilu reikanin she'bahen melei'im mitzvos k'rimon*" (*Berachos* 57a). A Jew who appears to be empty of Yiddishkeit may, in fact, be as filled with mitzvos and goodness – or the capacity, the predilection, the potential, the inner desire, for mitzvos and goodness – as a pomegranate is with seeds.

On Simchas Torah, many shuls have visits from remotely marginal Jews. Often it is because they want their children to experience *something* somehow connected with Judaism. Typically, their day-to-day lives have very little if anything at all to do with Yiddishkeit – at least on the surface. Below the surface, sadly sometimes far below, in a Jew, there is *something*. That something, held in check usually by ignorance and faulty upbringing, is often manifest in the drive to goodness of the spirit. And then sometimes something rushes to the surface.

In our shul on Simchas Torah, I saw a young man come in with two women. Typical Russian Jews who had not been fortunate enough, as many have been, to find their way back. But there they were, impassive, looking. Someone walked over with a Torah and offered it to the man to hold and to dance with.

He seemed electrified. He turned to the two women, who had not noticed, and walked over toward them proudly with the Torah in his arms. Seeing him thus, they *ran* toward him, stretched out their arms, and touched the Torah to kiss it. Their instant reaction was no less electric than his. This was so obvious that it stopped me in my tracks.

*Ana*. Ribbono shel Olam, lead us. Guide us, direct us. At whatever level we are, lost or found, near or far, our souls are connected with You, and like the servant who is the child of a servant, raised in service, we want only to be Yours, to be freed of the shackles of the distracting mundane world and mundane mindset, so that we can follow You, even if we don't even know it yet.

For we are Your children, Ribbono shel Olam. Don't give up on us. Lead us, even those of us who are the most remote, or who *seem* to be. For even the *reikanin she'bahen*, the "empty ones" of Klal Yisrael, even those on the far reaches, are as filled with mitzvos and with goodness as a pomegranate is with seeds.

*Parashas Noach 5782*

# Lech Lecha

## Battling the Mosquito

My mother told me, when I was a young boy, about a letter she saw when she was herself a young girl in Kolbesov. Her neighbor received it from her son, who was, in the early part of the twentieth century, a *chalutz* in Eretz Yisrael.

He was somewhere in a desolate rural area, draining swamps and trying to bring the land back to life. His own life – and that of his fellow pioneers – was harsh, hard, backbreaking, physically miserable, and fraught with danger. Even more dangerous and enervating than the threat from hostile Arabs was the incessant attack from the unrelenting mosquitos, who gave them no respite, and whose mission, it seemed, was not just to buzz and bite without letup, but to spread malaria, from which all too many did not recover.

My mother remembered, all those years later, how he expressed himself. It's so hard, he said, so miserable, that even the mosquitos who tormented them no doubt pitied their victims even as they bit them.

But even so, he would not give it up for anything. He knew, and his colleagues knew, what they were accomplishing. The joy of that, bolstered by the camaraderie in their holy endeavor, made it all worthwhile.

The Land of Israel is today a beautiful garden, lush and lovely and fruitful and truly *eretz chemdah*, a most desirable and bountiful land. It is easy, today, to forget what it took, in human terms, in labor and sweat, in danger and disease, in self-sacrifice and privation, to make it happen. It could not have happened without divine help, and it needed, as well, the human element willing to do it. Arabs, in their hostility, watched them and thought they were crazy, a fair target. The flowering of the land under Jewish hands, after so many years of absence, is truly miraculous, as is the fortitude and determination of those who put their lives into it.

They had a precedent. Thirty-five hundred years before, their forefather, Avraham, heard the divine call to stake out a presence in what was to become the Land of Israel. He led a somewhat nomadic existence there, traveling up and down the land, back and forth, establishing that presence. The locals, in their hostility, watched him and thought he was crazy.

The Midrash presents it this way: Canaanites saw Avram and declared, "Look at that crazy old man! He's walking all over the land like a crazy person!" They gnashed their teeth, they muttered and sputtered; they swore, "If I can, I'll kill him!" Of course, they could not harm him, and eight generations later (hinted at by "haCanaani az ba'aretz," with the word az [אז], "then," having a *gematria* of 8) , Avraham's descendants returned to claim the land that God had granted them and their forebear had prepared for them. Avraham was the trailblazer.

In every walk of life, in every human accomplishment, we stand on the shoulders of those who came before us and prepared the way. This is so commonly forgotten, often even derisively dismissed. Every generation thinks *it* discovered America, so to speak.

In our lives as Jews, we are taught this, but we don't always remember it or recognize it in virtually every sphere of our existence. Our sacred texts, we are certainly aware, have been painstakingly transmitted to us through all the generations, studied and analyzed, explicated, and applied to the new situations of life every step of the way. Beyond that, it is our very existence, our way of life that owes its continued presence on this Earth, in human terms, to the incomparable, unshakable dedication and sacrifice of all the generations that have come before, in the face of sometimes unbearable hardship.

That hardship may have been in the form of a teeth-gnashing Canaanite, an Egyptian slavemaster, idolaters, a Greek, a Hellenist or even turncoat Jews, a Roman, a churchman, a Crusader, a Cossack, hostile neighbors, Nazis and Communists, marauding Arabs, poverty and hunger, heat and thirst, the defeatism of helplessness and hopelessness – even the unrelenting, incessant, enervating bite of a mosquito.

To the dedicated heroes who came before us, from Avraham Ha'ivri, who started it all, to his successors, the stubborn stalwarts of every generation; to those who struggled, in every generation, to transmit the holy legacy of their forebears; to those who fight *milchemes haTorah*; to those who stand bravely in the defense of our Holy Land and its people; to those who fought the mosquitos and the swamps and built the land that is today so lush and beautiful; to those who fought the wilderness of America and built the Torah life we can live today, we owe everything – we owe the very essence and the strength of who we are, who we are so blessed to be.

*Parashas Lech Lecha 5781*

# Amar Rabbi Akiva

Amar Rabbi Akiva, Amar Rabbi Akiva, ashreichem Yisrael
*Amar Rabbi Akiva, Amar Rabbi Akiva, ashreichem Yisrael!*

Amar Rabbi Akiva, Amar Rabbi Akiva, ashreichem Yisrael
*Amar Rabbi Akiva, Amar Rabbi Akiva, ashreichem Yisrael!*

Ashreichem, ashreichem, ashreichem Yisrael
*Ashreichem, ashreichem, ashreichem Yisrael!*

Ashreichem, ashreichem, ashreichem Yisrael
*Ashreichem, ashreichem, ashreichem Yisrael!*

Lifnei Mi atem metaharim u'Mi metaher eschem
*Lifnei Mi atem metaharim u'Mi metaher eschem!*

Avichem she'ba'Shamayim, Avichem she'ba'Shamayim
*Avichem she'ba'Shamayim, Avichem she'ba'Shamayim!*

V'omer, v'omer Mikveh Yisrael Hashem
*V'omer, v'omer Mikveh Yisrael Hashem!*

Mah hamikveh metaher es hateme'im, af Hakadosh Baruch Hu metaher es Yisrael
*Mah hamikveh metaher es hateme'im, af Hakadosh Baruch Hu metaher es Yisrael!*

Ashreichem, ashreichem, ashreichem Yisrael
**Ashreichem, ashreichem, ashreichem Yisrael!**

If this song was not part of your growing up, sadly, you missed something foundational, intensely so. The song leader recites each line, and then the group thunder-
ously responds, with great fervor and growing excitement, voices reinforced by
movement of body and soul. I remember the picture of the young fellow, an older
teenager, who led the singing, when I was a much younger boy and first learning
it. Really, absorbing it. Feeling it. Overcome by it, as its meaning was translated,
by our souls, from words to utter identification with its meaning and its message.
It drove home, into the deepest place of our national identity, who we are, Whose
we are so blessed to be, and Who, by our heritage and by our choice, is ours. On

and on we sang, with growing fervor, identifying completely with the concepts, until we could finally sing no more. Into a kind of heavenly *mikveh* we plunged, immersing ourselves completely, giving ourselves over completely, identifying completely as God's beloved children.

It is from a *mishnah* in *Yoma* (8), a lesson from Rabbi Akiva, who knew much about suffering and difficulty, who traveled a long and painful road from ignorance to greatness and finally to martyrdom and immortality. A striver who struggled heroically his whole life to elevate his soul, to bind it to God, and to bring the rest of us with him on that journey, the fulfillment of our very purpose in this world, and to *appreciate the great privilege* that is ours in so doing.

No surprise that this is the same Rabbi Akiva who teaches (*Avos* 3:18) that beloved as man is to God that He created man in His image, even more so is it a gift that He gives man to *know* and thus appreciate this loving gift; that beloved as Yisrael is that Hashem considers us His children, even more so is it a gift that He gives us to *know* and thus appreciate this loving gift; that beloved as we are to God that he bestowed upon us the Torah, the greatest holy beauty and wisdom possible in this world, even more so is it a gift that he gives us to *know* and thus appreciate that the Torah He gave us is the greatest holy beauty and wisdom possible in this world.

This journey starts with a journey taken 3,759 years ago by our forefather Avraham, who separated himself from the rest of mankind, and in so doing, he separated us, as God told him "*Lech lecha*," and he went. His personal journey started years before when as a child he recognized and sought God, struggling from then, preparing himself for the call that transformed the world.

Avraham knew what he was getting us into. At the Bris bein Habesarim, he saw Krias Yam Suf and Matan Torah; he saw Gehinnom; he saw Bavel and Rome; he saw the glorious entry into the Land of Israel; and he saw exile after interminable exile. He saw the tzaddikim and the *chachamim*. He saw the Torah fulfilled, and he saw it foolishly set aside. He saw the greats. He saw Rabbi Akiva. He saw the struggles, and he saw the heights. He saw it all, and as exalted as it was – and is – it also filled him with dread. The price we pay for that rare, exalted, lofty status is a long and terrible fall should we falter, and falter we do. And he saw how great the gift was.

And Avraham Avinu saw his legacy lasting into forever; he saw Mashiach and his era; he saw his children, in an unbroken chain, clinging fiercely to God, come what may, as did Rabbi Akiva in good times and in terrible times, even in martyrdom, as did countless others throughout the generations. He saw and heard

Jewish children, in good times and in the face of all adversity, jumping up and down, singing at the tops of their voices, "*Ashreichem Yisrael! Lifnei Mi atem metaharim u'Mi metaher eschem! Avichem she'ba'Shamayim!! Ashreichem, ashreichem, ashreichem Yisrael!*"

*Parashas Lech Lecha 5782*

# Vayera

## What the World Needs

According to the Hal David/Burt Bacharach song, love is what the world needs now. Love for everyone. There's too little of it. From our own national perspective, in this context, "love" translates to what we call *chesed*, an expression of love and goodness, kindness and caring for our fellow human beings. The Creator makes it very clear, in Bereishis, that *each* human being, of every nationality, is created *b'tzelem Elokim,* in the image of God. He wants us to be aware of that (it can be easy to forget!). The history of the world, as described in Bereishis, tells us of an epoch in which immorality, meanness, thievery, and corruption reigned – *va'tishaches ha'aretz lifnei ha'Elokim va'timaleh ha'aretz chamas*. It was so lacking in love that it was utterly destroyed in the Flood. The Torah then tells us about how Avraham came along ten generations after that with the cure and revolutionized civilization, making the rest of history possible.

The world stands on three pillars, as we have been taught, and the Avos established them: Avraham epitomized *gemilus chesed,* Yitzchak represented *avodah (tefillah),* and Yaakov Torah. But the first, fundamental ingredient is the *middah* of *chesed,* without which the others could not in practicality exist. It's unlikely that *maamad Har Sinai* would have been possible had the people not already been spiritually prepared by a tradition of *chesed.* And in the end, we are told, while we as a nation cannot exist without Torah and *avodah,* it is *chesed* that will be our ticket to redemption. Of course, to our understanding, Torah, *avodah,* and *chesed* are all derived from the same Source and are intertwined with each other. But it begins and ends with *chesed.*

Much of Parashas Vayera is devoted to teaching us *chesed* and its power. From our perspective today, Avraham's *chesed* seems very laudable but not so rare. In fact, he grew up in a world that did not know *chesed,* certainly not as a way of life. He had no role models and no one to teach him. He was doing what he understood God wanted, but in human terms, Avraham *invented chesed.* What a great and kind person does today he does only because Avraham showed the way.

Three days after a painful and especially delicate operation, his *bris milah*, the ninety-nine-year-old Avraham sits at the opening of his tent, looking for travelers to host. God, wishing to spare him, has made the day unbearably hot, so that no one will venture out. Avraham is disappointed. His *chesed*, and that of Sarah, is not only to offer travelers food, drink, shade, and rest, but to engage them in such a way that they come to learn about God, to bring them *tachas kanfei haShechinah*, an ultimate *chesed*.

The *pesukim* are filled with expressions of *chesed*. He greets them and addresses them with the greatest of respect. He tells them that they are honoring him by accepting his hospitality. He *runs* to prepare their repast. Sarah *rushes* to bake bread for them. The guests are made to feel that their hosts really mean it, which they obviously do. They are serving God by serving their fellow man. When they leave, Avraham escorts them on their way.

And we know where they are going. To destroy Sedom v'Amora. The Torah tells us what God is thinking at this point. I should tell Avraham my plans for Sedom, Hashem says, because he will transmit tzedakah and *mishpat* to his children and future generations. He will teach them the power of tzedakah and *chesed*, to offset *din* in *mishpat*. Hashem knows that the loving Avraham will now pray to Him on behalf of the sinners of Sedom. Perhaps this is why He informs Avraham of His plan – so that Avraham will pray for them, despite who they are, as an expression of his *chesed*, thereby establishing this *middah* as a lasting legacy for his children.

That no one except for Lot and his daughters would survive is beside the point. The point is *chesed* and its power. The point is having Avraham "push" Hashem as hard as he dared, and then some, in order to help people. And *maaseh avos siman la'banim*, that is part of our legacy. That is what Hashem wants us to do as well. Hopefully bolstered by Torah and *avodah*, we must bring to bear the power of *chesed* and "push" the Ribbono shel Olam when we need to.

How big a role did Lot's *chesed* play in his being saved? It's true that in large measure, he was spared for Avraham's sake, but he did learn from Avraham; he did everything he could to shelter, host, and then save the travelers (the *malachim*). And, as *Bereishis Rabbah* teaches, Hashem appreciated and now rewarded Lot's *chesed* to Avraham, when he heard him tell Pharaoh that Sarah was his sister rather than his wife. He would have been rewarded nicely for telling Pharaoh the truth, but he protected them instead.

*Olam chesed yibaneh.* Our world begins with and is built upon *chesed*. But for Avraham's *middah* of *chesed*, which he implanted, along with his faith and dedication, in his future generations, *in us*, all the rest could not have followed. Without Torah and *avodah*, we are nothing and could not exist as a nation. Without *chesed*, without tzedakah, without kindness and caring, without empathy *and acting upon that empathy*, without self-sacrifice for our fellow man, we could not even have gotten started and could not have become Klal Yisrael. We would be unrecognizable. A Jew without *chesed*, we are taught, is someone with questionable *yichus* as a Jew.

And so permit me to close with another song with a great message. Written for the Christian world, it too is a direct legacy from Avraham Avinu, the *av hamon goyim*. The real source of its message is, of course, the Torah and the values all of mankind has learned from its teachings, its mandates, and from the example of our holy Avos and Imahos. How much more should we, the actual children of those forebears and the bearers of their eternal legacy, take it to heart and to practice.

The song, by Tommy Coley and Shorty Sullivan, posits that you can't claim to love God if you don't love your neighbor. If you gossip about him, if you have no mercy, if you don't help him when he is in need, then in fact you don't love your neighbor and you clearly don't love God.

*Parashas Vayera 5780*

# Akeidas Levi

Have you been to Italy? It's a pretty big country, a long boot extending south and east from the Alps into the Mediterranean. And it's got Sicily and Sardinia. It's, well, very Italian, top to bottom. Most people don't realize that Italy actually only became a country in 1861. In the decades prior to that, it was many different states: the Kingdom of Sardinia, Lombardy-Venetia, the Duchy of Parma, the Duchy of Modena, the Duchy of Lucca, the Grand Duchy of Tuscany, the Kingdom of the Two Sicilies, and not least, the Papal States, extending from Rome eastward and northward past Bologna toward Venice. The pope of the Roman Catholic Church was, in effect, the king of this latter country, which he ruled absolutely (to the dismay of liberals and many intellectuals in the realm).

Schoolchildren, when such things were still taught, learned that the heroes of Italian unification were the long-struggling Garibaldi, Mazzini, and Cavour. An argument can be made that the final catalyst for successful unfolding of the push for unification and the undoing of the Papal States was a six-year-old Jewish boy from Bologna, Edgardo Levi Mortara.

Momolo (Shlomo) Mortara was a middle-class shopkeeper who, with his wife Marianna, had seven children. On the night of June 23, 1858, the papal police entered their apartment and seized little Edgardo, under the orders of the local inquisitor upon the direction of papal authority. Edgardo, they told the horrified parents, had been baptized. Under Church law, he was a Christian and could not live with Jews, even his own parents.

Of course the Mortaras protested that their son had never been baptized, to no avail. Desperate efforts to clear up the obvious error were firmly and utterly rebuffed. Edgardo, weeping and screaming, was carried off under force of arms. He was quickly whisked off to Rome, where Pope Pius IX took a personal interest in him and in shielding him from his family and the Jewish community.

It later emerged that a sixteen-year-old girl who worked for the Mortaras, Anna Morisi, illiterate and morally debauched, had told a friend that she had sprinkled some water on the child and pronounced him baptized. The friend told her priest, who passed the information along, and Edgardo was seized. She could not have known the right words to say to baptize someone – a requisite for a valid baptism. She said that the corner grocer told her the words. He vociferously denied having done so.

The family struggled for years but could not extricate their son from the pope's grasp. This was far from the first time that such a horror occurred; it was a known and feared risk of life in that time and place. But this particular incident gained the attention of liberalizing forces in Italy, France, elsewhere in Europe, and even the United States. Protests, diplomatic efforts, appeals of various kinds, and legal action all fell on determinedly deaf ears. It was a major international scandal that played a role in undermining the legitimacy of the papal kingdom and the loss of Vatican control of all lands beyond the Vatican itself when Italy was finally unified under King Victor Emmanuel II.

The Mortaras and the Jewish nation never did succeed in recovering Edgardo. He lived his life as a Roman Catholic priest, dying in Belgium in 1940 at age eighty-eight.

Edgardo and so many other Jewish children like him were sacrificed on the altar of our tortured exile.

Avraham's ordeal was a test. Yitzchak survived it, as did his father, Avraham. But his mother Sarah did not. The Midrash in Vayera tells us that God does not test the wicked, only the righteous. Our people have been tested in every way, innumerable times. Sometimes the tested need to make a choice of actions, as did Avraham. And sometimes, all too often, the choice is one of faith, of remaining steadfast. *Va'yidom Aharon.*

Please God, oh, please, dear God, Father in Heaven! May we never be tested. May we be counted among the righteous, but, as Avraham begged the Ribbono shel Olam after the Akeidah, *no more tests!* We have already had innumerable *akeidos*, sacrifices beyond counting. Avraham and Yitzchak showed us the way – that it is possible in the face of anything to remain strong and hold fast, to cling to God and to be His, come what may.

We cannot know what "Akeidas Levi" – the ordeal of the Mortara family and their countless Jewish brethren in suffering – accomplished. But we can be sure that our Father in Heaven *yasim es dimoseinu b'nodo lihyos*, bringing us closer to that time when tests and *akeidos* are but a memory of the dim past as we sit safely and securely in God's loving embrace, when we are joyfully entirely His, even as He is ours.

*Parashas Vayera 5783*

# Chayei Sarah

## Married before God, Married for God

My maternal grandfather, Shloime Nussbaum, *a"h*, learned that he was engaged to be married when the Dzhikover Rebbe, the Ateres Yeshuah, told him that he was. It was fine with him, as the Rebbe had assured him and his parents that it was "*a gitte zach*" (a good thing). Indeed, it was. When the nineteen-year-old Shloime and the seventeen-year-old Brandel got married two years later, having met just once, it became a love match famous all over the region. They were devoted lovebirds. It was indeed *a gitte zach*. They went through good times and then the most terrible of times, but they survived together in utter love and devotion.

My mother and father, *a"h*, met and later married when my mother, who lived in the small town of Kolbesov, traveled to the relative metropolis of Reishe to do some shopping. While there, she needed to make a phone call. Attention, young'uns: believe it or not, there were no cell phones, not even unsmart cell phones, in 1937. Nor were there ready-access phone booths in that Polish "metropolis." But there was, in the old town square, the large wholesale commodities emporium of Pfeffer and Reich, owned by two brothers-in-law in the well-known and highly regarded Reich family. She entered and asked to use the phone. Shimon Reich graciously assented, of course. Eleven years and a Holocaust later, I appeared on the scene in their refuge in America as their second son. A more dedicated and devoted couple would be hard to find.

My mother was actually my *shadchan*. We knew the family, of course, as we had mutual *mechutonim*. Sue Hilsenrad was an excellent girl, and her parents were very fine people with good values that they inculcated in their children. My parents had nixed various other *shidduch* suggestions because those families either did not seem to have the right values or were too rich (a remarkably wise and dedicated stance for a poor family to take).

Now, here I will admit it: I did not have to be convinced, as I was quite aware of this girl, whom I had first seen (and assessed as absolutely remarkable) in a

God-sent blitz of insight when I happened to first lay eyes upon her when I was fifteen. Somehow, I understood, in that first moment, what she was. When they picked me up off the floor (so to speak), I filed it away for later on in life. I was, after all, a fifteen-year-old yeshiva boy and years away from such matters. But the time did come, thank God, and the rest is blessed history.

We don't know anything about how Avraham and Sarah got together to be married, although they were close relatives. What is clear is that they were the devoted couple who essentially introduced God into the consciousness of mankind, the first-generation creators of Klal Yisrael. The Torah tells us that she was very beautiful and that Avraham was well aware of it, even though their prime relationship was in building a holy world together.

We know more about how Yitzchak and Rivkah got together and how they too complemented each other in *kedushah* as, devoted to each other, they took Godliness and the development of Judaism to the next step. The Torah tells us here too that Rivkah was very beautiful, even as the main focus of their lives was spiritual, on a plane we cannot begin to understand. We also know that their son Yaakov, the distillate of the greatness of the Avos, loved his very beautiful wife Rachel passionately, even as he and his wives set their twelve holy sons, *shivtei Kah*, on the path to bring Klal Yisrael into actual existence, destined to encounter God at Sinai and to bind all of us with Him for all time.

Of course, the primary role of the Avos and the Imahos was spiritual, their level of purity and spirituality and holiness so great that only they could have accomplished the bringing of the Nation of Israel and the Torah into the world. But all this was based on actual marriages, which God designed to be the vehicle – a holy vehicle, if we are wise enough to make it so – to make the goodness and the accomplishments of human existence possible.

Goodness and kindness to each other – mutual support – are absolutely essential to make this work. But the Torah also makes sure to let us know that God also created, along with marriage, the blessing of marital love. It is the motor that drives the engine of accomplishment and building the world and the goodness possible in that world. It is a good, a necessary, a desirable thing. It is magical, and it is one of God's greatest gifts to mankind. It is *a gitte zach*. It is so powerful, in its goodness, that it is a necessary component in driving everything else.

And that is perhaps why, when the Torah describes the first encounter between Yitzchak and Rivkah, as she arrives from Aram Naharayim to become his wife, as she sees him davening in the field, as she sees him, this complete tzaddik, communing with the God she never encountered in her idol-worshipping father's home but Whom she already knew in her pure and holy heart, she is so overwhelmed, she is so smitten, she falls so utterly in devoted love, the Torah tells us not that she *descended* from her perch on the camel, but *va'tipol me'al hagamal*, she literally *fell* off (Bereishis 24:64). In that first look, she understood what Yitzchak was about, she understood what she was getting, she came to understand what her world-building role with him would be. And so they presumably picked her up off the floor (so to speak) and presented her to her *chasan*.

*And Yitzchak brought her to the tent of his mother Sarah, he married her and she became his wife, he loved her, and Yitzchak was comforted, in Rivkah, for the loss of his mother.*

And so, by the grace of God, our world was built.

*Parashas Chayei Sarah 5779*

## Yes to a No That Means No

The passing of Sarah Imenu also marks the apparent "passing of the baton" to Yitzchak. Avraham still lived for many years afterwards, but in the Torah, it's all about Yitzchak. He was Avraham's successor. He excelled in everything, especially in purity, piety, and prayer; with Rivkah alongside him, he brought the development of Klal Yisrael to the next step.

Avraham and Sarah's task, with Yitzchak, was to raise him to be perfect so that he could fulfill his role. In this, they were "lucky": he was. The age of the Avos is long over. But the truth is that every generation of Jews has the task to raise their children to be good Jews, who will carry on our faith and our peoplehood. But despite the best of intentions and even the best of efforts, the sad reality is that it doesn't always turn out that way. And even when it's good, it isn't always easy.

The age of the Avos is indeed long over. Yetzias Mitzrayim and Matan Torah were long ago. The prophets of Israel spoke their words millennia ago. But they are all still with us; the teachings of the Tannaim and the Amoraim can be heard today everywhere there are Jews who are Jewish, because we have a *mesorah*, an unbroken chain of witnessing and teaching and passing on, from parents to children and from teachers to students.

The *mesorah* – and the utter faith in its eternal truth that makes it all possible – can be discerned already as Yitzchak and Avraham walk along *together* to the Akeidah with a common purpose and equally determined. It was Avraham who received the commandment directly from God to bring Yitzchak as an *olah*. Yitzchak did not. And yet Yitzchak was as resolute in this as was his father: *Va'yelchu shneihem yachdav* (Bereishis 22:6). And in so doing, Yitzchak established the unbreakable strength of *mesorah*: Avraham was his father, his rebbe, and the *navi* of Hashem. For Yitzchak, it had the same strength as if he had heard it from God Himself. This very same strength of *mesorah* has perpetuated Am Yisrael, Toras Yisrael, and *daas Yisrael* until this day.

Hence, the heartbreak to the Jewish parent when a child, *lo aleinu*, drops out or teeters on the brink. Of course, we are infinitely far from the level of Yitzchak Avinu and cannot expect that of our children or of any of us. And we also realize that human nature is such that for many people, that feeling just does not seem to come naturally or easily, and that the life of the spirit is not smooth sailing for everyone, even with the best of upbringing. But that upbringing certainly makes a huge difference, usually the determining difference. Effort, dedication, self-sacrifice, setting a good example, *sincerity*, and wisdom in Jewish parenting are still no guarantee, but they go a very long way in nudging that elusive factor, *mazal*, in the right direction. It usually pays off very well indeed.

Good parenting has always been a major human challenge, but the stakes and the challenge are particularly great in the *chinuch* of Jewish generations. The *parashah* that describes the success of the first generational transition, from Avraham to Yitzchak, is accompanied by a *haftarah* that describes a tragic generational failure for a very great Jew, one of the greatest Jews of all time, David Hamelech himself, who had sons who, *nebech*, did not turn out at all as he wanted them to.

David's oldest sons, Amnon and then Avshalom, went very wrong and had their lives cut violently short. Kilav (also identified as Daniel) was apparently a very worthy person, but not up for becoming king, and he appears in fact to have died young as well. Along comes Adoniyah, and, while David is still alive, and although the succession was promised to Shlomo, he preens and boasts and declares that *he* will be king. He gets himself a royal chariot, a troop of honor guard horsemen, and fifty guys running before him wherever he goes (think of the political candidates these days who walk down the street with shouters going before them, calling out, "Ladies and gentlemen! [oops, it's no longer PC to use those terms!], Future Senator Aardvark! Senator Aardvark! Greet your future senator! Senator Aardvark!"). He set about having himself actually crowned and declared king of Israel.

The *navi* tells us several factors (aside from any inherent character flaws) that helped bring this about, that shaped his thinking. He was the oldest surviving son of David, he was really good-looking and knew it, he surrounded himself with powerful bad actors whose day had passed and who now sought to manipulate themselves back into power by stroking his ego and manipulating him, and, first and foremost, *his father had apparently never said no to him*. During his upbringing and beyond, David had never criticized any of his bad behavior. His sense of entitlement was boundless, and he had no training whatsoever in self-restraint. There was no real "no" in his upbringing. *V'lo atzavo aviv mi'yamav leimor, madua kachah asisa?* He was never denied anything, nor was he reprimanded or punished for anything. His father didn't want to make him sad.

We have all witnessed parenting where there is hardly ever a no, and even a no does not usually remain a no once the kid starts to whine. Some parents, it seems, are more afraid that the kid won't like them than they are of how such a kid will turn out.

There is no doubt that some kids are *so* difficult, and the challenge to parenting is so great and so baffling, *nebech*, that one cannot blame the parents. How does one know what to do and where to draw a line? *Lo aleinu*, that challenge is terrible – and not as rare as we would like to think.

But all too often, we see otherwise regular kids damaged by really bad parental judgment. As kids-at-risk professionals sometimes say, how do you get a kid who doesn't know the meaning of no to learn to say to *himself* the many nos that a frum life requires? And what type of marriage material do they make? What type of parent?

The association of the *haftarah* with the *parashah* appears to relate primarily to the parallel stories of succession of leadership of Klal Yisrael. But it also highlights a huge contrast in worthiness in considering succession and a timeless lesson in parenting, and, applied wisely, lovingly, and when necessary firmly, the character-building power of no.

*Parashas Chayei Sarah 5780*


# Mommy

A husband and wife visited the doctor for a routine checkup. The husband overheard the wife, who is in good health, softly tell the doctor that she had no wish to outlive her husband. The husband was deeply moved; as a successfully and happily married man, he understood it.

There are various midrashim and *gemaras* that talk about the demise of Sarah Imenu so many years before her husband Avraham. We know what the Satan did, in making her think that Yitzchak was actually slaughtered at the Akeidah, even though he was, in fact, alive, well, and never in actual danger. But how was it up to the Satan to decide how long Sarah should live? Life and death are in God's hands, and Sarah was certainly front and center in God's attention, the beneficiary of His promises and His blessings.

*Bava Kama* (93a) and *Bereishis Rabbah* (45) teach us a very sobering lesson: Do not, in your interactions with anyone, no matter how justified you think it may be, invoke God's judgment. It is a dangerous and fraught thing. How commonly do we hear, "There's a God Who sees how you've harmed me! There's Justice in the world! You'll see! God sees what you're doing! You'll get yours! God will judge between us and punish you for what you've done to me!"

All these statements may be true and justified. But don't make them. Sarah did, and it cost her thirty-eight years of her life. Whoever invokes *middas hadin* will not emerge intact, without penalty from that very same *middas hadin*. For Sarah was worthy of living as long as Avraham, but when she declared, *"Yishpot Hashem beini u'veinecha"* regarding Avraham (Bereishis 16:5), invoking *middas hadin*, bringing the attribute of strict judgment into their lives, her own life was diminished by thirty-eight years.

How much more careful should *we* be.

But there is also, interestingly, another dimension to Sarah's dying before Avraham did. *Midrash Sechel Tov* says that (time period aside), it was a kindness for Sarah to predecease Avraham. She would have had no wish to outlive him. In fact, the Midrash continues, it was common for the great *tzidkaniyos* to pass away before their husbands, not to leave them lost and grieving widows.

And there is a deeper dimension still to the role of wife and mother. We are all aware of the special, profound bond between mothers and their sons. Yes, their bonds with their daughters run deep too, as do those of fathers and their daughters, and fathers and their sons. It's such an interesting part of the system God put into creation.

One of the saddest scenes on a battlefield, *lo aleinu*, is said to be that of mortally wounded soldiers calling out, "Mommy, Mommy!" as they lie dying. May Hashem protect us.

It is the way of the world, Rashi tells us, that a man is especially bound to his mother. And when she dies, if he is blessed, he finds his comfort for that loss in his wife.

When Eliezer brought Rivkah back with him to marry Yitzchak, encountering Yitzchak in the field, he told him the entire miraculous story of his finding her, the perfect wife for him, a union clearly ordained and facilitated by God.

The Torah tells us that Yitzchak took Rivkah into the tent of his mother Sarah; he took her to wife, he loved her, and in her he found consolation for the loss of his mother (24:47).

Chazal tell us that Yitzchak had been mourning his mother the entire three years since her death. He knew that Sarah had died, prematurely, in her grief for him when she thought that he had died at the Akeidah. When he went into her tent and saw that the supernal light that had filled it in her lifetime had gone dark, he tore at his hair in grief. When he brought Rivkah there, and he saw that with her, the light had returned – and more, the protective heavenly cloud hovering overhead had returned as well, and the breadbasket was blessed, all as it had been when Sarah was alive – he finally found comfort and consolation in his worthy wife.

Kesav Sofer looks at this further and understands that during those three years, Yitzchak mourned inconsolably not just his mother's physical death, but he feared that without her there to teach the girl he would marry, no girl of any background could possibly become a worthy life partner for him, who together with him would build Klal Yisrael. Upon meeting Rivkah, however, he realized what a *tzaddekes* she was in her own right and that with her, he could fulfill his mission in this world. Knowing so well – as only a close and devoted son, an absolutely pure soul, could know – what his mother was, Yitzchak thought that there could be no mother for Klal Yisrael or wife for himself like Sarah. And then he found the fulfillment of his mother in the wife Hashem sent to protect and nurture him through life as only a mother and wife could. And when there is no longer a mother, it is all up to the wife.

Yitzchak saw, as well, *b'ruach hakodesh*, that with her he would have a son named Yisrael, and in this he took great comfort. Imrei Noam tells us that this is hinted at in the *gematria* of *va'yinachem Yitzchak acharei* (וינחם יצחק אחרי) equaling that of Yisrael (ישראל).

But they had a long road yet to get there. For twenty years, there were no children. They each prayed fervently, all those years, for a child. And they so valued each other that they also prayed fervently, Rivkah that in her life she would have children *only* with Yitzchak, and Yitzchak, that in his life he would have children *only* with Rivkah.

Leaving one's parents and making a life with a wife is the way of the world; it is the normalcy of life, a normalcy of extraordinary power. The Torah tells us so immediately in Bereishis, in describing God's design for healthy family life: "Therefore a man shall leave his father and his mother and cling to his wife, and they shall be of one flesh" (3:24). A man is formed by his parents but lives his life with his wife. A wife is not her husband's mother, but the safety and the loving yearning that are a necessary and precious part of the healthy human makeup, learned in a mother's loving embrace, can be found after her death only in a wife, if the man is so lucky. She is his wife, but, in a healthy way, there is an element of mommy in her too. If he is so lucky. And if she is.

The great prophet of consolation, Yeshayahu Hanavi, describes the scene in the future, when God will finally bring peace and safety and consolation to His people Israel and to Israel, His land, and to Jerusalem, His city:

> For so says Hashem, behold I will extend to you peace like a flowing river, like a flooding stream. You shall be borne, and dandled on the knees [like a beloved child].
>
> Like a man whose mother consoles him, so I will console you, and in Jerusalem you will be consoled [כאיש אשר אמו תנחמנו כן אנכי אנחמכם ובירושלים תנחמו].
> (Yeshayahu 66:12–13)

To the mommies of this world, to the precious wives who succeed those mommies, who are *not* our mothers, but who, when they're really good at it, are a healthy bit of mommy too, we men owe everything. We owe our sense of self, our sense of safety, our power and ability to act and to build in the world, our very sense of being men, our purpose, our drive, our hope, our sanity, our safe refuge from the storms of life, the very softness and the sweetness of life, the meaning of selfless love and giving in their purest form, the caring wisdom that sustains us, the rational voice we need to hear, the loving heart without which life is no life at all.

*Parashas Chayei Sarah 5781*

# Toldos

## Why Esav Loves Yishmael, Even as He Despises Him

My mother weighed less than eighty pounds when my parents smuggled their way into the American sector of Berlin shortly after the war, seeking asylum in the refugee camp there, at Schlachtensee. My father, a six-footer, weighed somewhat more, a scrawny version of his normally well-built self. They had nothing but each other, a little child on their arms, little more than the clothes on their backs, memories of life and family that were no more, and the hope of starting life anew in the Land of Israel. Their native Poland, which they had just fled, was not only the graveyard of their murdered families, it was also the site of the ongoing hatred, murder, and pogroms, as well as the hopelessness that drove them out.

Here's how Lieutenant General Sir Frederick Morgan, formerly of the British Army and then chief of the United Nations Relief and Rehabilitation Administration (UNRRA) generically described the surviving Jews: "Well dressed, well fed, pockets bulging with money." They were there not fleeing for their lives, he maintained, but were in Germany as part of a Jewish Zionist conspiracy.

Morgan made these remarks quite publicly. There was some protest from Jewish organizations, but as a protected close associate of the British high and mighty, he got a pass. His real crime, as related by David Nasaw in his recent book on the displaced persons of World War II, *The Last Million: Europe's Displaced Persons from World War to Cold War* (Penguin Press, 2020), was that he was indiscreet enough to say out loud what so many in Washington and London were thinking.

The doors to "Palestine," closed to Jews by imperial Britain even when that resulted in the slaughter of millions, remained closed to the pitiful remnant of survivors with nowhere else to go, when no one would take them. Britain refused even an emergency humanitarian permit for 100,000 Jewish survivors languishing in camps in Germany, even after the UN vote for partition but before Israel was established, even only into the designated Jewish area, declaring that such an act would be, as Arthur Creech-Jones, the colonial secretary, put it, "so manifestly unjust to the Arabs that it is difficult to see how we could reconcile it with our conscience."

The British countered American pressure to let at least some Jewish survivors into Palestine with the assertion, quite true, that America wanted the Jews sent there because they didn't want them in New York – or anywhere else in America. The doors to America were at that time closed to them as well.

Most people today, if they even heard of the ship *Exodus*, think of it in terms of the romanticized version of the story, as depicted in the book and movie by that name, in which, after initial cold bureaucratic reluctance, the British relent in a humanitarian gesture and allow the more than four thousand Jewish survivors huddled on its decks and in its cramped hold to disembark in Haifa. That's not what happened. The ship was boarded in the Mediterranean by British forces, who killed several of the resisting Jews. The ship was turned back to Europe, initially to its port of embarkation in France, but then forced to carry and unload its cargo of human misery *onto the accursed soil of Germany itself*, to make a point: *You Jews don't tell us what to do, or what you can do; we tell you. And Palestine is not yours.*

Of the hundreds of thousands of non-Jews in the DP camps, many, such as the Baltic Latvians and Lithuanians, as well as Ukrainians and others, were, in fact, well fed and well dressed, having fled to Germany only as the Red Army approached, because they had served the Germans well in the killing squads and the SS. They could not go back home because of their high crimes. They later denied it, of course, but it was well established. They were readily welcomed in many countries as clean, often skilled workers, and, of course, good Christians, untainted by Jewish heritage.

Esav at work. The very name "Palestine" for the Land of Israel is an invention of Esav's *einiklech*, the Romans, who invoked the Plishtim – who at one time had inhabited the southern coastal region – in order to erase the memory of the Jewish People from their own homeland, after their brutal destruction of the land and the people in putting down the Bar Kochba revolt. In many ways, it worked very well, even as we sadly see, until this very day. Even now, many on the political left, not only in Esav's contemporary home base in Europe but even in America, are loath to even mouth the word *Israel* and refer to the land as "Palestine." Esav is still at work, sympathetic to (even if now quietly contemptuous of) Yishmael, making common cause against Yaakov.

In his hatred for his father and his brother, the Aggadah tells us, Esav went to Yishmael with a proposition that they join forces. *Your brother Yitzchak dispossessed you*, he told Uncle Yishmael, *and my brother Yaakov has dispossessed me of what is rightfully ours. Your father Avraham loved you with all his heart, until Yitzchak swayed him against you and took over the full inheritance. The same happened with me: my father used to love me, but my brother somehow swayed him into blessing him with what was* my *rightful inheritance.*

*Now, I can't kill my father,* Esav told him, *but you can. You kill Yitzchak over your inheritance, and I'll kill Yaakov over mine. That's acceptable behavior. We'll be rid of those Yids and take over everything, the entire Abrahamic enterprise, the land, the wealth, the blessings.*

Yishmael didn't trust Esav or his judgment. So Esav tried to soften him up by marrying his daughter Mochalas. It gained Yishmael's sympathy, perhaps even his intentions, but not his actions – at least at that time. Over the ages, Esav and Yishmael have been at longstanding war with each other. And yet, Crusades and mutual contempt are put aside as they continue to make common war against Yaakov.

The dust from Yaakov's epic wrestling match with Esav still fills the air, even as his existential struggle with Yishmael threatens to consume that air. Esav and Yishmael, by any name, are still hard at work. We wrestle on, as we must. We struggle on, as we must live. We do what we can, by human means as Yaakov did, and by calling out in prayer to God, also as Yaakov did. But if there is one lesson from our long, complex, and often tortured history – Tanach describing one empty and futile foreign alliance after another as nothing more than a brittle reed that snaps and collapses, modern history reinforcing the lesson that looking to nations we think will help us is more often than not just a disappointing pipe dream – we have no one to truly rely on but our loving Father in Heaven.

And may the sincerity, the intensity, the wholeness of that reliance be such that He gathers us up, now, today, in His loving hands and delivers us, rescues us, frees us from those who have spent millennia hating and plotting – sometimes separately and sometimes in tandem, sometimes with a snarl and sometimes with a deceitful smile – and brings us home.

*Parashas Toldos 5781*

# Strategic Flight

The young couple, married for a year, had not yet been blessed with a child. So they did what their people have always done: they went to the Rebbe for a *berachah.* In 1939 Poland, there was not much else they could have done.

Upon hearing their request, Rav Alter Horowitz, the Dzhikover Rebbe and the husband's kinsman, grew agitated. He rose from his chair and went to the window. It was a clear day with a blue sky. He pointed at that clear sky and said, *"De himmlen zenen azoy farvolkent*, the sky, the heavens, are so darkly overcast, and you want to have a child now? *Besser nisht yetzt.* Better not now."

That was January or February 1939, more than half a year before the war. When war did come, the German blitzkrieg suddenly swept into Poland and swept away a thousand years of Jewish life in Poland, murdering in every cruel way nearly every Jew in its dominion. With rare exceptions, only those who managed to flee ahead of the onrushing Germans had any chance of survival. Virtually everyone who stayed was murdered. By and large, people with young children could not flee, and certainly not with babies. Having a baby or a small child was virtually a death sentence.

And so my parents' lives were saved in this manner by their Rebbe, who would not bless them to have a child at that time. He himself perished among the millions. Childless, my parents did flee, and despite the many travails and horrors they suffered through, they survived, and I am here to tell you about it. Those who fled had at least a chance. Not everyone who ran survived – far from everyone. But almost no one who stayed survived.

Some years ago, an older man sat in my exam chair and recounted to me how as a sixteen-year-old boy, when the war broke out, with everyone fearful, knowing of the Germans' hatred and cruelty (but incapable of imagining just how bad it would actually be), he told his mother that he wanted to flee eastward, away from the Germans. She was afraid to let him go, a young boy running into the danger-ous unknown. She wanted him to stay with the family, some measure of safety. *Let's brave it out here at home*, she said. *We'll manage.* Whatever would befall them, she said, would be his destiny too. He ran, and he survived. He never saw his par-ents, his brothers and sisters, his grandparents, his cousins, or any of his neighbors again. (My non-Jewish assistant, a Ukrainian young woman, did not understand the Yiddish words we were speaking, but from experience, she understood what we must have been talking about, with tears pouring down both our faces. She'd seen it before. Later she freely admitted that her people by and large hate my peo-ple, but she had no idea why.)

It was the hour of the cruel Germans. They were ascendant, and, in their hour, they did as they pleased, with no stopping them.

After Yaakov snatched Yitzchak's *berachah*, his mother Rivkah told him *brach lecha*, flee. Run away from Esav.

Why? She must have reasoned that given his destiny, his very purpose in life, God would surely protect him. But she acted otherwise. She understood something about life, about the world and how it works, a wisdom, a practical cleverness about survival that she passed on to Yaakov and thus to us as well.

The world can be such a dangerous place. There are times when danger and evil are ascendant. God tells us in such times, *distance yourself from that danger and live to fight another day* (see Yeshayahu 26:20). Fight evil we must. But know when to advance and when to strategically withdraw. It is a critical life skill. The Midrash cites many examples (including, *k'v'yachol*, God Himself!) of the otherwise mighty and the righteous who survive and ultimately prevail, as they read the situation and act accordingly, as the hour of power passes from the evil to them. But in evil's hour, lie low. Don't be reckless.

And so, rather than rely on miracles, Yitzchak and Rivkah sent Yaakov fleeing the danger of Esav, even if that meant falling into the clutches of Lavan. No shortage of miracles accompanied Yaakov in his flight and for the many years until his return. But that was God's gift, not Yaakov's expectation or demand.

Yaakov's parents and Yaakov himself did the normal and reasoned thing, even though he was Yaakov and might have expected miracles. It was also the wise thing.

Ah, to know what the wise thing is! What a blessing that is. It requires us to think, to reason, to observe and to learn, to intuit. To be well advised. To be blessed.

Part of Yaakov's skill in life was cleverness in dealing with adversaries, demonstrated time and again. He was a man of perfect faith who was also prudent and practical, a combination of skills he passed down to his descendants, skills that can buy life spiritually as well as save life physically. Yaakov combined the powers and the attributes of his *temimusdik* father and his practical, realist mother.

This is the *parashah* of Yaakov's blessing. For Yaakov – for us – to survive Esav, to survive Lavan and every would-be assassin throughout history requires that blessing. To be pure and good with God. To be clever. To think, to reason, to observe and to learn, to intuit. To shun recklessness. To be *oysgecheshbont*. To be well advised. To be blessed.

*Parashas Toldos 5782*

# Vayetzei

## Smart and Not Smart

If you had to draw up a list of people in history who were capricious, the Avos certainly would *not* be on it. And the Ribbono shel Olam certainly is not. Now, whether it was Yitzchak Avinu or, as some hold, God Himself Who chose the name Yaakov, the name of the perfect tzaddik who established Klal Yisrael and whose face appears, in some manner, on the very throne of God, would not be, I submit, solely based on the curious and simplistic observation that his hand was grasping his twin brother's heel as he was born.

You know that it is far deeper than that. The whole story of the complex and eternally ongoing struggle between Yaakov and Esav is alluded to and hinted at in the Torah *parashiyos* that relate the events in their lives. We draw the conclusions and the lessons.

And so while *ekev* (heel) is the identified source of the name Yaakov, the word, with its various associated and derived metaphors, also refers to footsteps, creating a trail or a path, a footprint, consequences, results, things that are consecutive, and so on.

Esav taught us that it may also refer to matters of intelligence, wits, even the capacity to defraud. When he learned from his father, Yitzchak, that Yaakov had snatched the *berachah* of the *bechor*, which had been meant for Esav, he gave out a terrible cry of anguish and said to his father, bitterly, "His name is called Yaakov, and *va'yakveni*, he *outsmarted me* twice!" (see Onkelos and Rashi, Bereishis 27:36). Smart. According to Esav, *too* smart.

Yitzchak, fearing mightily that he had done something terrible in blessing his younger son rather than his firstborn, his *bechor*, and hearing that something *else* had happened ("he outsmarted me *twice!*"), asked Esav what that was. Esav told him about how he had sold the *bechorah* to Yaakov years before. Amazed at the turn of events and God's obvious hand in the matter, his having given the *bechor's* blessing to the one who rightfully owned it (Yaakov), Yitzchak declared, "*gam baruch yihyeh*, indeed he [Yaakov] will be blessed!" (27:33).

Yes, Yaakov was very smart. He was *ish tam yoshev ohalim*, the scholar, the thinker, the intellectual who read and studied and thought all day. And now, as he prepared to flee to Charan and his wily uncle Lavan, he was worried.

Sitting in the safety of his relative isolation, he was shielded from the seductive power of alien ideas, which can seem pure and wonderful and idealistic but may in fact be the work of the devil, worthy of his nasty uncle Lavan, made to sound nice and virtuous by his clever uncle Lavan or by Lavan's neighbors in the outside world, but in reality corrupt, devoid of justice and certainly of holiness. And thus when Yaakov returned from his twenty years with Lavan, his message to Esav included the declaration that *im Lavan garti*, I lived with Lavan, but I absorbed none of his corrupt ideas.

I had a rebbe who taught me that when a Jew is far from Torah, he is capable of any bad thing, just like anyone else. Only the *koach haTorah* can keep us pure and good. I mentioned this once to a smart man, someone who grew up *frum* but had lapsed somewhat and lived his life in a largely secular world, mainly among non-*frum* Jews, whom he held to be ethical people. He was rather annoyed by this statement – he didn't believe it – but he was wrong. Many people think that the goodness and the *chesed* that is part of the Jewish DNA protects the Jew, even the Jew who has wandered off, from being as bad as the bad neighbors whose society he has joined. We all wish it were true; we like to think it is true; we all know stories about how it is sometimes true, and indeed, sometimes it is true; but really, all too often, it is not. So sadly, it is not. The Torah, the Neviim, and the Kesuvim all refer to Jews whose birthright was goodness and holiness, but who perverted that birthright and embraced evil.

Have you heard of Genrikh Yagoda (Henoch ben Gershon from Rybinsk)? Or Izrail (ben Moshe) Leplevski from Brisk? Or Lev (Label Rosenfeld) Kamenev, Grigory (Hershel Apfelbaum) Zinoviev, Lazar Kaganovich or Label (ben David) Bronstein, better known as Leon Trotsky? Lev Raikhman? Boris Berman? There were, sadly, horribly, many others. Very many. I hate to say it, it hurts terribly to say it, but mostly they were Stalinists (Trotsky was ideologically opposed to Stalin and was forced out and later axed to death in Mexico), perpetrators and enablers of mass murder and misery on a scale unknown in twentieth-century Europe until the Germans outdid them – *but not by as much as you might think* – in the name of the Soviet Communist Revolution.

They thought they were being smart. Having done away with God, in their ideology, they brought to life Dostoyevsky's wry observation (in *The Brothers Karamazov*) that without God, *everything* is permissible. They probably even made themselves believe they were doing something good for the sake of mankind.

Most of them (and their families) were themselves murdered in the Great Terror of the 1930s. A high number of the Jews who did every bad thing to prove their loyalty were themselves erased, *liquidated*, and replaced by ethnic Russians. At one point, when the Great Terror began, fully one-third of the high-ranking NKVD officers were Jews. Within a couple of years, they were themselves murdered, the percentage of Jews down to 4 percent.

And we cannot leave out the infamous Yevsekstiya, staffed by Jews under the chairmanship of Semyon (Shimon) Dimanshtein, whose mission it was, by every violent and vicious means, to utterly erase Judaism – even "cultural" Judaism – from the Jews of the Soviet Union. As insiders, they knew whom and what to target. As we know, they were highly successful. Even so, Dimanshtein and many others from his organization were later executed in the Great Terror, by the very regime and morally bankrupt system they served and helped create. *Azoy.*

My Tante Rivke used to say a teaching she learned back in the Old World: "*A Yid tur zich keinmul nisht oysglitschen*" (A Jew must be very careful not to slip and fall). Sure, literally, don't fall on the ice. But the real lesson was in the metaphor that the slippery slope can be far more slippery and far steeper than one thought, and the consequences catastrophic and often irreversible.

Jews certainly have no monopoly on being smart, but there are many smart, thinking Jews. And sometimes they are smart and obviously stupid at the same time. They stupidly seek wisdom and truth where it is not to be found and forsake the very wellspring of truth that is their inheritance. Today's many Jewish names and faces in the Boycott, Divestment, Sanctions (BDS) movement, Jews for Justice in Palestine, Jewish Voice for Peace, J Street, Peace Now, and many other "progressive" organizations think they are being preciously virtuous in their militant antagonism to Israel and really, to Judaism. The kindest thing one can say about them is that aside from being utterly ignorant, they are stupid – even if some of them are otherwise intelligent – "smart."

Yaakov Avinu left the holy and pure home of Yitzchak and Rivkah and came face to face with a world full of dangerous, seductive ideas. Communism, socialism, secular Zionism, Bundism, atheism, and any number of other isms may not have existed then, but the danger to an earnest, sensitive, and thinking person from alien ideologies dressed up as something virtuous is very great. Even Yaakov Avinu feared it. So, certainly, should we.

Yaakov returned to the Land of Israel and his father's home *shalem*, whole. *Im Lavan garti, v'taryag mitzvos shamarti.* Even for Yaakov, it was a major accomplishment. One critical lesson of Yaakov's twenty-year sojourn with Lavan is that Jews, who are especially vulnerable to the world of ideas, must never look elsewhere for truth or wisdom when *hi chochmaschem*, the Torah, which is our God-given legacy, is the ultimate source that defines what is true, what is good, what is virtuous, what is holy, what is our purpose in this life, what is our role in this world.

*Parashas Vayetzei 5779*


# Know When to Hold; Know When to Fold

Why did Yaakov run away? Because his parents told him to? OK, so why did they tell him to? Because Esav was out to get him? OK, but he was Yaakov Avinu, so close to God, destined to father the twelve tribes of Israel, as ordained by Him. Surely no harm could come to him. Lavan was going to protect him?

Remember that Yosef spent an extra two years in captivity because he relied on human intervention on his behalf – a normal strategic move – rather than just God alone, as was appropriate for someone on his level. But Yaakov was on a still higher level!

So why did he have to run away? Should he not have just relied on Hashem, as Yosef was faulted for not doing?

We all understand that life is not so simple, the world is not so simple. So many forces are at work that knowing the right thing to do is maybe not always so simple, even for the Avos. We know from bitter experience that the world is a dangerous place, even for – often especially for – the innocent.

Do we confront evil when it is ascendant, or do we hide from it, hoping to survive and thrive another day? The key, it seems, is discerning when it is indeed ascendant, for that may not be the best time to confront it.

Every army that has ever made a strategic withdrawal has done just that, making that withdrawal in the face of overwhelming disadvantage, in order to live and fight another day. In cosmic terms, the reality of the world is that every dog may have his day, and every villain may have his hour: don't count on miracles, even if you are Yaakov Avinu, if you have any other choice. Don't try to force God's hand.

In that apparently dark place where Yaakov lies down to sleep, not realizing that he is, in fact, at the very gates of Heaven, God appears to him and reassures Yaakov of his safety and his blessing, that he has God's many promises to protect him, that he will thrive. But God doesn't say *it's OK, go back home, nothing will happen to you*. Rather, Hashem promises Yaakov that He will be with him wherever he flees to. But flee he must.

Bravery and recklessness are not the same thing. Faith guarantees merit, but not necessarily the desired outcome.

Twenty years later, upon his return, before encountering Esav again, Yaakov worries that *"katonti mi'kol hachasadim"* (32:11), that his protective merits may have been diminished, used up, by the *chesed* he's been shown until then. Even in his faith, he has a healthy (and normal) fear of the power of evil let loose. And we know about it – the Torah tells us about it – because it is something we need to know.

This was not my original question. The Midrash asks it. It then quotes a *pasuk* from Yeshayahu (26:20), warning the people, as the destructive enemy looms, "Go, My people, into your inner rooms and close the door behind you. Hide, for a while, until the anger passes."

God is telling us that in this world, when evil has its moment of strength, its *shaah chatzufah*, when the *middas hadin* is predominant, during its *hour*, don't try to stand up to it. Give it space, *ten lah makom*. Even I, says Hashem, *k'v'yachol*, *step back at such a moment*: "*Heshiv achor yemino*" (Eichah 2:3). *When, because of your sins, the forces of evil were unleashed against you, I did nothing. I stepped back (even though I would want to protect you).* Evil was having its hour.

Evil has, sadly, had many such hours in our history.

But whoever steps back at such a time may live to ultimately triumph. The Midrash then provides examples of those who did not step back when they should have and were lost (Navos with Achav), and those who did step back and triumphed (Avraham, Yitzchak, Moshe, David at various times). And now Yaakov, who fled from Esav because that was the strategically right thing to do at that time, and who ultimately prevailed.

God was telling Yaakov, and through him us, that there is an ebb and flow in history. He will bless us completely, but His protection also is affected by what we do to keep the *middas hadin* at bay. That is up to us. Human beings tend to slip and fall, and we must be prepared for that, but people also know how to pick themselves up again, and we must prepare for that as well.

In the end, however, in Yaakov's revelatory dream, God showed him something that made him declare, "*zeh shaar haShamayim*," this is the house of God, the very gates of Heaven (Bereishis 28:17). Hashem showed Yaakov what would later transpire on that very spot, at the summit of Mount Moriah. He showed Yaakov the Beis Hamikdash that Shlomo built and its later destruction by Nevuchadnezzar. He showed him the Beis Hamikdash that the returnees from Bavel built and its later destruction by Titus. And He showed Yaakov the third Beis Hamikdash, to stand on that very spot, that will stand forever, spreading peace and blessing, finally, over all of mankind.

But on the road to get there, in that terrible struggle (which didn't really have to be such a struggle, except for that devil, human nature!), we need a roadmap. The Torah is that roadmap, but there is more to the roadmap, a practical and strategic wisdom derived from the Torah but also from the accumulated wisdom of our forefathers, in dealing with that struggle. You have to know, borrowing from a popular song, *l'havdil*, in a totally different context, when to hold your cards and when to fold, when to walk away and when to run.

May Hashem bless us in all our struggles, private as well as communal. The Avos showed the way. It's time for those terrible struggles to be consigned to the past, please God! May we have the wisdom, and most of all the merit, to just stand tall.

*Parashas Vayetzei 5781*

# Vayishlach

## In the Land of Eureka

Ever been to Syracuse, New York? Except for passing through the train station on my way to Toronto, many years ago, neither have I. But recently, I was in Siracusa, the original Syracuse, on the island of Sicily, an old Greek settlement. That's where Archimedes, thousands of years ago, supposedly figured out principles of physics and the laws of buoyancy while sitting in the bathtub, as well as the principles of levers and fulcrums. Famously, he is said to have cried out, "Eureka! Give me a place to stand, and a lever long enough, and I can lift the world!"

I can't trace the lineage exactly, but the sages commonly identify Rome with Esav. I don't know if the connection is actually genetic or if it is cultural, nor can I comment on how much of that connection lingers today, in Rome and Italy, but it was in that land that I heard a story that I immediately connected to the story in Vayishlach. Yaakov was left isolated, alone, having gone in search of small but important items that were missing, and he had a violent encounter with the mysterious "man" identified as *saro shel Esav*, Esav's "angel," who had come to damage or destroy him by interfering with his ability to pass on his holy legacy to succeeding generations. Yaakov bested him, and here we are today.

Jews had lived and thrived in Sicily for many years, going back to very ancient times. An important crossroads of the ancient world, Sicily has been invaded many times, by many nations, each one leaving its mark. As elsewhere, the Jews managed to get by for the most part. It all came to an end with the Inquisition; the Jews left, and Sicily has been essentially *Judenrein* for five hundred years.

Some years ago, there was some excavation in and under an old building that was being transformed into a boutique hotel. Deep down, they found unaccounted-for moisture, and, as they dug further, finally, a natural spring. But the spring did not feed a water source for drinking. It fed a group of five *mikvaos*, each one perfect and beautifully constructed into the rock, each one fed by the spring below, with no need for the device of a central collection *bor* feeding pools by halachically acceptable artifice. These were real-deal natural *mikvaos*, built *al taharas hakodesh*, reached by a

46

winding stone staircase long ago dug out of the natural rock. There was an old sign on the wall, etched in stone, in Hebrew, about the specialness of the place. Now right side up, it was found upside down. Evidently, at some point in the past, it had fallen down; with no Jews left to know the difference, it had been put back upside down.

On our way there, walking through the old streets of what had once been the Jewish quarter of Siracusa, a fellow traveler, a Sephardic fellow, told me a Yaakov and Esav story. It says a great deal about Yaakov and about Esav, and about the seemingly never-ending wrestling match between them, the dust of which struggle still fills and clouds the world. This man had an uncle who was a Polish Jew, who as a young boy still in his teens had somehow survived the Holocaust and lived to see the liberation of his concentration camp by American soldiers. A soldier found him, starved and emaciated, orphaned, alone. A Jew himself, the GI asked the boy what he could do for him. The boy replied that he had not put on tefillin in years, and that is what he wanted above all else. The soldier reached into his knapsack and pulled out his own tefillin, giving them to the boy. He told him to keep them; he himself would manage.

The boy eventually made it to Israel, where he married, raised a family, and lived his life. Those tefillin, given by a son of Yaakov Avinu to a son of Yaakov Avinu (the small but important item Yaakov went back for?), were, for the rest of his life, that fellow's most prized, appreciated, and precious possession.

In the fullness of time, the boy, later the man, passed on. Years later, his daughter saw a war documentary on TV. An old man recounted how as a soldier liberating the concentration camp, he had come upon a young boy who was certainly hungry, but who was hungrier still for the holy legacy of his forefathers. The old soldier recounted how he had given that boy his own tefillin and had never seen him again; he did not know what had become of that boy. Other details in the story matched up as well.

The daughter managed to track down that old American veteran and made a pilgrimage to the United States, where she returned to him his tefillin. She told him that he had saved her father's life in more ways than one. She told him about the generations of loyal Jews that had emerged from that encounter.

In the nearly four thousand years since that desperate midnight wrestling match, Yaakov has been building *mikvaos*, Esav has been destroying them, and Yaakov has been rebuilding. Yaakov has been careful to preserve and save holy things, however small; Esav has been destroying them, and Yaakov has been retrieving them, even if getting beaten up in the process, and passing them on. Yaakov has been building generations, Esav has been trying to destroy them, and Yaakov has been preserving and propagating them the best he can.

More often than not, Yaakov is left damaged and limping. He takes a terrible beating in that seemingly eternal wrestling match, the pattern for which was set so long ago. In the end, Esav cannot altogether destroy him, try as he might. And as it did then, in the end the sun will shine for Yaakov, healing him and making him whole. In the end, we are promised, *v'alu moshiyim b'Har Tzion lishpot es Har Esav, v'haisah l'Hashem hameluchah* (Ovadiah 1:21). That healing sun will shine for us too. We will no longer be locked in that terrible, painful struggle; the God of Israel will be acknowledged by all, and we will, in that warm light, be made whole.

*Parashas Vayishlach 5780*

# Connecting the Dots

What's with the dots we sometimes come across in the Torah, sitting above the letters? There might be more letters than dots, more dots than letters, or exactly the same number of each.

We all understand that they represent hidden or esoteric meanings to the plain text, which carry a greater message than the simple meaning of the text itself. They are not particularly a secret, but decoding them does require study of the rabbinic sources to find reference to the Masoretic teaching regarding a particular instance.

Of the ten such words in the Torah, one famously appears in Parashas Vayishlach. Yaakov and Esav approach each other in their tense reunion, twenty years – and a lifetime of experiences – after Yaakov fled Esav's murderous wrath over Yitzchak's *berachos.* Yaakov expects that Esav will likely try to kill him, and he has prepared in various ways.

At the final stretch, Esav sprints toward his estranged brother, embraces him, falls upon his neck, and kisses him, *va'yishakehu* (וישקהו), as they both weep. Each letter of that word, *va'yishakehu,* has a dot above it. Rashi tells us that some interpret it to mean that Esav kissed his brother, but insincerely and unlovingly (why would he do that?). Others maintain that although Esav's hatred for Yaakov (in every generation!) is a given, well established, at that moment his feelings were stirred, and he kissed Yaakov with all his heart.

Why, indeed, would he do that? *Midrash Tanchuma* tells us that Esav indeed set out with his army of four hundred thugs intent on attacking and destroying Yaakov, as he had plotted and consoled himself for the past twenty years. God would not let that happen. Along the way, Esav's army was encountered by a battalion of angels who challenged them, "Who are you?" Esav replied, "We are

Avraham's grandchildren." The angels thereupon attacked them and beat them thoroughly. Esav, a bad actor but no fool, then called out, "I am Yaakov's brother!" and the attack let up.

Esav continued on his war march and encountered another band of angels, and the same thing happened. Then again, and then yet again. It went on all night. By this time, well beaten up, Esav changed his tune (out of fear and not love!) and approached Yaakov peacefully and "full of love," however insincere.

A broader picture of the ongoing struggle between Yaakov and Esav, with its incredibly complex, convoluted inverse power structure, wherein Yaakov will be ascendant only when he acts like Yaakov and not like Esav, but will be under Esav's dominion when he acts like Esav and not like Yaakov, is offered here in the *Midrash Rabbah*. It's based on those dots above the letters.

Rabbi Shimon ben Elazar says that wherever the letters outnumber the dots, the straight meaning of the words predominates in our understanding. Where the dots outnumber the letters, the esoterics of the dots predominate in the deeper meaning. Here, however, the number of letters and the number of dots are the same. This suggests, Rabbi Shimon says, that as bad as Esav was, at that moment he was actually moved by brotherly emotion and his kiss was sincere.

Rabbi Yanai asks him the same question you just asked: If so, why do we need the dots here altogether? In your scenario, they apparently add nothing to the meaning. Rather, he says, this parity between the letters and the dots serves as a metaphor for and a precursor to the age-old, ongoing struggle, the eternal wrestling match between Yaakov and Esav, the pain, the anguish, the hurt, the frustration.

Esav, he says, that wicked knave, despite having suffered all night because of his bad intentions, knowing he would, in this, harm himself, could not restrain himself. As they embraced, he tried to assassinate Yaakov by biting him in the neck, by ripping out his throat. Famously, Yaakov's neck, as Esav's teeth sank in, turned to stone, to marble (as did Moshe's neck several generations later when Pharaoh tried to have him beheaded). Esav broke his teeth.

They both cried, *va'yivku* (ויבכו), Esav for his broken teeth and Yaakov for his neck. They also cried, I think, out of pain, fear, and frustration for a hurt-filled struggle that will *never* end, as long as the world continues as it is, a desperate wrestling match that to this day fills the world with the dust of its violence, the cries of those strugglers, Esav and Yaakov, the attacker and the attacked, echoing painfully, mournfully, tragically through the ages.

*Parashas Vayishlach 5781*

# Yaakov Injured

It was during his presidential campaign that Governor Mike Huckabee visited us here in Manhattan Beach. I don't think it was during the week of Parashas Vayishlach, but he spoke of Yaakov Avinu's violent wrestling match with his strange opponent, whom we have been taught represents the malign forces of Esav. Jacob, he said, was left limping for the rest of his life.

Now, Governor Huckabee is, I believe, a good man, moral and upright, a good Evangelical Christian, an ordained Baptist minister. As far as I can tell from whatever I know about him, he is a *Yidenfreind* (friend of the Jews). I think he would have made a great president, especially for us Jews. As biblically minded as he is, though, there's no reason for him to be familiar with the teachings of Chazal.

And so I quietly pointed out to him that Chazal have taught us the ancient traditional understanding that Yaakov limped for a bit, but then when morning came, *va'yizrach lo hashemesh*, the sun shined *for him*, the healing power of the sunshine was enhanced for him and cured him of his injury. And that is why it says *lo, for him*.

Governor Huckabee was, I think, impressed, realizing that there is a world of understanding that we, Klal Yisrael, are privy to about our Scriptures that the rest of the world, including its Bible scholars, have no clue about. It is our *mesorah*; it is ancient, unbroken, and authentic. He understood, he intuited, I think, that what I told him is true. His face told me that he recognized the truth of the source.

That said, Mike Huckabee was also not wrong about Yaakov Avinu limping, although not in the way he meant it.

In that dust-raising violent encounter that dark night so many years ago, in that bitter and desperate struggle, Esav, through his mysterious proxy, struck Yaakov a lasting and debilitating blow.

The anatomic identifier the Torah gives for the site of Yaakov's injury, the *yerech*, the thigh, is also used by the Torah to allude to adjacent anatomy related to the organs of procreation and generational continuity. In this context, it refers to the future generations of Klal Yisrael.

Esav – here in the form of his *malach*, elsewhere in any and every form history has managed to conjure up, tries to undo Yaakov and the bond between him, his generations – *us* – and the Ribbono shel Olam. In this he has failed, and he has also succeeded wildly.

He has failed because we are still here as God's committed and special nation, and we will always be. The future of *va'yizrach lo hashemesh* is ultimately ours. He has succeeded because of how many, over all the generations, have been torn away. It's been estimated that but for those who have been eliminated from Klal Yisrael over all the generations, we might have been as numerous today as the Chinese. I don't know if that's accurate, but the number has to be very great. There are millions of non-Jews out there, halachically and in every practical way *goyim*, who are *mi'zera Yisrael*, descended from Jews, remotely and not remotely. Lost to us. Lost to Yaakov Avinu. *Neshamos* torn away from us and from what might have been their legacy.

Yaakov limping, his *yerech* damaged, is the ten lost tribes of Israel. It is those who disappeared into Bavel and other such places. It is those lost to the Hellenism of Greece and later Roman culture. It is the schismatic sects, some of them quite large, who have gone lost. It is the untold numbers massacred by the Crusaders, the adults and especially the children dragged to the baptismal fonts of Spain and Portugal and other accursed places in Europe. It is the Inquisition, which persisted until 1834 (!). It is the entire cities of Jews in the Arabian Peninsula, Islamicized or murdered by Muhammad and his followers. It is the hundreds of thousands murdered by Ukraine's national hero Bogdan Chmielnitzki and his hordes. It is the victims of the countless pogroms and the burnings. It is the Edgardo Mortaras of history, Jewish children seized by the church. It is the blood libels. It is the Cantonist decrees in Russia that cruelly seized so many hapless Jewish children. It is the untold numbers of Jews – the masses of Jewish youth especially – who threw away their Judaism in favor of any number of other empty isms: socialism, communism, Godless secularist Zionism, radicalism, liberalism, progressivism, secular Yiddishism, anarchism, now *woke*ism, anything but Judaism. It is the majority of Jews today who are so remote from their holy legacy that many are barely discernible as Jews. It is the majority that now intermarry. It is the Reform movement that destroyed vast communities of religious Jews and taught their children and adults to eat pig and to violate every law in the Torah. It is the redefining of Judaism as really being only about social justice. It is the Soviet system that failed at so much but succeeded in tearing millions of Jews, whole generations, away from Judaism. It is the hatred all around us, the hostility everywhere.

It is the Holocaust.

Somehow, the priceless *berachah* that Yaakov received is diminished by all this loss, a curse, a violent blow that Esav was somehow empowered to strike back with. Yaakov wins but is left limping. Esav's bitter cry upon discovering his disenfranchisement – which he entirely deserved, and which needed to happen – had power and effect even beyond what he could have imagined.

*Al ken lo yochlu Bnei Yisrael es gid hanasheh asher al kaf hayerech ad hayom hazeh ki naga b'chaf yerech Yaakov b'gid hanasheh.* For this reason, the Children of Israel will not eat of the *gid hanasheh*, the cattle analog of the site of Yaakov's injury, *to this very day*.

Why not? Because Yaakov sustained something of an injury, indeed a temporary one? In its superficial understanding, it doesn't seem to make much sense. I submit that it is because of the deeper significance of that injury, one that affected Yaakov far more severely than getting punched or kicked in the thigh, one that has horrifically tormented us in every generation, that leaves us panting and gasping with unspeakable pain and loss, one that left Yaakov, even in victory, and us *ad hayom hazeh*, partially broken, damaged, limping.

We are *maaminim bnei maaminim*, and we have faith in God and His grand plan. But with all that has happened, in any way that we mortals can understand, we cannot ever be quite whole. We can hope and pray for the future, but however bright that will be, the past cannot be undone. We can remain steadfast in our faith and in His goodness and His justice. But we are mere mortals. Even as we are on one level restored, we remain, on another very human level, damaged and limping.

*Ad hayom hazeh*, yearning, praying, waiting for, finally, *va'yizrach lo hashemesh*.

*Parashas Vayishlach 5782*

# Gene Pool

The Avos and Imahos had DNA very much on their minds.

Presumably they didn't actually know about the double helix, about deoxyribonucleic acid, ribonucleic acid, messenger RNA, the base pairs adenine and thymine, guanine and cytosine, when uracil kicks in, or for that matter, mitochondria or the hexose monophosphate shunt. They probably could tell you nothing about chromosome pairs; but about genes, in their practical application, they could tell you a great deal. They understood what it takes to create and build Klal Yisrael and to sustain it.

And so Avraham married Sarah, the only woman in the world who with him could make it happen, as did Yitzchak in marrying Rivkah.

Now, let's say all the good genes of Avraham and Sarah went to Yitzchak, and whatever bad genes they inherited went to Yishmael.

Yitzchak was perfect, but Rivkah, while personally perfect, carried bad "genetic" baggage from Besuel & Co. Famously, she figured that the good, from Yitzchak, went to Yaakov, and the bad, from her, went to Esav. Well, she thought, if so, even a Canaanite girl could have done that. *Im ken, lamah zeh anochi?* What did they need her for?

Well, without Rivkah, Yaakov could not have been Yaakov, but just as well, any good that would throughout history emerge from Esav – and there has been – could not happen without Rivkah's positive input.

And with regard to Yaakov's children, the *shevatim*, what about the lode of nasty input from Lavan? That would badly taint the nation about to be built. The Imrei Noam tells us that when, in parting, Lavan kissed them goodbye, he aspirated, he drained them of all his negative influence, his *zuhama*, and absorbed it all back into himself, leaving them pure and pristine, ready to build Klal Yisrael.

Now Yaakov, about to encounter Esav, is worried about Esav's power not just for now but in future generations as well. So permit me a bit of fanciful speculation.

Esav was coming Yaakov's way with an army of four hundred thugs.

Esav was given dominion over Yaakov at any time that Yaakov – or his future generations – falls short. In this, Yaakov was ominously prescient. *Hatzileni na mi'yad achi, mi'yad Esav*: Save my descendants, Ribbono shel Olam, from Esav's descendants, who will attack them with Esav's power (*Bereishis Rabbah* 76:6). We have seen, tragically, how that has played out over the generations.

Esav inherited "good" genes, which he chose to suppress. Yaakov was afraid not only of Esav's bad genes and bad traits, but also of the potential for good within him that perforce bodes poorly for Yaakov, whose standing falls when Esav's rises. Indeed, Yaakov kept Dinah hidden from Esav not just to protect her from him as a *rasha*, but to protect himself (Yaakov) and his future generations from Esav as a potential tzaddik, lest Dinah, in her *tzidkus*, so influence Esav for the good that she turn Esav around into a tzaddik. Given the terms of Yitzchak's *berachos* to them both, that could be catastrophic for Yaakov. (See Torah Temimah on this.)

We Jews are a nation with a common history and a common destiny, children of common ancestors. We are a tribe, but strictly speaking, genetically, there has been a measure of outside input over our long history, from nearly every nation. We have remained, in our fierce and determined loyalty, largely genetically intact, but not 100 percent so. Interestingly, that is part of our mandate, to gather up the *nitzotzos hakodesh* that the Creator scattered in the world and bring them home, to us and through us. Those external physical genes are foreign, even as we absorb them; the good internal spiritual "genes" we have absorbed are not so foreign, their essential benignity not alien, but welcome.

And so it's interesting to think, in the context of *hatzileni na mi'yad achi, mi'yad Esav*, something about the genetic makeup of Ashkenazi Jewry. Whereas the Sephardic world, in its various manifestations, is for the most part descended from

Babylonian Jewry, with its own story and genetic history, it was mostly the Jews of Eretz Yisrael who made their way into Europe to become the Ashkenazim. It didn't all happen at once. It is estimated that more than 100,000 captives were dragged from Judea to Italy after the fall of Jerusalem in the year 70 CE, and many more again after the Bar Kochba revolt.

Those who survived the arenas, the gladiatorial bloodbaths, and those who were spared those fates knew lives of slavery, servitude, and subjugation. In the nature of such things, a certain amount of Roman/Italian DNA found its way into the gene pool. In the centuries after, there were tremendous pressures placed on the remaining Jews in Israel, who were still a majority of Israel's population until de-Judaizing campaigns eventually reduced their numbers. Italy (Rome) again was a portal for entry into Europe.

Italy itself is genetically highly diverse, which is no surprise, given Roman history. It is said that genetic diversity within Italy is thirty times greater than the genetic difference between Portuguese and Hungarian populations. Chazal identify Rome with Esav. I can't say how much of that relates to actual physical DNA, and how much is spiritual. But spiritual will do.

Is our absorption of some measure of Roman DNA a kind of reclamation of whatever might have been good or positive in Esav's *einiklech*, somewhat akin to what Lavan did with Yaakov's children, but in the opposite direction? Perhaps an answer, part of an answer, to Yaakov's prayer of *hatzileni na mi'yad achi, mi'yad Esav?*

Who knows? Who can know? Perhaps the important and highly stressed mitzvah of *V'ahavtem es hager* is not just about kindness and acceptance of those who forsake their previous lives and come to join us and take shelter *tachas kanfei haShechinah*. Perhaps it is also in part Hashem's answer to Yaakov's prayer, that over history we be saved, in a broader, spiritual sense, from the evil of Esav by absorbing whatever potential good was still vested in him, potentiating Yitzchak's *berachah* and bringing us closer to completion of our mandate in this world.

Our path has been a long and tortuous one. The twists and turns, the ups and the downs defy the imagination. Maybe one day *Tishbi yitaretz kushyos v'abayos*, the Ribbono shel Olam will make it all clear to us. Meanwhile, Yitzchak's *berachah*, Yaakov's determined nation building, and our fierce loyalty sustain us while we await God's loving final Redemption.

*Parashas Vayishlach 5783*

# Vayeshev

## Joseph H. Pollyanna

If your brothers were jealous of you and couldn't stand you, and you dreamed a dream in which you ruled over them, and you started to tell them about it and they didn't want to listen, would you annoy them and antagonize them further by insisting, perhaps whining and pleading, that they stop and hear all about it? And then when they were really put off by it, and you dreamed again, essentially to the same effect, that you were going to be boss over them – and your brothers were mature, accomplished men, great men, powerful men, and angry with you – even if you think it's important, would you insist and persist in antagonizing them even more, to the breaking point?

Why would Yosef do that? He was young, but surely he was not a fool. Later on, he would be the viceroy whose hardheaded cleverness saved Egypt and consolidated Pharaoh's wealth and power.

Why would he stand up to the six brothers who were Leah's sons, defending not only the other four brothers whom they shamed, who were the children of the two maidservants-turned-wives, Bilhah and Zilpah, but also pointedly standing up for the honor and position of those two ladies? Even though Scripture itself referred to them as *shefachos*, here, where Yosef extends himself for them, the Torah very specifically refers to them as *neshei Yaakov aviv*, with full honor, a position that Yosef insisted upon.

And he did so even though they apparently did not stand up for him: those four, the sons of the "lesser" wives, the very brothers he went out of his way to befriend and defend, were in on his being thrown into the pit and then sold into slavery. It's possible they felt bad about it but, in awe of the senior brothers, they went along with the travesty, apparently not loyal or appreciative enough, or strong enough, to do what's right by him (see Ohr Hachaim).

What was there about Yosef that made him different in this way?

There is a reason that Yosef stands out in Jewish parlance with the rare title Hatzaddik. Much has been written about his unusual righteousness, his uncommon empathy that moves him repeatedly to tears, his repaying his brothers' treachery with kindness, his resistance to all manner of temptation, physical and spiritual.

I submit that part of that picture – the very mindset that was central to the personality that made Yosef who he was – was his *intentional* stance as what we would call today a Pollyanna, a kind of naïveté born not of foolishness but of uncommon goodness. He certainly was no fool, but he determinedly looked upon his brothers, at their core great men all, as being above succumbing to the wrongheadedness that they eventually were guilty of. His *tzidkus* made him look upon others more kindly than they deserved, even though he probably knew the real truth about them.

Rather than foolish or just naive, this stance is, when appropriately placed, one of determined moral courage and optimism. It is a vote, with one's very life and well-being, for optimism and positivity, in seeing, in assuming the good. Set in the *parashiyos* that lay out historical patterns for the future of Klal Yisrael, it is, perhaps, part of what has allowed us to see a bright future even in periods of the greatest darkness.

In this cynical world, it's a rare person who does that. I know that such people exist, as we scratch our heads in wonder that they insist upon persisting in that attitude, even though they are often the victims of those they had judged kindly, but should not have. And they do so again.

They are beacons of light in the cynical darkness, wrong perhaps about others' intentions, but so right about brightness of the spirit. That brightness, that holy naïveté, marked and forever set apart Yosef Hatzaddik, the story of whose *tzidkus* always ushers in the beautiful holiday of Chanukah, the time of our redemption, the brightness in this dreary world we call the Festival of Lights.

*Parashas Vayeshev 5780*

## Shivisi Hashem l'Negdi Samid

Alfred Dreyfus was a thirty-five-year-old Alsatian Jew, a family man and a French patriot, who was a career artillery officer in the French Army when he was convicted of treason and sentenced to be publicly degraded (to the howling of the mob screaming, "Death to the Jews!") and sent to rot in the hellhole penal colony known as Devil's Island in French Guiana.

It was 1894, and France was fearful of an aggressive, militaristic Germany. Military intelligence detected evidence of espionage, and, needing a scapegoat, they selected the Jew Dreyfus to serve that need.

The more it became clear that Dreyfus was innocent, the more the old guard doubled down, intent on destroying him. Antisemitism, of course, played a major role; "protecting the honor of the army" was the excuse given to further railroad a decent and loyal man, rather than to admit error. That was, apparently, a perfectly acceptable strategy in that culture. Real evidence was suppressed, fake evidence was produced; the real culprit, when identified, was falsely exonerated, as Dreyfus and his family were destroyed, satisfying the old-boy network, even while raising a hornet's nest of violent antisemitism throughout France. In this, these "old boys" thought they found honor.

That Dreyfus was much later exonerated and reinstated in 1906, somehow still alive and somehow still willing to serve (and he served honorably throughout World War I), speaks much about the man's dedication to his country, but poorly of the institutions running it and the corrupt, amoral culture that pervaded it.

Institutions often speak of honor but really serve expediency, and when corrupt, are willing to destroy innocents in the name of an imagined "greater good," in addition to simply covering up an embarrassing truth. Even their amorality they portray as a tool of serving that "greater good." *What's one man compared to the harm that will otherwise happen?* they reason. Borrowing a well-known tactic of the Satan, they even portray their evil as a higher virtue.

There was a film, some years ago, fictional but frightfully realistic, portraying a high government official in Washington, with the connivance of others, destroying exculpatory evidence, lying under oath, and having a dedicated career Marine officer with thirty-five years of distinguished service be the fall guy, on trial for his life for the "murder of innocents" in a Mideast country, terrorists who actually shot and killed US Marines, because the truth was inconvenient to his policy goals, which, in his arrogance, he equated with America's best interest. From the safety and comfort of his high office, he had no trouble convincing himself that sacrificing the innocent and loyal Marine's life was worth it. Perhaps unfortunate, but in his mind it served a greater good and was therefore actually a virtue.

Such stories are altogether too common in human society, where hubris reigns, where arrogance rules, where people are pawns to be sacrificed, where covering up fundamental errors is more important than life itself – as long as that is someone else's life. People in high places often think that makes them high people, above the truth and above the law. Because of their great importance, because they identify the nation's or a particular institution's interest with their own, preserving their own position becomes equated with preserving the institution or the nation itself. Certainly worth the sacrifice of…*someone else.*

*What's one man compared to the harm that will otherwise happen?*

There is, of course, a common denominator at play in all these scenarios. These villains forget that God is watching them.

That God is, in fact, watching, that scapegoating the innocent to protect the "honor" of anything or anyone is immoral, amoral, evil, and virtually never acceptable is the key to a brief but world-altering conversation related in Parashas Vayeshev. In fact, the concept behind it, encapsulated in that verse from Tehillim (16:8) that is to be found front and center in many shuls, *Shivisi Hashem l'negdi samid* (I set [or I envision] Hashem before me always), is actually behind at least two key occurrences in Vayeshev.

In a particularly enigmatic tale, Yehuda the son of Yaakov, a very great man destined to be the father of the Davidic line, finds himself in an acutely embarrassing situation with Tamar. She is apparently guilty of what is legally tantamount to adultery, and, as the equivalent of a *bas Kohen* for that era, faces the penalty of death by burning. She is, in fact, innocent. But to reveal that would cause Yehuda grave public embarrassment. *Tzaddekes* that she was, this she would not do. She was prepared to die by fire rather than to cause Yehuda to be publicly shamed.

But that doesn't mean she wanted to die. She left it up to Yehuda to acknowledge his role in the situation, which would exculpate her. *Haker na*, she says to him, *please look and recognize* certain objects that he had given to her, acknowledgment of which would cause him great shame and embarrassment.

The Gemara (*Sotah 10*), paraphrased by Rashi here, adds another layer of meaning to *haker na*, with emphasis on the word *na*, please. Look, Yehuda, *please look, recognize your Maker, Who is watching always and knows the truth of my innocence, and do not look away from me. Speak up on my behalf (which I won't do, as I will not be the agent of your embarrassment, no matter the cost to me), and save three lives (mine and the twin sons I am carrying)*.

Yehuda, tzaddik and prince, rose immediately to the occasion. He publicly declared that she was right and he was wrong. *Tzadka mi'meni*, a play on words: literally, she was more correct and more righteous in this than I am, and indeed it was *mi'meni*, *from me*; I am the father of the twins growing within her. *Shivisi Hashem l'negdi samid*, a powerful and profound lesson and legacy for all future generations.

Could Yehuda have convinced himself that the *kavod* of Beis Yaakov should not be sullied by such scandal – the future of Klal Yisrael at stake, there's too much to lose – even if it meant harming one person? The "honor" of the nation of Israel is at stake! *What's one person compared to the harm that will otherwise happen?* (Not to mention his own public humiliation.) Not Yehuda, or he wouldn't have been Yehuda.

Later in the *parashah*, Yosef, a healthy young man in his late teens, far, far from home, with much to complain about in the home he was torn away from, immersed in a vile and immoral culture, is targeted relentlessly by Mrs. Potiphar to sin with her. As she is wearing him down, he sees before his eyes the image of his father, which really represents awareness of what God wants and expects of him. Our forebears and our revered teachers are the human links in the chain that connects us to God, a connection that is at the same time also quite direct and personal, between us and God. *God is watching*, he reminds himself. He flees her grasp and spends years in the dungeon as a consequence. God is watching: he is Yosef, son of Yaakov Avinu, a child of the Avos and Imahos. Of that he must always be aware, and that is the guidepost of his life.

Could he have rationalized giving in, in such difficult circumstances? Not Yosef, or he would not have been Yosef.

It is – or ought to be – no different for any of us. The declaration *"Shivisi Hashem l'negdi samid,"* prominently displayed in so many shuls, the constancy of awareness of God, the holy, priceless legacy of our forebears, is what makes us the Children of Israel. Otherwise, we would not be, we could not be, who we are, what we are, who we need to be, what we need to be, who and what we were created to be.

*Parashas Vayeshev, Chanukah 5781*
*May the light of Chanukah open our eyes, that we may indeed see, envision at all times, feel the Presence of our Father in Heaven before us, that we may live and serve Him as befits His chosen children.*

# Human Beings, Exalted but Human

An individual is an individual. Each person has an individual nature and is responsible for his or her own actions, which are a personal choice and not determined by one's sociological group. And yet, it's also clear that some groups have different attitudes and behavior patterns from other groups, and clearly, those typical patterns are reflected in the behavior patterns of individuals within a given group and can be suggestive –even if not predictive – of typical behavior.

Lots of Jews are easygoing. But that's not the first word that comes to mind for a people that we all know can be, well, difficult, even as they also stand out as remarkably wonderful. We won't prejudge any individual based on stereotypes (which after all exist for a reason), but when people do fit the stereotype, we are not at all surprised.

Something of a paradox, it seems, but really not. That's how the world works; that's how we are created.

In Vayishlach, and especially in Vayeshev, the complexities of the Jewish People, patterns that we recognize when we look around us, are introduced. The web of complexity grows from this point on, from Mitzrayim and Yetzias Mitzrayim, through the forty years in the *midbar*, settlement of the land, and our history there, at times glorious and at times depressingly disquieting.

The Torah recounts the events that it does, describing relationships between non-Jews and Jews, and between Jews and Jews, patterns that will be repeated in history over and over.

It can also be deeply disconcerting to see what appear to be serious human foibles exhibited in the Avos and the *shevatim*, whom we know to have been the foundational tzaddikim upon whom our nation is built, who were closer to God than any subsequent generation, whose example we try to emulate, whose behavior we try to live up to.

Somehow, many of us do seem to emulate the foibles, such as they are.

Look at all those described generations. They weren't exactly easy people. Look around you at our people today. Easy people? By and large phenomenally good. But easy?

Yaakov Avinu was the distillate of what the Avos represent.

What was someone like that thinking when he showed such favoritism to one son that they were set up for the tragedy that followed?

What were the *shevatim*, holy men all, thinking when they conspired to kill their brother, instead sold him into slavery, and brought such sorrow upon their father?

What about all the rest of it?

Clearly it was God moving history according to His divine plan. The foibles, I think, are quite intentional, part of the plan and the lesson.

The Torah tells us things we need to know. We need to know how we came to be, our relationship with God, and the organic continuum from the very beginning, through all the generations (us!) until forever. Why all these things apply to *us*.

And we need to understand about human nature. People, even the greatest, can have their foibles. In our belief system, no one walks on water.

On looking at others, no matter who, and at ourselves, we need to remember that.

And when we look at the foibles of other groups as well as our own, we need to remember that while individuals are responsible for their own actions, every one of us, Jew and gentile, is God's child, and their groupings are also God's children. That is how God, Father of us all, created us. And He wants us to love them.

*Parashas Vayeshev 5782*

# Miketz

## The Confused Dark Night before the Dawn

My *zeide*, Shlomo Nussbaum, *a"h*, was born in Dzhikov, but after he got married, at age nineteen, to Brandel Hoffert, he moved to her hometown of Kolbesov, where they set up their household. The Rebbe arranged for one of his Chassidim, a major lumber merchant in Hungary, to teach young Shloime the business. In time, my grandfather was able, with just a look, to assess a forest for how much lumber of what type and grade it would produce. He was quite successful. His partners were Betzalel Orgel, the senior member, and Yisrael Blitzer. Because of the nature of the work done at a lumber mill, the enterprise also lent itself to milling wheat as well, producing flour.

And so the mill, with its need for power, and therefore his house as well had electricity and telephone service well before most people in that little town did. I think his phone number was 2 or 3.

One day, the phone rang. It was an urgent message from the Dzhikover Rebbe. Shloime must, without delay, give a particular amount of money to tzedakah, which he immediately did. The Rebbe later on called to confirm that it was done. When informed that it was, the Rebbe gave a sigh of relief and told him, "Oy, Shloime, you don't know what you saved yourself from with that tzedakah." The Rebbe never explained what it was about, nor did my grandfather ask. Clearly, the Rebbe perceived a threat of some kind hanging over my *zeide*, who then, in whole-hearted faith, did what he had to do.

And this was why I reacted as I did early one morning, years ago, when I awoke from a terrible dream about one of my friends. It left me terribly upset. I know that there are many who would discount such a dream altogether as being of no account, and there are those who would advise making a positive interpretation of the dream to deflect its negativity. But I just got up and ran over to the friend's house and urged him to give tzedakah right away, which he did. Nothing bad happened, thank God. I have no idea, of course, whether that played any role at all.

Virtually everyone has had, at one time or another, a troubled night. Such is life. What happens afterward is one of the defining dramas of human existence. In the terrible *tochachah* spelled out in Parashas Ki Savo (Devarim 28:67), Moshe relates the terrible things that will befall Israel should they leave God's path. The troubles mount up so badly that in the morning, the people long for the night before, because however bad it was then, it was not as bad as now; at night, they long for the morning before, because however bad it was then, it wasn't as bad as it is now. It just gets worse. The long night holds no prospect of anything better in the morning.

Contrast that with the opposite (Tehillim 30:6), in which the righteous may go to bed at night awash with tears and worry, but, by the grace of God, the morning brings with it the joy of relief: *ba'erev yalin bechi, v'laboker rinah* (בָּעֶרֶב יָלִין בֶּכִי וְלַבֹּקֶר רִנָּה).

Yosef's dreams were full of portent and meaning, but initially at least, they brought him, his father and his brothers, nothing but trouble. The nights he dreamt of his own special place in the world aroused, by day, such anger and resentment in the brothers that they were followed, in turn, by years of the nightmare of enslavement and imprisonment. In the end, however, as was God's plan, came the joy and relief of reconciliation and renewed life.

Pharaoh's Sar Hamashkim, his Sar Ha'ofim, and finally Pharaoh himself all had troubled nights of dreams. They dreamed dreams with real meaning, and they did so in order that Yosef could play his unique role in that divine plan and fulfill the destiny revealed in his own dreams. And the rest is history.

The troubled, turbulent nights of life, whatever time of day they actually occur, whether they are occupied by dark dreams, actual nightmares, or dim foreboding, are preludes to an uncertain dawn. That dawn could turn out, God forbid, worse than the foreboding itself, or it could be the joyful nullification of it. Sometimes we are lucky enough to have a Yosef Hatzaddik or a latter-day tzaddik help shepherd us through it. Mostly, however, we have the formula laid out for us in Toras Moshe Rabbeinu, in which we are taught that the path to life is to do good, to care for and to love one another, to be charitable with our spirit as well as with our treasure, to absorb the Torah and to follow its dictates, and to face that dawn, come what may, with utter, wholehearted trust and faith in Him, as we have been taught, *Tamim tihyeh im Hashem Elokecha*, be wholehearted with Hashem your God, and you will be His.

*Parashas Miketz 5778*

## To Hear a Dream

Charlie had too many oysters, washed down with too much beer. That night, he had crazy dreams. It's a reasonable assumption that his dreams meant nothing more than that he overdid it.

Meredith was a far more conservative and constrained person. Almost ascetic, contemplative, and spiritual. She also dreamt, something not rare for her. She knew that much of it somehow reflected her day-to-day concerns. And sometimes, she was convinced, her dreams bore a message, and she thought a lot about what it might mean for her.

We all dream. I don't think normal life would be possible if we did not. We'd probably go crazy. Mostly we forget them as soon as we awaken. They are a biological function. Sometimes they linger, and sometimes we are haunted by them. Sometimes, convinced that they have meaning for us, we act upon them or at least consider doing so. (Remember the old joke about Motke who was really bad at math, but who was destined to be lifted out of poverty? He went to bed thinking about the upcoming lottery. In a dream, he saw seven sevens dancing before his eyes, and when he awoke, recognizing a sign from God, he ran right out and bought lottery ticket number 42, which won first prize and made him rich. His arithmetic was terrible, but the Sender of Dreams counted on that to get him to win.)

But how do we know if there's a real message in a dream, or if it's…just a dream, a *gurnisht*, which is the most likely. And yet we know, and the Torah has let us know, that dreams can and on occasion do carry messages. The Gemara offers advice on how to "manage" a dream, on the possibility that it has predictive content. Chazal tell us to immediately interpret it positively, no matter how frightening it might be, preferably invoking a positive *pasuk* from Tanach to back up that interpretation, lest a "negative" *pasuk* come to the fore and turn it bad.

Yosef the Dreamer also interpreted dreams, as that tzaddik was endowed by God with the power to discern His messages delivered through dreams. And the various dreams the Torah tells us about in these *parashiyos* were very much pointed and filled with meaning. And when speaking to Pharaoh – Yosef's first statement to the king in whose temporal power it was to raise Yosef up – he told Pharaoh that it was not him, Yosef, who gave meaning to dreams, but rather, Almighty God. And the meaning of these particular dreams was not affected by subjective interpretation but was the objective intent of God.

Well, we know about Pharaoh's dream, its interpretation, and all that came out from that. But let's go back a bit to the dream of the Sar Hamashkim, Pharaoh's cupbearer who was to survive, which Yosef interpreted while imprisoned with him and the doomed Sar Ha'ofim.

The Egyptian official dreamed of a grapevine with three branches that blossomed and bore fruit before his eyes, fruit that he squeezed into Pharaoh's cup as wine. Yosef told him that the three branches are three days, after which he would be restored to his former post as cup bearer to the king. Remember, this is the same *pasgudnyak* (nasty guy) who, upon being saved, promptly dismissed Yosef from his mind, did not help him as promised, and only two years later, when it was useful to him, told Pharaoh about Yosef, also making sure to denigrate him in the process. No matter, he served his purpose. God's will be done.

Now let's see what symbolism the Gemara (*Chulin* 92a) finds in that same dream. Rabbi Eliezer Hamoda'i says the grapevine represents Yerushalayim. The three branches are the Beis Hamikdash, the king, and the Kohen Gadol. The blossoming, *porachas*, refers to the *pirchei kehunah*, the blossoming young Kohanim in training coming into their own, and the ripened grapes, the *nesachim*, the wine offerings on the Mizbe'ach.

Huh? What does any of that have to do with Pharaoh, the Sar Hamashkim, or even Yosef at that time and place, or altogether in that context? And yet, of all the symbolic interpretations offered in the Gemara, Rabban Gamliel seems to prefer that of Rabbi Eliezer Hamoda'i, saying that we need it *adayin*, still. Ongoing. "*Adayin tzrichin anu es Hamoda'i.*" What's the connection?

The Torah Temimah wonders the same thing. He explains that all those things, Yerushalayim in its greatest glory, start here with Yosef, his own dreams, and especially his God-inspired interpretation of the Sar Hamashkim's God-sent dream, which launched his ascent to leadership that resulted in the rest of the story. And then he makes a remarkable statement: Yosef was dragged down to Egypt so that the rest of his family would eventually follow, become enslaved and then finally freed hundreds of years later, so that they would eventually be brought back into the Land of Israel, the Beis Hamikdash would be built, Yerushalayim and Israel would be in its glory as all those things in the interpretation of Rabbi Eliezer Hamoda'i would come into being. The *haftarah* of Miketz reflects that period, during the reign of Shlomo Hamelech.

Think of that. They had to *leave* Eretz Yisrael and suffer so that they could eventually *re-enter* it and flourish. Avraham Avinu's arrival in the land was enough to establish our claim to the land, but not enough to cement our national hold on it. We had to leave the land, suffer, be formed as a nation – a special, Godly nation – and then return to claim it. But now that claim is eternal. That was and is God's plan.

God has many messengers and many means of delivering His messages. Sometimes it's as obvious as Moshe on Har Sinai, witnessed by all of us. Sometimes it's the voice of a prophet calling out his message in the marketplaces of Jerusalem or Shomron. Sometimes it's the inspiration in the heart of an individual. And sometimes it can be a dream, even one dreamt by a bad but potentially influential official, even one down on his luck and rotting in jail, but then interpreted by a pure servant of God in a manner that leads, eventually, no matter the many twists and turns in between, to the ultimate glory, those twists and turns known only to the all-knowing God Who directs all of history, the destiny of nations and of every individual within those nations, everything, *everything*, even the silly dreams we have, and also the dreams upon which our entire world, the world we have and the world we pray for, is built.

Part of the wisdom of life is knowing how to listen, how to be attuned, always, to His message.

*Parashas Miketz 5782, Yerushalayim Ir Hakodesh*

# Vayigash

## Surgeons Must Be Very Careful

Surgeons must be very careful
When they take the knife!
Underneath their fine incisions
Stirs the Culprit – Life!

*Emily Dickinson, 1859*

Chances are you have been one, or possibly both, of these two people: Two guys shake hands. One is actually greeting and looking at the other. The other guy is looking over the shoulder of the person he's shaking hands with, seeing who else is there who is more interesting or more useful than the useless *shmegeggy* who's shaking his hand at the moment.

Nasty. I would guess that most of us have been, at one time or another, in the *shmegeggy* position, and that many of us have been guilty, at least on some occasion, of being in the nasty position. Many people who have done it are really not like that, are really nice, but somehow it happened. Perhaps just distracted. Sorry. Didn't mean to do that. And there are those who live that way, because they are, in fact, not nice people.

One recent Shabbos, I was the *shmegeggy*, and the other fellow was, I know, actually the nicest person. It can happen. A mindless, unintentional lapse. No hard feelings at all. But it made me think about another person with a different kind of problem.

That other person is a well-respected rabbi and scholar. He certainly seems nice enough, if somewhat aloof. I was once at a talk he gave and afterward went up to him and asked a question. Normal procedure. There was nothing bad or challenging or provocative about the question or the way it was asked. It wasn't, I believe, a stupid question (*and if it were?*). After his curt reply, I was immediately struck by an overwhelming feeling of regret that I had asked him anything.

67

I couldn't understand, at first, why I felt that way. Please understand that I am not judgmental, I'm not challenging, I like and appreciate people, especially Torah scholars, I had no problem with his talk, and I said nothing to indicate that I did. And yet, as I reflected, his response was some kind of subtle but, I thought, unmistakably dismissive put-down. It was so not understandable to me that I concluded that I must have thoroughly misread him, and I put it out of my mind. I was mistaken. Had to be.

Months later, I again attended the same man's talk. Afterward, I asked him a question, having put that first incident out of my mind. Don't think it didn't happen again. It did. Unmistakably. And on another occasion, without asking a question, just when I said hello, there was a snide remark. I don't get it. I'm not paranoid. It was real. I had never heard (or said) anything at all negative about this rabbi. Perhaps because I'm not a member of his congregation, and he doesn't depend on me, he allowed his apparent haughty arrogance to come through. This was not the kind of response I normally elicit from people. And certainly not what one would expect from a Torah scholar, and a respected one at that.

On yet another occasion, I was chatting with a great older lady, a remarkable Holocaust survivor with whom I have a relationship. A woman breezed by and interjected her grand greeting to the lady, blowing me aside as if I were not there. OK, that can certainly be unintentional. But by her manner with the great lady, it was startlingly clear that what she was actually doing was *bestowing herself* on that lady, her greeting being a brief act of *noblesse oblige*, after which she breezed on by, her little entourage in tow.

Then, surprise, surprise, I heard someone address her by name, identifying her as the wife of the man described above. They say poverty follows the poor. I suppose haughtiness also follows the haughty.

Let me say right here that these two are probably, in reality, very fine people. And yet they came across, each of them, as if they are not. They let it happen. It's hard for me to write like this about a rabbi. But no one is immune; this applies to everyone, especially a rabbi, the public face of Torah Judaism.

No one should act haughty or grand with other people. And the more one commands respect by virtue of one's position in life, the more one has to be oh-so-careful about this. Rabbis – and in the broader world, clerics, doctors, public officials, people in positions of power over others – beware: you *are indeed* held to a higher standard in the mensch department. You do not deserve to occupy your position of public trust unless you behave decently, with respect, with kindness, with caring, with compassion, with honesty, with appropriate humility to the people who need you, who depend on you, and who look up to you. God put you in that position to serve, not to be grand. Your dignity, which you deserve, is not a license to inflict indignity on others. It is, rather, among the greatest opportunities in this life.

Watch truly great people, and you will see this principle in action. Learn from them.

Yosef Hatzaddik had to test his brothers' sincerity, but his heart, from the moment he saw them, was filled with love and goodness, with a generosity of spirit that remains to this day an ultimate example and model for *tzidkus*. He was the cleverest, most powerful, and arguably the most prestigious and influential man in the world at the time, and at every turn, it seems, he is so overcome with love and compassion that he must weep. He weeps for their despair; he weeps for their shame; he weeps when, after Yaakov's death, he thinks they fear he will harm them; weeps for his brother Binyamin, upon whose portion of land in Israel, many hundreds of years later, both Temples will be destroyed. He protects them in whatever way he can from the hurts of the world and makes it clear that he considers it his great privilege to do so, and he does so with utter kindness and compassion, with respect, preserving their dignity. So should we all be. That's why the Torah tells us about it.

Surgeons – or anyone else in an analogous position – must be *very* careful when they take the "knife" (*you fill in the blank*)! Underneath their fine "incisions" stirs the Culprit – *Life!*

*Parashas Vayigash 5780*

# He Prayeth Well Who Loveth Well

The face of the man sitting opposite me conveyed an impression of earnest and kindly empathy. It was no surprise to learn that he is engaged in a profession in which he is dedicated to listening to people's problems, *really listening*, and devotedly helping people all day long.

How did he get that way? Is it built into his nature? Is it the result of how he was brought up? Nature or nurture? Well, I think we all understand that it is both, and the person that results is a function of the interplay of the two.

Of all the people in the Tanach, many are identified as tzaddikim, but only one has that description incorporated into the name we call him by: Yosef Hatzaddik. The Torah relates much about him that qualifies him as a tzaddik, but those fine and admirable attributes are not unique to him. The Torah does go to considerable lengths, however, to make clear to us those aspects of his character that make him stand apart.

Yosef had every reason to be angry with his brothers, to be unforgiving, to be cruel, to make life miserable for them, *to rub it in*, even if he did save them, except for one main reason: it would have been totally out of character for him to do so;

not because he was spineless – after all, he was the powerful viceroy of Egypt who ran the country and cleverly centralized wealth and power in Pharaoh's hands – but because he was, by virtue of nature and of nurture, a kind, loving, and soft-hearted person, emotional, prone to emotional weepiness (*my favorite – and if you know me, you'll know why*), attributes which he melded together with his faith and *yiras Shamayim* to make him the remarkable figure known as Yosef Hatzaddik.

Yosef was raised by Yaakov Avinu and – until she died when he was about eight – by the selflessly generous Rachel Imenu, whose kindness and empathy for Leah caused her to switch with her when she was supposed to marry her beloved Yaakov. Small wonder that he was special, with such parents. But, as we know, that is not enough. The "devil" is always at work, and our challenge is to confront that devil trying to make us bad, or less good, whispering in our ear that under the circumstances, we would be entirely justified, even righteous, to do things *his* way.

Yosef Hatzaddik was who he was because he was born with the capacity to be that way, he was raised by parents who taught him that way, *but mainly because he made himself that way.* His love was limitless.

And so this gentle, kindly man, sitting across from me, as we were talking about this, pulled from his pocket a well-worn inscription that was his mother's chief moral legacy to him. I don't know much about how *frum* the home was or any other circumstances of his upbringing. But he grew weepy as he read to me his mother's oft-stressed lesson in life, on what was important for a person to be the kind of person God put us here to be. Of how to relate to other people, indeed to all of God's creatures. Of how to endear oneself to God, by endearing oneself to His children.

And so she would read to him from Samuel Taylor Coleridge's *Rime of the Ancient Mariner*, lines of wisdom in life that would translate into his own dedication to serving others with love:

> He prayeth well, who loveth well
> Both man and bird and beast
>
> He prayeth best, who loveth best
> All things both great and small
>
> For the dear God who loveth us
> He made and loveth all.

*Parashas Vayigash 5779*

# *Reishis Chochmah*

It is said, and I certainly believe it's true, that Jewish children achieve a high level of religious understanding and sophistication considerably earlier in life than do most other groups.

Other groups may instill rote teaching or practices, but few, if any, invest the intellectual immersion into the principles as well as the practices of their faith system the way we do and always have. That has been a remarkable strength for us, not just in our continuity, but in standing up to our persecutors – and tragically sometimes in knowingly giving our lives for our faith. Think of the Chanukah story of Chana and her seven sons. Each had a *pasuk* and a philosophical teaching to bolster his faith as he faced martyrdom.

May we and our children never be tested. Let's dwell on everyday life. If we choose wisely, and if we make the required commitments in how we raise our children, they are, or at least ought to be, powerhouses of budding Yiddishkeit. But we also know that the reality isn't always that way. There are no guarantees in life. Things can happen and sometimes do.

And so we must, as parents, invest in our children by providing for them, first and foremost, a living, loving example of how Jewish life and faith should be lived. One that is not cosmetic but entirely genuine. One that is joyful and enthusiastic, not grudging but happy. Kids know when parents are not sincere. And remember my famous dictum: the good things you do in life, *if you're lucky*, your kids will also do. The bad things you do, they will almost for sure also do.

And we must, of course, be ever so careful and vigilant in educational choices for our children. The spirit in a school, the *ruach*, is critically important. Is it a school where they will be imbued, *happily*, with real *yiras Shamayim*? That is of prime importance before they even get to the academics, as important as that is. We all know cases of parents foolishly choosing schools based on other considerations instead, such as politics (e.g., Zionism, emphasis on Hebrew language – *as important as that is* – but not so much on fervor for lived Yiddishkeit), what's fashionable in their circles, what others will say (I remember one fool being so angry that his rabbi sent his sons to a traditional yeshiva rather than to a co-ed Ivrit b'Ivrit day school where Chumash or Gemara were subjects, much like any other – important, perhaps, but not apparently as important as Zionism, and certainly not as important as getting into a prestigious college – that he declared that rabbi *no rabbi of his*), or what might be less difficult for their preferred lifestyle (no criticism from the children for substandard religious standards at home). And very little is as important as who the child's friends will be. Not surprisingly, many children of parents who had other priorities turned out not as they'd hoped or naively expected.

And then there have been those who were so taken up with their own religious and studious endeavors that they failed to pay enough attention to their children, who went off in a far different direction. Sadly, there have been many such examples.

Of course, sometimes the opposite miraculously occurs. A gift from God, and a gift from wonderful children. It's not just up to the parents. A reminder to parents: children do have minds and personalities of their own. We can encourage but not guarantee their performance. And we know, of course, that children may start out well and then fall down, or God forbid drop out later in life, a crisis of maturity and adulthood. And some children start out very weak and unmotivated but then flower beautifully, an inspired choice of maturity and adulthood.

Blessed is the person who was raised right and then, with maturity, raises himself right and grows from there. That is the ideal we aspire to. *Oy* for the person who wastes his childhood years on foolishness and then lacks the basis for a well-grounded maturity. *Oy* for the person who had a great upbringing, but once out on his own, lets go of the momentum he was given and, in his freedom, runs after foolishness.

Yosef Hatzaddik was only seventeen years old when his brothers, who were supposed to be his protectors, role models, and teachers, betrayed him. He spent years in the most difficult and depraved circumstances, with only a limited number of childhood years' *chinuch* to sustain him, not only as a Yid, but as a tzaddik. In his case, that was enough. The home of Yaakov Avinu was the ideal environment to grow up in. During that harrowing time, he not only remained true to his heritage, but he grew in *tzidkus* and in *middos*. His unbelievable graciousness to his brothers who did him wrong was a function of his upbringing, his *chinuch*, his kindly personality, and his unswerving faith in and understanding of the God of his fathers, Whose *hashgachah* brought them to this point. *"V'ata al te'atzvu v'al yichar b'eineichem ki mechartem osi hennah, ki l'michyah shelachani Elokim lifneichem"* (Bereishis 45:5). Do not be vexed, my brothers, for having sold me here, for it was to sustain our lives that God sent me here before you.

In the dramatic buildup before Yosef finally reveals himself to his brothers, when, as the viceroy of Egypt, he tells the brothers that he will keep Binyamin as a slave, Yehuda makes his powerful and emotional case. He offers himself – a far more powerful person – as a slave in his brother's stead. *"Ki eich e'eleh el avi v'hanaar einenu iti, pen er'eh vara asher yimtza es avi"* (44:34). For how can I go up (from

Egypt) to my father *(how can I face him?!)* and the boy (Binyamin) is not with me, lest I see *(that I cause!)* the misery that will then envelop my father.

Yosef can't stand it anymore. Overcome, he banishes all the Egyptian retainers from the room, that his brothers not be shamed before them, and reveals his true identity, lovingly and forgivingly comforting them in their resulting embarrassed discomfiture.

The simple meaning of that *pasuk* is, of course, as it says. Yehuda would be unable to face his father. But like everywhere else in the Torah, the choice of words conveys meaning on many levels beyond the simple *peshat*.

Our *darshanim* bring us a valuable life lesson from this phrase. It is one that every Jew must ask himself as he conducts his life. *Ki eich e'eleh el Avi v'hanaar einenu iti?* How will I go up to my Father (in Heaven, after 120), when the precious and opportunity-filled days of my youth are not with me? I wasted them with foolish, childish pursuits rather than building a basis for my eternity. Or I utilized that time well but then did not follow through and keep it up in my adulthood, conjuring up excuse upon excuse for frittering it away, or simply because I had the freedom to do so and chose foolishly. Or *hanaar einenu iti* may refer to one's children who did not receive the attention or the education they should have, and they are thus no longer *iti*, with me, spiritually.

We need *mazal* in everything, especially in how our children turn out, but it's certainly not just *mazal* alone that determines how they turn out. And we need *seichel* in the choices we make in life, so that we have done everything we can that we ourselves turn out right, that our children turn out right, and through them, all our future generations forever.

Indeed, we pray never to be tested. But of course, all of life is a test, even the good times. One lesson from Yosef Hatzaddik is that *chinuch* is virtually everything, starting with how we ourselves behave, how our children see us, the choices we make for our children while we still have the power of choice on their behalf, the choices we make for ourselves. For in the end, *sof kol sof*, there is no escape: *e'eleh el Avi*. We will, every one of us, inevitably go up to Him. How we face Him – and from that perspective, how we face the generations that follow us, how they turn out as a result of the choices we make – is the primary challenge of our lives.

*Parashas Vayigash 5782, Yerushalayim Ir Hakodesh*

# Vayechi

## Chesed shel Emes

It was never quite clear to me why Yosef had to spend an extra two years in prison for having asked the Sar Hamashkim to remember him and to mention him to Pharaoh. What was he supposed to do? Rely on miracles? We're not supposed to.

There are those who maintain that a tzaddik of Yosef's caliber should place his full faith in God and not ask others to do anything. But I have not been able to quite understand that. The full weight of our tradition and teaching tells us we must do what we can, and, of course, pray and trust in Hashem. But we are not supposed to just sit back. When the rowboat approaches the proverbial drowning man, he's not supposed to send it away, saying, "Don't bother; God will save me without you." The Sar Hamashkim, about to return to Pharaoh's service and with access to Pharaoh's ear, was an obvious opportunity – and, like the proverbial rowboat, presumably sent by God. After all, what was the point of that whole dream thing with the two officers of Pharaoh's court?

So, is it that the tzaddik shouldn't ask anybody for help, even someone in a position to help?

Or is it that the tzaddik may, in fact, ask someone to help, but may not ask a bad guy, as the Sar Hamashkim was? Rashi seems to favor this approach, quoting a *pasuk* to the effect that one should trust in Hashem and not in bad people.

Is that what Yosef did that cost him two extra years of imprisonment? Is it possible that he placed his trust in that guy rather than in Hashem? We can be sure that was not the case. Rather, I think, perhaps Yosef did what he was supposed to do, but not in the way he should have.

Yosef uses a particular grammatical form in asking the Sar Hamashkim, as it's rendered in the Torah, *zechartani*, "remember me." And then he asks this Egyptian courtier to do him a *chesed*, and, in that same form, *hizkartani*, "mention me" to Pharaoh, and thereby, again in that form, *hotzeisani*, "get me out" of this place (Bereishis 40:14).

*L'aniyus daati*, I think that's the key to Yosef's error. It's one thing to tell the Sar Hamashkim that he, Yosef, is an innocent victim of kidnapping who wound up in this terrible circumstance, and can he please put in a good word for him with Pharaoh. Of the operative words, I think *zechartani* and *hizkartani* are not so bad. Yosef Hatzaddik asking the Sar Hamashkim for *chesed*, is, I think, problematic, but most serious of all is *hotzeisani*, "get me out of here." I suggest that Chazal's criticism is that it would have been better to say to the Sar Hamashkim, *The God Who sent you that dream, the God Who revealed its meaning to me, the God Who will now spare your life and have you released from here and return you to your high office, will, in His great chesed, also get me out of here.* That was undoubtedly what Yosef was thinking but apparently did not actually say to that haughty and ungrateful Egyptian.

Fast-forward twenty-six years. Yaakov Avinu senses that his life is drawing to a close, at a considerably younger age than his father or grandfather (with all he suffered, no surprise). He does not want to be buried in Egypt, and he must ask Yosef to assure that he will be carried back to Israel and laid to rest in the Cave of Machpelah.

There is an interesting recapitulation of grammatical form in this request, evocative of Yosef's language when he petitioned the Sar Hamashkim. *Al na tikbereni*, don't bury me in Egypt, *u'nesasani*, carry me to the Land of Israel, and *kevartani*, bury me in Me'aras Hamachpelah with my forebears and with my wife Leah (47:29–30).

Yaakov understands that Yosef may have reason to chafe at this request. Yosef's beloved mother, Rachel, snatched away when he was still a little boy, was hastily buried at the roadside, *not at all distant from Hebron*, where, it seems, she could have easily been brought to Me'aras Hamachpelah. Yaakov Avinu, acting as God's agent in history, did as he understood was necessary. But that might still have been hard for Yosef.

And so Yaakov asks Yosef to do him a *chesed*. But now it's Yaakov Avinu talking to Yosef Hatzaddik. There is an additional element to this *chesed*. It is *chesed v'emes*. It is the right thing to do, for Yaakov, for Yosef, for Klal Yisrael, for history. And Yosef Hatzaddik, whose *tzidkus* in his gracious and loving treatment of the brothers who sold him into slavery is his defining characteristic, responds readily, eagerly, and earnestly. And thus we have also established the principle and the practice as well as the terminology of *chesed shel emes*.

Do someone a favor, and you can reasonably expect that someday he will return the favor.

That greases the wheels of society. *Chesed shel emes* typically and specifically refers to performing an act of *chesed* on behalf of someone who will never be able to return the favor, because that person has died. The honorable and respectful burying of the dead is classic *chesed shel emes*.

We are taught, as well, that there actually is reward for this *chesed* on behalf of someone who, having died, cannot return the favor. One who undertakes this effort on behalf of others, who respectfully tends to the deceased in the ways they need to be tended to, can be assured that when his time comes, others will do the same for him.

Well and good. Except that in this world, it doesn't always turn out that way. How many *chevra kadisha* members were slaughtered just a generation ago, with no one to deal respectfully with their remains? What was left of them, bodies or ash, was unceremoniously dumped, along with the remains of the millions of their fellow victims. And the same holds true for many of the martyred in our history. Where is their *chesed shel emes*?

Part of the *gezerah*, the decree on those generations that suffered martyrdom, is that the many who cannot in any way be considered individually deserving of being so martyred were martyred anyway. The only way we can cope with that is to understand that there is a plan and a plane of justice that is utterly beyond our ken, and, in our faith, we put our trust in God. Ultimate justice is in His hands. We must leave it to God to reward those who fulfill His will.

But still we act. We revere the memory of the martyrs, we recite Kaddish, we observe known yahrtzeits precisely and communal yahrtzeits at designated times (as is done here in Israel on 10 Teves), we mourn for them on Tisha b'Av, we elevate their souls in Heaven by retaining our faith and trust in the very God Who allowed them to be martyred, no matter how much we chafe under that burden. And, I submit, the better Jew we are, the more we connect and care, the greater that chafing burden.

Yaakov, feeling his life force waning, turned to his loyal son Yosef, the outstanding tzaddik, and asked him to do a difficult thing. The political and practical aspect, getting Pharaoh to sanction it, was the lesser challenge. Yaakov feels the need to explain himself to Yosef. He knows that Yosef is hurt and presumably resentful over the treatment of his mother, her having been buried in apparent haste at the side of the road. It appeared as if Yaakov could not be bothered to transport her the relatively short distance to Hebron (or even the closer Beit Lechem), yet he now asks Yosef to carry his remains from Egypt for proper burial in Me'aras Machpelah, alongside his mother's rival wife, Leah. Furthermore, Yaakov reveals, *you, Yosef, having done this for me, will yourself be buried in Egypt. But I am asking of you* chesed shel emes. *Do it anyway.*

Yaakov reveals that he had reasons for doing what he did, following God's guidance, and not out of disrespect or lack of concern for Rachel's honor. Her presence there would help her exiled children, so many generations later, as they were being led into captivity past that very spot.

And from that vantage point, she has continued to be a consoling presence for the Children of Israel in their many troubles, to this very day. And for many people, the powerful, emotional pull, the tug at the heart, the consolation of Kever Rachel is far more powerful than even that of Me'aras Hamachpelah.

Yaakov taught Yosef that we may brood and we may chafe, but there is a larger picture and a perspective known only to God. Yosef himself, despite his begging plea, had been sold into slavery at age seventeen by his own brothers and had endured years of imprisonment and hardship. He was terribly wronged, but what had he done wrong to deserve that? And yet later, he consoled those brothers in their shame by telling them that even though none of them could see it when it was happening, in the end it was clear that it was all God's plan to give them life and to build the nation. And so Yosef Hatzaddik readily understood and was reconciled.

But Yosef would have undoubtedly done as he did, as graciously and as lovingly as he did, with the *kavod* that he did, with the *chesed shel emes* that he displayed, regardless of any explanation, for that was who he was. And in the end, having lain buried in Egypt for so long, his own bones were raised and, in *chesed shel emes*, carried with the Children of Israel into the Promised Land.

And it is particularly telling, I think, that the place designated for his burial was not near Hebron, where he grew up, but in Shechem, where it all started, where he was cruelly thrown in the pit, and where he later, as viceroy of Egypt, stood and blessed God for having performed a miracle on his behalf on that spot. The *miracle*? Being thrown in the pit and then sold into slavery? In Yosef's eyes, yes, for that is from where God sent him on the incredible journey to be the savior of his nation, to be the epitome of *chesed*, to embody *chesed shel emes*, to become known forever afterward as Yosef Hatzaddik.

*Parashas Vayechi 5778, Yerushalayim Ir Hakodesh*

# Shadow

No offense (especially to my children who live there, and even seem to really like it), but I still haven't quite figured out why some people prefer to live in a *dorf*, a *shtetl* like Monsey, when they could be living in a normal place like Brooklyn. Don't get me wrong: they have beautiful *kehillos*, shuls and yeshivos, and nice trees. In many ways, it is very nice indeed. OK, so it doesn't have the elegant ambiance of Coney Island Avenue, and there's hardly a funeral parlor in sight, and it has much too much fresh air. Still, it has some nice – if simple – things going for it. But try walking on a road at night – say, on Shabbos – and you'll wonder what they see in pitch-black roadways, with no sidewalks and only an occasional light. Kind of primitive, don't you think?

As you walk on such a dark road, hoping not to trip, when you finally approach a light, you know there must be a shadow behind you but dare not turn around and look, lest you find you are being followed by a disease-laden tick or a crazed wild turkey, waiting to pounce. So you look straight ahead toward the light, finally able to see the road. As you reach the light, directly under it, there is no shadow. One step forward, and the shadow appears. It is short and truncated at first, but with each step, as you get further from the light, the shadow grows longer and longer, until it begins to fade and finally disappears altogether. You are back in the darkness, alone with the potholes, the wildlife, the disquieting mystery of what might be lurking out there.

It is at such a moment that the wisdom of Monsey (and places like it) becomes apparent: it's the shadow, along with the profound lesson shadows have to offer.

David Hamelech longed to build the Beis Hamikdash. It was his lifelong dream. God told him no. Too much blood, too much history. David's son and successor Shlomo would build it. But David did as much preparatory work as he could, including marshaling the resources of the people, gathering gold and silver and other precious commodities from the enthusiastic nation. At the end of his life, with twelve-year-old Shlomo at his side, he gathered the people with their fabulously rich gifts for the House of God and gave them what would be his final oration and instruction.

He asked the people to recognize that the young and tender Shlomo, chosen by God to be the next king of Israel, had a tremendous task before him and needed the people's help and support. He praised God Who created all and is the source of all wealth and power. All this wealth brought by the people was from God, Who bestowed it upon them. "For who am I," proclaimed David, "and who are my people that we can have the power to donate like this? It is all from God! What we donate now to You [for the Beis Hamikdash] we received *from* You! We are but temporary dwellers in this world, as were our forefathers. We are but a passing shadow on the earth, without hope [of somehow remaining alive beyond our given time]" (I Divrei Hayamim 29:14–16).

Much has been said about that shadow that is a metaphor for our time on this earth and the impression we leave on it.

Young Shlomo must have been listening intently, as he later famously wrote in Koheles about the apparent empty vanity of life, *hevel havalim*, which passes like a shadow, unless man invests his pitiful efforts for the good, through Torah and mitzvos, through doing God's will and fulfilling his purpose and mission in the "blip" that is his life.

"*Ki mi yodea mah tov l'adam ba'chaim...v'yaasem ka-tzel*" (Koheles 6:12). Who is wise enough to know what to do with the "shadow" (the life, the impression a person leaves on the world) we are given? *Midrash Rabbah* asks, what kind of shadow does a human make? Sadly, not like the shadow of a wall, which has some permanence, not like the shadow of a tree, which may be broad and pleasant and long-lasting, but rather, as David said, *k'tzel over*, like a passing shadow, like the shadow of a flying bird that flits by so rapidly, it has no lasting quality at all. And finally, the Midrash says, not really even like a bird, but like the wings of a bee, which are so small and gossamer and move so quickly that they make no impression at all.

And *Metzudas David*, on Divrei Hayamim, reminds us that the nature of a shadow is that it grows longer the further one moves from the light source. One's shadow grows longer and longer as one's sun sets, as one grows further removed from the light source of life, until it finally reaches a point where there is no light; then the shadow, and in this context the person who cast it, are altogether gone. And there is no hope for it – no one is exempt.

And so we must very well contemplate how, in this fleeting life, we can try to cast the most profound shadow, the most lasting and effective, the most meaningful shadow possible, lest, before we know it, it is gone altogether, leaving no more impression and no more effect than the small, gossamer wings of a bee, which move so quickly that they make no impression at all.

*Va'yechi Yaakov b'Eretz Mitzrayim*, Yaakov lived in Egypt for the last seventeen years of his life (Bereishis 47:28). *Va'yikrivu yemei Yisrael lamus*, the time for Yisrael to die approached (47:29). Interesting how the Torah here sometimes refers to our forefather as Yaakov and sometimes as Yisrael.

Kesav Sofer looks at the meaning of these choices. Yaakov was about to die – indeed he did die, as everyone must. And yet, the Gemara (*Taanis* 5b) declares that *Yaakov Avinu lo meis*, Yaakov our forefather did not die, citing a *pasuk* that refers to him as if he were still alive. Yaakov didn't die, in a manner of speaking, Kesav Sofer says, because he had his son Yosef, who was so much like him, carry on after him, his moral power still effective in the world. But while Yosef may have approached the exalted level of "Yaakov," he did not reach the even more exalted level of "Yisrael," which no one could. And thus, the Torah declares here that it was the time for *Yisrael* to die, for upon *his* passing, no one could replace him.

And yet, Yisrael also did not quite die, for here we are. *Am Yisrael chai.*

David Hamelech spoke about life being but a passing shadow, but the imprint he left was so strong and so lasting that today we declare, indeed we sing, *David Melech Yisrael chai v'kayam!* King David is alive and exists still!

And it is the very existence of our nation – still recognizable as the very same nation with the same faith as that founded by our forefather Yisrael so many generations ago, with so much that might have undone it – that attests to the power vested in mankind and bestowed upon our people by the Creator to somehow, on some level, in a fundamental way, escape the inevitability of death that is every mortal man's lot, by transforming those gossamer bee's wings into a massive wall, a broad and towering tree, by our actions, by our choices, by our faith, by the stubbornness with which we have been both cursed and blessed, to cast a giant shadow.

*Parashas Vayechi 5779*

## Zoll Shoyn Zein de Geulah

The young yeshiva boy, about nineteen years old, was having a bit of technical trouble feeding dollar bills into the turnstile in the *mikveh* on Erev Shabbos. Waiting my turn to enter, I quipped, "It doesn't take Confederate money." I got a blank look, followed by the apparent realization on his part that he should know what I'm talking about, but he doesn't.

So I asked him who won the Civil War. Pause. Then his sheepish response: "Egypt?" I asked him where he went to school. (Note: he was not *chassidish.*) He was reluctant to tell me. Then he told me, but insisted that the fault lay with him, not the school. A really nice and sweet boy, he seemed intelligent, was very polite, and later made sure to wish me a good Shabbos.

Now, there's insularity and there's insularity. How insular do we have to be to be insular enough?

In every immigrant group I encounter, the children always speak better English than the parents and are far more aware of what's going on. There's one group only, in my experience, in which the parents have to come along to the doctor's office and do the talking, because the young fellows are unable to express themselves in the English language. The parents usually have no foreign accent, but their children do. The parents' vocabulary may be somewhat limited (or may in fact be rather sophisticated) but the sons' is much worse. The educational system set up for them assures that.

How insular is insular enough? I'm thinking of a very "*yeshivish*" boy who derisively dismissed the study of mathematics as a total waste of time. "But it's the language of creation," I replied. "What if it helps you understand how the world works? What if you one day need it?" If he must learn it, he told me with a dismissive and skeptical wave of the hand, he could do it later in life. His mother, a professor of mathematics, held her head down and looked at the floor, clearly embarrassed.

How about having no clue about – and therefore no real appreciation for or connection to – what was done for us by the many thousands of brave young men who stormed the beaches at Normandy, and other horrible places of military slaughter, running headlong into murderous machine-gun fire knowing it was likely they would die, so that we today can live our peaceful Jewish lives in freedom and safety? So that we can sway and pray and learn Torah?

How insular is insular enough? Does avoiding eye contact with your non-Jewish neighbors and never saying hello make you a better Jew? Is it "good for the Jews"?

An Italian American colleague told me of his *frum* Jewish next-door neighbor who never, ever greeted him in any way. Never looked at him. The doc decided to force the issue. He walked up to the man, looked him in the eye, and said, "Good morning!" The neighbor was shocked. He returned the greeting and walked on. The doc, who wisely and benignly understood what it was about, persisted. He made it a project. They eventually became cordial friends, although at a proper distance (not drinking buddies!). This doc understood that the neighbor was not being distant out of malice, but from a kind of inward insularity. Most people, however, don't understand that, and sometimes very bad feelings result, something we don't need.

How insular is insular enough? Is being more ignorant about basic American history and civics than your average low-intelligence American know-nothing a desirable thing?

When our forefathers, Yaakov's little tribe of seventy souls, went down to Egypt and settled there, they excelled as they grew. They took hold of the land of Goshen, as they grew, but the land of Goshen, of Egypt, also took hold of them. *Va'ye'achazu bah* (Bereishis 47:27). They possessed – and they were also possessed by – that alien land. Some became *too* Egyptian. That is the universal story, to some degree, of the Jewish diaspora.

There is a fine line, a balancing act, that is always at play. Get too familiar, and you have the estimated 80 percent of the nation disappearing into Egypt, never part of Yetzias Mitzrayim, lost forever, a pattern we have seen over and over. Too insular, and you generate the hard feelings that you are utterly alien, uninterested, perhaps a parasite, and a target, potentiating any other hatred and resentments that are always part of the package of our exile. This dichotomy, it seems, is a built-in constant.

Our challenge, one of very many, is to decide really how insular is insular enough – and that we do need that insularity in order to survive has been proven, tragically, in the huge numbers of young Jews lost to the nation – and how much is excessive, off-putting, and counterproductive in various ways, including to the young people who bear its potentially unbearable burden even as they are ostensibly shielded by it.

We languish yet in Galus. Even in Israel, the alien effect of the Galus, felt nearly everywhere, has laid waste to so many Jewish families, and that pernicious influence threatens normal kosher families as well. A major part of our Redemption, I think, will be not just the reality of Redemption in the usually understood way, but freedom also from the burden of fear that every family harbors, on some level, for the spiritual life and safety of its children, and the sometimes odd, stultifying aspects of culture that fear helps create.

There are very many reasons, urgent and pressing reasons, for our constant prayer and plea. This too, an outgrowth of our civilizational angst, is yet another reason: Ribbono shel Olam! *Zoll shoyn zein de Geulah!*

*Parashas Vayechi 5780*

## Mitaso Shleimah

The seventeen years that Yaakov lived in Mitzrayim, the last seventeen years of his life, were, Chazal tell us, the best years of his 147-year life. This despite his being old and nearly blind, a widower, and exiled from the holy Land of Israel.

We are told that prior to that peaceful period, Yaakov's was a life beset by troubles. Esav, Lavan, Esav again, Dena, Yosef, etc., etc. Famously, we are told, as soon as he finally settled back in the Land of Israel, hoping for some peace at last, he was hit with the whole Yosef affair, which lasted more than twenty-two years. That was his lot.

Nowhere that I have seen, however, is reference made, in this context, to a different period of Yaakov's life. For his first fifteen years, he grew up in the home of and was nurtured by not just his parents Yitzchak and Rivkah, but also his grandfather Avraham. Then, when the brothers were fifteen, they essentially parted ways, with Esav out hunting and cavorting, and Yaakov secluded in the *beis medrash*, the *ish tam yoshev ohalim*, the *talmid chacham*.

The incident with Yaakov's grabbing the *berachah* occurred *forty-eight* years later. That's a nice stint in *kollel*. And when he did run away, he hid out for the next fourteen years, before going to Charan, studying Torah in the *beis medrash* of Shem and Ever, a place where he would never run into Esav. Only then, at age seventy-seven, did he head off to Charan and to the house of Lavan. It was his duty to create the twelve *shevatim* of Klal Yisrael, and that is what he undertook there. This timing also explains his hurry in marrying, seven years after that. He had to get started.

So were not those years spent in tranquil Torah study also very good years? Why are just those last seventeen years of his old age described as his best years?

A large part of Yaakov's travail in his later years had to do with his children and family. Rachel's initial barrenness, then her early death, Reuven's indiscretion, Yehuda's matter with Tamar, the abduction and rape of Dinah, Shimon and Levi's violent reaction to that, and above all, the seething anger in the home culminating in the loss and apparent terrible death of his beloved Yosef. His grief was so great, so profound, and so permanent, his sadness so spiritually debilitating that the Shechinah deserted him, deepening his depression even further.

And yet…

And yet, I suggest, it was his family, his children, *with* all the troubles, *the very source* of his travail, that made possible the level of peace and fulfillment he finally came to know at the end of his life. The price was so high, but with them, he was able to fulfill the mission for which he was put on earth. Part of his suffering was that with all the history and the drama, it was not always clear to Yaakov that he had succeeded in producing offspring who were *all* worthy to be the *shivtei Kah*, an absolute must.

In the end, he came to see that they were all, without exception, holy and worthy. He realized that *mitaso shleimah*, his "bed" was complete, whole, every one a tzaddik, including Reuven, Shimon, and Levi. He even found that Yosef's children, Menashe and Ephraim, born and raised in Egypt, were utterly unaffected by that depraved culture and were as worthy to be *shevatim* as their uncles. In fact, they were raised not only by Yosef, but by the *tzaddekes* Osnas, identified in the Midrash as the daughter of Dinah.

We are most vulnerable through our children. And it is through them that we can achieve our greatest fulfillment. However great Yaakov was before, however pure, it was his suffering – and in particular, his suffering as it related to his children – that solidified his perfection as the father of Klal Yisrael. Thus, his best years were not necessarily his easiest years, but his most fulfilled years, when he could see that his work was, in fact, done, his holy mission accomplished. And he was able to enjoy that for seventeen years.

Raising children can be the most wonderful and rewarding experience in life, or the most painful, *Rachmana litzlan*. Many people have some measure of both, although we pray that the good far outweigh the bad. We cannot control everything. The responsibility is very great. Children see virtually everything you do, *and they notice*. The holy Avos and Imahos as related in the Torah, and our holy forebears throughout the generations, have shown us the way. We do, hopefully, what we must do, and we pray that God will bless our efforts, as we aspire to that greatest *berachah*, that it may be said of us, as it was of Yaakov Avinu, *mitaso shleimah*.

*Parashas Vayechi 5781*

# Rapture

I didn't go to the *mikveh* for two years. In normal times, I'm a regular. I missed it, but I feared in COVID times that it was not safe.

I did not attend shul for about a year. My shul mates know that my return from COVID seclusion was a gradual and cautious one: alone upstairs masked, alone upstairs unmasked, downstairs at the open front door masked, then unmasked. Finally, having survived thus far, back to my regular seat masked, and then finally unmasked.

And I originally thought this whole thing would last a few weeks altogether.

I did not kiss a *sefer Torah* in all this time. As much as I want to, you never know who touched the spot you are kissing, just before. Yes, it's kind of strict, but I believed it was the right thing for me to do.

One can conjure up all manner of metaphors or substitutes for kissing the Torah. Learning, davening, intensity. Rapt attention. Emotion.

In my shul in Yerushalayim, I saw something that gave me another perspective. It was during *hagbahah* right after *krias haTorah*. Everybody rises and says *v'zos haTorah*. Some people point with their pinkies. We honor and lovingly revere the Torah, our sacred guide for life, God's inestimable gift to us, and this moment is an expression of that.

I happened to glance up. I think I caught a motion that drew my attention. Right above us, in the women's gallery, stood a middle-aged woman. As the Torah was lifted and displayed, her eyes intensely focused upon it, she placed both hands to her mouth and then spread them broadly in a gesture that was simultaneously adoring and benedictive, her face gently but unselfconsciously quietly rapturous. *Loving.* Cherishing. It was clearly absolutely genuine and heartfelt. And I was blessed to see it and to learn from it.

Avraham, Yitzchak, and Yaakov, the foundational fathers of our nation, are, with their foundational *middos*, introduced to us in Sefer Bereishis, now drawing to a close with Parashas Vayechi. We are taught about them – the Torah tells us about them, the *meforshim* tell us, rather than just listing the mitzvos – so that we understand who we are, where we come from, how and why we are unique among the nations, and who and how we have to be. And, of course, why this holy land is, unapologetically, ours.

Each of the special *middos* of Klal Yisrael is traced to the Avos whose particular strength and innovation those *middos* were. *Chesed. Avodah. Torah. Emes. Temimus. Tefillah. Yirah.* Dedication. Self-sacrifice.

*Middos* that set us apart, define us, and make life as Jews possible.

And then the Torah tells us more detail about one person than any other in Bereishis, spanning five *parashiyos* and describing key elements of his character, even though he is technically not one of the Avos. And that is Yosef Hatzaddik.

Yosef's personality is presented as none other. And we are told about aspects of his life – like those of the Avos – that we need to know. He wasn't one of the Avos, but, Chazal tell us, he could have been. He was on that level. And he is the only figure in the Torah, indeed in all of Tanach, to be identified for all generations as Hatzaddik.

Yosef took all that was handed down until then and stamped it with love, deeply emotional love, the loving application of all those *middos* established by the Avos to our daily lives, our interactions with others, especially our own brothers, no matter how difficult, judging them as kindly as possible. Again and again, the Torah spells out that Yosef is overcome with emotion, that he weeps. And this is the combination – overwhelming love of God and His Law combined with overwhelming love of one's fellows, one's brother Jews – that renders him Yosef Hatzaddik and a key role model for all time. He shows us the practical application, under all circumstances, of the fundamental principles: his life is a guide for life as a Jew.

It is that life, that lesson, I submit, that drives our dedication in every sphere. It is what drives the *masmid* to push himself to the limit. It is what drives even poor

Jews to be phenomenal *baalei tzedakah v'chesed*. It is what drives dedicated Jewish men and women, boys and girls of all ages, to remain steadfast, no matter what. It is what makes us stop whatever else we may be doing and jump to our feet when the Torah is raised and proclaim its centrality in our lives.

It is what makes an ordinary Jewish woman in the ladies' balcony grow lovingly rapturous as she gazes at the Torah and what makes someone like me realize how blessed he is to be part of this holy and unique heritage, how lucky he is to have been shown the image of that holy Jewish woman, to appreciate a moment that might, God forbid, become rote and routine becoming, instead, an emotional, even tear-filled moment of holy love. Indeed, of rapture.

*Parashas Vayechi 5782, en route from Eretz Yisrael*

# ספר שמות

# Shemos

## Jews in High Places

The grateful people of Egypt, saved from starvation, proclaimed to Yosef, "You have given us our lives! May we find favor in your eyes and be servants to Pharaoh!" (Bereishis 47:25). With his clever planning and skill, Yosef marshalled the resources available and kept them alive through the terrible years of famine. In the process, he served the people well, even as he served the king of Egypt, whose power, wealth, and landholding he increased greatly. Yosef and his Jewish brethren stood in the highest regard.

And then it all changed. There arose a new king in Egypt "who knew not Yosef" (Shemos 1:8). Because that is inconceivable, except perhaps in the case of a foreign invader, Rashi and others understand this to mean that he chose to forget Yosef, to pretend as if he knew him not, who, in his magnified wealth and power, preferred to pretend that it was not Yosef who accomplished that for him. In this sense, there is nothing new under the sun.

And so Pharaoh threw off any sense of obligation to Yosef, and by extension to Yosef's tribe. But what of the people of Egypt, presumably grateful to Yosef for their lives?

Pharaoh appealed to the xenophobic nature most ethnic groups and native communities are prone to. *Those Hebrews are a fifth column. They are not like us. They are not loyal. They will double cross you when it suits them. They will join with our enemies and force us from our land.*

The irony here is that the king of Egypt had already taken their land in exchange for food during the famine. So now he deflected their resentment and pointed at Israel as the plotting culprit who can be blamed.

*What have you done for me lately?* It is an altogether too common human trait to diminish or extinguish any sense of obligation to someone by finding some serious fault that negates any good the person may have done. In turning against Yosef, Pharaoh and the Egyptians inevitably also turned against Klal Yisrael, with disastrous results. A small, vulnerable people seen as essentially foreign are easy prey. And the Jewish People in particular, for a host of historic reasons, are especially vulnerable.

And here we have to be especially careful. In this world, Jews in high places are themselves targets, along with their fellow Jews. That is not to say that Jews should not strive or serve. But that is why historically many have felt it safest for Jews to keep a low profile. And that applies to Jews whose service to society has been thoroughly honorable and aboveboard.

This vulnerability does not only apply to high officers and policy makers (and there have been many examples lately of highly placed officials of Jewish origin who have arrogantly promulgated terrible and embarrassing policies, foisted upon a public that they deemed too stupid to know what's good for it) but historically, Jewish theoreticians have put forth ideas with disastrous consequences for whole nations, such as the Soviet Revolution, the excesses of which were for the most part not carried out by Jews, but for which Jews, with some justification, could be blamed.

And what shall we say of prominent public figures who are obviously of Jewish origin whose behavior is so sordidly unsavory? Sadly, there have been many of those in the news lately.

It appears to be a reality that, if not unique to Jews, is certainly particular to them. The situation of one Jew, especially a prominent one, winds up affecting them all. Perhaps this is a lesson to us. If the world sees us this way, we should also. And thus the poor among us should make us all feel their want. The infirm among us should make us all ache. The sad among us should make us all sorrowful. And the joy of one Jew should be celebrated by all. For tribe that we are, family that we are, the lot and the fate of one is the fate of all.

*Parashas Shemos 5778, Yerushalayim Ir Hakodesh*

# Where's Yer Moses Nowww??

I can't vouch for it, but there is supposed to be a classic, memorable line in the movie *The Ten Commandments* (1956, starring Charlton Heston as Moses), spoken by the evil and contentious Dathan (Doson of Doson and Aviram infamy), played by the inimitable Edward G. Robinson (born in Romania as Emanuel Goldenberg and buried in Beth El Cemetery in Brooklyn). Robinson played lots of tough guys in films and plays, and he brought his tough-guy persona and famous bad-guy intonation to the role.

At some time of difficulty during the tumultuous period around the Exodus, Robinson's Dathan is supposed to have said to the people, in his best cynical tough-guy-from-Brooklyn voice, "Where's yer Moses nowww?"

Well, I don't know if it's in the movie or not. It's not exactly in the book (the Book) either, but it might have been. Who knows? We know there were plenty of cynics in those days (not that they've gone away since).

It always struck me as remarkable that, according to Chazal, we learn from the words (in Parashas Beshalach) *V'chamushim alu Bnei Yisrael mi'Mitzrayim*, literally meaning that the Children of Israel were armed, a midrashic teaching that only one-fifth of the people merited to leave Egypt. The rest, undeserving, too far gone, died during the three days of darkness. *And that nasty Dathan and his partner in crime Aviram were among those who did make it out!* Wow. Those others must have been bad indeed.

So Doson and Aviram, although unnamed in the Torah here, play a major role in Moshe's development into Moshe the redeemer and lawgiver. They were the ones who witnessed Moshe killing the Egyptian taskmaster he found beating a Jewish slave and proceeded to inform on him to the Egyptian authorities. This resulted in the death sentence for Moshe, who then had to flee and then ultimately returned as the promised redeemer.

Now let's look at how Moshe slew the Egyptian. *Midrash Rabbah* (Shemos 28) offers three versions. One is that he hit him with his fist (*egrof*). The second is that he used a trowel (*magrefah*) from the mortar work the Egyptian made the slaves do. And the third is that Moshe killed him by uttering the Ineffable Name of God. This is why, the Midrash continues, the informers (Doson and Aviram) challenged Moshe: *Halhorgeni ata omer?* (Shemos 2:14). Literally, do you plan to kill me too, as you did the Egyptian? Midrashically, do you plan to kill me with a verbal utterance (the Name of God) as you did to the Egyptian?

And so as I sit here in Yerushalayim, this land and this city so special, so blessed, and yet so set upon by the evildoers in the world, we contemplate the perennial confusion of what to do about it. As in days of old, the old dilemma: *V'anachnu lo neda mah naaseh* (II Divrei Hayamim 20:12). We don't know what to do. There are many points of view, but what's the right thing?

There are those who say that the best response is with force of arms, a fist (*egrof*). That is certainly necessary and appropriate, as we all understand. But alone, it is not enough. There are those who say we can beat them with technology and tools of innovation (*magrefah*). Undoubtedly, that is also necessary and important. But that too is not enough.

The *Avnei Azel*, who brings his own wise and tragic historic perspective to bear, tells us that in a war, you need the practical weapons of the world – you need the fist, and you need the technology. But they alone will not suffice for us to prevail. For us, success is only possible if behind that fist and behind that high tech stands the Ineffable Name of God, invoked in faith and in purity by His children, who turn to him for all things and in all times, in peace and in war, in times of plenty as well as in times of want, in safety as well as in danger, when the sun is shining as well as when it rains rockets and opprobrium and curses and threats and accusations and boycotts, despite the alienated cynics and the skeptics among our own people, loyal children who reply to those cynics and to those of all nations who cynically challenge, "Where's yer Moses nowww?" He is here beside us. The Torah and mitzvos he taught us are our way of life; we invoke the help of the God of our Fathers, and in His great Name we employ the fist and the technology and any other weapon that will defeat you, for He is with us.

*Parashas Shemos 5779, Yerushalayim Ir Hakodesh*


## Unser Glück

"I die for Germany!"

Absolutely incredibly, this witnessed declaration in extremis was shouted out by a German Jewish woman as she stood at the edge of the pit in the Rumbula Forest just outside Riga, Latvia, a second or two before she was shot, one of about twenty-five thousand Jews shot there between November 30 and December 8, 1941, by German troops and their eager Latvian assistants.

Many German Jews were murdered by their countrymen not on German soil, but deported east for that. To a large percentage of German Jews, Germanness was about *Bildung* and *Kultur*. It was more important to very many of them to be German than it was to be Jewish; "German" was their primary self-identification. To their murderers, Germanness was primarily about race and the Jews of Germany an utterly non-German stain on the nation that needed to be cleansed.

A great tragic irony of German Jewish history is the plaint expressed in the highly cultured salons of the German Jewish intelligentsia in the early 1800s, typified by the declaration of the hyper-Germanified Rahel Levin (who got baptized to marry Karl August Varnhagen von Hense), "It is our misfortune [*Unglück*] to have been born Jewish." She and her ilk did everything they could to erase that stain. One hundred years later, banners festooning Nazi rallies and Hitlerian events mirrored that sentiment and declared *die Juden sind unser Unglück*, the Jews are our misfortune.

How could they have been so foolish?

And yet, they were hardly the first. There is a haunting scene in rabbinic literature describing a small Jewish child hugging and kissing its idol, even as it lay dying amidst the destruction of Judea by Babylonian forces – a fate brought upon it by its habitual idolatry, among other sins.

Yaakov's small tribe of seventy souls came to Egypt out of necessity. They did not expect to stay any longer than necessary, but there they still were 210 years later, having grown, miraculously, into a nation of millions. By God's decree, they had to suffer their bitter bondage, after which God redeemed them and led them out to the Promised Land, amid great miracles. That generation, despite all their missteps, stood at the foot of Har Sinai, declared *naaseh v'nishmah*, and heard the very Voice of God.

We also know from rabbinic teaching that very many of that generation did not leave Egypt at all, but, assimilated too far into Egyptian culture, never made it out. They disappeared during *makkas choshech*, the plague of darkness, so that their shame and the shame of the nation not be made public. The Torah, in its narrative, says nothing about it. And yet we know it.

There is, I think, a lesson there. We must know about these things in order to learn the hard lessons that we need to learn in order to survive as a nation, even as we prefer not to dwell upon or highlight it. It is our shame, a colossal failure on the part of a significant part or our people. These failures have appeared and reappeared many times, in many forms, throughout our long and difficult history. But the story of those failures is the sad story of the dropouts, not of the Nation of Israel, which has persevered beyond all normal bounds. We live, and we will live.

There is a direct, glorious line from Yaakov Avinu and those precious seventy ancestors to every one of us today. The long, incredible history of Klal Yisrael, its march from enslavement in Egypt to the ultimate, final Redemption, from Yosef's promise of *Elokim pakod yifkod eschem v'he'elah eschem min ha'aretz hazos* (Bereishis 50:24) to all the prophecies of Moshiach and the peace and tranquility he will bring, is our story. The dropouts are a sad and tragic byproduct of the human capacity for foolishness, even stupidity, as well as the result of long exile and terrible suffering. But we are here.

We are here. That we are the Children of Israel is our great good fortune. It is our *Glück*. The blood of the Avos, of the *shevatim*, flows in our veins. Their destiny is our destiny. Their closeness to God is our closeness to God. We pray not to be tested, but tested many of us are and many have always been. With our faith, our strength, and with no small measure of courage, we hang on, and like our steadfast forefathers in Egypt, we wait, with utter confidence, to be redeemed.

*Parashas Shemos 5780*

# Ivri

The day after the Germans entered Kolbesov, they came looking for Shlomo Nussbaum. Specifically, by name. They came to his house, led there by the Nussbaums' close neighbor and good friend, a fine Polish Catholic. My grandfather was a prominent member of the *kehillah* and a man of means. Understanding that he would be a target, my grandparents had already fled; they ultimately survived. The German strategy was often to decapitate the communal leadership, targeting such individuals well before they went after everybody else.

They gathered a group of prominent men, pointed out by their Polish neighbors, in a field belonging to my grandfather, and shot them.

The Jews, about 10 percent of the population of Poland (and in some towns and cities a very high percentage: Warsaw was about 30 percent Jewish), had been an integral part of Polish life and civilization for nearly a thousand years, deeply intertwined with its identity, economy, and overall culture. Religiously and socially distinct, they were nevertheless very much a part of Poland and Polish life.

Even the antisemites (no shortage of those, of course, also part of the culture) understood that the Jews of Poland were the Jews of *Poland*. But *other*. Other. Not *really* Polish, the thousand years of their presence not making them any more actually Polish than they were when they arrived centuries earlier, fleeing the persecutions in western Europe.

And so, although with noble exceptions (kind and brave people who risked and sometimes gave their lives to shield Jews), the same Poles who themselves suffered terribly under the German occupation also often cooperated with the Germans in the persecution and murder of the Jews. To say so today in Poland is virtually a crime. (There are honest Polish historians who are today persecuted for telling this truth.)

Otherness – being targeted and persecuted for being other, for not really belonging – is no stranger to the history of the Jews in our various, seemingly interminable exiles. And it has a long pedigree.

*V'eleh shemos Bnei Yisrael haba'im Mitzraimah* (Shemos 1:1). Who *are coming* into Egypt. Much has been made of the Torah's use of the present tense to refer to an event that, as Rav Yosef Dov Soloveichik points out, occurred 210 years before the Exodus. Yaakov and his sons, who are described here as coming to Egypt, were long gone. But as long as they had been there, well settled in the land, they were still viewed by the Egyptians as strangers who had arrived that day. Not belonging. Not part of Egyptian society. Alien. Other.

The essence of antisemitism throughout history, Rav Soloveichik says, has long been that the Jew is everywhere a stranger, not belonging, an interloper, unwelcome. Ivrim – from the other side of the river, apart from everyone else. This has sadly, tragically, played out all over Europe and elsewhere. The ancient city of Alexandria in Egypt (long before Christianity) had so many Jews, who were so much part of its civic life. But that did not save them from the pogroms that destroyed Jewish life there.

Of course, in certain fundamental ways, we do keep ourselves identifiably different, without which we could not survive as Jews. Famously, the Children of Israel in Egypt had stubbornly maintained their identity, keeping their Hebrew names, their Hebrew language, their Hebrew clothing, and their God. Reuven went down to Egypt, the Midrash says, and Reuven came up from it. The Jews who left Egypt spoke the same Lashon Hakodesh as those who arrived hundreds of years before, and as fluently. Ivrim – the legacy of Avraham Ha'ivri.

And herein lies the tension. Jews typically think of themselves as an integral part of the places they inhabit (messianic hopes aside), participating in, building, and working as part of the larger society, while at the same time maintaining – we stubbornly insist on maintaining – our specifically Jewish identity. But sometimes, the Rav says, society insists that we terminate our unique Jewish identity and disappear into the whole, to live like the rest of society in order to be accepted (maybe; it certainly didn't work in Germany, or even, for a long time, for the conversos in Spain), and this we cannot do. We are Ivrim. In this sense, we stand on one side of the river, even if everyone else in the society around us stands on the other.

*Haba'im Mitzraimah*, coming into Egypt, participating in the broader society, we can do. But Pharaoh saw us as incorrigible outsiders, as strange today as we were when we first arrived long before, unwilling to give up our core identity and beliefs in favor of Egypt's, and therefore dangerous, unwelcome, disloyal, a potential fifth column who might join forces with Egypt's enemies. Ivrim, to be persecuted, subjugated, enslaved.

Some years ago, I attended a fair in Jerusalem with vendors offering local wares of various kinds. One young Arab seller had great pictures of old Jerusalem scenes. As I looked at them, he asked me, in Hebrew, if I speak Hebrew. In truth, it was a fair question, as so many Jewish tourists do not. But it also offended me deeply. That this gentile should speak Hebrew better than most non-Israeli Hebrews (Jews) was painful to contemplate, as realistic as it was. I looked him in the eye and replied, a little testily, *"Ani ish Ivri. B'vadai ani medaber Ivrit."*

In fact, I make it a point to address Arabs in Israel in Hebrew. Many converse well enough. Some, hostility in their eyes, insist on English even if they know Hebrew. Them I can't abide, because I know what they are doing. They are refusing to recognize our connection to this land.

And so, if Hebrew, Lashon Hakodesh, is an important factor in that connection, in our very identity as the descendants of the Children of Israel in the Land of Israel, the Ivrim of the land of the Ivrim (*ki gunov gunavti me'eretz ha'Ivrim*, I was stolen away from the land of the Hebrews, said Yosef [Bereishis 40:15]), why do most Jews outside of Israel itself have little or for the most part no Hebrew at all?

Obviously, for the same reason as the tragic failure of so many, today, in the basic identifiers that kept our forefathers a distinct people while in Egypt, and which made them worthy of redemption: Hebrew language, Hebrew dress, Hebrew names, and tying it all together, Hebrew faith and practice. They were, and remained, Ivrim. The terrible widespread falling away from Judaism in the last two hundred years has been tragic beyond description. But it didn't start as a total separation. Rather, it was a gradual and progressive nibbling away that led from one step to another, reaching, in our generation, to indifference, national self-destruction, assimilated disappearance, and even overt hostility in so many of our misled brothers and sisters. Ignorance – having been raised in an utter vacuum regarding Judaism, lack of education – leads to lack of self-awareness, lack of caring, lack of Jewish *self*. For some, even self-loathing.

I often speculate, if the generations who came before who gave up on keeping Shabbos and did not Jewishly educate their children had foreseen the later consequences of their choices, after a couple of generations, with intermarriage and disappearance from the fold becoming the norm, with their descendants often sympathizing more with our enemies than with our own, would they have acted differently? I would like to think yes.

Our forefather Avraham the Ivri, set himself apart from the rest of mankind and dedicated himself, and us after him, to that particular devotion to God and to the goodness mandated by Him that is now known to us as Judaism, Yiddishkeit. It was the force of that commitment, reinforced by concrete acts of dedication, by which our ancestors merited to be redeemed from Egypt, brought to Sinai, and into the Promised Land.

The world sees us as Other. Historically, where segments of our people have tried too hard to blend in beyond recognition, tragedy has ensued. The Germans especially hated the Jews among them who looked and acted German. The world evolves. Civilization evolves. We don't dress like our long-ago ancestors did, but among strongly committed Jews, there is a strong tendency to dress identifiably like other Jews, in whatever form that might take, to speak like other Jews, to identify by Jewish names, to remain passionately loyal to God and His Torah. Because the world is right, even if for the wrong reasons. We *are* Other. Not in an antisocial way, not in opposition to the society around us, but in the course of self-identity, self-preservation, and self-fulfillment.

For we are Ivrim. It is that commitment, that dedication, the sometimes painful price we pay for standing apart, that will bring us, we pray, as it did for our forefathers redeemed from Egypt, into the Promised Land.

*Parashas Shemos 5782*

## Strangers in Our House

Did the Spanish, after the expulsion of the Jews from Spain, hate and persecute the New Christians, Jews who had submitted to baptism and who lived as Christians, because they did not trust them and suspected them of being secret Judaizers (apparently true for some Jews, but not the case for many others)? This is the popular view, and it is the position of historian Cecil Roth. Historian Benzion Netanyahu (Benjamin Netanyahu's father) – citing many precedents – held that even the most Christian of the formerly Jewish New Christians was generally despised by the Spanish on "racial" or ethnic grounds, a visceral hatred. I was fortunate to have a talk with Professor Netanyahu about it one day, having met him casually in the military cemetery on Har Herzl, when I chanced upon a memorial ceremony for his son, Yonatan, who fell at Entebbe. I had, in fact, just finished reading his book on the subject. He traces this hatred back many centuries and through many civilizations, a hatred aimed at a peculiar nation, Israel.

These *parashiyos* in the Torah lay out a pattern that is repeated over and over in history, between Jews and gentiles and between Jews and Jews.

Much has been said about the Torah's use of the present tense to name the children of Israel who had arrived in Egypt generations previously (*haba'im Mitzrayma*). One observation is that even after the Jews being in the land for 210 years, and being very established there, the Egyptians still considered them foreign inter-lopers, as if they had arrived that very day.

Of course, that measure of apartness that at least a core of Jews maintain every-where in their travels – a pattern established in Egypt – also played a role in their meriting to be redeemed, despite their otherwise serious descent into assimilation. We have been witness, in our time, to Jews disappearing in droves *Rachmana lit-zlan*. But it's not for the first time. Think back to the Chanukah story.

It's not dwelt upon too much, especially in the popular understanding, but while the chief enemy was the Greek culture, philosophy, and pagan mindset – all antithetical to Judaism – a major enemy force was the elite Jews who much pre-ferred to live as Greeks and to leave the "outmoded" faith and ways of their unen-lightened forebears behind. It was, in fact, a civil war. It was a turncoat Jew whom Mattisyahu slew in the act of sacrificing a pig to the Greek *getchke* that sparked the Maccabean uprising.

Tragically, this pattern has been repeated from time to time over history. The "Reformers" in Germany wanted to be – and acted – more German than the Ger-mans. The "elite" among them mourned their misfortune, their *Unglück*, that they were born Jews. It didn't help them. They were swept away, despised aliens, along with their long-caftaned, bearded, and *peyos*-adorned Jewish brethren.

So it appears to be a matter of perspective. Among the Jews, in whatever *galus* they are in, there are those who understand completely that while they may be loyal citizens and good neighbors with the non-Jewish majority, "in it" together with them in much of daily life, they are in fact in a fundamental way apart, different.

Hence, the sons of Israel who arrived in Egypt 210 years before are as if they are currently arriving – *haba'im*. Their names, their mode of dress, their language, their faith remained unchanged. They knew who they were. They may have been in Egypt, they may have excelled there, before the enslavement, in every endeavor, but they were the Children of Israel. Reuven, Shimon, and the rest. They – their generations – merited, on this basis, to be redeemed.

And there are those Jews who place their assimilated identity over that of their inherent one. And there comes a tipping point beyond which there is no return. Chazal tell us what happened to them – the many of them – during *makkas choshech*.

From the gentile perspective, throughout history, we may have been very much a part of the local scene, for a thousand years or more, but we were always *other*. Sometimes, this was not especially hostile, but for the most part it was, often unbearably so. It is a hatred, *Chazal* tell us, a *sin'ah* that was born at Sinai, where we, in fact, became permanently different from the rest of the world. (We like to think, and we hope, that the United States, foundationally different from other countries, is a noble exception, on a national level, at least in principle.)

Rav Soloveichik understands Pharaoh's words to his people regarding the Jews to mean that despite their presence – apparently quite loyal – in Egypt for over two hundred years, despite their full participation in society, they must be viewed as a fifth column that arrived only today – *haba'im*. They are strangers, they are dangerous, they are disloyal, they are out to get us, *they are not us*. They are not Egyptian, and we must undo them.

The title above is taken from the title of a book, *A Stranger in My House*, by my brother, עמו״ש, Dr. Walter Reich (Holt, Rinehart and Winston, 1984) about the seemingly intractable problem of the Jews and the Arabs of the "West Bank" – Judea and Samaria – each seeing the other as unwelcome strangers in what each view as their own home. The situation is somewhat different, but the title is apt.

The Jews of Eretz Yisrael are, in fact, home. We pray that our Father in Heaven will bring the rest of us there speedily, *b'vias goel tzedek*, and in the process obviate that problem of whose house it is. Meanwhile, still a majority of Bnei Yisrael continue to reside in *galus*, in houses that may be comfortable, that may feel like home (and I still maintain that this blessed country, the United States, is different, despite recent fears, for it is uniquely built on better, more just principles than any other nation in history), but among others who can, at any time, God forbid, come to look upon us, as did the very Egyptians who so benefitted from us, from our loyal efforts, from our neighborly toil, as *other,* different, as strangers in those homes, unwelcome, threatening, foreign, to be put down.

Our best protection, as we learn from our forefathers in Shemos who merited redemption, is for us to remember always who we are, where we come from, whose children we are, Who is our God, how we present ourselves, how we comport ourselves, and how we speak – what is our true language, and with the power of thought and language, what we say. That we are Bnei Yisrael, stalwart sons and daughters of those stalwart sons of Israel, whose names we still bear proudly to this day, *haba'im*, constant, always cognizant of what Hashem, our Creator and Redeemer, expects of us. To be Am Segulah, a unique, loyal, dedicated, unashamed, special nation unto Him.

*Parashas Shemos 5783*

# Va'era

## Farchapt

Grim-faced, tense, visibly worried, they sat on the edge of their seats watching the news broadcasts of the Arab leadership in the countries surrounding the nineteen-year-old State of Israel haranguing the vast crowds, calling for the destruction of Israel and the death of its Jews.

The wild eyed masses of Arabs shook their fists, jumped up and down, and in a frenzy of hate, vowed to do just that. I remember it. Their eyes rolled in their heads in the passion of their bloodlust.

It was May 1967, and we were all nervous and frightened. But more than the youth, my parents' generation, especially those who, like my own family, had seen it all before, who had lived it and somehow managed not to die in it, unlike most of their loved ones who had been swallowed up and destroyed just a few years before, who feared terribly that yet another holocaust hovered over our people, with a largely indifferent world watching. And they were well justified in that fear.

And so from time to time, when particularly villainous people were shown spewing their hate and bloodlust against our people, my mother and my uncles and aunts would curse those murderers with the Yiddish expressions generally reserved for such terrible people. "*Farchapt zollen zei veren!*" Literally, I understood it to mean that they should be grabbed (to *chap* [*khap*], to grab), I assumed, by the proverbial devil, or some such bad fate. I never did explore the origin of that particular curse.

I thought of this lately because I recently read a short book about our poor brothers, the little Jewish boys, officially from age twelve but some as young as eight, or even five, in Czarist Russia who, from about 1820 until about 1855, were stolen away from their families and conscripted into the Russian army for a period of at least twenty-five years, the count *starting* when they reached age eighteen. The primary purpose of this terrible decree was to de-Judaize them, in addition to filling the ranks of the army. The evil czars had tried for many years to erase Judaism from their realm, wielding both carrot and stick, in an effort to get the

Jews to adopt the Russian Orthodox Christian faith. There were Russian children who were also taken for long periods of army service, but the Jewish children were particularly targeted.

The Russian government enacted terrible, harsh decrees in order to keep the stubborn Jews in miserable poverty. It also offered rich rewards, including generous land grants, to Jews who would be baptized. Not a single Jew came forward, not even when the rewards were greatly increased. And so Czar Nicholas I and his ministers, may they rot, decided to steal their children into the army, away from their families, and force them, with the harshest of tactics, with the cruelest torture and beatings, to accept baptism. Countless Jewish children died terrible deaths from the freezing cold, the forced marches, the beatings, the backbreaking labor, the starvation, the unrelenting torture. The Russian authorities were amazed at the religious sophistication of these little boys and their tenacious resistance. They found that those who debated religion with the children were easily out-argued and intellectually defeated. And so they resorted to brute violence. While many brave children held on, many, *nebech*, could not. And who can blame them?

The parents of young boys were frantic with fear and inconsolably frantic when their children were caught and marched off. They would call out to them, tearfully, pitifully, helplessly, *"Gedenk az du bist a Yid!"* Remember you are a Jew.

Many, many such children were lost to our people. Most of those who survived and held on to their Jewish identity, after twenty-five years of this brutalization, were far removed from normal Jewish civilization and could not successfully reintegrate back into the fold. Many lost all recollection of their families and even of their real names.

And then there was an even darker side to this story. Each town, each shtetl, each district, had a quota of children to produce to be Cantonists, as they were called. It was often left up to the *kehillah* to decide which children should go, and here the darkness turns darker still.

Years later, the accursed Germans forced the Jews in the lands they occupied to form councils of elders, or *Judenrats*, to rule the ghettos, as well as a Jewish police force, ostensibly to maintain order, but really to facilitate the work of the Germans in exterminating the Jews. There were many Jews who served in these ways in an altruistic effort to help their brethren and ease their terrible burden of suffering to the extent possible. And then there were those who were just thugs, or who saw this as an opportunity to save themselves and their families (although that virtually never happened) and who behaved badly – even very badly. We pray that we never be put to such tests, and, except perhaps for the most egregious cases, one must be careful about judging others. But human nature will generally result in those with power and influence, in such trying circumstances, using that power and influence to deflect the suffering onto others. And so it happened with the terrible plight of the Cantonist boys and their families a hundred or so years earlier.

There is a terrible, dark substory to the Cantonist tragedy. It was not unusual for the leadership of the *kehillos* – and these were generally not the poor folks – to try to save their own families by facilitating the destruction of others. Families tried to hide their little boys in various ways. But the *chappers*, the grabbers, were on the prowl. And those *chappers*, paid thugs whose job it was to catch and turn in little Jewish boys, were, by and large, *not goyim*.

It was one of the worst things that could happen to a Jewish family. And so it occurred to me, this week, that the terrible wish of bad upon others that I heard from my parents' generation years ago, in the dark days of fear before the miracle of the Six-Day War, which was always directed at the enemies of our people and never at Jews, that they should be *farchapt*, was a historical echo, a lingering, dreadful epithet that still, so many years later, evoked the horror of that terrible time in which *chappers* terrorized the Jewish People. The worst fate at that time was to be *farchapt*.

In the system Pharaoh employed to subjugate and enslave the Children of Israel, intermediaries, Hebrew officers, were appointed to enforce the slave labor and to maintain quotas. The penalties for not meeting those quotas were severe. Bad as things were for the Children of Israel, those officers, the *shotrim*, among them, could not bear to see their brethren hurt beyond the bitter fate that was already theirs. And so they undertook to bear the beatings and the lashings that would otherwise be meted out to the people upon themselves. And for their loving self-sacrifice, for their suffering on behalf of their brethren, for their absorbing the extra measure of pain and terror themselves, these good, loving souls were later appointed to be the first Sanhedrin of the Children of Israel in the *midbar* in their march to freedom.

Oy, oy, may we never be tested. Even the best of people, to all appearances, under terrible circumstances, may be unable to stand up to the test. *Hashem yishmerenu.* But those who do are the immortals of our people.

And so, a story.

Years ago, I took an El Al flight from Zurich to Tel Aviv. Sitting next to me was an Israeli woman who told me about her family and their history in Israel. Her great-grandfather arrived there in the late 1800s as a lone *chalutz* from Russia. His name was Linievich. Over the succeeding years, the family had tried, without success, to locate any relatives they may have in Israel. They scanned directories from all over Israel and found none. The apparent reason for that was that Linievich was not at all a Jewish name, but quite Russian.

The great-grandfather, a Cantonist child, had altogether forgotten what his real name had been, or anything else about his family. He took the name Linievich from his Russian sergeant, who had been kind to him. He only knew that he was a Jew and was determined to remain a Jew, and that he would do so in the Jewish homeland, the Land of Israel. As difficult as life was then for those pioneers, it was a far cry from the days of his captivity as a Cantonist child in the Czar's army, where he served for twenty-five years.

This woman went on to relate that one day the family, descendants of that Cantonist *chalutz*, unable to locate any relatives, read in the paper of the arrival in Israel of the American undersecretary of state for Near Eastern affairs, Sol Linowitz, for diplomatic consultations with the Israeli government. *Linowitz*, they thought. Linowitz – *could it be an Americanized version of Linievich?* The ambassador was, after all, also a Jew. And so they traveled to Jerusalem and staked themselves out in the lobby of the King David Hotel, hoping to get to speak with Mr. Linowitz.

The undersecretary of state walked in with his entourage. They approached him and managed to get his kind attention before the security people could shoo them away. They told him that their name was Linievich, that their family was originally from Russia, and that they knew of no relatives. Could the ambassador, given his name, perhaps shed some light on some possible family connection and maybe some information about their origins?

Undersecretary Linowitz told them that he didn't really know much about the origin of the name or where in Russia his family was from. He only did know that his great-grandfather had been a Cantonist.

Many, many have been the travels and the dreadful travails of the Children of Israel. *In fire und flamen hut men unz gebrent, in vasser hut men unz dertrinken.* In hellish fires did our enemies burn us, in deep waters did they drown us. And yet we are here, clinging to our God and to each other. There have been so many terrible tests along the way, some too difficult for many to bear. And yet here we are.

The *shotrim* in Egypt, who bore whatever pain they could for their suffering brethren, showed us the way. Even with our many shortcomings, we still cannot know the Mind of God, why He has chosen the path He has sent us on, why it has been so fraught. But on each step of that difficult path, even as there have been those who could not withstand the test, there have been others, outstanding in their love and their leadership and their self sacrifice.

The soaring language of redemption that opens Parashas Va'era tells us that the God Who, for His own inscrutable reasons, led us into Egypt and bondage also redeemed us from it in the most glorious way; that He sees our suffering; that He sends us true leaders in every generation and has established for us in history a role that will, in the end, be as glorious and triumphant as Yetzias Mitzrayim, a time when we will stand together in mutual love and support as did the *shotrim* for us in our darkest hour, and as we stood together unified in utter brotherhood at the foot of Mount Sinai.

*Parashas Va'era 5778*

# Who, Me?

Moshe Rabbeinu is the towering figure in Jewish history. There was no one like him before or after. But there is something the Torah clearly wants us to know about him: his mortal humanity.

Twice the Torah tells us that this great man was the child of an aunt-nephew marriage, one that would later be forbidden by Torah law as semi-incestuous. The Torah also spells out that exalted and exceptional as they were, Moshe and Aharon were conceived and born in the way all people are, the product of normal marital activity, very much human. Moshe was capable of anger and errors and Aharon of hesitant indecision at critical moments.

That they became the greatest Jews of all time, that Moshe was the vehicle for divine Revelation and could speak with God at will, that Aharon was the purest of the pure and chosen to be the founding Kohen Gadol of Klal Yisrael was the result not of an undeserved free gift bestowed upon them and the world, but rather because they so worked upon themselves, they so built themselves up in holiness, they tried so hard that they merited the prophecy and the exalted offices they held.

And in case one is (understandably) incredulous, the language of the Torah doubles down, so to speak, by specifically identifying the Moshe and Aharon identified above as the sons of Amram and his aunt Yocheved as being *the same Moshe and Aharon* who were called upon to stand before Pharaoh and bring about the release of the Children of Israel and then again specifying, *the very same ones* who, upon the order of God Himself, spoke to Pharaoh and demanded the release of Bnei Yisrael.

The lesson here for us is that people often look at those who have achieved such greatness and cannot relate to them or to what it takes to achieve whatever greatness they are capable of. Thinking that those high achievers are so different from them, many people don't aspire – they don't try at all. But they are wrong.

The Torah is teaching us that every one of us can achieve greatness. Moshe Rabbeinu himself was not Moshe Rabbeinu until he achieved the self-perfection that made that possible, raising himself above the mundane to the point that God would then do the rest. We cannot all be a Moshe or an Aharon, but there is also virtually no limit on how we, any of us and each of us, can raise ourselves up from the low earthiness of our origins and reach for the stars, indeed to become the stars each of us has the potential to become.

Who, me? Yes, indeed. You.

*Parashas Va'era 5779, Yerushalayim Ir Hakodesh*


# A Tough Crowd

The turmoil blown up by the terrible *magefah*, the coronavirus pandemic, laid bare some rather surprising (or maybe not quite so surprising) quirks among our people.

There are many things that can be said about their behavior that I will not go into at this time. But think back to the dark, dark time, a time of fear, a time when people were dying in droves, and medical science, despite all its advances, could barely cope. There was so much we didn't know, but basic medical precautions against spread were our first line of defense. That much was obviously true.

Like all medical facilities, my office observed a strict mask rule. Yet nearly every day, and sometimes several times a day, as I walked into an exam room, I saw the patient sitting there with the mask down or off altogether. I would stop in my tracks and not go in. The patient would have to wait to be seen in another room when one became available, and the air treatment equipment in that room would be turned up to the max to cleanse it.

More often than not, patients looked at me incredulously when I told them I couldn't enter the room. They knew the rules very well when they came in. They just didn't want to listen. The rules don't apply to them, it seems, even in MY house. My favorite excuse: "I was on the phone!" As if any idiot (me!) should understand that the basic rules of health hygiene and precaution don't apply when you're on your cell phone.

The other main excuse I would hear is "you weren't in the room" – as if whatever potentially deadly viruses they may have filled the air with would now magically disappear when I walked in.

These people are not stupid, and they are not, for the most part, ignorant. They are just willful, self-absorbed, they know better (I especially enjoyed the occasional eye roll), and they are just unwilling to follow the rules.

Don't get me wrong: I love and respect my people. But why, when this happened, was it almost never a non-Jew? And don't get me wrong: I love and respect our women. But why, when this happened, was it almost never a man?

I can't and won't comment (publicly) on the woman thing (*ah, you've figured that one out already on your own: it's in part a function of their strength*) but let me offer some insight on the Jewish thing.

Paradoxically, it relates to one of our great strengths as a people, which is, in applied living, also our Achilles tendon.

No generation of Jews saw open miracles, the very clear Hand of God at every turn, as did the generation of the Exodus from Egypt. God made the terms of His Covenant with us very clear. Follow the rules, live as He requires of us (and a very nice life that is), and we will be blessed, always, in every way. Violate the Covenant, and the price will be terrible. At every step, we were given warning after warning, from when we were still in the *midbar* until the very end, when exile and destruction and the loss of the Beis Hamikdash loomed.

Did we listen? *Nooooooo.*

There were many prophets during all those generations, but the *navi* par excellence of preaching, warning, as well as of loving consolation, is Yeshayahu Hanavi. His tenure ran many years, and he suffered badly for most of that time from an angry, resentful, unheeding nation. Indeed, he came to a bitter end at their hands.

There is an astounding midrash in *Vayikra Rabbah* (10:2). Yeshayahu tells us (6:8) how he was first called to his mission. He sees a divine vision, and then God asks, regarding the mission of prophecy to the Jewish People, "Whom shall I send, who will go for us?" Yeshayahu answers, "Here I am; send me." The Midrash tells us the back story. Yeshayahu is sitting in his *beis medrash*, at peace, when he sees the prophetic vision and hears God's query. Yeshayahu answers, he'll go. God warns him, *I sent Micha, and he got beaten up. I sent Amos, and he got beaten up.* Yeshayahu replies, he'll go. Then God says to him, *Yeshayahu, it's not so simple: banai tarchanin, sarbanim. My children are difficult people who don't want to listen to authority and don't want to follow the rules. If you can accept upon yourself to be beaten and abused and shamed and cursed, then go on this mission. If not, don't go.*

Yeshayahu replies, *al menas ken: This is what I expect. I fully accept this as part of my mission to my beloved Klal Yisrael. I will go.*

And that is why Yeshayahu was who he was and who he remains for us for all time.

But that was not the first time in our history that such a conversation took place.

There is an enigmatic *pasuk* in Parashas Va'era (Shemos 6:13) in which Hashem tells Moshe and Aharon to *command* (*va'yitzavem*) Bnei Yisrael and Pharaoh that Bnei Yisrael must leave Egypt. Sure, Pharaoh needed to be commanded to send them out. But did the Hebrew slaves need to be commanded to leave their bondage?

When Moshe initially arrived and declared to the nation that the time of deliverance had arrived, they believed him, and they bowed before God in praise and thanksgiving. Pharaoh resisted, of course, and doubled the workload of the slaves. Exhausted by the labor, an exhaustion exacerbated by a disappointment that left them spiritually drained – *kotzer ruach v'avodah kashah* (Shemos 6:9) – the people didn't listen to Moshe when he approached them again.

God then tells Moshe to return to Pharaoh and tell him, yet again, to send the Jews out of Mitzrayim. *If the Jews themselves won't listen to me*, responds Moshe, *how can I expect Pharaoh to listen?* And Hashem tells him, *Tell them both – Pharaoh and the Jews – it's not optional for either of them! Pharaoh to send them out, and the Jews to leave.*

Hashem now tells Moshe and Aharon (*Shemos Rabbah* 7:3): *Banai sarvanim hem, ragzanim hem, tarchanim hem.* My children are contrary, angry, and infuriating, burdensome, difficult, hard to handle, hard to take. They don't want to listen to authority. They resent being told what to do. They think they know better. They will challenge you and try to grind you down. A tough crowd. You must accept this – these conditions – if you are to lead them out of slavery, to Sinai and Matan Torah, and into the Promised Land. You must accept this (*al menas ken*), even if they curse you, even if they stone you.

This is how they are: those same obnoxious traits are really side manifestations of their great strength, the strength and determination to stubbornly withstand all that history will throw at them (*and how much history has thrown at them!*) and still remain Mine. Ultimately their loyalty is with Me, and yes, with you too, but they won't make it easy (*for either of us, k'v'yachol!*). They are the most remarkable people, who will make their mark on the world in every sphere of human endeavor like no other nation can or ever will. They are, at their core, good and pure and holy and brilliant. They do need loving and patient guidance and training in how to express those strengths. In a seemingly paradoxical way, it is their very toughness that serves as a vehicle for their survival in a very tough world, by which their essential goodness can thrive and triumph.

They are, many of them, like sabras, those prickly fruits that are tough and thorny on the outside, protecting the sweet, soft, luscious fruit within.

They are shining stars in a cold firmament. They are as filled with mitzvos and *maasim tovim* as a pomegranate is with seeds, even the least of them. And each time God describes them in the context of their quirks, to Moshe and Aharon, to

Yeshayahu, to anyone and everyone, He describes them first and foremost as *banai*, My beloved children. I gave them those *kochos*. I instilled those strengths into them with creation. It is their challenge to use them only for the good. They don't always use it as they should, and that will cost them. But without those *kochos*, those tools, they could also not be who they are, the nation whose mission is becoming who they were created to be, the sweet and luscious fruit.

*Parashas Va'era 5781*

## Blimp

Cigars come in many shapes, and each one has its own special characteristics and name. There's a whole "*toyreh*" on it. The *parejo*, for example, is cylindrical, with different subtypes having rather specific length and diameter specifications. The *figurado* can be torpedo-shaped or pyramidal. Some cigars are blunt-ended, and others need to be clipped (or bitten). But ask anyone who is not a cigar aficionado what the classic shape of a cigar is, he will likely describe the type called the *perfecto*, with both ends tapered and bulging in the middle.

You'll soon see where this is going.

To call something or someone "cigar-shaped" is actually not that specific, even though the meaning is commonly understood to be more or less shaped like a blimp. Call it a dirigible (from the French *diriger*, to steer), or a zeppelin, or a blimp. Although there are some differences, the idea one gets when visualizing a blimp is like a somewhat exaggerated version of the cigar in question, tapered at the ends and bulging in the middle.

Now, I don't smoke *perfectos* (or anything else), I have never eaten a blimp, and I have certainly never eaten at Blimpie's. *So why do I have a natural tendency to assume that shape?*

Come on, you fellas (and wives) know exactly what I mean. Most of us eat more of what we shouldn't than we should, and most of us don't get away with it. We become shaped like a real *perfecto*. Like the Goodyear blimp. How healthy is that?

Now let's look at two quite complementary shapes. The cigar/blimp is broad in the middle and tapered at the ends. The second image is the opposite, tapered in the middle and broadest at the ends. It depicts what happens to formerly wide-open arteries with atherosclerosis, hardening of the arteries, critical narrowing of the blood flow passages, precursor to heart attack or stroke, *lo aleinu*. They tend to go together, it seems. No guarantees either way, of course, as there are so many other factors at play in different individuals. But by and large, they go together.

Cigar:

*Perfecto cigar (under license from Shutterstock.com)*

Many of us:

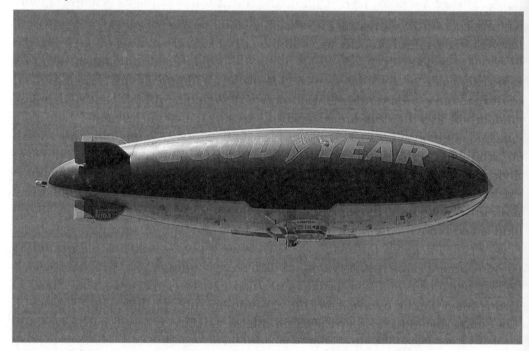

*The Goodyear Blimp (Tmxv4128, public domain, via Wikimedia Commons)*

The walls of the artery are thickened with plaque, so that the passageway for the blood (the "lumen," the channel in the middle) becomes increasingly narrow. *What do you need that for?* It's not confined to people who are blimp-shaped, but there is an obvious correlation.

God forbid:

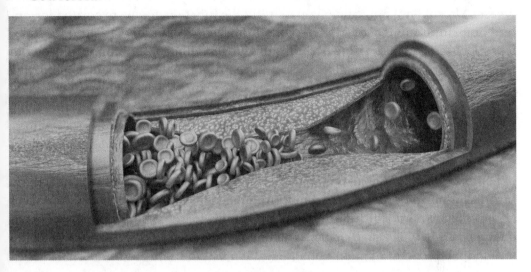

*Atherosclerosis (under license from Shutterstock.com)*

In Egypt, two things happened to our ancestors more or less simultaneously. They were suddenly quite free, and they were loaded up with a slew of complex mitzvos and obligations regarding the Pesach *korban*, the Pesach holiday, chametz, and matzah, Rosh Chodesh, *petter rechem*. It's good to be free, but freedom has obligations, and only a fool takes undue liberties with the freedom he has; he is likely to inflict harm on himself or on others, or both.

As the process of redemption played out a bit later on, the pursuing Egyptians were swallowed up in the Red Sea, and Israel was finally, totally, miraculously free. They then needed water, but the local water was bitter. Miraculously free, they nevertheless whined and complained before Moshe had a chance to wondrously sweeten the water for them by tossing in a God-given antidotal piece of wood. They drank, and God gave them more mitzvos on the spot, including the intricate laws of Shabbos.

And then He told them something remarkable: you must, in your freedom, especially in newfound freedom, learn to restrain yourselves, lest you come to profound harm. Unfettered freedom, taken by the individual or by society as utter unrestrained license, *will make you sick*, even kill you. It is good to be free – you should be free, you should indeed have free choice – but know that choices have consequences, and all choices made are not equally valid.

I am giving you laws, mitzvos, that will not only have you act in a way that pleases Me, that not only allow you to fulfill the function you were created for, and thus constitute the most physiologic path for you to follow for your well-being, *but will also train you to control yourselves* and thereby become, to the extent such things are possible, masters of your own fate. And if you do this, God says, if you follow these laws and these statutes, the various terrible maladies inflicted upon the Egyptians will not befall you, *for I am Hashem, your Doctor, Who heals you.* Physically *and* spiritually.

It's true that in the physical realm, we each have our own nature and metabolism, and keeping fit and healthy is certainly easier for some than for others. Many of us have to battle our own metabolisms in ways that for others are no problem at all. And this is true in the spiritual realm as well; the battle of the spirit, which each person must wage, is a greater challenge for some than for others. That's just how it is.

God knows who we are, each of us, and what our struggles are. There are no guarantees in life, as anyone who has been around a bit in life can tell you, and so we must make the effort, fight the good fight for our spiritual and physical health, persevere, and have faith that the Almighty Creator helps us in those efforts, recognizes those efforts, blesses those efforts, watches over us, personally and as a nation, and manifests for us His attribute of *Ani Hashem Rofecha*, I am Hashem, your Doctor, Who heals you, physically and spiritually.

*Parashas Bo 5779, Yerushalayim Ir Hakodesh*

## L'havdil: Distinctly Holy and Not So Wholly Distinct

I had to avert my eyes.

The grieving woman in the exam chair in front of me, a Jewish grandmother crying over her deceased granddaughter, was showing me, on her cell phone, a picture of the poor dead girl. I felt bad for her, of course, and, as I must on occasion do, I look respectfully and sympathetically at the picture of the lost relative for a while before looking back at the patient and offering any solace I can. It comes up sadly often in a doctor's practice. But this time, I immediately had to look away, as the young woman in the picture was "dressed" in a way that made it necessary for me to look away. The grandmother was utterly clueless, and not just about that.

The girl apparently died of a drug overdose. This woman had *given her* her apartment in Florida *to live in with "some guy"* whom she or the girl's parents knew nothing about, other than that he might have used drugs. So far, except for the actual death of the girl, apparently nothing was, to them, particularly wrong or unusual about this arrangement.

Just a couple of rows up in the picture archive on the phone, a powerfully familiar photo flashed by. I started to ask her why she had a picture of Rav Aharon Kotler on her phone. A second look made me realize it wasn't Rav Kotler after all, but actually a "cross" between Rav Kotler and Rav Moshe Feinstein, a kind of composite. It was obviously a real-deal Litvishe-type holy and pious Jew, most likely a *rav*. I asked.

"Oh, that's my *zayda*."

It was not the right time or place to challenge her, but I couldn't help gently asking her whether she saw anything odd or jolting about the juxtaposition of the two pictures, and what might have led from one to the other, what catastrophe happened in between the generations that made this tragedy possible. The poor woman didn't even understand my question. She was completely clueless. And when I asked her the grandfather's name, after a brief hesitation, she again said, "*Zayda*"; she wasn't sure what his actual name was. She knew him in her childhood, but was so removed from who and what he really was that she had no idea other than that "He went to temple."

When the Israelites stood at the edge of the Yam Suf – hemmed in by the sea on one side and the attacking superpower, the Egyptian army, bearing down on them on the other – only a miracle could save them. God was going to cause the sea to split for them. Utterly contrary to the laws of nature, this was to be a major miracle indeed. But were they worthy? Various midrashic sources describe how the angels of Heaven exclaimed, "Why are you saving these [Bnei Yisrael] and killing those [the Egyptians]? What's the difference between them? These worship *avodah zarah* and those worship *avodah zarah*! These are in a morally low state, and so are those!" Why the miracle – contrary to the otherwise immutable laws of nature – not only to save these but to kill those?

God replies that even if they appear to be the same, even if they appear to act the same, they are, in fact, not the same. There is, at the core of a Jew's *neshamah*, an innate connection to God, a faith, inherited from his forebears. If stimulated, however deeply it might be suppressed, it starts to glow and to blossom, no matter how many *klippos*, how many layers of separation there might be.

In introducing the fourth plague, *arov* (marauding wild and destructive animals that burst into Egypt, ran about everywhere and filled the land, but stopped abruptly at the edge of Jewish habitation), Hashem says that He will, in this, separate the land of Goshen from the rest of Egypt, for no wild animals will enter there, and that He will emplace *pedus*, a distinct and obvious division, between the Children of Israel and the Egyptians. *Pedus*, of course, also means "redemption." The context here, however, is that of *division, separation, distinction*. To make a *hevdel*, such as we do ceremonially with Havdalah, at the conclusion of the holy Shabbos.

In that prayer, teaches Rav Soloveitchik, we bless God, Who *has separated between the holy and the profane, between light and darkness, between Israel and the nations, between the seventh day and the other days of creation*. Upon analysis of these examples of separation, some are more obvious cases of distinction than others. As between light and darkness, that difference is obvious to all; even plants and animals make the distinction.

The *havdalah* between holy and profane is much different. The eye cannot perceive it. It requires a special intuition. It must be sensed, perceived with the heart and with the spirit. Once both types of *havdalah* are mentioned, the most obvious and the least obvious, the unique *havdalah* of *bein Yisrael l'amim*, between Israel and all other nations, is introduced.

Sometimes, when Israel lives as a holy nation, that distinction is as obvious, to all, as is the distinction between light and darkness. The contrast between Am Yisrael and the other nations is clear to anyone. When the Jew abandons God, however, that distinction may no longer be obvious at all, or even apparent. And yet, says Rav Soloveitchik, mired in sin as the Jew may be, deep in the Jewish soul there remains something holy and mysterious, which can neither be erased nor destroyed.

Yes, the Israelites worshipped idols in Egypt along with their Egyptian oppressors. In this regard, one could barely discern a contrast between them. But God did separate between them. Beneath the profanity, He discerned the holiness that He Himself had implanted there. God discerned the *pedus*, the distinction, the *hevdel* that existed on a deep spiritual plane, and He saved His people. He then granted them *pedus*, redemption.

The word *pedus* appears three times in Scripture. Once here, where it is spelled פדת (*chaser*, without a *vav*) and twice in Tehillim (111:8 and 130:7), where it is spelled פדות (*malei*, with the *vav*). Baal Haturim explains in all three places why: whereas in Egypt, the *pedus* served to rescue our people specifically from the *makah* of *arov*, and it was still far from the final Redemption, the later references to *pedus* do address the long-term promise of our final Redemption.

It is a long and frightfully difficult road that we have traveled. Along the way, we have been good and we have been bad. Sometimes we stand out and shine, light amid the darkness. But the long dark *galus* has made many of us crazy, and sometimes the holy spark is so deeply hidden, it is barely discernible, if at all, to the undiscerning eye. But even then, we have God's promise that it is, in fact, there, waiting to glow and to blossom, and that He sees it within us, no matter how far we have fallen.

So many, so many, are *nebech* lost along the way. The tragedy of those who were reachable – as every Jew is – but were never reached! God's *cheshbonos* are known only to Him. These weeks of the *parashiyos* of Shovevim ([שובבי"ם] Shemos, Va'era, Bo, Beshalach, Yisro, Mishpatim) remind us of God's compassionate readiness to reach down to us, to recognize and hopefully reignite the spark of holy distinctiveness within *every* Jew, no matter how far he has fallen.

It is a gift, but it is not an altogether free gift. He is waiting for us to open our hearts to Him, to invite Him in, and to let Him do the rest.

*Parashas Bo 5780*

## Quand on n'a que l'amour

I walked out of the Paris hotel and approached the cab idling there waiting for a fare. A white-gloved hand, attached to a fellow in a doorman's outfit, beat me to the cab door and opened it for me. Especially because even under a baseball cap, who and what I am is so readily identifiable, I gave him a rather generous tip, which he deftly transferred to his possession. He then proceeded to look at my money in his hand, now his money; twitching the ridiculous pencil mustache on his upper lip, in a practiced move, he regarded it as if it were not money but a camel turd I had placed there.

A Parisian acquaintance later told me it had nothing to do with my being a Jew and a lot to do with my being American, not French and not Parisian, and the fact that I had given him something for doing practically nothing, something he could enjoy resenting me for.

Ah, human nature. You certainly don't have to be French for that, but there is apparently something in French culture that makes things like that happen. Perhaps that's why it has been said that many French resent the Americans; they cannot forgive us because, with our blood and treasure, we saved them twice in the twentieth century. Maybe that's why when Paris was liberated from the Germans in August 1944, the road from Normandy to Paris littered with 226,386 Allied casualties, including 72,911 dead, Charles de Gaulle haughtily declared that "Paris has liberated itself." (De Gaulle, who had no modest opinion of himself either, is said to have hated the British for burning him at the stake when he was Joan of

Arc.) And he never forgave Israel – Jews who might be pitied as losers but were not tolerable as winners – for winning the Six-Day War.

No, this is not at all unique to the French, but is, to varying degrees in different people and different cultures, an apparent constant of human nature. As a wise man back in the shtetl observed, when he heard that someone was badmouthing him, "Why is he talking bad about me? I never lent him money; I never did him any special favor. I never did anything for him. *Why is he talking bad about me?*" A bad trait, a very un-Jewish one, but a common human weakness.

Many of the whites who actively fought apartheid in South Africa were Jews. Famously, many of the strongest white opponents of racism in America were Jews. They put their lives on the line, and some even gave their lives. Israel risked much and expended much to actively bring black Africans from Ethiopia who identified as Jews in a massive airlift to Israel and to integrate them into Israeli Jewish life. But by and large today, from loud and strident pronouncements flung at the Jews and at Israel from all too many (but certainly not all) prominent black voices, it is the Jews who are guilty of every bad thing, who are the problem throughout the world.

Human nature.

Yosef the Israelite kept Egypt alive during the great famine, both the people and the state itself. He kept Pharaoh on his throne and even made it that much stronger. The upshot, after things quieted down, was the Egyptian determination to "know not Yosef" and the cruel enslavement of the Children of Israel.

Amid all the drama of the Exodus, there is a substory subtly hidden in the text. Remember the Sar Hamashkim, Pharaoh's wine steward whom Yosef generously helped when they were both in the dungeon? Although he promised to help Yosef, he made himself forget about him and let him languish years longer in the pit. Only when it was useful to him did he tell Pharaoh about Yosef and his abilities, actually trying to denigrate him in the process.

Fast forward to the final plague, *makkas bechoros*, the smiting of the firstborn of Egypt: *It happened at midnight, Hashem struck down all the firstborn in the land of Egypt, from the firstborn of Pharaoh on his throne to the firstborn of the prisoners in the pit, even the firstborn of the cattle* (Shemos 12:29).

No house was spared. All of Egypt, every class, was complicit in, profited from, and supported the enslavement of the Jews. This from the same people who had been saved by the Jew.

But why the prisoners in the pit, slave workers who toiled by day and were locked up in the pit by night? What did they do to deserve that?

Chazal tell us (*Midrash Rabbah*, Rashi). There's another nasty human trait that is not too different from the theme above: people rejoice in the downfall of the righteous (one of the important themes in Dostoyevsky's *Brothers Karamazov*); they also rejoice and take comfort from the suffering of others that is greater than their own suffering. Those who are laid low like to find others who are even lower than they are and to hold them in contempt for that, feeling somehow superior in that contempt.

It seems that in the great upheaval in Egyptian society brought about by the Ten Plagues, the tearing apart of Egyptian societal norms by the very idea of a nation of despised slaves overturning the "natural order," wrenching their freedom from their Egyptian masters through their all-powerful God, even the lowliest prisoners in the pit had something to say. They hated the Israelites, whom they held to be even lower than themselves, but who had uppity ideas. They lobbied the Egyptian rulers *not* to allow the Jews out and offered to extend their own period of servitude indefinitely if only Egypt would not allow the Jews their freedom. Such is gratuitous hatred in the dark pit of the hateful and resentful mind.

The revolution let loose in Egypt that day, the day of the Exodus, was one of the spirit as well as of the flesh – the freedom not just from physical bondage but from enslavement of the spirit to man's baser instincts. Our forefathers set out, on that day, not just away from the *kur habarzel*, the roiling smelting pot of depraved Egyptian culture that was at the core of their bitter, backbreaking slavery, but onto the road to Sinai, where they, and the world, were transformed forever.

They marched toward a world of *chesed*, of gratuitous *love*, of fairness, of goodness, of good-heartedness, of tzedakah of the spirit as well as of coin. They learned, and we have been taught – the whole world has been taught – that we can, and we must, suppress our baser resentful nature, banish it, and shine with loving-kindness. They marched toward a world that has been lovingly handed to us – we who are alive today to benefit from their travail – with an ideal of life so high and pure and rare that it is, in large measure, summarized deceptively simply in a single, timeless, utterly revolutionary phrase, a mitzvah central to our identity as a nation and as human beings created in God's image, *v'ahavta l're'acha ka'mocha*.

*Parashas Bo 5781*

# Ivri, Forever Ivri

At the end of his journey, just before he passed on, Moshe gathered all the people and charged them with remaining loyal and steadfast with God, His Torah, and with each other. *Atem nitzavim*: you are all standing here together today before God, all of you, the great ones and the plain ones, the leaders and the flock, of every stratum of society, the men and the women, the little boys and the little girls. Everyone. We are all equally in this together, for all time. For when it's great and glorious, and, God forbid, when it is the opposite. Those are the terms of our nationhood; that is integral to our relationship to God; that is what connects us to the Avos; that is what will keep us until the end of time. We are, all of us, the children of Avraham Ha'ivri, who set himself and thus us apart. Ivrim. It is a package deal.

Moshe repeatedly speaks to Pharaoh in the name of the God of the Ivrim. He could have referred to Him as the Creator, the Master of the universe, or any of a number of universal titles that refer to the Ribbono shel Olam. But Moshe emphasizes Hashem's particular relationship with the particular nation whose mission is and always will be to be fundamentally apart. Ivrim, on the other side of the metaphorical spiritual and cultural river.

Pharaoh may have understood this better than is apparent, even to the extent of its historical implications.

There are certain passages in the Torah that are presented in a way that makes them somewhat cryptic, not so obvious in their meaning. Moshe and Aharon come before Pharaoh and declare, yet again, "Thus says Hashem, the God of the Ivrim, how long will you refuse? Send forth My people and they will serve Me. For if you refuse, tomorrow I will bring a plague of locusts throughout your land" (Shemos 10:3–4). *It will be terrible.* Pharaoh's servants advise him to accede. Pharaoh asks Moshe who would be going. *Mi va'mi haholchim?* (Shemos 10:8). Moshe replies, famously, *bi'ne'areinu u'vizkeneinu nelech* (Shemos 10:9), all of us, everyone without exception, men and women, old and young, boys and girls, with all our things. We are all in this together.

Pharaoh replies in one of those cryptic passages that require interpretation, essentially, *no.* I do not agree to send the children, *and nor should you want to take them: ra'ah,* something that forbodes blood and death, is awaiting you in the desert (Shemos 10:10).

Rashi quotes a famous midrash, that Pharaoh, through his astrology, foresaw in some way the bloody end that Bnei Yisrael might have had for their sin with the Golden Calf, but he did not foresee that God would spare them and that the blood he saw would instead be the blood of the circumcisions performed by Yehoshua before their entry into the land. Moshe, in praying for their forgiveness, specifically brought up this prediction of Pharaoh's, asking Hashem not to let that *rasha* have been right.

But there is another dimension to this obscure wording. Pharaoh was warning Moshe not just about blood in the *midbar*, but blood throughout the ages.

Remember Pharaoh's complaint, and that of every one of our haters and oppressors throughout the ages. These people cling stubbornly to their ancient ways and refuse to integrate into the mass culture. They refuse to disappear. They insist on being different. They dress different, they talk different, they act different, their religion is different. They are not us, no matter how long they exist in our land; they will never be, they are not loyal, they think they are special, they think they are superior, they think they know better, they look down upon the rest of us, they conspire with our enemies, their ideas are anathema to us, they are not to be tolerated. They must be wiped out, erased – if not culturally, then physically. All of them. The children are as bad as the adults. They are indoctrinated so young that we cannot do anything with them. They are bad from birth. Their fate is decided by their birth.

They are all in it together. Some may bend our way, but the nation as a whole never will.

And somehow, he understood part of why that would be so. Not only is it inherently ingrained in their national DNA, not only is it a function of their famous national stubbornness, but it is also built into the very nature of their steadfastness: they are absolutely convinced. This makes possible the ongoing perpetuation of our faith and knowledge of our past, alluded to in the *pasuk, l'maan tesaper b'oznei bincha u'ven bincha es asher hisallalti b'Mitzrayim v'es ososai asher samti vam: vi'datem ki Ani Hashem* (Shemos 10:2). Rav Yehoshua of Belz, who battled against the so-called Haskalah (the "Enlightenment" movement, which spread nothing but darkness on Klal Yisrael as it sought to tear Jews away from their holy roots), interprets this to tell us that the only way true faith can be instilled in our children is if we ourselves are absolutely and genuinely complete in our own faith, *vi'datem ki Ani Hashem.*

Our own obvious certainty, sincerity, and steadfastness, clearly seen by our children, clearly *experienced* by our children, deeply felt by our children, will be ingrained in them. And while throughout history there have been people and segments of Klal Yisrael who have, *nebech*, fallen away, *the nation as a whole never will.*

Pharaoh, Rav Soloveitchik suggests, in an ongoing theme in his analysis of the sweep of history foretold in these *parashiyos*, as much as warned Moshe that Jewish children will pay in blood and suffering for the stubbornness of their elders. *Separate them out*, he said. *You go off into the wilderness and worship your God, if you must, but leave the children here. (Without you, they will be mine!)* His mock concern for the Jewish children – the same children that his nation had thrown into the Nile at birth, had mixed into the mortar for bricks – was, of course, a ploy, in an effort to undo what he had come to understand as the recalcitrant nature of this nation that saw itself, that defined itself, as Ivrim, every soul of every age forever bound organically to each other and to their God, Elokei Ha'ivrim, come what may.

Moshe, of course, would not hear of it. Without that organic oneness of all the generations, we would have long ago disappeared, and with us, the very purpose of creation. There is a price, but one far outweighed by the benefit. And we know the rest of the story.

*Parashas Bo 5782*

# Beshalach

## Armed and Dangerous

God famously led the children of Israel out of Egypt by a circuitous route, lest they be forced to fight the Plishtim, and, in fear and panic, retreat back to Egypt. And yet those very same *pesukim* tell us that they left Egypt fully armed. A week later, when the Egyptians caught up with them at the Yam Suf, they again didn't have to fight; God did that for them. So why did they have to carry arms with them, and why does the Torah make such a prominent point that they did?

Of course, they needed to be able to defend themselves if attacked along the way, as indeed they were by Amalek within a very short time. And they would presumably need arms in case of resistance upon entering Canaan, as indeed they did. But why, upon their triumphant exodus, when no one could stand in their way, would the Torah tell us that these former slaves armed themselves? Was it on their own initiative? Did Moshe direct them to? Was it a divine command? Whatever the source of that initiative, it was important enough for the Torah to make significant mention of it.

Where the Torah provides historical narrative, it's not primarily as a history book (although the history it does provide is irrefutably accurate), but rather to provide a context for us to understand our relationship with the Ribbono shel Olam as well as with each other and to teach us things He wants us to know. And, as we know, the experiences and actions of the Avos and the early progenitors of our nation, as related in the Torah, serve as a model for what the future holds for us, how to comport ourselves, and what we can expect in this world and of this world.

When Yaakov Avinu, upon his return from Lavan and Charan, prepared for his reunion with Esav, he approached that dreaded encounter by covering all the bases he could. He prayed. He divided his camp strategically. He prepared for war. And he pushed diplomacy, with nearly obsequious, undeserved graciousness toward Esav. And that clever diplomacy, in the end, brought about a peaceful, successful, on-the-surface-loving meeting with the evil Esav, who apparently never bothered him again. Yaakov was, in fact, ready for war, if need be, but he did everything he reasonably could to avoid it. And he succeeded.

It can be said that an important lesson in life was imparted in the juxtaposition of the verses that tell us of the Israelites' preparations for war and the prudent course of avoiding it if possible. Their resultant course of travel was far from the direct route to the Land of Israel, but God led them on that circuitous route because it was better for them not to have to fight at that time. Fighting would eventually come, and they would stand in their own defense, but God also knew that they weren't yet psychologically ready.

The classic understanding of that psychological unpreparedness for war is that the Israelites, as recent slaves, at that time lacked the self-confidence to wage war. But let me suggest that there can be another way to look at it. This nation, although until recently enslaved, also knew that they were the children of the exalted Avos and the beneficiaries of the many great promises made to those Avos. They had just experienced the unbelievable reality of witnessing God defeat the great empire of Egypt on their behalf. They were, it seemed, invincible, with God on their side. And so perhaps they were actually more confident than they should have been about an upcoming battle with the Plishtim. God had defeated the Egyptians for them, but perhaps it was not yet the time for the defeat of the Plishtim (and it wasn't, apparently, for another several hundred years). A sudden defeat at the hands of the Plishtim this soon after the Exodus would have been dispiriting to the nation in the extreme, and they might indeed have retreated back to Egypt.

Their readiness for war – necessary but perhaps unrealistically optimistic – might have led them to a mindset that was, in the long run, not good for them. Being armed does not necessarily mean ready, and being ready does not necessarily ensure victory, as experience has so many times painfully taught. And so they were taught Yaakov Avinu's strategy: war is best avoided when possible.

Terrible as they inevitably are, wars are sometimes foolishly sought by overconfident people who have forgotten what war really is. And so the Civil War in the USA, at its outset, was greeted jubilantly in many quarters as a great heroic adventure. And the militant excitement, even the joy, that accompanied the outbreak of war in Europe in 1914 was followed, as in all wars, by untold misery and carnage.

But beyond the wars of nations, as individuals in daily life, we face questions all the time of conflict that may be dealt with either cleverly and peacefully or with confrontation, struggle, and, on some level, personal destruction. Sometimes we have no choice. Sometimes there is nobody rational to talk to in the inevitable conflicts in life, and we have to "go to war." But it is usually much better – even if we are well armed like our forefathers marching out of Egypt – to go the extra mile, if we can, to take the longer, even circuitous route, to avoid an avoidable fight. In our dealings with each other, it is best to do whatever we can to avoid the demoralizing, disheartening, and destructive effects of that terrible scourge, *machlokes.*

*Parashas Beshalach 5778*

# Netzach Yehuda

Walk into any serious, busy *beis medrash*, and you will see a major manifestation of the energy of the Jewish People. The energy, an aspect of what is often called *milchemes haTorah* – the "battle" of Torah, the back-and-forth argument between study partners over meanings and the teachings to be derived from such intense study – fills the spirit as well as the ears. The energy is visible, even palpable, as it is audible. The energy is not quite about the argument, as vigorous as that might be, but it is a function of what drives that argument, which is not truly an argument but a loving joint effort, a joint struggle to fulfill the Jewish mandate to know God's will. It is Jewish energy made manifest.

But there is more to the overall energy of Jews, Judaism, indeed the Jewish nation than what one encounters in the *beis medrash* or the shul, as important and as central to our nationhood as that is. It is to be encountered in the life of the nation as it lives its life *as* a nation. Aspects of this are to be found all over the world, wherever Jews live as an organized *kehillah*, but nowhere is it as obvious or as active or as energetic or as *obviously natural* as it is in the Land of Israel.

Let's put aside all the problems and factional issues that drive Israelis (and drive us nuts at the same time). I wish to describe a scene I witnessed – indeed, experienced – at the recent *tekes* (ceremony) at the Kotel for the induction into the Israeli army of a large group of boys from an array of seriously *frum* backgrounds. Our English friends' grandson was among them. The Netzach Yehuda battalion of the Nachal Haredi is an integral part of the Kfir Brigade of the Israel Defense Forces, frontline troops defending the nation. Time and again, one hears the soldiers of this and similar groups speaking so devotedly and proudly of the holy privilege of defending the people, the nation, and the Land of Israel.

Afterwards, one could see family groups standing proudly with their sons and groups of friends. I have written before how I don't care for the term *charedi* to describe the perceived religiosity of someone based apparently just on a mode of dress. There is, of course, a role – an important one – for a uniform as part of a self-identifying mission statement, but externals are externals and easily donned for a variety of possible purposes, while being truly *"charedi l'devar Hashem"* depends on what is in the heart and the soul, what is the actual practice, and not on the cut of the garment.

Even so, it was fascinating and emotionally moving to see these groupings and their interactions. *Charedi*-looking parents and siblings with their *charedi*-looking inductee. *Charedi*-looking inductees with less *charedi*-looking families, and every other possible combination. Ethiopian immigrants standing and posing for pictures proudly with their thoroughly Israeli children. Friends with friends. What was obvious was not just about the army. It was the pulsing vibrancy of daily life in the Holy Land, where God, working through otherwise improbable history, is in the process of gathering together Jews from all walks of life, of every appearance and skin color, of every type, *together*. Very Jewish, very excited, the whole throng throbbing with excitement, emotion, and the energy of Jewish national life in the Promised Land of Israel.

As usual, it made me cry. Particularly gratifying to me, as a father, is that I saw my daughter, precious soul, doing the same.

We have been a nation for a very long time without a land and without an army. *Tzahal* is one of the miracles of rebirth. But we know as well that it is not the military might of an army that is the deciding factor, but the will of God. And so we encounter in this *parashah* a Jewish army of ex-slaves who have weapons but lack the will, fortitude, or confidence to fight. Even though they had just experienced such miracles done on their behalf against the very same enemy, it is God Himself Who leads them away from potential battle until they are psychologically ready. But now, hemmed in between the sea and the granite mountains of the desert, the Egyptians bearing down on them, they are frightened. God tells them to do what they have to do; the rest is up to Him. He will take care of it for them.

*Mah titzak Elai?* (Shemos 14:15). Why are you standing and shouting out in prayer when you need to move? Some explain it to mean that they, including Moshe, should not stand in prolonged prayer when it is time strategically for them to *act* – in this case, to march forward (into the sea!). Others emphasize the *Elai* part: *this is on Me*, says God. And perhaps we can also explain it as unifying both approaches.

Generations later, when the Jewish People are beset by a multitude of invading enemies and don't know what to do, how to best defend themselves, they pray, *V'anachnu lo neda mah naaseh* (II Divrei Hayamim 20:12). We don't know what to do. We are paralyzed with fear and indecision, feeling impotent. There too God tells them to leave it up to Him. He will take care of it. And, as at the Red Sea, He did.

*Mah titzak. Mah naaseh.*

Literally, *mah* means "what." But *mah* (מה) is also *mem-heh* (מ"ה), *milchemet Hashem* (מלחמת ה'). Hashem's war. The war He wages on our behalf.

When we are faced with war, God forbid, we need to do what a normal army does, and we need to beseech God to grant us victory, for without His will, there can be no victory. And even when it is God's intention to grant us victory – even miraculous victory, *Hashem yilachem lachem*, God will do the fighting for you, so to speak – we need to do what is humanly necessary, and we need *tze'akah* as well. *Mah – milchemes Hashem – titzak Elai!* Call out to Me! Shout out in prayer to Me at the proper time, and then, in the proper time, go to war; hopefully, please God, may it be His will, *Hashem yilachem lachem*, God Himself will carry the fight for you.

*Shemos Rabbah* (21:1), on *mah titzak Elai*, speaks of Yitzchak Avinu bequeathing unto Yaakov the power of *hakol kol Yaakov*, the voice (prayer), and to Esav the power of *hayadayim yedei Esav*, the arms (the sword). Each nation was proud of its particular source of power, and each was good at it. But that is not to say that Yaakov/Israel, in this world, can rely on prayer alone, so he must also know how to protect himself with arms as needed. And Esav, brutish thug that he is, who normally lives by the sword, can, if he will, turn to prayer as well.

Bilaam tried to turn the power of the Jews against them. He knew that *ein kocham ela ba'peh*, their power is in their mouths, their ability to pray. So he tried to undo them by turning that very force against them, to weaponize the spoken word, with the curses that he tried to utter. He could not, of course – God did not allow it – and later, he got his comeuppance: the Torah tells us specifically that in the subsequent battle with the Jews, he was killed *by the sword*, the weapon of choice of the world he came from.

So when the Children of Israel cried out to God as the Egyptians approached, and then Moshe undertook to pray, Hashem chided him for it, saying that He had already heard the peoples' prayers. Done. Now was no time for Moshe to pray, but to act.

The Midrash continues with the most wonderful teaching. When Jews pray, in today's world, they don't all pray in one place or at one time. They have congregations all over the world, wherever they are, all davening at different times. An angel of our loving God then collects the prayers of His children from all over, and the Ribbono shel Olam crowns Himself with them, *k'v'yachol*, proudly and lovingly. He declares, *Look what a beautiful crown My children have made for Me!*

And He loves and desires the prayers of all, equally. Come see, says the Midrash, the difference between how God pays attention to requests and entreaties and how humans do. Typically, when someone is approached by a poor person, a street person, someone who is down and out, someone generally held to be of no account, he may pay him scant attention. If, however, approached by a wealthy big shot, high and mighty, he will listen very well indeed. Not so the Ribbono shel Olam. To Him, all prayers are equally attended to. Men and women, rich and poor, freemen and slaves, from all walks of life. And thus when our forefathers – the plain people, the *amcha Yidden* – stood at the edge of the Yam Suf, with Pharaoh's mighty army bearing down on them, they called out in prayer: *va'yitzaku el Hashem*. When Moshe then undertook to pray, Hashem told him, *Stop! My children have already prayed to Me. No need for you to do so. I will take care of it. Now is the time for you to act!*

There are, sadly, many spiritual deficiencies in Israeli society, including – even especially – in the army. There is, in the secularist upper echelons, a prejudiced fear of the influence of the newer breed of dedicated *frum* fighters. It doesn't fit their preferred narrative, and invoking God's protection makes them feel uncomfortable, as if it were somehow unwarlike, because it differs from the chest-thumping swagger of the military types who arrogantly imagine that it is *kochi v'otzem yadi*, their own brute strength that assures victory.

Notoriously, one of the most respected and talented commanders in the army, a real star, had his career sidetracked – and effectively ended – not long ago because he had the temerity, when sending his troops into battle in Gaza, to publicly invoke God's protection as they faced the murderous enemy. But I believe that as the strength of the religiously motivated grows, the future belongs to those who also understand our past, where we come from, why and by what right we are here, and by Whose grace we live.

It is also clear that the most motivated and dedicated soldiers in the Israel Defense Forces are those precious boys who, at their induction, proudly clutch in one hand the Tanach and in the other the rifle that they are presented with, in their hands both holy weapons, as they take their solemn oath to defend Am Yisrael with all their might, with their spirit, with their lives.

May Hashem bless them and, together with *all* the precious and dedicated soldiers of Israel, God's beloved children, keep them safe and bring them home. And may the precious and abundant energy of Klal Yisrael be ever more channeled to accomplish the wonderful and wondrous things that we, as individuals and as a nation, were created for.

מי שברך אבותינו אברהם יצחק ויעקב
הוא יברך את חילי צבא ההגנה לישראל
העומדים על משמר ארצנו וערי אלקינו
מגבול הלבנון ועד מדבר מצרים
ומן הים הגדול עד לבוא הערבה
בכל מקום שהם ביבשה באויר ובים
יתן ה׳ את אויבנו הקמים עלינו נגפים לפניהם!
הקדוש ברוך הוא ישמר ויציל את חילינו
מכל צרה וצוקה ומכל נגע ומחלה
וישלח ברכה והצלחה בכל מעשה ידיהם
ידבר שונאינו תחתיהם ויעטרם בכתר ישועה ובעטרת נצחון
ויקים בהם הכתוב "כי ה׳ אלקיכם ההלך עמכם
להלחם לכם עם אויביכם להושיע אתכם."
ונאמר אמן

*Parashas Beshalach 5779, Yerushalayim Ir Hakodesh*


# Middas Harachamim

*Rachamim!*

We need *rachamim!* Without Hashem's *middah* of *rachamim*, how can we survive at all?

Our forefathers' redemption from Egypt came about after Hashem revealed to Moshe that while He had appeared to the Avos through other Names, He did not make Himself known or fully understood by them through the Name Y--H, commonly associated with His *middas harachamim*. Now, therefore, Hashem said, *Go tell Bnei Yisrael that I, Y--H, will now redeem them; I will fulfill all My promises to them, as this Name encompasses.*

They were promised redemption, back in Yosef's time: *pakod yifkod Elokim eschem.* "Elokim" is commonly associated with *middas hadin.* That redemption actually came after Hashem declared that he would now act on their behalf as Y--H.

And so it's interesting that we learn in Parashas Beshalach that *lo nacham Elokim derech eretz Plishtim*, that upon the glorious Exodus, rather than go straight to Eretz Yisrael by the quick and geographically easier route, Elokim had them go south, deep into the wilderness, headed for a difficult and extremely roundabout route. The stated reason – lest they encounter war with the Plishtim and flee back to Egypt – seems odd considering that the same God Who utterly overcame the mighty Egyptians on their behalf could certainly deal with the Philistines. Indeed, a generation later, when they did enter the land, God clearly did miraculously fight for them. That Elokim led them away from the direct route is stated three times in rapid succession.

Furthermore, just as soon they turn away from the direct route, God's name is henceforth presented in the narrative as Y--H, as He leads them into the desert. But in turning the Jews away from the quick route, Hashem manifested Himself *davka* as Elokim.

Rav Soloveitchik says that in this, "Elokim" represents the natural order of things, a slow process. Had "Y--H" been used, he says, the whole journey would have lasted but a few days, Moshe Rabbeinu himself would have led them into the land, Canaan would have surrendered immediately, there would have been no *churban*, no exile, no historic tribulation. Everything would have been handed to them, for all time. But that's not how God wanted it. We must also do, we must make our choices, we must deal with consequences. The long, slow, and terribly difficult road we have been and still are on all these years, waiting for Redemption, is reflected in the perspective of the Name Elokim.

But, on that longer road, there was Krias Yam Suf (and what would Jewish homes today do for art on the wall but for that?), there was the *mon*, there was *maamad Har Sinai* (the Torah would have been given some other way), there were the innumerable and constant miracles in the *midbar* that Y--H provided, along with all the problems they faced – problems of their own making – and the resultant punishments. But it was for them to choose, their behavior was decided by them, as it has always been throughout the generations, as it is for us today.

We were not put here to live our lives as contented cows in a rich pasture, with nothing to do but live our biological functions. The power and the opportunity to choose good over bad – to be tempted but to use one's free will to triumph over that temptation, to pay a price, if need be, to choose that which is right, to earn merit before our Creator – is, indeed, one of the greatest gifts that the Creator bestowed upon mankind, and in the context of our own lives, upon us, the Children of Israel, with our own unique rules of life and our own unique relationship with our God, Who is known to us by multiple names, most prominently Y--H and Elokim.

Sometimes the Hand of God reaches down to help us in a breathtakingly obvious way. And sometimes, it requires much faith to understand that God is there with us, even in the most painful depths, as He, in His wisdom and His judgment, directs events. And, in His *chesed*, He allows us, *k'v'yachol*, by our own choices in life, to influence His.

The privilege of our particular, special relationship with God is very great, but it has a price beyond just the consequences of our choices. It earns us the unending enmity of our foes. It is true that the closer we cling to God and His Torah, the more He is likely to protect us, but there are just too many (and it apparently doesn't take very many – witness the case of Achan in Yericho) who, for various human reasons, stray too far from the path God has laid out for us, indeed created us for.

And so we move from the beginning of Parashas Beshalach to the end of it, and *Va'yavo Amalek*. Amalek, child of Esav, is the quintessential Jew hater, a trait most common to Esav but not limited to him.

Rav Soloveitchik identifies Amalek as "man-Satan," the enemy of man who enjoys causing misery and injury to all people, but who is particularly preoccupied with venting his gratuitous hatred upon the Jew, finding therein his greatest delight. This man-Satan may adopt many guises and sociopolitical programs – socialist, capitalist, fascist, reactionary, progressive, religious-clerical, or secular-atheist, but the Jew remains his central preoccupation.

The Jews in Persia thought they were OK until they discovered that Amalek-Haman, the man-Satan and his minions, were seeking their utter destruction. The very existence of the Jew is intolerable to them. This pattern has been repeated so many times in history, reaching an unparalleled crescendo just a generation ago. And after a "moment" of relative respite, the forces of unrelenting hatred are being heard again, including in places previously thought safe.

The early secular Zionists, who were so far from Torah that they simply could not understand this issue at all, thought that if the Jews "normalized" and set up their own "normal" state (ideally, complete with thieves and loose women, they argued) there would be no more Jew hatred, and certainly not in or about that Jewish state. Blind fools that they were, so outside the context of Torah Judaism they had placed themselves, they could not fathom the real cause of this hatred. Today, it is clear that our enemies, the man-Satan that forgot to go away when the majority of Jews became much less obviously Jewish or different, cannot abide not just the existence of the Jews as a political institution, the State of Israel, but they cannot stand the existence of the Jews altogether.

Parashas Beshalach opens with the Jews' triumphant march out of Egypt, *b'yad ramah*, seemingly invincible. But God steers them away from what seemed the quick and hopefully easy path. It would not be so easy, as the Philistines' time had not yet run out, even as the Canaanites' had. Many great dramas, good and bad, had yet to play out, as they did on the alternate path they took. The choices and behavior of the Israelites made a difference. The miracles and the victory at Yam Suf were totally gratuitous, a gift from God in fulfillment of His promise. Beshalach closes with Amalek's attack and the ensuing battle. God granted victory there too, but the pattern and manner of that victory were telling and set a pattern for future generations.

Amalek had sniped at the weak periphery of the Israelite camp, probing for a full attack. It made no sense for them to do this. Israel was no threat to them at all, and the whole world feared the Jews, knowing that God's might was with them. Why would they attack, and how could they expect to win? In the classic example offered by Chazal, in their hatred they knowingly jumped into a boiling cauldron not just to inflict harm on Israel, regardless of the cost, but also, in the process, to cool the waters so that others could then jump in to continue the war against the Jews, against God, and against the relationship between Israel and God.

And so, with God on their side, Israel went to war with Amalek. But this battle was very different from the encounter with the Egyptians at Yam Suf. The Egyptians enslaved the Jews not out of gratuitous hatred but for economic and nationalistic reasons, coupled with the arrogant pagan disregard for human dignity common to much of the world at the time, before the Jews taught such values to the world. The Amalekites, however, scions of Esav, were driven by pure hatred, a perverse passion that still reverberates in the world.

At Yam Suf, Israel needed to do nothing but have faith in God and in Moshe as God's messenger, and to walk across the seabed, munching on divinely provided treats along the way. The rest was up to God. With Amalek, they had to organize a battalion of soldiers under Yehoshua's captaincy and actually do conventional battle, wielding swords and spears, giving and receiving blows. But even then, more was needed.

Moshe sat on a high perch overlooking the battle. When he held his arms up high, the Jewish soldiers prevailed. But even Moshe could not hold his arms up indefinitely, and when he let them down to rest, the enemy started to prevail. So Moshe's brother Aharon and his nephew Chur stood by his side and held his arms up.

Asks the Gemara (*Rosh Hashanah* 29a), what's this? Did Moshe's raised arms wage war, weaken the enemy, and bring victory? Clearly, not directly. Rather, Yehoshua's army, tzaddikim all, looked up to Moshe for inspiration, and continued their gaze upward to where Moshe was pointing – to their Father in Heaven. Fighting for their nation and their families, they utterly and completely dedicated their hearts to Him, placed their faith and their trust in Him, and He granted them victory.

*Lo nacham Elokim derech Eretz Plishtim*, Elokim did not lead them by the quick route to the Land of Israel. They would have encountered a struggle they were psychologically unprepared for, the need to actually go out and do battle without lightning bolts from Heaven striking down their enemies for them. The scare and then the salvation at Yam Suf, the scarcities of food and water, their whining complaints followed by the miraculous appearance of food and drink had to come first. Life for individuals and for the nation will not be that of the contented cow in pasture, with no effort. The struggles, of life, and of all of Jewish history to follow, not just those common to mankind, but those unique to Bnei Yisrael, without which there can be no merit and no gain, are central to the very nature of life in this current phase of creation.

We pray that those struggles not be, for us, too difficult. We pray that our loving God will do for us as He blesses Himself, so to speak, *k'v'yachol* (*Berachos* 7b), *she'yichbeshu rachamai es ka'asi v'yigolu rachamai al middosai v'esnaheg im banai b'middas rachamim v'ekanes lahem lifnim mi'shuras hadin* (שֶׁיִּכְבְּשׁוּ רַחֲמַי אֶת כַּעֲסִי וְיָגוֹלּוּ רַחֲמַי עַל מִדּוֹתַי וְאֶתְנַהֵג עִם בָּנַי בְּמִדַּת רַחֲמִים וְאֶכָּנֵס לָהֶם לִפְנִים מִשּׁוּרַת הַדִּין), that Hashem will let his *middas rachamim* predominate over His *middas hadin* and bless Am Yisrael accordingly, and especially that the time will come soon when the ultimate successor to Moshe Rabbeinu, Mashiach Tzidkeinu, will usher in the ultimate phase of creation, when, basking in divine blessing, we will need struggle no more.

*Parashas Beshalach 5780*

# Yisro

## Altar Ego

It was a unique moment in all our history. Never before, and never after, it appears, have all of us, every single Jew, been perfect, all at the same time. At Sinai, as we stood at the base of the mountain, we were, in effect, on the very mountaintop.

That's when God admonishes us to build an altar, the *mizbe'ach*, as a tool in reaching out to Him when we are no longer so. Upon it we will offer the *korbonos* that are dedicated to Him, but which really speak to *us*, are there for *us*, to set our hearts and minds and spirit, our consciousness and our conscience, in perspective to our God. With the *mizbe'ach* we approach Him, but with it He is also telling us something about how, in order to do so, we are to approach each other.

The *mizbe'ach* in the desert is referred to as *mizbe'ach adamah*, made of earth. The walls were copper-clad wood, but the mass was the clods of earth that filled it. Later, in the Mikdash in Jerusalem, it was to be made of stones. But those stones had to be whole, uncut, unhewn, untouched by any metal tool, rough with imperfections. And there could be no steps to its top, only a ramp.

A person bringing a *korban* to atone for his sins sees the sacrifice consumed in the fire and comes to realize that he himself, for his sinful act – itself a rebellion against divine authority – deserves to be so consumed. But God, in His kindness, allows us to bring the sacrifice instead so that we may contemplate our place in the world, our relationship with our Maker, and return to Him. We stand on clods of earth, or rough stones, to remind us that man is himself derived from a clod of earth and is destined to return to such a state. God, we are but clods of earth! Tolerate us! Forgive us!

But, in judging our fellow man, whom we are often quick to criticize, judge, and condemn, we had best remember that the clods of earth we are standing on – the rough, imperfect stones – are so designed to remind us not only of our own limitations and imperfections as we appeal to God to forgive us on that very basis, but also of the limitations of our fellow human beings, as we regard them and judge them. Awareness of our own humble position obligates us to judge our fellows no more strictly than we would ourselves wish to be judged.

Metal tools, otherwise used as instruments of war, have no place in building this *mizbe'ach*. That would be utterly inconsistent with the message of love and tolerance, peace and forgiveness, the message of life that the *mizbe'ach* should arouse in us.

And finally comes a most profound lesson in sensitivity. One is to climb to the top via a ramp, an inclined plane, with no steps, in order that *lo sigaleh ervascha alav*, that your "nakedness" not be revealed in ascending. The imagery in the Midrash is that one who climbs steps exposes his *ervah* as he does so. But even though the Kohen's uniform includes trousers under his robe, apparently obviating this problem, it is called *"karov l'giluy ervah,"* an action that approaches such exposure.

And herein is the lesson that caps all the above. Stones have no consciousness, no feelings, no sense of hurt or shame, cannot suffer humiliation, and neither care nor are affected in any way by anyone's *ervah*, exposed or not. And yet the Torah tells us to be very careful not to embarrass them, as these stones, inanimate as they are, are there to serve our purpose before God. Well, then, what about our fellow man, created in God's image, who thinks and feels, who is pained and damaged by humiliation, who cares very much indeed?

All the more so, we must be careful never to cause hurt, through word or deed, even a hint, a wink and a nod, even something as remote as unintended but careless disrespect. We approach that *mizbe'ach* as we approach God for our very lives and those of our families. Through these lessons, God reminds us, among other lessons, that the road to Him leads directly through our fellow man.

*Parashas Yisro 5780*

# Shalom

You never know where life will take you.

Most people, in the history of the world, lived out their lives within a few miles of where they were born, the course of their lives utterly predictable, with some variations, and little different from the lives of their folks.

And then there are those whose lives wound up being startlingly removed from where they started. As the world progresses, as mobility, in its various meanings, has increased, the potential for such transformation has also increased. But even so, barring major upheavals, most people live, in a general sense, fairly predictable lives. And then again, you never really know what's coming. Wars and upheavals do that, as does life itself, even mundane life.

There are myriad stories of rags to riches in the world. There are stand-outs, like Abraham Lincoln, born in a poor cabin on the frontier, barefoot and penniless, who had to use charred sticks from the fireplace and the back of a shovel if he wanted to write something, going on to achieve world renown and immortality.

But within each individual life, from the most mundane to the most unusual, the seeming vagaries of life and our ability to hold on to it are boundless. You really never know where life will take someone, *anyone*, or where or when it might... drop him. Just like that.

The pandemic that recently gripped the world, especially in its early phase, shockingly did just that, all over the place.

A vibrant young friend who worked in my operating facility met a shocking, violent, and sudden end, *lo aleinu*, on the Belt Parkway.

You never know. There are things we cannot control. And there are, it seems, some things we can do to try to tip the balance in favor of life. Certainly, trying to win merit before God is key, but we also know that God's *cheshbon* goes so far above and beyond human reckoning that we cannot hope to understand how that works. We can only take comfort in the faith that it does.

There are some mitzvos and activities, such as tzedakah or *kibud av va'em*, that we are taught do buy us life, although in what manner and in what amount, we cannot know.

Prayer can buy us life. When we think of prayer, most of us envision formal davening, such as Shacharis or Minchah. Or Tehillim. But we also understand and have been nurtured to know from earliest childhood that for us, prayer and a prayerful awareness of our Father in Heaven is a constant. He hovers ever near us, waiting for us, listening, wanting us to reach out to Him constantly, with our lips and with our hearts, in all things in life. And for that He has imbued us – our mouths – with the power to affect the world. Everything we say counts, to a greater or lesser degree. *Ein kocham ela ba'peh.*

And so the Jew understands to be very careful with the words that come out of his mouth, as they can affect life – for himself, for his family, as well as for others. We also see the difference a single letter in one word can make, famously related in *Berachos* 64a. David said to Avshalom, *"lech b'shalom,"* go *in* peace, and Avshalom shortly thereafter died a grisly death. Yisro sent off Moshe with *"lech l'shalom,"* go *to* peace, and Moshe went on to become Moshe Rabbeinu. The words we utter and even their nuances have power, sometimes even over life and death.

When Yisro advises Moshe to appoint worthy judges to share the burden of adjudicating the many issues a nation as driven as the *yotzei Mitzrayim* were (and have remained), for Moshe alone cannot handle it, he says that only in this way can the nation successfully arrive at their destination, the Land of Israel, *b'shalom*.

*B'shalom*, Yisro says – not *l'shalom*, as when he sent off Moshe to success, but *b'shalom*. Why the difference?

I believe it harks back to that *gemara* in *Berachos*, in which, after admonishing us not to say *lech b'shalom* to the living, only *lech l'shalom*, it tells us not to say *lech l'shalom* when taking leave of the deceased at the cemetery, but only *lech b'shalom*.

When Hashem told Avraham, in the Bris Bein Habesarim, of the difficult but formative travails his children would have to undergo, He said, *Know that your children will be foreigners in a land not theirs, a term of four hundred years, during which they will be enslaved and tortured. I will then judge their enslavers, and they will leave that land with a great fortune. But you, Avraham, will not have to witness any of that. V'ata tavo el avosecha b'shalom; you will die a good, peaceful, and fulfilled death (both his father Terach and his son Yishmael ultimately did teshuvah); you will arrive in Heaven b'shalom.*

The endpoint and the journey are different. When Moshe started out on his – and Israel's – epic journey, Yisro's blessing of *lech l'shalom* was the right message. When a person's mission in this world is done, and his loved ones take leave of him as he is put to rest, *lech b'shalom* is the right message. When the *dor hamidbar*, whose mission was to live the Exodus, with the miracles in Egypt, at Yam Suf and in the *midbar*, to stand at Sinai and to hear the Voice of God as He revealed Himself with our eternal legacy, arrived, finally, in Eretz Yisrael, their mission was done. *Al mekomo yavo b'shalom.*

The ability to speak is a prime differentiator between man and beast. Man is *hamedaber*. That power of speech is, in turn, endowed with power far beyond just making spoken language. It is a bridge between the mundane and the sublime. It can evoke power from above, and in giving us speech, the Creator also invited us to do just that, to affect the world and all that is within it with our speech. To pray. To bless. And if one chooses, *Rachmana litzlan*, to hurt.

The power to bless and to heal is the flip side of the power to curse and to injure.

In every human encounter, we have a choice to make. To love and to bless, even as we want to be loved and blessed, or God forbid the opposite. To soothe and to heal, to help make whole, or God forbid the opposite. To love our neighbor as ourselves, or God forbid the opposite.

Until our mandate in this life is done, when we are sent off into the afterlife to meet our reward with the parting blessing of *lech b'shalom*, we have the blessed opportunity, a chance so precious, to bless and beautify the lives of others and thus beautify and bring blessing into our own lives in this world and the next, with a kind word, with a smile and a blessing, with a compliment, with a good wish, with a friendly greeting of *shalom*, with a loving word in parting, with a heartfelt *lech l'shalom*.

*Parashas Yisro 5781*

# For Our Children

I have a relative whose daughter got married after a year-long engagement. He told me that it was the worst year of his life.

With all that time to pick at and to bicker over ridiculous details of the wedding event, it was nonstop fighting over foolish disagreements about meaningless details and decisions. In particular, mother and daughter (the only daughter in the family) were at each other's throats, screaming in fury, endlessly, it seemed, over nothing important. It's years later; I hope their relationship recovered. I don't know if any of this misery spilled over into the relationship between the bride and groom.

These relatives live their lives by and large not too connected to our own communal norms and habits. In our traditional custom, at least in this era (it's been different in the past), for good reasons, it's typical for an engagement to last about three months, enough time to make all the necessary arrangements. (Too much time, if you ask me. If you're asking me, all you need is to find a place to live, get the basics, and arrange as simple and inexpensive a wedding as possible. Funny, though: I don't remember *anyone*, even regarding my own children's weddings, asking me.)

The Ribbono shel Olam led the Children of Israel out of Egypt and toward the Promised Land not by the shortest, most direct route, but initially in another direction altogether. The given explanation is that with the quick route, they would have encountered war well before they were ready for it. There is much involved in being ready.

How long does it take to be ready? Well, Krias Yam Suf and seeing the final and utter destruction of their enemies helped. Ultimately, they reached Sinai in the third month after their departure from Egypt. Like a bridegroom who seeks to please the bride before the wedding with gifts, nice words, and all manner of attention, God prepared them during this time with ongoing miracles (not that they always seemed properly appreciative). It was a kind of wooing period that was not too short and not too long.

*Midrash Tanchuma* brings an interesting parallel. There is a halachah that a woman who is a convert, or released from captivity, or widowed/divorced waits three months before she can marry. The given reason is that there should be no question of paternity, should she give birth. But there is also the need to mentally and emotionally separate from what was before in order to properly bond with what comes next. Like the Children of Israel, there is much involved in being ready, in order for it to come out right. About three months seems to work. To prepare, to grow into it, to savor it, to feel confident and certain about it.

Much was at stake. The commitment at Sinai – and it was huge – was not just about those present then, but about every Jew who would ever live afterwards until the end of time. It was about every one of us today, about our children, and their children for all generations to come.

God told them that He has chosen them to be his special, treasured nation. *Segulah mi'kol ha'amim. Mamleches Kohanim. Goy kadosh.* That's quite a commitment for the Ribbono shel Olam to make to a people who He knew would, just forty days hence, after the once-in-the-lifetime-of-the-world Revelation of Matan Torah, be dancing around a golden calf. In His infinite love and mercy, in His love for the Avos and in His love for *us*, He did it anyway.

But wait! What guarantee, He asked them, what guarantors do I have that this is a forever commitment, your pious cry of *naaseh v'nishma* notwithstanding? I know what you will do in the future, I know about your failings, not once but repeatedly.

Our forefathers, truly great despite their various weaknesses and failings, had an answer that satisfied God and cemented the deal forever. To the Ribbono shel Olam's question – who will be your guarantors that the Torah will be with you forever – they answered, says the Midrash, *Our children!* And Hashem responded, *They are the best guarantors of all!* Thus, says David Hamelech, *Mi'pi olelim v'yonkim yesadita oz*, from the mouths of babes, even suckling infants, You have established strength (Tehillim 8:3). This is the ongoing strength, the guarantor of our eternity.

The Midrash goes further. Our forefathers brought out their wives and children, even the unborn babies in their midst, who all saw the Revelation, who heard it, who experienced it and proclaimed that they would uphold the Torah and keep the Covenant alive forever.

*Do you guarantee it with your lives? Do you agree to bear the burden of responsibility, even punishment, if your fathers fail?*

*Yes!* they cried.

*Anochi Hashem Elokecha.*
*Yes!* they cried.
*Lo yihyeh lecha*, you shall have no other gods.
*Yes!* they cried.
And so for all the *dibros*, crying out their eternal commitment to each one.

And God told them, He told those children, *it is for* your *commitment, and in* your *merit, that today I give the Torah to Israel. The reward is very great. But understand that the price of failure is also very high.* And the price of such failure, God forbid, is paid not just by the parents who failed, but by the children, *Rachmana litzlan*, of those parents who failed.

The terrible, terrible reality is that Jews who forsake the Torah thereby bring such terrible harm to their own children, in many ways. We have seen this countless times in our long and sometimes tortured history.

The highs are very high, the pinnacle of human spiritual and temporal existence. It is, for the most part, ours for the having, if we are smart enough, individually *and collectively*. That has been, for much of our history, an elusive goal.

Walk into virtually any *cheder* or *beis midrash*, and you will see the power and the beauty of this eternal commitment in action. But we also see, *nebech*, all around us, so many who just don't get it, who don't understand, who have been robbed of their beautiful gift from God and from their loyal forebears, who don't realize the harm they are doing to their own children as well as to ours, to the whole nation, who are good on the inside but don't understand what it takes for a Jew to be good in the manner he was created for.

With love, we must reach out to them, each as best we can. There are such heroes among us who dedicate their lives to doing so. They are the heroes of *kiruv*. To those heroes we owe our gratitude and our support, for they are saving our lives, saving our children, saving our future.

*Parashas Yisro 5782*

# Mishpatim

## My Palestinian *Mechutan*

On Shabbos, Parashas Mishpatim, my family was preparing to usher its newest member into the Covenant of Avraham Avinu, with his *bris milah*. In that rite, a Jewish male is *perfected* by removing a bit of tissue. Thus, in its natural state, a boy's body is considered to be *imperfect* for a Jew, even if for everyone else it is the natural state (if all is normal) that can be considered perfect.

Achieving that perfection is so lofty an attainment that the child must experience the holiness of a Shabbos first in order to be able to receive that elevation.

Similarly, we understand that the Creator gave us a beautiful world, but even in pristine nature, it still requires human beings to cultivate and develop it – *l'ovdah u'l'shomrah* – for it to be brought to the state it was designed for. Thus, part of the plan of creation is that it is up to humanity to continue and to complete acts of creation. It is our prime mandate, and the goodness that derives from that is a reason for creation itself.

We know that of the many mitzvos we have, there are those for which the reason is given, those for which the reason is not given but for which a rational reason may be discerned, and then there are those whose purpose remains an utter mystery, their fulfillment an act of pure faith.

I believe that there are also mitzvos that were *not* actually given – expectations of us by our Creator that are not specifically contained in the *taryag* (613) mitzvos of the Torah or the seven mitzvos that apply to all human beings – but are nevertheless where, I submit, God wants us to go, a level we need to attain for mankind to perfect itself and to achieve the mandate inherent in what God put us here for. It is part of continuing and completing acts of creation. And just as more primitive man could not achieve things modern man can, so too society at large has a mandate to develop itself morally and ethically. Thus, *l'aniyus daati*, there are societal and civilizational achievements that are possible – and expected – now, that might not have been expected of society in an earlier stage of its development.

In the avalanche of laws laid out in Parashas Mishpatim, immediately subsequent to Matan Torah, which govern how we are to relate with each other, the first is about servitude. It is interesting to note that this set of laws, about *eved Ivri*, is the segue to an entire system of law and ethics affecting our lives in nearly every way. But if it's about *ethics*, about decency, fairness, justice, and goodness, how is it possible that our holy Torah – the defining source of what, in fact, is decent, fair, and good – permits slavery? True, an *eved Ivri* is not a true slave in the full sense of the word, and even full-fledged slavery is not really slavery the way we usually think about slavery (with perhaps more obligations on the part of the owner toward the slave than the slave toward the owner), but the institution of slavery is, in fact legal. And that it is, at least on paper, permissible, is mystifying, even as it is disconcerting.

If that revolution in human behavior, the Torah, outlawed eating pork, if the Torah separated out one day of every week to be given over to the spirit, with work forbidden, if the Torah outlawed charging our brethren interest, if the Torah forbade *avodah zarah* in any form, if the Torah mandated that we share what we have with the poor, if the Torah had room for 613 commandments, if the Torah is about goodness and decency, why did it not also include, as part of that revolution, the outlawing of slavery?

I would suggest that it is omitted precisely because it is so important, so central to human decency, that forbidding it would be, in a sense, the "easy way out" as far as human beings perfecting themselves is concerned. It is a far greater accomplishment for slavery to be outlawed, for racism and bigotry to be viewed with horror and disgust, for decency and fairness to be the expected norm as a function of human ethical development *derived* from the Revelation at Sinai, but the end result of human *choice*. Human beings serving God and fulfilling the function they were created for by following the ethical dictates commanded to them by their Creator to their logical and desired conclusion. It's about what God wants of us: goodness taught and so well internalized that it becomes self-driven.

And so, a word about goodness and decency. I had five wonderful *mechutonim*. Americans all, three were born in the United States, one is Israeli, and one Palestinian. A recent Shabbos was the fifth yahrzeit of the Palestinian.

Lest you be confused, until the recent past, when a "nation" of Arabs now commonly called "Palestinians" was contrived, with a fabricated history, for political purposes to fit the narrative of our enemies, the term *Palestinian* referred primarily to Jews living in pre-State Israel, then called Palestine.

Yossi Eisenstadt, *a"h*, was a Palestinian by birth. He was an aristocrat by lineage. But mainly, he was a prince, by virtue of his lifelong striving for self-perfection.

Quietly and privately excellent in his devotions to God, he revealed his excellence in how he related to other people. And like the child who is perfected by his bris, like the beautiful earth perfected by its fruitful development, like society going beyond the bare legal requirements and striving to achieve the full measure of man's potential for goodness, my Palestinian *mechutan*, the beloved and sorely missed Yossi Eisenstadt, may he rest in peace, perfected himself like few other people. The beautiful family he left behind (and I am especially grateful for his Akiva, who is now my beloved son too) bears testimony to his accomplishments. The feelings of others toward him and about him bear testimony to his exemplary character and to the very excellence of his striving for personal excellence. *Yehi zichro baruch.*

*Parashas Mishpatim 5778*


# Cast Your Bread upon the Waters

The enemy had already been at the gates and beyond.

Nearly nine hundred years after Israel's triumphant, God-led exodus from Egyptian bondage, the kingdom it had forged in the Promised Land had fallen to such a low and decadent state that the split-off northern kingdom of the ten tribes had already been gone for over a hundred years, its people lost altogether. The southern kingdom had already been defeated and subjugated by the powerful Babylonians, its king carried off into captivity and a new puppet king, Tzidkiyahu, appointed in his place by the conquerors. They had been warned by God's prophets but would not listen.

Tzidkiyahu and his courtiers did not take well to being puppets and rebelled. Babylon turned on them with a fury. In a gesture to God, the sinful and haughty nobility, at the king's urging, solemnly undertook to reform a widespread cruel and vile practice. They had taken fellow Jews as slaves or indentured servants, but refused to release them from their servitude after the mandated six-year term as the Torah commanded. In their fear, in their time of duress, they had solemnly pledged and undertaken before God to release all their Jewish servants and never to enslave a fellow Jew again. As soon as the immediate crisis passed, they arrogantly sent out their goons and recaptured their former slaves and put them back under the yoke.

Yirmiyahu Hanavi confronts the king and the nobles (Yirmiyahu 34). *The word of God: I made a covenant with your forefathers on the day I took them out of Egyptian bondage, that any such indentured Jewish servants must be freed no longer than after six years (and the terms of the servitude must be benign). But you desecrated My Name and violated your solemn pledge to let them all go, cruelly re-enslaving the recently freed slaves.*

*For violating the freedom of your poor brethren, I will repay you,* declares God, middah k'neged middah, *measure for measure, with freedom: freedom from Me, from My protection. I will make you "free" – free for the sword of the enemy, for pestilence, for famine, for exile, all of which will have free dominion over you. The Babylonians will return, destroy, take the king into captivity, and "free" the land of its inhabitants, leaving it empty and desolate.*

Nearly nine hundred years before, the escaped Israelite slaves stood on the shores of the Yam Suf and saw their Egyptian enslavers lying dead in heaps. At that moment, they truly became free, in their minds as well as in fact. Very shortly thereafter, they stood at the foot of Har Sinai and encountered God's Revelation; they entered into an eternal covenant with Him, sealed in the spectacular experience of Matan Torah and the Aseres Hadibros. Immediately afterwards, as Moshe begins laying it all out for them, the very first mitzvah, in Mishpatim, is the mitzvah of *eved Ivri*, the strict and humane laws governing the indenture of a fellow Jew who has fallen low.

The whole story, the saga of the so-called First Commonwealth of the Jewish People, begins with a lesson and a requirement regarding human dignity and decency toward our fellow man, in the context of the *eved Ivri*, and ends, tragically, with an utter failure in that same endeavor.

It is quite apparent from the *navi* that had they held true, had the haughty and arrogant, heartless aristocrats shown the humility and the humanity, the decency toward their brethren that God asked of them and that they had indeed sworn to do, the tragedy would likely have been averted.

They should have remembered as well the lesson of Yisro, who came running to Israel's encampment after Krias Yam Yuf, for it revealed a powerful lesson and a justification of his life.

Yisro, according to the Gemara (*Sotah* 8a), was one of Pharaoh's advisers, who, when confronted with the Egyptian plan to drown the Jewish boys at birth, fled rather than be part of it. A spiritual seeker, he tried every religion, worshiped every *avodah zarah*, until he concluded that it is all naught, except for the God we know as the Ribbono shel Olam. He took Moshe as his son-in-law and continued to hover on the periphery.

Krias Yam Suf and the drowning of the mighty Egyptian army was for Yisro the clincher. *B'kedera she'bishlu bah nisbashlu* (in the very cauldron one cooks in, he is cooked, *Sotah* 11). The drowned Egyptians, who had years before drowned the

Jewish children, wound up getting "cooked" in the very pot in which they had cooked their little victims. Yisro declared, "*Ata yadati!*" (Shemos 18:11). *Now I know for sure that it is indeed the Ribbono shel Olam Who created and rules the world, and, in His utter and absolute control of the universe, typically metes out reward and punishment* middah k'neged middah, *measure for measure.*

God expects more of us than He does of any other nation, for we experienced Him in Egypt, at the Yam Suf, in the Wilderness, and especially at Sinai. All mankind is given the moral wherewithal to behave with justice, kindness, and consideration toward others, starting with their own kin and extending outward to all. But our own nation was given, in the Revelation, a special, supercharged boost, which is infinitely more sinful to suppress.

We lost our freedom with the terrible Destruction in the time of Tzidkiyahu Hamelech and Yirmiyahu Hanavi (and to this day have never recovered it), for a variety of terrible moral and spiritual failures, but the cap was the moral and human failure toward our fellow Jews, a mandate for which was the first requirement presented to us, a fundament that puts everything else in perspective, when the glow of Sinai was still upon us.

*Parashas Mishpatim 5779*

# Divine Servitude

The little kid did not stop crying. About thirteen or fourteen months old, he was so agitated that he seemed not to know what he wanted. He reached for my water bottle repeatedly. Each time his mother or I handed it to him, he threw it down and cried some more. He was distraught.

His young mother, sitting opposite me in the exam chair, could not calm him down. She was the patient, not he; it wasn't fear of the doctor. I was, in fact, able to examine her, but she was upset and distracted by his behavior. She said that he was a good baby and never did this – until recently.

*Has anything at home changed?* I asked.

*Come to think of it, yes,* she replied.

And what she told me made me understand what the kid really wanted, even if she did not wish it to be so. She had recently started to go to work, dropping the kid off at childcare. Since then, he has been doing this. About a month.

Now, I have to be careful here. We have become surrounded, in the broader society, by a "woke" "cancel culture." Say the wrong thing, and you are not only dismissed as wrong, you are "cancelled," losing all credibility as a serious person, and are to be dropped.

I wouldn't want to lose my *"frum* cred." Yes, we do have some version of being religiously "politically" judged operating in our society. Sure, you can have a reasoned opinion and are free to express it. But say the "wrong" thing, and there are families that will thereafter not consider yours for a *shidduch.* You clueless, ignorant fool, you just don't get it. (You probably even pronounce the name of the *mesechta* correctly, *"Yoma,"* instead of the more frumly but not grammatically correct *"Yuma,"* thereby labelling yourself as not too religious!) You may be a generally OK person, but you don't really pass muster to be taken fully seriously. It will not be spoken, but that is how you may well be judged. But I'll spell it out anyway: The kid wants his mommy. And he deserves to have her.

The father of the child is in *kollel,* and the mother brings home the money. I suggested that she and her husband ask his *rebbe* or *rosh yeshiva* if they are doing the right thing. "But we're doing it for Torah!" she replied. Ask the *rebbe,* I countered, if the Torah "wants" them to do this to their child. Is there another way? The system may be OK for some, but it certainly is not OK for all. It may work well for some, but it does not for all. Perhaps this mommy should find a way to stay with, love, protect, and nurture her vulnerable little child.

In previous generations, in Europe, a young scholar who was supported in his learning for a period of time, typically by his father-in-law, "ate *kest,*" the term used for this arrangement (*er hut gegessen kest*). Usually the young couple lived with her parents for that time, lessening the financial burden. But young mommy stayed with her babies to raise them. That scenario is not too likely now, but perhaps society can organize a system to keep a deserving family afloat without putting vulnerable and love-needing Jewish babies into the less-than-fully-loving hands of *not their mommy.*

Immediately after Matan Torah, we encounter, in Mishpatim, an avalanche of civil law, which is, for Jews, actually religious law. There is no distinction between the two.

The very first subject is servitude. We all know the lesson, the message, that we who heard at Sinai that we are servants of God should have no master other than Him. One who finds himself in a condition of indenture should not choose to remain there when that term is up. And the dignity of even someone in a servile position is such that the obligations of his "master" to him probably exceed his own to the "master." A young girl who is indentured to a family is actually being set up for a marriage, with the safety, the security, the food, clothing, and shelter she needs, and, mandated by Torah law, *affection*, the comfort of loving marital intimacy, a basic human need implanted by the Creator.

A spouse who uses that intimacy, by withholding it, as a weapon, a cudgel, is not only cruel and callous, but, if a man, is in direct violation of Torah law, and if a woman, in violation of the teachings of the Torah and is considered rebellious. A marriage is not and should not be a prison for either spouse, and no one should ever be that close to someone he or she despises. Such a marriage cannot be sustained and must be dissolved. But if that marriage is a healthy or at least viable one, the message is clear that that closeness is an inviolate personal obligation upon each spouse to help the other with that fundamental human need which, in a Jewish marriage, can only be provided by the spouse. It may not be used as a weapon. That is a treacherous violation of marriage.

As much as we are servants, really, only of God, Mishpatim begins with talk of forms of indentured servitude to other people because, I suggest, we must remember that even so, the reality of life is that we are also servants of and in a manner of speaking, morally indebted to the significant others in our lives to whom we are accountable. Without that, we would have no life.

The husband and wife, the parent and child, the fellowship of society, have their inherent, built-in social contracts that have been put in place by the all-wise and all-benevolent Creator. Usually, dispassionate reflection makes clear what is the right thing to do. The marriage vows, in return for exclusivity, place upon us a responsibility to perform, a kind of benign servitude, in all spheres, graciously, lovingly, and generously, all things that one marriage partner is supposed to do for the other. And by bringing a child into the world, the parent, in a kind of benign servitude that is one of the greatest privileges in all of life, owes that helpless little one far, far more than any societal formulaic construct, even the most worthy. And that, no doubt, is what the Creator expects of us.

*Parashas Mishpatim 5780*

# Terumah

## "Al-Fikr Kufr"

Max Weber, a late-nineteenth- and early-twentieth-century German sociologist and political philosopher, in his classic work, *The Protestant Ethic and the Spirit of Capitalism*, postulated that the great economic growth and success of Western Europe was a direct outgrowth of societal changes brought about by the Protestant Reformation. It may well be that societal pressures for change made the Reformation possible, but in either event, a new and different ethic had a major impact on how Europe and therefore advanced sectors of society developed and prospered.

Not to dwell upon alien theological issues that we need not concern ourselves with, it is certain aspects of the role of the individual in the theological and economic life of society that are particularly relevant.

The Roman Catholic Church did not want individuals studying or even reading the Bible on their own. Only the Church may do that, with the priests telling the faithful what they need to know. And the priests were told what the hierarchy wanted them to know.

One of the revolutionary innovations of Protestantism was the freedom of the individual to think and to study the Scriptures for himself. Associated with that was the fostering of a spirit of diligence, hard work, frugality, and delayed gratification, which, coupled with ambition, gave rise to the "spirit of capitalism" that made Protestant Western Europe and North America centers of striving, innovation, and economic success.

With the opening of the opportunities for reason to flourish, it flourished and grew throughout all sectors of society.

In another part of the world, in another society, the battle between the rationalists and the doctrinaire literalists in the Muslim theology was long before won by the literalists. The human intellect, they hold, is fickle and defective. Human reason has been described by mainstream Muslim theologians as a cancer upon Islam, and those who disagree have found themselves punished, exiled, or worse.

Thus, the Islamic principle of "*al-fikr kufr*": the very act of thinking is tantamount to being an infidel. And along with thinking go education, reason, and innovation. The name of the Islamist group Boko Haram literally means that non-Islamic teaching is forbidden. Societies dominated by this mindset are, as a result, typically plagued by innovative backwardness.

Now stop and think about our system of Torah. We have Torah She'b'chsav, Torah She'b'al Peh, we have a world of Midrash, we have six orders of Mishnah, twenty volumes of Talmud, a veritable ocean of analysis and learning over all the generations of Judaism, we have traditions as varying as black is from white, and all are true and legitimate. We declare that *shivim panim la'Torah*, the Torah has many parallel ways, which may all be within the Law. The utter rationalist is as at home as is the romantic spiritualist. The very word *chiddushim*, the product of novel and innovative thinking, is the hallmark of Torah striving and excellence. The preferred method of Talmud study is in pairs, so that the study partners can battle it out, truth emerging from the intellectual ferment. This represents a high ideal in scholarship and extends to the rest of life as well. We seek growth and development. All things are studied, analyzed, and examined. How different is our ethic, even in the most religious endeavor, from the alien concept of *al-fikr kufr.*

But the sea of the Talmud has within it a potential trap. We intellectualize about the Torah because we strive to know God. That is the goal. Sometimes, however, it is possible for the intellectual game to so overpower the spirit that is behind its pursuit that the spirit may get lost in the process. And thus we have the sad history of *maskilim* in history who have proverbially (and apparently actually) pored over a Gemara or a *Ketzos* on Shabbos with a lit cigarette in hand. God was somehow lost in all that intellectual ferment, rendering it essentially hubris of the worst kind.

There is a remarkable passage in *Midrash Tanchuma* on *V'yikchu Li terumah.*

*Amar Hakadosh Baruch Hu l'Yisrael:* God says to Israel, "The Torah is Mine, and you have taken it." Well and good. *Lo ba'Shamayim hi.* The Torah is no longer confined to Heaven, and it is for Israel to use, to learn, and to develop. To delve and to research and to think and to reason over. To adjudicate and to litigate. To master and to *pasken*, to decide the Law.

*You have taken My Torah,* God says, *and that is what I want. But one more thing: V'yikchu Li. Take Me too. Study the Torah that you may come to know Me, to the extent that a human can know Me. Delve into the Torah so that you may know My will, to the extent that a human can know My will. Immerse yourself in the Torah so that you may be imbued with the spirit, the goodness, and the holiness that it is imbued with. Strive in the Torah so that in so doing, you are worshipping and serving your Creator.*

There is much to do in this world. It is for you to build it and to excel in it. The Torah will guide you and teach you how the human mind and spirit can be harnessed to that end.

Use your reason and your intellect, every one of you. But never forget where the Torah and your intellect came from, and why they were given to you. *Take My Torah, My beloved children, grow and prosper. But please, in all that you do, in all that you accomplish, never forget the spirit. Never forget to take Me too.*

*Parashas Terumah 5778*

# That God Dwell among Us

Imagine this scene. I'm a nine- or ten-year-old kid visiting my father in his small grocery store in Williamsburg. Right outside, there's a loud argument going on. A Satmar kid, maybe fourteen, is very angry with another Satmar boy. The thing escalates until, unable to contain himself, the boy hurls his ultimate insult at his adversary: "Ben-Gurion!"

The argument had nothing at all to do with Israel or with David Ben-Gurion. The name Ben-Gurion was used as a curse word.

At that point in my life, I didn't quite get it. I knew that the Satmars didn't like the secular Zionists, although I didn't know very much about it. I knew that Ben-Gurion and his colleagues were not *frum*, but I was unaware until then of the extent of the hard feelings. I did not have the historical perspective. Lots of Jews were not *frum*, but their names were not used as curse words.

My father explained it to me a bit, without going into too much detail. This was not my parents' point of view, nor their way. I have, over the years, had occasion to meet or see up close Ben-Gurion, Levi Eshkol, Golda Meir, and Abba Eban. I was certainly polite and respectful, given their accomplishments and their high office in the State of Israel. I was also young enough not to have learned yet things about some of them that might well have colored my reaction to them.

There is, sadly, a long and weighty history there. This is not a specific Satmar thing, but they have been prominent voices in this. In fact, when scoping out the land upstate where the future Satmar village, Kiryas Yoel, would be built, the Rebbe is said to have declared that he didn't much care where it would be, as long as there would be no "Tsionistin" there.

The Rebbe's animus was not directed at the simple non-frum, these days for the most part themselves victims of their upbringing, and not even at those who may love Israel as the Holy Land but who do not support the secularist agenda. What many people today are not aware of is the intense, zealous, unrelenting – even all-consuming – war with the Ribbono shel Olam and His Torah that was waged by some of the biggest luminaries of the historical Zionist movement.

In Europe, they did their utmost to ridicule what we understand as the Torah way of life and to tear the younger generation away from it. In this they succeeded to a great and horrifying degree. In the Land of Israel, it was aimed at redefining what it means to be a Jew and doing their utmost to tear young immigrants, both from Europe and from the Arabic lands, altogether away from Torah Judaism. That included, incredibly, known cases of cutting off their *peyos,* forced *chillul Shabbos,* ridiculing Yiddishkeit and its *frum* adherents, and intentionally directing them to settlements where the Torah would be expunged from them.

In Europe, the utterly secular Zionist "visionary" Theodor Herzl, at least for a while, thought that the answer to the Jewish "problem" was mass conversion to Christianity. Judaism as we know it had no role in the national life of his conceived "Judenstaat." Ben-Gurion is said to have declared that the Knesset should henceforth replace the Talmud and *Shulchan Aruch* as the source of Jewish law. He had the committed secularist's arrogant and disdainful contempt for the Jewish faith and for those who did not share his socialist view. He expected Judaism as we know it to disappear in Israel. For political reasons, he did manage to compromise with the religious here and there.

It is painful for us, lovers of Zion and of Israel, who appreciate all the wonderful things about it, who support it most strenuously, to contemplate these sad truths about many in the founding generations whose efforts resulted, by the grace of God, in our beautiful and magical Israel. Somehow, in His inscrutable plan, they merited to be among His instruments in bringing it about. Rav Kook, *a"h*, had a philosophical rationale built around that.

Our forefathers in the Sinai desert, fresh from Matan Torah, were called upon to create a resplendent *mikdash* to accompany them in their wanderings, which would serve as a precursor to the "permanent" Mikdash in Jerusalem. Parashas Terumah enumerates the grand components to be fabricated, from the donations of Klal Yisrael. *Let them build for me a Mikdash,* says Hashem, *and I will "dwell" among them.*

Four hundred eighty years later, King Shlomo indeed built the most magnificent wonder, the Beis Hamikdash. The prophet Achiah Hashiloni comes to Shlomo with the word of God: *This House that you are building, if you walk in My ways and follow My mitzvos, I will fulfill My word to your father David; I will dwell amongst Klal Yisrael, and I will not abandon them, but* only *if you live according to My statutes, no matter how beautiful the building may be.*

The people eventually broke faith, and God "departed." The Mikdash was lost. For our sins, the second Beis Hamikdash was lost as well. In the future, however, God promises (see *Midrash Tanchuma*, Pekudei 11), in the third Beis Hamikdash, *may it be built speedily and in our day*, God will never depart. He will dwell forever among His people.

Israel is beautiful and wonderful and miraculous, but it is not the Beis Hamikdash. That seems almost as elusive as ever. Venture outside the religious areas, and the spiritual and religious destruction wrought by the enemies within is painfully obvious. Israel is strong, but we are so, so vulnerable, so at risk. The Torah nation within the larger nation, which Ben-Gurion and his like-minded cohorts were sure would soon disappear, is miraculously larger and stronger than ever and represents the best hope for Israel's survival.

The precious Israel Defense Forces, may Hashem protect them, as capable as they are, as dedicated and as brave as they are, do not and cannot guarantee Israel's survival. Only the Ribbono shel Olam can. In our time, after thousands of years and so many generations, the end of our wandering and suffering in Galus appears to be, we pray, somewhere in reach, please God. We cannot know God's plan, but the miracle of modern Israel also cannot be an accident, a quirk of history.

Our forefathers in the desert wholeheartedly contributed to the building of the Mishkan, and God dwelt in their midst. The Erev Rav did their best to damage them, and they did grievously, but in the end goodness prevailed. Settled in the land, the Erev Rav of their time did their best to lead the people astray, and to a painful extent they succeeded, at great cost to the nation. The later Second Commonwealth fell as well, as the covenant was betrayed. God withdrew His obvious presence.

We have enough enemies from without. That we should have enemies and destroyers from within, including those who posture as "good" and dedicated Jews, a latter-day Erev Rav, is particularly painful. The mass of good-hearted and otherwise loyal Jews who are simply ignorant, unlearned, unobservant, victims of their faulty upbringing, are in large measure casualties of the war waged upon Judaism by turncoats of every anti-religious persuasion who arrogantly believe that they are smarter than God and certainly smarter and more enlightened than the greatest *chachmei Yisrael*.

*V'asu Li mikdash v'shachanti b'socham.* We pray for the day that all of Klal Yisrael will finally see the truth and will band together as one, as they did at Sinai, and let God in, so that He will at last, this time forever, dwell among us, never to depart.

*Parashas Terumah 5780*

# A Gift Like None Other

The heady days of June 1967 were preceded by weeks of angst, fear, and worry. Who could predict that there would be such miracles? All we could see, in human terms, was a world of wild-eyed Arabs, many millions of them in many nations, screaming, jumping up and down, brandishing weapons and promising to destroy Israel and murder its Jews. Of course we hoped and prayed. We prayed hard. We could not believe that our God would permit that, *chalilah*. *Oy*, but it had happened before, and not so long before. We prayed and we hoped that Israel was prepared as well as humanly possible. But aside from the military preparations in Israel, we heard also that thousands of graves were being dug, even in city parks, in case, God forbid…

When the Ribbono shel Olam reached down with His mighty arm to protect us, when it was obvious to the whole world that the God of Israel intervened for His children, when even the most cynical, unbelieving Jews had to set aside their disbelief (for a while, anyway), Jews around the world stood taller.

And we witnessed something interesting. Put aside physiognomy – some Jews look so Jewish on their faces that most people familiar with our nation would correctly guess that they are Jewish. But for most Jews, it's their presentation to the world that makes their Jewishness obvious, apparent, or, when the individual so chooses, not at all apparent.

In those heady days, everybody who was Jewish wanted to be identified and recognized as Jewish. They have God on their side. Men could wear yarmulkes. But I remember that women who by their dress were not obviously identifiable as Jews started wearing Jewish symbols, such as a Star of David necklace, on the outside of their clothing even if they had worn such ornaments inside before. They wanted it known to all who they are.

Too bad, for so many it didn't last.

Several generations ago, Jews in the Ashkenazi and Sephardi worlds could readily be identified by their clothing. It was a major change, in many places, when Jews otherwise committed to Judaism began dressing and presenting in the manner of the surrounding peoples. All too often, this led to further decline in the Jewishness of those families, and for this reason it was bitterly disapproved of. Today, many fervently Jewish Jews can be instantly recognized from a distance for who they are, for whom they identify with, making it quite obvious with their Jewish uniforms of various types. Many others make it quite obvious even with less blatant "uniforms."

A uniform may serve to broadcast to others, but most significantly, it serves to broadcast to its wearers a constant reminder of who they are and what is expected of them.

The Ribbono shel Olam expects us to identify with Him in every aspect of our lives. Who we are, whose children and whose descendants we are, how and by what lofty principles we live our lives, what governs our actions and our choices, what motivates us, should be plain on our faces, in our presentation to the world, in our behavior. We are Hashem's nation, and He is our God.

And so in a once in all of history event, He revealed Himself to us at Sinai and presented us with the greatest gift possible, His Torah. The dramatic, earth-shattering events at the mountain, the long list of civil laws in Mishpatim which are actually divine law, and the ritual requirements laid out in Terumah and Tetzaveh are all of the same source, with the same objective: in making Hashem ours, by internalizing Him through His Torah, by identifying and presenting ourselves to the world as well as to ourselves as reflecting, in every aspect of life, His will which is absorbed within us, our Father in Heaven lovingly makes us His.

Chazal teach that with *V'yikchu Li terumah,* Hashem is telling us that in giving us His Torah, He is also, *k'v'yachol,* giving us Himself: My gift to you, My *terumah,* is Me. *V'yikchu Li.* Take Me. When you acquire Torah, when you toil in Torah, when you live Torah, when you absorb My Torah, when you reflect the special and unique qualities the life of Torah makes possible, when before all the world it is obvious that you are a special people imbued with the holy refinement that is My gift to you, then part of that gift, part of that countenance with which you greet the world is, *k'v'yachol,* an aspect, a reflection, a manifestation, of the God of Israel Who, by this gracious gift, is within you.

*Parashas Terumah 5783, en route to Eretz Yisrael*

# Tetzaveh

## Through Our Children Do We Endure

Turbulence and discord hounded David Hamelech through much of his life. He had much trouble with his own children. One son violated his own half-sister and was in turn killed by her brother. Another son, despite being favored by his father, openly rebelled and sought to depose David and seize the throne, bringing many along with him in his plot. Avshalom's death in the course of the rebellion utterly broke David's heart. David's first son with Bas Sheva, from a notorious and embarrassing union, died in infancy. There followed another son, Shlomo, also named by God Yedidya. And in David's old age, another son, Adoniah, never disciplined by his father for bad behavior, took it upon himself to seize the throne, surrounding himself with powerful coconspirators and sycophants. David had said, and Nasan the Navi had prophesied, that Shlomo would succeed David. The likelihood of Shlomo, and even his mother, surviving in a reign by Adoniah was slim indeed.

The aged and enfeebled King David lay wrapped in blankets that failed to warm him. Encouraged by Nasan the Navi, who saw what would happen unless David intervened, Bas Sheva approached the king, told him what was happening, and pleaded for her son. Given the problematic nature and origin of her relationship with David, her very position and standing, and those of her son, were awkward and weak. By prior arrangement, Nasan then appeared and confirmed Bas Sheva's story of Adoniah's attempted usurpation, of having himself proclaimed king without even informing his father, the actual reigning king. Can it be, Nasan asked, that David had gone back on his word to have Shlomo succeed him, a succession about which he, Nasan, had actually prophesied as Hashem's will?

David immediately rectified the situation and had Shlomo officially proclaimed the successor king. Adoniah and his conspirators withered away, to be dealt with later.

In gratitude, Bas Sheva bowed low before David and blessed him that he should live forever.

Could she really have meant that? He was, essentially, on his deathbed. Was she mocking him? Not only would he of course not actually live forever, but if he did, it would undo her son Shlomo's destiny. Why would she say that? Interestingly, the Targum renders the blessing as one of *endurance* – in Eternity – rather than actual temporal life. And that was the very point of David being succeeded by Shlomo, *yedid Hashem*. For through Shlomo and his line, David's legacy on earth and position in Heaven would indeed endure forever.

In fact, David's very improbable and embarrassing entanglement with Bas Sheva was at least in part the result of his God-inspired perception that through her would he be able to achieve greatness, paradoxical as it seems. And it was that very expectation that she had in mind when she advocated for her son in the dramatic scene above.

This story has a dramatic parallel in Moshe's mandate to appoint his brother Aharon *and Aharon's sons after him, and their offspring after them, forever*, as the Kohanim. The Midrash says that Moshe felt bad. Is it possible that Moshe, the most humble person alive, the most giving and the most loving, was actually jealous of his brother? Remember when Hashem told Moshe at the outset of his mission to travel into the desert toward Egypt, where he would encounter his brother Aharon, who had set out to meet him? That the more senior Aharon would rejoice, not just openly but in his heart, that the younger Moshe had been chosen? Was Moshe less altruistic or modest than Aharon? Was he so power hungry?

Of course not. In fact, Moshe resisted Hashem's mandate for seven days at the burning bush. *Not me! There are more worthy people! My brother Aharon is!* Finally, Hashem grew angry and told Moshe, *Enough! It's you! Now go.*

Moshe paid a price for those seven days of arguing with Hashem. When the Mishkan was established, Moshe inaugurated it by serving as the Kohen for the first seven days only. As much as his soul yearned to be so close to the Ribbono shel Olam in His service, that was it. Enough. Now he had to delegate it to Aharon, and to Aharon's children after him.

And this exactly, says the Kesav Sofer, is what this really was about. Aharon would be perpetuated for all eternity through his children, who would succeed him in the *kehunah*. But Moshe knew that he himself would not have that. His children would play no role at all, and his line would disappear.

Forty years later, when it was time for Moshe to pass on, Hashem told him to climb Har Ha'avarim, Har Nevo, where he would die *ka'asher mes Aharon achicha*, just as Aharon had (Devarim 32:49), Rashi tells us that this alludes to Moshe's desire to expire just as Aharon had, *b'neshikas Hashem*, with the kiss of God on his lips.

But that *ka'asher – you too,* as it were – has a lot more meaning than just the means of the soul departing the body. Moshe had also longed for a death like Aharon's *in that Aharon did not quite die* – he did not just cease to exist – as he was succeeded by his sons and all the generations to follow, who perpetuated Aharon's existence through their continuing his legacy. And Moshe mourned the fact that he did not have that.

Hashem was telling Moshe that that was not the case. True, his sons were not his successors in leadership and never played any significant role, but Moshe's true successors were, are, and will be for all time all of Israel who perpetuate Toras Moshe. With every mitzvah that every Jew does throughout all the generations, with every act of *talmud Torah,* Moshe Rabbeinu is alive and is among us. Perhaps Moshe's great modesty kept him from seeing this, at least initially, but in fact the *zechus* of all Israel, including Aharon and his sons, all depends on Moshe. In this way, he lives in perpetuity.

But this is not just about Moshe. It is true for all of us. *Bra mezakeh abba.* One benefits from righteous posterity (*Sanhedrin* 104a). Kesav Sofer expounds further. A man is called a *holech,* literally *a walker.* He "walks" from level to level, up or down, according to his actions. Once he is dead, that's over. He can no longer do anything for himself. He can no longer "walk" anywhere, do anything, or in any way affect his status. He is utterly stationery, static – except for what his children do to help his status. *Bra mezakeh abba.* One who leaves behind children who continue in his own righteous path is, in Heaven, like a walker among the stationary.

Before he died, David told Shlomo, his designated successor, *anochi holech b'derech kol ha'aretz. I am about to walk the path that every human being must eventually take. Cling to the ways of Hashem, be true to Toras Moshe, and you will succeed in every way.* Implicit here is also that through Shlomo's righteousness, David would, in a heavenly kind of way, continue to be a "walker," reaching ever higher.

Bas Sheva understood that David's eternal "life," his legacy and his line, depended on Shlomo not only surviving but on his becoming king. And thus she bowed low before David and blessed him that he should live forever. And he has. *David Melech Yisrael chai v'kayam.* Moshe Rabbeinu, our teacher, through his legacy, the Torah, is *chai v'kayam,* he is alive wherever Jews are, indeed wherever people of every background perpetuate his teachings.

And we, the *amcha Yidden,* Jews high and low, who are dedicated to the Ribbono shel Olam through the perpetuation of Toras Moshe in all its manifestations, who through the hard work and the sincerity of our devotions and the example we set for our children, can, if we are so blessed, aspire to perpetuate our own existence in the higher spheres after we are gone from this one, to remain holy "walkers" among the stationary, as our children, as their children after them, and those after them, follow the path of Godly righteousness that we, by that example, teach them.

For it is through our children and the good works that we and they bring to the world that we endure.

*Parashas Tetzaveh 5782*

# Ki Sisa

## The Backstabbers: They Smile in Your Face

One of the worst things we ever did as a nation was the sin of the Golden Calf. We have never stopped paying for it. How did it come to that?

When you ask, many will say, yes, very shortly after the nation stood at Sinai and heard the very Voice of God, *k'v'yachol*, as He revealed Himself to them, after they proclaimed *naaseh v'nishma!* the people turned around and worshipped a golden calf instead of God.

Does that make any sense? Can that be true? Is it that simple? Can Aharon, however unwillingly, have been a part of that? The *meforshim* think not.

Forty days had passed from the awesome, earth-shattering events of Matan Torah at Sinai, and Moshe had not reappeared. They were subsisting on the *mon*, the only food available, but no *mon* fell onto Mount Sinai, where Moshe had gone. He had no food. By their reckoning, even if they knew Moshe was to return in forty days, the deadline had passed; *he must be dead*. Fearful, they ganged up on Aharon (*va'yikahel ha'am al Aharon*; Shemos 32:1) and demanded new leadership that would lead them to safety – not a regular person, but a superhuman figure, indeed a supernatural one. It was, in fact, a grievous act. There is no supernatural intermediary power between us and God (as in some religions). Thus, Hashem says to Moshe, "*saru maher min haderech asher tzivisim*," they have quickly strayed from the way I have commanded them (32:8).

They demanded of Aharon, *aseh lanu elohim*, provide for us *elohim*, to lead us and tell us what to do. They were not seeking a false god, but some kind of intermediary with supernatural powers, a replacement Moshe, to lead them, which was bad enough. What Aharon did was *not* abetting idol worship, which would have been for him an impossibility. He was buying time to get them past this, until Moshe would reappear (the next day).

Enter the Erev Rav, the "mixed multitude" of non-Jews who escaped from Egypt on Israel's coattails. Egypt was a tightly locked country. There were, in

Egypt, many enslaved people who had no hope of escape until the miraculous Exodus of the Jewish People. They accompanied Israel out of Egypt, and they were the source of trouble and instigation throughout the forty years in the wilderness. Moshe, in his goodness and charitableness, had accepted them and allowed them to come along, on his own authority, without asking God. In so doing, thinking he was doing good by bringing them under the "wings of the Shechinah," he sowed the seeds not only of Israel's downfall, but, as we shall see, his own.

It was the Erev Rav *who* started this process with the *egel*, and it was the Erev Rav who, seeing the Golden Calf emerge from the crucible, exulted and cried out to the Jews, "*Eleh elohecha, Yisrael!*" They did not say, "This is *our* god," but rather, "This is *your* god, O Israel!" And when Hashem told Moshe about it, He said "*shiches amcha,*" *your* nation, rather than "*ha'am,*" *the nation*, that *you* took with you out of Egypt, has brought about destruction. *You, Moshe, by allowing the instigating rabble to exert a bad influence on the vulnerable Jewish ex-slaves, have unwittingly played a role in this.*

*You thought you were doing something good and noble* (and an argument can certainly be made that he was), *but the "grateful" no-goodniks, ingratiatingly smiling in your face to get what they want, have stabbed you in the back and brought Israel to the edge of destruction.*

By morning, they had gotten a number of the real Israelites not just to demand a supernatural replacement for Moshe Rabbeinu, but to sin along with them in every wicked way, including the cardinal sins of murder and illicit carnality, along with the idol worship that veneration of the Golden Calf had become.

The number of Jews guilty of outright *avodah zarah* was actually relatively small. Ibn Ezra points out that the three thousand who were later killed for this constituted but one-half of one percent of the adult men, and a little more than one-tenth of one percent of the whole nation. And yet we have all paid a terrible price throughout the ages for this act of rebellion, for allowing ourselves to be seduced into sin by the smile-in-your-face backstabbers, who have plagued us throughout the generations.

When Israel prepared to enter the Land of Israel, they were warned not to be overly solicitous toward the evil nations that were to be displaced. Allowing them to stay and wield their wicked influence on the Jewish People – and that is virtually certain to happen – would spell doom for the Jews, who, corrupted, would lose their own virtue, their standing before God, and their very rights to the land. As my father, *a"h*, a very good man, taught me, excess of anything is no good, even of goodness. "*Afilu tzi git iz oych nisht git.*" It will likely lead to unexpected and undesirable outcomes, often the very opposite of goodness.

The Erev Rav, allowed in out of Moshe's kindness and his desire to bring them *tachas kanfei haShechinah*, into God's camp, ruined things over and over for Klal Yisrael. The very people Moshe was kind to, who appealed to him to take them along, stabbed him, and all of us, in the back, and indeed played a role, ultimately, in God's decision to deny Moshe entry into the land.

The Torah doesn't tell us what became of the Erev Rav as Israel entered the land and set up their national state. It is commonly understood that they exist among us as the rotten and seditious "Jews" whose bad actions have damaged us throughout our history. In our time, we see them not only in those who labor to turn Jews away from Judaism, but in those backstabbers who "smile," who publicly proclaim their "Jewishness" and their veneration of "Jewish values," who claim precious virtue by arrogantly and cruelly siding with and aiding our enemies, who seek to destroy us.

And let us not forget the corrupt world of Esav out there, the ultimate backstabbers who publicly deny antisemitism, even decry it, who smile in our faces, but who are in fact world-class practitioners of it.

In the end, it was Moshe's appeal to Hashem way back then, *Va'yechal Moshe*, that we read from the Torah on our public fast days, that saved us then and continues to save us now. In the end, it is an eternal relationship between us and our Father in Heaven, which the backstabbers and all the others may try to chip away at but cannot undo. In the end, there are no intermediaries and no third parties, supernatural or otherwise, but just us: our Father and His children, some of whom who may at times be swayed, some of whom may get lost along the way, some of whom may rebel, but whose core will never be lost, will never turn away, but, like the Levi'im after the *egel* so many years ago, will always rally to the call *"Mi l'Hashem eilai,"* who will never let go, but who will, for all time, cling to Him with a might, indeed a ferocity and a determination that is beyond all human understanding.

*Parashas Ki Sisa 5779*

# Saving Ourselves

There's an old Yiddish expression about a situation in which everything went bad, no matter how hard one tried, no matter how hard one prayed: *Es hut gurnisht gehulfen, nisht kein poideini, nisht kein matzileini.* Nothing helped, not even, proverbially speaking, the prayer recited each morning before Shemoneh Esreh, in *al harishonim.* "*Podenu u'matzilenu.*"

When something goes bad, *Rachmana litzlan*, really bad, it's hard to think and we take little comfort in the idea that it could have been even worse. That's only natural. Could the Holocaust have been worse? Well, the Germans might not have been stopped at El Alamein and could have swept into Eretz Yisrael, where they had plenty of potential collaborators. Stalingrad might have gone the other way. The Allied landings in Normandy might have been repulsed, their armies slaughtered, thrown back into the sea. The monumental and decisive battle of Midway could easily have turned out the opposite, Japan triumphant. The Germans rather than the Americans might have figured out how to make an atom bomb.

These are things that are unknowable to us, reserved for the Most High. We are left to deal with the adversities in life, may they be few and mild, do the best we can (and we do have to *do*), and to have faith.

When the devastation of Superstorm Sandy struck, hard hit as we were, we had a quantifiable and for the most part not life-threatening catastrophe to deal with, and, with God's help, we did. Faced with the possibility of a plague, God forbid, we become, it seems, powerless and largely helpless. We are not in control, no matter how hard we try. We must do the best we can (and we do have to *do*!), but many overlook the full meaning of doing the best we can.

So consider the position of our forefathers as they camped at the foot of Mount Sinai, just a short time after the most monumental moment in history, when they, of all people before and after, had been chosen to hear the revealed word of God, in His own "voice."

They messed up about as terribly as one can possibly imagine, with the Golden Calf. It should have been, and nearly was, over for them. Moshe stood up for them, as Hashem knew he would. In fact, that was why Hashem chose Moshe – *insisted* on Moshe – in the first place, knowing that he, of all people, would persevere and succeed at their defense. For them, he would even "stand up to" God if he had to, just as Hashem wanted him to.

As God acceded to his entreaties and his arguments, aware that it was a moment of favor before God, seeing his chance, Moshe went for it: "*Hareni na es Kevodecha*," he asks of the Ribbono shel Olam. Essentially, reveal Yourself to me; let me understand You. Hashem replied, of course, that this is impossible for a human being. *Lo yirani ha'adam va'chai. Instead*, says Hashem, *I will teach you something of great importance that you need to know.*

*I will teach you how to pray to Me, how to approach Me in supplication on behalf of Bnei Yisrael, and how they in the future can and should pray to Me.* Moshe had resorted to invoking *zechus avos*, the merit of the forefathers, and he worried that once that *zechus avos* was used up in the gravity of their sins, there would be no further hope for Klal Yisrael.

*This profound manifestation of Me*, Hashem informs him, *I will reveal to you, Moshe. But it will be limited; great as you are, loyal servant as you are, holy as you are, you are also a human being, and can "see" only so much.* God stationed him in the cleft of the rock and, *k'v'yachol*, passed before him, "covering" Moshe's eyes as He did so, to protect him, letting Moshe catch a kind of glimpse, an inkling, from "behind." And as He passed, so to speak, Hashem taught Moshe the Thirteen Middos of Rachamim that are the backbone and basis for all our supplications before Him. He taught us how to invoke those *middos* of *rachamim* which always elicit at least some degree of positive response, even if there are no other merits, not even *zechus avos*. *V'chanosi es achon, v'richamti es asher arachem.*

Moshe's understanding heretofore had been that God might respond with *rachamim* if that was His judgment, or He might not at all. Here Hashem says to him, *Hineh Anochi kores bris neged kol amcha. I pledge to you My Covenant with Klal Yisrael: when the Jewish People turn to Me and invoke My middos of* rachamim, *whatever else happens, whatever else it is My Judgment that must occur, however bad it may seem for them, this prayer, this supplication, will never go entirely unanswered. That will never happen, no matter how bad it looks. Pray to Me in this way, and it will always turn out at least somewhat better than it would have.*

The power of prayer is very great. The power of invoking the Yud Gimmel Middos is particularly great.

Chazal have taught us that if the nations of the world only understood what the Beis Hamikdash accomplished for *them*, rather than destroy it, they would have posted guards around it day and night to protect it. Similarly, if they only understood what Yaakov Avinu meant for the world, their whole behavior would have been different. What shall we say about Jews who, at least nominally, understand about the power and efficacy of prayer, and in particular the Yud Gimmel Middos (or about *Yehei Shmei Rabbah*, etc.) but all too often behave as if they really don't get it?

Sorry, I have a pet peeve (I'm not too peevy, but it's not my only one). What greater, more awesome time is there, when our lives and the lives of our families are in the balance, than the Yamim Noraim, the Days of Awe? If we are in fact believers, then presumably we really *do* believe it. The hallmark of Selichos at that time is the repetition, multiple times, with great intensity, of the Yud Gimmel Middos Harachamim as we beg the Ribbono shel Olam to bless us, our families, and our nation with life, health, peace, and prosperity. We really mean it, right?

We really believe it, right? We actually believe there is a connection between our actions and our prayers and what happens to us, right?

*Oyb azoy*, if so, how come so many people who do come to Selichos arrive regularly so late that they get to say few if any of the Yud Gimmel Middos? Even worse, in a shul with a tight minyan, their absence often means that there is no minyan at all until very late, and thus no recitation at all, or very few recitations of the all-important Yud Gimmel Middos Harachamim? I'm thinking of a fellow, all *frum* and learned, who is a habitual latecomer to shul. On one occasion that stands out, his arrival for Selichos on Erev Rosh Hashanah made the minyan (he was the tenth man) – but only after *thirteen* opportunities for the Yud Gimmel Middos were lost. *No one* said it, as we had no minyan until his arrival. When I pointed out to him (nice and friendly, of course) that his apparent indifference cost us as a congregation a total of 130 opportunities to implore God with the most powerful tool of prayer we have (ten people times thirteen recitations each), he looked at me as if I were the annoying and naive alien from Pluto who doesn't understand how things really are. During Aseres Yemei Teshuvah, he continued to come late, with the same effect.

The Sephardim and the Ashkenazim who daven Nusach Sefard recite the Yud Gimmel Middos daily as part of Tachanun. Many congregations who daven Nusach Ashkenaz recite it on Mondays and Thursdays along with the expanded Tachanun of *V'Hu Rachum*.

Life is an unsure place. Whenever we face a particularly frightening unknown, one which we cannot quantify and, try as we might, cannot really control, we don't know what to expect, we hope and pray for the best, but we also know that it can be, God forbid, terrible. What can we do?

Certainly during a pandemic, as recent experience shows, we can follow the medically advised procedures and protocols. One who willfully does not, against best medical knowledge, is not only a fool but a knave who irresponsibly places others at risk. Sadly, we have seen that. (And sadly, also, we have seen medical pronouncements that turned out later, it appears, to have been politically driven, something utterly unacceptable.)

Above all, we can and must use the tool that has been in our hands since the beginning of our nation, handed down from our forefathers, *prayer*. As they reeled in remorse and mourning over their egregious sin, our loving Father in Heaven taught Moshe how best to pray to Him, that he teach Israel how in the future to save themselves.

Such prayer never goes completely unanswered, even if in what way may not be apparent to us. Of that we are assured. May we all have the wisdom to do as we should, and may Hashem bless us, His People everywhere, with His *middah* of *rachamim*, in full measure, in every way.

*Parashas Ki Sisa 5780*

# Vayakhel-Pekudei

## Normal

In the minute or so that my car radio was on, I heard the announcer, a relationships guru and arbiter of contemporary mores, proclaim that "nothing is abnormal." He then repeated for emphasis, "*nothing* is abnormal."

He was being ever so *au courant*. A process that seems to have begun in the sixties, with youthful revolt against authority, rooted in protests against the Vietnam War, grew and picked up steam over the years into a general overturning of societal conventions and has of late become a dizzying torrent of negation, discarding, and ridiculing of much of what has served to civilize mankind and to keep it moral.

Religion, faith in God and His laws, marriage, decency, morality, have come, in certain loud and prominent segments of society, not only to be objects of ridicule, but are also scorned as being hateful, and, in this warped ideology, *morally unacceptable*. Whoever disagrees is considered a bigot of the first order and is to be accorded no respect. In fact, for the first time in American history, a citizen's right to practice his faith has become subject to rendering that faith subservient to the new "theology," under penalty of law.

There is no objective truth, in this worldview, no objective right and wrong, no objective morality, no objective standard of decency, no objective standard of normalcy. The only objective truth is the acceptance of this particular credo as truth. The only objective normalcy is the absence of objective normalcy. And you'd better not disagree.

Each year on the Shabbos after Purim, we read Parashas Parah, which contains a formula for reversing the most stringent form of ritual impurity. This *chok*, the logic of which is beyond us, serves not only to restore *taharah*, but also to affirm our faith and fealty by observing a ritual ordained by God and that we carry out only because of that faith and fealty. And thus we are doubly purified.

The *haftarah* for Parashas Parah, from Yechezkel Hanavi, tells of the moral decline of ancient Israel and the consequent desecration of God's Name by their bad actions. Amorality and the acceptance of amorality pushes Israel as far away from God as can be. In the end, however, God will redeem them – not because they deserve it, but for His Name's sake. He will sprinkle them with the *mayim tehorim*, an allusion to the Parah Adumah; He will purify them and bring them back to the Land of Israel.

And then the very issue that brought about all the trouble, the sinfulness, the acts of rebellion, the willful throwing off of the yoke of Heaven, is addressed. *I shall give you a new heart*, God declares, *I will implant a new spirit within you. I will remove your hearts of stone and will give you a real heart, a true heart, a heart of flesh. I will place My spirit within you, and you will go in My ways. You will dwell in the land that I bestowed upon your fathers; you will be My people and I will be your God.*

The world around us has gone mad, and we need a fix. Significant sectors of society are distancing themselves as far from God as can be, at an ever more rapid pace. The youth are caught up in it. The weak and the alienated of our own people are drawn along with it. They have thrown out what God has told us is right and moral and brazenly, self-righteously, proclaim the very opposite as right and moral. We need help.

We need God to look down upon us in pity and to save us, and the rest of civilization as well. If not for our own sake, then for the sake of His Name. For the sake of Avraham, Yitzchak, and Yaakov. For the sake of Sarah, Rivkah, Rachel, and Leah. For the sake of the generation that placed its trust in God and marched out into the wilderness, who stood at Mount Sinai and declared *naaseh v'nishma*. For the sake of the countless generations of the faithful who endured every hardship, every unspeakable torture, for His Name's sake.

We need Him to remove the stone hearts from within us and replace them with hearts of flesh that beat and resonate with holiness because that is what He asks of us, and that is how we serve Him.

As we prepare now to observe and in a sense to relive the pivotal event of history, our Exodus from Egyptian bondage and our elevation to the unimaginable heights of Revelation at Sinai, we need to be sprinkled with the *mayim tehorim* that will restore our spirits, that will restore decency and goodness and morality to a crazy world, that will restore that very basic but bewilderingly elusive value to civilization, *normalcy*.

*Vayakhel-Pekudei 5778, Shabbos Parashas Parah*

# God's Shining City Waits

The young boy did something foolishly and seriously bad. And his timing could not have been worse. A family excursion to their absolutely favorite activity was planned for that very day. A loving father, wise enough in his parenting to be appropriately strict when strictness is due, had to teach the boy a painful lesson. The boy could not go, but had to stay in his room.

The son cried and protested, promised and cajoled, but the father stuck to his ruling. It had to be. For the sake of the boy, it had to be. They had been through this before. Angry, hurt, and dejected, the boy slunk to his room, sat in a corner, and wept.

At some point, he realized that he was not alone, and not the only one crying. Incredulously, he saw his father sitting nearby, eyes red, cheeks wet.

"Why are you here? What about the trip?"

"Mom and the other children went."

"What about you?"

"Without you there, my beloved boy, what pleasure can I possibly have?"

*Midrash Tanchuma*, on the completion of the Mishkan, which later was succeeded by the Mikdash in Jerusalem, cites various Scriptural sources that the Ribbono shel Olam, in His great love, created in Heaven a Mikdash and a Jerusalem that correspond to that on Earth. In the multitude of our sins, we caused our Jerusalem and our Mikdash to be destroyed. The very God Whose judgment decreed that destruction, because that painful punishment was necessary to save us in the long term, Himself sits in mourning, as it were, and refuses to take any "pleasure" in the Heavenly Jerusalem; He refuses to "enter" it, as long as His beloved children below are bereft of theirs.

Yeshayahu (52:5) reveals God's sentiment: *What is there for Me here? My people have been taken away! Without you there, My beloved children, what pleasure can I possibly have?*

The building of the Mishkan in the *midbar*, physical focus of our connection with God, was the beginning of a long and tortuous process, a powerful, seemingly never-ending struggle with ourselves with our *yetzer hara*, our abiding love of God and our propensity to fail and to fall, the duality of the cycle of growth and the spiral of decline, of destruction and of rebirth, of despair and of hopeful anticipation, of war and of peace, of turbulence and of tranquility, of utter loneliness dispelled by the palpable nearness of our loving Father in Heaven, Who had to punish us but Who nevertheless hovers near, cries along with us, soothes us, holds out the promise of ultimate rebirth, of the return to that *Mikdash*, and lovingly, comfortingly, lets us know, that without us there, what pleasure, *k'v'yachol*, could He possibly have?

*Parashas Pekudei 5779, Rosh Chodesh Adar Marbim b'Simchah*

# ספר ויקרא

# Vayikra

## Kosher

You probably remember that no-goodnik in Monsey, a highly respected Yid, a *talmid chacham* and a Daf Yomi *maggid shiur* who made his living as a purveyor of strictly kosher chickens to his God-fearing brethren, who, some years ago, was found to have been selling them *treif* for God knows how long.

How in the world does that happen?

And he wasn't the first. There have been cases, sadly, all along. Some stand out in their notoriety. There was a terrible case in Prague, a few hundred years ago. And the Midrash tells a story. There was a butcher in Tzipori who notoriously sold *neveilos* and *treifos* to Jews. Once, before Yom Kippur, he ate and drank, as all Jews are supposed to do. He drank too much wine, went up to the roof, fell down, and died. Dogs came to lap up his blood. The town's residents asked Rabbi Chaninah if the butcher's remains should be rescued from the dogs. He responded that the Torah says that *treif* meat should be fed to the dogs. This villain fed *treif* to Jews, cheating the dogs of their due. They should let him lie there and let the dogs get what's theirs.

It's one thing to fall victim to one's urges, to have that moment of "temporary insanity" and partake of a forbidden pleasure or some similar sinful indulgence, however wrong that is. It's quite another to feed fellow Jews *treifos* and *neveilos* on an ongoing basis. That's unimaginable – or would be if we didn't know that such a thing exists.

How does that happen? I think we have to postulate that there is something fundamentally wrong with the perpetrators, a kind of social psychopathy that can only be accompanied by a total lack of *yiras Shamayim*. Such people, regardless of their outer trappings, no matter how learned they are or how apparently religious, are not, at their core, religious people. They are not believers. And they are arrogant. *Gasei ruach.*

There is a powerful midrash on *Va'yikra el Moshe*, with that humble small *aleph*. It says that *neveilah* is better than a *talmid chacham* "*she'ein bo daas*" (who has no *daas*). Moshe – who of all people could have been proud and assertive; who was the father of all prophets, all wisdom, and all prophecy; who took Israel out of Egypt; who was the instrument of countless miracles in Egypt and at the Yam Suf; who was brought up to the heavens to receive the Torah; who built the Mishkan – still did not approach God, in his humility, until God called to him. *Va'yikra el Moshe*. Moshe's character was such that he was the most humble man alive.

So one way to understand this midrash is that it applies to someone who, despite his learning and his training, has an ingrained character flaw. He is arrogant. And because of that arrogance, that hubris, he is likely to *pasken* on questions he is incompetent to decide but is too arrogant and too proud to admit it. And thus, he may, in fact, be feeding Jews *neveilah*. Can one be God-fearing and do that? Can one really be a believer and do that? Arrogance places one very far from God.

The midrash is explained further that he is worse than *neveilah* because while the *neveilah* became *neveilah* through no fault of its own, this person is *misnabel* – he makes something bad of himself, something *neveilah*-like but lesser than *neveilah* – because his own actions bring it about. In fact, taking it further, it is said, based on a *gemara* in *Pesachim* (117), such a person is better off openly dealing in *neveilos* than falsely declaring them kosher.

The Ateres Yeshuah nails this objectionable person in another way, highlighting another manifestation of faulty character. *Talmidei chachamim* typically earn their livelihoods from the public, who give them money to live and, if they are in positions of leadership, to distribute to the poor. There are those who, receiving this money, distribute what they have been given to distribute, but give none of their own money, reasoning that they don't have to. This, says the Ateres Yeshuah, is evil and negates their very rights to the money that they are given.

Blessings devolve upon those who earn their living through hard work, in the marketplace, and then share their hard-earned money with tzaddikim who are thus able to do their *avodas hakodesh*. A *talmid chacham* who does not give to the poor from his *own* income, sourced from the *baalabatim*, has no power to bring blessing upon those who give him money. And thus he is robbing his donors of *berachah*. This is a *talmid chacham she'ein bo daas*. He would be better off, as the *gemara* says, dealing with *neveilos* in the marketplace than doing what he does. *Neveilah* is better than he is.

*Wow*. These are powerful condemnations. Considering the reverence we have for our *talmidei chachamim* – and considering that when we look upon them, we see refined, exemplary Jews, our leaders and role models – where does this *midrash* come from? Why does it even exist, especially as it was written by *talmidei chachamim*?

It's because they were smart, and they were honest, and they had tremendous insight into human nature. Betraying a trust, personal or public, is egregious. And, sadly, there are, in this world, people in positions of trust who do not deserve that trust, people who are lacking something in their characters. People who have no *yiras Shamayim* but, for reasons of advantage, wear the costume of those who do. I remember seeing a comment by the Vilna Gaon on the question of what became of the Erev Rav who caused us such trouble in the *midbar*. He said they are the bad Jews among us, including *rabbonim* who are not worthy of that role or title and who lead people astray.

This whole idea is disconcerting. Certainly, it is normally a safe assumption that a *talmid chacham* is worthy of our reverence and trust. Being steeped in Torah refines people as no other influence can. We see that all the time. And yet we know there is a known entity of the *zaken mamre*, the "*talmid chacham*" who leads people astray, into Reform or other such schismatic groups, whose internal compass is utterly askew, a compass that points to himself rather than to the right direction.

With this midrash, Chazal are warning us. Honor and revere our *talmidei chachamim*. They are the repository of *Toras chayim*. But human nature is a funny thing. Watch out. If you see arrogance, if you see subpar *middos*, if you see *gasus ruach*, look to someone else for leadership or to *pasken* even technical *she'elos*.

The Torah makes sure to tell us that the same Moshe Rabbeinu who received the Torah from God Himself was the most modest and humble man on earth. That is no accident. It was a necessary condition, and the Torah is telling us so. Look at our greatest leaders. They have been kind and humble and giving. You will never find arrogance or haughtiness bound up with greatness.

There are those who might fool some or even lots of people some of the time or even much of the time. But expect them, like the feeders of *neveilah* – in actual or in spiritual form – to Klal Yisrael, to be ultimately exposed.

We are a nation that reveres its Torah leaders. We pray that we be blessed only with leaders who are *tocham k'varum*, whose inner *yiras Shamayim* exceeds their outer trappings, whose character is molded and refined by the Torah they have absorbed, whose role model is Moshe Rabbeinu in all his ways, who are entirely kosher, even as we strive to be, to the best of our ability, entirely kosher.

*Parashas Vayikra 5782*

## Haman and Perhaps Not Haman

The young woman, an ophthalmology resident working in the next examination space at the clinic during my residency, a non-Jew – very much a non-Jew – was surprised and amused. She understood much of my Yiddish conversation with my own patient. She had never heard Yiddish spoken before. An exchange resident from a German university, she was, in fact, about as German as you can get.

Actually, she was quite nice, and we became pretty good friends. We never discussed the obvious, the German thing, although it was always palpably there. I was actually quite comfortable personally with her – *she* had done nothing wrong – all while acutely aware that her father and all her relatives of that generation were in all likelihood enablers if not actually active in the mass murder of my people. It was an odd dichotomy. I'm reasonably sure she was not an active bigot. And yet I found it oddly troubling that once, over a slice of kosher pizza, she mentioned that a then-famous tennis player named Solomon was Jewish. I had never given it a thought. Why did she?

A year or so later, I was privileged to do a prestigious fellowship at Harvard in ophthalmic plastic and reconstructive surgery. My mentor and program director was an immigrant from Germany, whose beloved older brother in the Wehrmacht died on the Russian front. The professor himself was too young during the war to be a soldier but was old enough to have been a member of the Hitler Youth. I don't know if he was or wasn't. We never spoke about that. He was very nice to me. His fellow before me, chosen by him, was, like me, a *frum* red-headed Jew from New York.

When I arrived in Boston, we sat down for an organizational meeting to set things up. With some trepidation, I knew I had to bring up the Shabbos issue. I did not; *he* did. He preempted me. "I'll cover Saturdays," he said. "You take Sundays." And that was that. We remained good friends until he moved back to Germany some years later. He hosted for me a catered kosher dinner in his house, and he ate in mine. He never gave me any reason to think him bigoted or hateful. Personally,

I liked this German, although with his bearing and German appearance, I had no trouble imagining him in an SS uniform, complete with a long leather coat, strutting with cold, imperious power.

Postwar Germany is post-Nazi Germany. But Germany is Germany. The large majority of NGO money today that is funding the relentless crusade to destroy Israel is from Germany. The virtuous rationale they proffer, as if it should be obvious to all: Given our Nazi past, they say, we have to fight Nazism everywhere. *So we have to fight the Nazis of today, the Israelis.*

The world is today, as I write this, horrified by Russia's brutal invasion of Ukraine and the suffering of the Ukrainian people. The Ukrainians are obviously brave and dedicated; they have been wronged, and for no apparent reason. They never harmed Russia. Russia has, historically, harmed Ukraine terribly, including the Holodomor (a manufactured famine) in 1932–1933 that swept away millions of innocents. This followed the similar famine of 1921.

There is no question who are the good guys here and who are the bad, who are the innocent and who are the guilty. One can only sympathize with and root for the innocent Ukrainian victims of this crazy aggression, the kind of thing we thought was unimaginable in this day and age. And yet…

Some years ago, I operated on a Ukrainian woman who, happy and appreciative, brought me a gift. It was a statue of Bogdan Chmielnitzki, one of the most notorious murderers of Jews in history, who, with his Ukrainian army, left a trail of murder, torture, mayhem, ruined families, destroyed lives, and destroyed communities in the infamous depredations of 1648–1649. Hundreds of thousands of Jewish lives were destroyed. He is the revered national hero of Ukraine, the very paragon of things Ukrainian, whose glorifying statue dominates the old central square in Kiev.

It was clear that she was either evil or ignorant, and I didn't think she was being diabolical. So I asked some of my Jewish coworkers who were from Ukraine. They said that she probably knows little about it, but that in general, it just isn't considered important. It's a minor detail of history – and maybe not so objectionable – that doesn't take away from his Ukrainian greatness.

In 2016, today's Ukrainian parliament honored the memory of and declared a memorial for national hero Simon Petliura, whose nationalists, in 1918–1921, murdered about fifty thousand Ukrainian Jews (as well as Poles and Roma). Later national hero Bandera's followers, especially in collaboration with the Germans, brutally abused and murdered untold thousands more. Ukrainians (as well as Latvians and Lithuanians) were especially notorious as active volunteer helpers to the Germans in the torture and murder of the Jews.

That was then. This is now. And yet…

It is easy to sympathize with beleaguered and terrorized people, and we should. We do. It is the morally and the emotionally correct thing. And yet…

It is so much easier to sympathize with the individuals, to root for them and their army, than it is with the nation that has been so cruel to us.

A young Ukrainian woman I have described previously (Toldos) who worked in my office told me that her people hate my people, although she doesn't know why. How could I explain it to her?

Parashas Tzav is given over to the details of *korbonos* of various kinds. The *todah*, a thanks offering, famously applies primarily to people who have survived a dangerous ordeal: sickness, imprisonment, dangerous passages across oceans and deserts.

And then there are times and places where people somehow survive all of those dangers and infinitely worse. They have stared into the three gates of Gehinnom and somehow survived and gone on. And those ordeals are virtually always man-made, inflicted by hateful, cruel people, cruel armies, and cruel nations.

I grew up among such survivors. They were by and large remarkably tolerant people. For all their loss and suffering, for all that was taken from them, for all the bitterness they were subjected to, they were not, by and large, bitter people. They were not prejudiced. They dealt kindly and civilly with all people they encountered, even individual members of nationalities that had hurt them. Unlike the haters and the bigots of the world, they understood the difference – or the potential difference – between individuals (who might be innocent) and nations that were guilty of the most heinous crimes. The bitter lessons in their lives taught them that.

Much has been said about growing up among war-damaged people secondarily damaging the children. That was not my experience at all. For me and others like me, growing up among survivors taught me to appreciate people, to recognize their humanity. To recognize that there are evil people and evil nations out there, many still intent upon hurting us, but also that even among those evil nations, not everyone is evil.

I learned that life is a complicated place. That when life proceeds normally, as it does, thank God, for us, as it did for the people of Ukraine until suddenly it did not, we must count our blessings, appreciate what we have, commiserate with those who have not, and for everything, with all our hearts, bless the Creator Who gave it to us, ask Him to continue to sustain us, to worshipfully say to Him, always, *todah*.

May there be love in our hearts, and may we thank Him for that as well.

*Parashas Tzav, Purim 5782*

# Shemini

## Calling

It was a well checkup – routine, really, without any abnormality noted or treatment required. The patient, an earnest and very fine young man, a Modern Orthodox type, upon hearing the good report, thanked me and then expressed his admiration for the privileged position I was in. He said that my work, even for a routine exam, was holy.

I replied that all work done honestly and for the sake of Heaven could be invested with holiness and considered holy. He replied that he understood the part about honesty and decency, but in the end, what he did in business was to shuffle money around, and even when done honestly, it was still just shuffling money around. He could take the comparison no further.

I meant what I said to him, but I also knew that he was right. Medicine is certainly not the only occupation that is a calling, but a calling it truly is, requiring a determination and a perseverance, a dedication and a responsibility that would make no sense to pursue were it not a *calling*. The depth, intensity, and difficulty of that responsibility are such that it is rarely fully understood by those who are not of that calling, even by those who are closest to us.

Sadly, there are those in the profession – thankfully not commonly – who do seem to be outside this parameter. In my experience, they are often the products of a different value system than we are accustomed to. But I do submit that among the colleagues I know, in the medical culture that I know and of which I am a part, the drive of medicine as a *calling* is paramount.

We see dedicated people in every sphere of life. We see rabbis and teachers who could not put up with what they have to put up with but for their calling to do what they do, to be what they are. What, other than a divine sense of mission, moves people to spend their lives among the sick and the miserable poor in the alleyways of Calcutta, or some other miserable place, sharing that misery as they try to alleviate it? What, other than a sense of duty, of calling, would have hundreds of firefighters race into burning buildings at risk of imminent collapse, even as everyone else is fleeing those deathtraps? How have soldiers, fighting for a cause, knowingly raced into a hail of oncoming bullets, knowing that death was likely? I cannot fathom that courage, but dedicated human beings have exhibited it.

The concept of being called plays a significant role in Parashat Shemini. Previously, God called Moshe – *Vayikra* – and now Moshe, upon God's instruction, called Aharon. It was Aharon's turn to take over the *kehunah*, a calling that would remain with his offspring until the end of time.

But first God called Moshe at the Burning Bush, a calling Moshe, in his humbleness, resisted strenuously. Moshe pleaded, "Send somebody else!" Both Moshe and the Ribbono shel Olam knew whom Moshe had in mind: Moshe's elder brother Aharon, who, Moshe argued, was superior to Moshe in every way, and more deserving. Hashem answered Moshe that indeed Aharon was greater, but this mission was for Moshe only. It was his calling.

Contrary to Moshe's concern for Aharon's sensibilities about being passed over, Aharon will, Hashem assures him, be *same'ach b'libo*, utterly and completely happy, in his heart of hearts, for his younger brother Moshe to be chosen for greatness.

And here the *Midrash Tanchuma* (Shemini 3) talks a bit about calling in Scripture. There is *kriah* (calling) for satiation: "I will rescue you [Israel] from your own spiritual uncleanness [*tumah*], I will call the produce of the land to be bountiful [*v'karasi es hadagan*] and I will not allow you to be hungry" (Yechezkel 36:29). There is *kriah* (calling) for hunger: "For God has called the hunger to come [and punish Israel] for seven years" (II Melachim 8:1). And there is *kriah* (calling) to greatness: Moshe called Aharon to the position of greatness that he so deserved.

Moshe might well have been the Kohen Gadol, with all that entailed for himself and all his future generations, but he lost that opportunity when he struggled with God too much – for seven days – at the Burning Bush. Back then, God had told him that Aharon would indeed be genuinely happy for Moshe, with all his heart. Now, when the *kehunah* was snatched away from Moshe after the first seven inaugural days of the Mishkan, and Moshe called Aharon to be elevated and to serve, Aharon at first demurred, for Moshe had labored greatly to establish the Mishkan and its divine service. How could he, Aharon, now become an interloper? Now it was Moshe's turn to reassure Aharon that just as he, Aharon, rejoiced in his heart for Moshe upon his being selected for leadership, Moshe now genuinely rejoiced in his heart for Aharon upon his assuming the *kehunah*, as much as he would for himself.

Not only would Moshe, who lived to serve God, not get to be the vessel of His service in the Mishkan, his descendants would lose out (and indeed, they have become untraceable), while Aharon's remain identifiable and special to this day.

*Amar Rabbi Shimon ben Yochai*: The heart that genuinely rejoiced upon his brother's elevation to greatness (Aharon's heart) will now be adorned with the precious stones and the breastplate of the Kohen Gadol, upon which are inscribed the names of the tribes of Israel.

Aharon's great strength was built upon his great and pure heart, which knew only goodness and love. Upon that, his character and resolve were built, and from that derived his eternal calling.

Some of us have a particular calling with regard to the kind of work we do. But each of us, every person and certainly every Jew, is called as well, to increase the goodness and the kindness, the love and the caring, the decency, the selflessness, and the devotion that the human heart is capable of, to illuminate and to elevate this world. We cannot all be a Moshe or an Aharon, but we all have the ears God gave us with which to hear that call, and we can each, in our own way, in our own spheres of life, find our calling, purify and refine our hearts, and answer that call to bring greatness stamped with our own signature into the world.

*Parashas Shemini 5778*

# Chosen

I did an audio double take when I heard the voice behind me, as one man said to his neighbor, in exactly the voice and intonation one would expect from a genuine "*grubber ying*," as they were discussing hiring a new *rav*, "The next rabbi needs to know he's *not* the boss. *We are.*" Did I hear that right? It was horrible.

He wasn't, in general, a bad guy, and he could also be kind and giving. But I knew him to be, in matters Jewish, utterly ignorant, and he was also sometimes arrogantly assertive, often when he was wrong. Here, he was being both at the same time. A successful businessman, he was accustomed to getting his own way (except, I suspect, at home). The reason for all this, of course, was that he had, in truth, no real idea what a *rav* is. Between his personality and his lack of education and knowledge, he qualified very well for that Yiddish description, *a grubber ying*, literally a fat young fellow, but meaning, really, an ignoramus who foolishly and brazenly displays his ignorance and rough edges.

It is sadly not rare for *rabbonim* to toil under such conditions, sometimes with even more "educated" congregants. Like the congregant in one shul – let's call it Congregation Anshei Entitlement and Privilege – who told someone close to me that they want to get rid of their rabbi because "he tells us what to do." The power of the purse in the hands of congregants sometimes puts their *rabbonim* in a difficult position indeed.

Of course the *rav* tells them what to do. That's his job. Even a congregation of learned individuals needs a *rav*. We sometimes encounter such a group of people who think they don't. In my observation, the more they think they don't, the more they really do.

And we also know that the more an individual is steeped in Torah, the more his judgment in general is guided by the *chochmas haTorah* in the right direction. We look to our *rabbonim* for that; hopefully that becomes manifest.

But we also know that in our religion, we don't do "infallible." Every human is fallible. That is an inevitable part of the human condition, no matter how exalted an individual might be. The devotees of some leaders don't like to admit that about their leaders, but it is a fact of life, built in by the Creator. Times of difficulty, challenge, and crisis are especially prone to put wisdom and leadership to the test. And integrity, and bravery.

Our leaders have much to take into consideration when making decisions with great communal ramifications, often more than individuals are aware of. We have all seen that in recent times. And the pressures put on those leaders sometimes affect their own livelihood as well as their quality of life. And yet, as leaders, they must make those decisions, they must make whatever stand their duty calls upon them to make. They must lead, for that is their calling as well as their duty. And then they must hope and pray that they are getting it right.

Moshe Rabbeinu built the Mishkan and inaugurated it, serving as interim Kohen Gadol for the first seven days. It was then time for Moshe to step aside and for Aharon to establish himself, and his heirs after him, as the Kohanim for all time. Chazal tell us that when the time came, Aharon tried to melt into the background, so to speak, rather than step forward to assume his leading role. *"Boshe"* is the term used, meaning shy, reticent, even embarrassed. Reluctant. Even afraid to step forward. "Why are you *boshe*?" Moshe asked him. *"L'chach nivcharta!"* *You were chosen for this!*

This role – difficult, demanding, and even dangerous as it is (think of Nadav and Avihu, who were that very day consumed by fire due to an error they made) – is his calling, his duty, his assigned role in this world. So too for the spiritual leader. It is his special, divinely ordained calling, however challenging. He needs to fulfill his role, even as the rest of us need him to do so, in times good and bad, when it is easy and when it is tough, to see what is right and to stand up for it, and to face the fallout if need be. And that, we know, can be hard indeed. Getting it wrong can be disastrous.

Sadly, there are those who needlessly and foolishly make it difficult for them. Who push them, sometimes with devilish force, thinking that they themselves are or ought to be "the boss," that it is the *rav's* duty to indulge them, even when he knows they are wrong (a possibility they apparently never consider).

And it is, of course, the *rav's* challenge to always know what is right. That's not always easy, indeed not always possible, as life teaches us. But step up he must, as did Aharon Hakohen, for it is for this that he was chosen. And it is for us to be as supportive and as respectful and as cooperative as is fitting for the one who is our spiritual leader, the one of whom it is said, in this sphere, *l'chach nivcharta*, for this you have been chosen. And God help him.

*Parashas Shemini 5781*

# Tazria-Metzora

## V'nahafoch Hu

God was obviously talking to us in the time of the COVID-19 pandemic. What was He saying?

Ah, a great question. It's interesting, isn't it, that thousands of years ago, during the times that we read about in the Navi, when our people were so terribly mired in sin, so guilty of all manner of abominations and idol worship, that they were still worthy, apparently, of having the prophets come and tell them exactly what God was saying, what their shortcomings were, and what they needed to do about it. Tragically, they all too often didn't listen, and the results were – and remain – devastating. But that was their choice, however bad. They knew, straight from the *neviim*, just what God was saying to them.

From our earliest days, at least some of us have had a hard time following orders. Remember the old joke about the Jewish rowing team that doesn't get anywhere because instead of one person calling out orders and everybody else pulling in unison, *everybody* calls out orders, and perhaps one person pulls? We have, *baruch Hashem*, many people who punctiliously follow religious instruction, who lovingly and zealously obey the word of God well beyond the letter of the law, who follow their rabbis' every instruction, but who, in other spheres, don't like being told what to do (in itself a great human strength) and find excuses not to, including not feeling bound to do so.

And we all have our different sensitivities. We can hear the same thing as others do, but hear it differently. But we did not hear a prophet of the Lord spell out for us exactly what God was saying to us in that terrible pandemic. And that, I suggest, may be exactly the message.

There was no shortage of people telling us what all this meant. "It's because of *this*!" "It's because of *that*!" "It's because of this *and* that!" It's because of *a*, *b*, *c*, *d*, and *e*. Well, maybe. People have their ideas about what's wrong with society, which would explain why we suffer. Sometimes they openly declare, *somehow knowing*, that *that's* the problem.

Chazal have taught us that *chayav adam l'fashpesh b'maasav*, a person must deeply and honestly examine his behavior, in times of trouble, to discern where he needs to improve himself. We have heard a fair amount from those "in the know" about what society is doing wrong. Maybe some are correct about some things, maybe not. But the obligation for self-examination and self-improvement, while it should extend to the *kahal*, is really directed at the individual. *Chayav adam. Adam,* one individual person.

God *is* talking to us. For the Jew, God is talking to us all the time, but sometimes, like during the pandemic, it seems He is sending us a loud message. He certainly has our attention at the moment – or He *should* have it, individually and communally. It seems to me that He wants us to know that He is, at each moment, sending us a message, but what that message is may not be the same for each person. *Chayav adam l'fashpesh.* Each of us should be looking into his or her own heart. Most of us, if we're not too dense, if we're honest, if we have some measure of insight into ourselves and our habits, understands more or less what that message is for ourselves. We need the honesty and the force of will to figure it out as best we can and to act on it.

In the history of the world, there have always been people who lived long lives. So many, however, died in childhood from infectious diseases that the *average* life expectancy was pulled way down. Add to that other illnesses such as diabetes that struck down young people, or heart disease in young middle age. The "conquest" of infectious disease caused the average life expectancy to skyrocket. Who was much worried about it in recent times? Along comes a virus bug and kills so many, *lo aleinu*, and shuts down the world, doctors apparently helpless, our lives utterly disrupted, healthy people fearfully hiding behind closed doors, behind masks and gloves. Who would have thought such a thing?

A particularly ironic twist was the Purim holiday that occurred at the beginning of the pandemic, normally a time of great joy. Purim represents the concept of *v'nahafoch hu*, that our forefathers in that time saw the world turned upside down in their favor, their pursuers themselves being pursued, their intended killers themselves being killed by the Jews, with fear and trembling turning to joy. To this day, this glorious reversal, this *v'nahafoch hu*, has been a central theme fueling our joyful Purim observance. And now *v'nahafoch hu* was turned on its head in a dreadful *hafuchah*: throughout Klal Yisrael, joy was replaced by fear and trembling, by mourning, lamentation, shock, and loss. Individual families and entire *kehillos* were decapitated, *nebech, Rachmana litzlan.* And we have to suspect that many of those terrible losses were set off during joyful Purim celebrations, when that virus had a field day. *V'nahafoch hu* turned horribly backwards, with a trail of orphans in its tragic wake.

So what we need, really, is yet another *v'nahafoch hu*, please God, flipping things back again in the right direction. In the Purim story, the Jews needed to fix themselves. They did, thank God, and the rest is history. What do we need to fix now?

There are some obvious and some apparent things, thinking of the Jewish People in general; there is no need to go into detail. As individuals, however, we also need to hear the message, the one directed to us individually, each of us according to what we need to hear. Remember the little *aleph* in *va'yikra* that represents the individual, the singular person, the "*aleph*," who needs also to listen carefully and to hear the Voice of God calling to him?

God has been speaking to us since Sinai. He continues to speak to us, to each of us, urgently and pointedly.

We need to get well, and somehow to heal. Parashat Tazria-Metzora concerns physical illnesses with a particularly spiritual basis, and how to get well from them. *Tzaraas* has various causes, but an underlying theme is *tzoras ayin*, a kind of meanness or even indifference to the troubles of others.

God punishes, *lo aleinu, middah k'neged middah*, a kind of cosmic measure for measure. We are not at all talking, *chas v'chalilah*, about those torn away in the pandemic and their poor bereaved families. We never know God's *cheshbon* in such things, and in this situation it is utterly unknowable. Like the fiery deaths of Aharon's righteous sons Nadav and Avihu, there is some higher purpose in this terrible national and personal sacrifice that He may or may not someday reveal to us. It is for us to derive whatever lesson we can, and like the bereft Aharon, as nobly as we can.

In the *haftarah* for Metzora, the terrible famine that had plagued Israel for years was, by the hand of God, about to be over. Four "lepers," sufferers from *tzaraas*, dying from hunger, came upon a huge bounty of food that had suddenly become available in the camp of the huge attacking army of Aram, as God had caused the Arameans to panic and flee for their lives, thinking falsely, miraculously, that the Jews were about to overwhelm them. Food was suddenly so plentiful that it was practically for free. The day before, the *navi* Elisha had prophesied that on the morrow it would be so. When the king's officer scoffed, asking sarcastically if God would suddenly open the windows of the sky and pour down food upon them, Elisha said that that scoffer would live to see it happen but would not himself live to benefit from it. That scoffing officer did see it come to pass, but was crushed to death in the rush of hungry people to get food.

Well, Hashem also rewards *middah k'neged middah*. In that story, the revealers of the sudden deliverance of Israel from the *tzarah* of hunger were *metzora'im*. *Tzaraas* is associated with *tzoras ayin*. The antidote to *tzoras ayin* is loving generosity, of the spirit *and of the pocket*.

A major Amora in the third century CE was Rav Shmuel bar Nachman (sometimes rendered Nachmani). It was in his troubled time that multiple catastrophes, including four major earthquakes, befell the land. *Taanis 8b* relates that a double calamity struck, with simultaneous famine *and* plague, an *epidemic*. In times of trouble, Jews naturally turn in prayer to their Father in Heaven for relief. And here they faced a dilemma: What to pray for?

There was an established custom that special prayers are not instituted for two different things but must be directed at one specific request. The Gemara offers explanations and scriptural hints why this might be so. Hence, their dilemma. It was suggested that special prayers be said for the elimination of the plague, as it had a higher and faster death rate, and that they would endure the famine as best they could. Rabbi Shmuel bar Nachmani replied that they should rather pray for relief from the famine, for when God sends plenty, He does so for the living. *"Pose'ach es yadecha u'masbia l'chol chai ratzon"* (God opens His hand to satisfy the desire of every living thing). Thus, Rav Shmuel reasoned, once God hears their prayers and relieves the famine, the plague will cease as well.

This is, thank God, not a time of famine for our society in general – but it may be for the many stricken families who lost not only a father and husband, but their breadwinner. They are lost – except for the *chesed* of Klal Yisrael who stand up for them. God wants us, in a human way, to emulate Him. *Mah Hu rachum, af ata rachum.* As God is Av Hayesomim, the Father of Orphans, *you too be the father of orphans.*

No one can replace the dead. How sadly terrible for those poor families and for Klal Yisrael. But by "praying for plenty" – and better, *by providing plenty* – perhaps we can, by doing *the very opposite* of *tzoras ayin*, merit, as in days of old, to put an end or at least a mitigation to an epidemic or other *tzaaros* as well, to protect ourselves and our families to the extent we can, by protecting, to the extent we can, those bereaved families. They are such hard luck cases, *nebech*, typically very young, large families, whose misery cries out to us as well as to Heaven.

I urge everyone, especially in troubled times, to contact any of the many reputable chesed organizations that are dedicated to helping tragedy-struck families, of which there have been and are so many, for so many different reasons throughout our history. It's one of the most meaningful and effective things you can do for yourself and your family.

When our forefathers gathered to inaugurate the Mishkan, as described in Parashat Shemini, the Torah says *va'yikrevu kol ha'edah va'yaamdu lifnei Hashem*

(Vayikra 9:5). Homiletically, this has been explained to demonstrate the power of closeness of Am Yisrael to each other, so that they stand most effectively and most powerfully before Hashem after *va'yikrevu*, they become close with each other in a loving and caring way. *Bava Basra* (10a) relates that *Rabbi Elazar yaheiv prutah l'oni v'hadar metzalei*, he gave tzedakah to a poor person before he davened, so that his davening should have more power and be more effective.

And many people, before davening, for the same purpose, preface their prayers with the declaration before God that they undertake to perform the all-important mitzvah of *v'ahavta l're'acha ka'mocha*, to love one's fellow as oneself. That is just what the Ribbono shel Olam has told us He wants to hear, and to *see us do*.

Parashat Tazria-Metzora falls around Rosh Chodesh Iyar. The letters of Iyar (אייר) are a mnemonic for *Ani Hashem Rofecha* (אני ה' רופאיך), I am Hashem Who heals you.

It's time already, please God. Hashem is speaking to the world, to Klal Yisrael, and remember that little *aleph* in *va'yikra*, to *each of us*, especially in crazily extraordinary, terrible times such as a pandemic. He is calling to us to do what each of us knows we need to do to correct and fine-tune our lives, to serve His purpose for us. But beyond those things, whatever they may be, even if the world may seem to be coming apart, we also know, because our Father in Heaven has told us, that *olam chesed yibaneh*, *chesed* will rebuild the world.

*Parashas Tazria-Metzora 5780, Rosh Chodesh Iyar, chodesh Ani Hashem Rofecha*

# Lepers

The boy, about twelve, broadcast clearly, before saying a word, that he was angry. And frustrated. And smart. It was all there on his face.

His mother brought him to examine his eyes and his visual system in the hope that I might find a remedy for his inability to read like other boys in his yeshiva. It wasn't his first eye exam. Others – I don't know how many – had been there before me. Eye exercises, prism glasses – various things had been tried, without real success.

The pressures on this child – and there are so many like him – were driving him and his distraught parents crazy. Our society is a world in which the written word is king, and its mastery is the key not only to success, sociologically speaking, but to any claim of regard or even self-worth.

This boy's failure in reading was destroying him and tearing down his family. Angry tears filled his eyes as he grimly submitted to yet another eye exam, knowing that his problem cannot be fixed by an eye exam.

In fact, there are specialized teaching techniques that can help many of these children learn and even read with greater facility. It is expensive and hard to come by, and the resources are not widely known. Some of the more commonly employed techniques are not regarded as effective by many authorities and lead to frustration and bitter disappointment.

The pain and the misery are real, and they are destructive. Our world, the Torah world, the traditional Jewish world, values scholarship above all. A rich older guy might get to "buy" some *kavod*, but the real regard is for the successful scholars. The *shidduch* prize is typically reserved for the prestigious young scholar. Worthiness in the yeshiva world is based on scholarship. The sports jock may do OK in the outside world, but it's not that way in ours.

How can a child in our world grow up with a normal sense of self-worth if the measure of worthiness is in an area beyond his abilities, regardless of how bright and inventive and otherwise worthy he might be? Regarded as a hopeless underachiever and not smart, he is, in a sense, almost like a leper, unless his school and his teachers are prepared to treat him from a different perspective. Fortunately, it has become far more common for yeshivas today to be institutionally sensitive to this problem, although not equally so nor equally able to cope with it.

After offering a possible resource referral, I suggested to the mother that she enroll him in an activity in which he might excel and see success, such as a chess club, where his native intelligence, driven by the ambition to succeed, might help him shine and feel good about himself. How can he otherwise grow into any kind of a fulfilling adulthood?

The enigmatic illness referred to in the Torah as *tzaraas*, commonly if imprecisely referred to as leprosy, appears, Chazal tell us, as a result of and as a punishment and an expiation primarily for *lashon hara*. But it also comes from *gaavah*, haughtiness, excessive pride. A person who speaks *lashon hara* recognizes that he is doing so. It's a bad thing, and he knows it. *Stam* pompous *gaavah* is foolish and makes one look ridiculous; most of us would realize it. But the devil is sneaky. He can coax us into *gaavah* about kosher things that make that very haughtiness seem appropriate and even laudable. I have seen haughty "*shpitz*" yeshiva fellows who know they're *shpitz* looking down their noses at lesser creatures. I am sure this is not very common, but it was disconcerting to see it. In their minds, I presume, they were upholding "*kavod haTorah*" (like the old joke, "It's not my personal *kavod* I'm talking about, it's my *kavod haTorah*, and my *kavod haTorah* is bigger than his *kavod haTorah!*").

There is, in fact, much to be proud of in the world of Torah, and its diligent pursuit by our brilliant (and less than brilliant but highly diligent) young scholars and older scholars is what keeps us alive as the nation of Torah and Godliness. Placing it at the highest rung of achievement is altogether right and has produced the matchless civilization that Torah Judaism is. But true *mechanchim*, true *yirei Shamayim*, true educators, also know that that's not all there is in God's beautiful nation. The same God Who created the Torah and gave it to us as a mandate to live by also created those special children for whom scholarship does not come naturally and placed them among us. They are otherwise quite normal, and they can be helped to achieve. They too need to learn and to grow, to be given every opportunity to do so and to excel as they can. They too need to feel happy and fulfilled, appreciated for who they are and who they can be, rather than to feel denigrated for who they are not.

The natural pride in producing excellence in Torah scholarship does not require the shunting aside of those who are hampered in this way, or for that matter, in various other ways. They are not irrelevant, and they are certainly not "lepers." They too need to be appreciated and cultivated. More often than not, lurking inside is a beautiful mind that can achieve much, often incredibly much, given the support and the opportunity. And that too is the beauty of Torah.

*Parashas Tazria-Metzora 5781*

# Kosher Phone, Kosher Talk

Do you remember when there were people out there who did not walk around with a telephone constantly in hand? The phones are ubiquitous, it seems, and people's attention seems to be focused on those phones when it should not be, often glaringly so.

Don't get me wrong. I have a cell phone too, and, in the world as it has evolved, I mostly need it on me, professionally speaking. But not much for conversation (except for other doctors, patients and their families, pharmacies, etc.).

Essentially, the image I am referring to is the patient sitting in the exam chair with the phone clutched in her hand. I gently remove it  (making sure that she won't faint) and place it to the side. And here is where one group stands out. Nearly everyone has a smart phone; many of the *frumer* do not. I see a variety of really old-style phones, primitive by today's standards. I am proud of these people for adhering to a standard designed to protect the community from the pervasive bad influences that plague the surrounding society. And it seems to me that these kosher phones are also somewhat more commonly held by kosher Jewish women than by men.

I asked a woman from Williamsburg recently, tongue-in-cheek, as I put her kosher "dumb" phone on the desk, now that she is protected from the sin of *lashon hara* with her kosher phone, how does she get the same protection with her regular phone at home? She told me with a straight face that she has it specially treated not to allow *lashon hara* or *rechilus*. Great answer to what she understood was a great question.

Which is the point. The kosher phone commendably won't let you look where you shouldn't look (if you're looking on the phone), but it won't stop anyone from saying what they should not say. One can talk all the *lashon hara* one wants even on a kosher phone, as unkosher as that is. I'm not sure which is the bigger problem.

There are various causes for *tzaraas, lo aleinu*; the most prominent one, the one that is associated most with *tzaraas* is *lashon hara* (*lo aleinu!*). And so the *Midrash Rabbah* in Parashas Metzora tells a story.

It starts, as the Midrash often does, by quoting the *pasuk, Zos tihyeh toras hametzora*, and by way of explication, relating it to another verse in Scripture: *Mi ha'ish hechafetz chaim* (Tehillim 34:13). It tells the story of a traveling salesman, a *rochel* (was he really a salesman, or was he actually "selling" this wisdom?). He was selling in the villages near Tzipori. He would call out in the marketplace, "Who wants to buy the elixir of life?" Hearing this, the people crowded to buy. Rav Yanai, overhearing, said to him, "Come, sell me a portion." The peddler replied to Rav Yanai that he and his colleagues didn't need it. Rav Yanai insisted, and the peddler produced a Sefer Tehillim and turned to the *pasuk, Mi ha'ish hechafetz chaim*, who wants life? *Netzor lashoncha me'ra u'sefasecha midaber mirma*. Guard your tongue from evil, your lips from speaking sinfully. Rav Yanai, excited by the realization, immediately cited the *pasuk* from Mishlei (21:23), *Shomer piv u'leshono shomer mi'tzaros nafsho*, he who safeguards his mouth (from saying what he should not) thereby safeguards his life. When Moshe taught the halachah of *metzora*, Rav Yanai says, he was also warning the people about the destructive effects of *lashon hara*.

There is a parallel story in *Avodah Zarah* (19b). Rav Alexandri would call out, "Who wants life? Who wants life?" When everybody crowded around, calling out, "Give us life!" Rav Alexandri would quote that same *pasuk* in Tehillim, continuing with the next phrase, *sur me'ra v'aseh tov*, turn away from evil and do good: If someone were to say, *OK, I'll watch my mouth, can I get by just with that?* No, staying away from bad is good, but not enough: one must *pursue* good as well. *Aseh tov: tov* is Torah. *Ki lekach tov nasati lachem, Torasi al taazovu* (Mishlei 4:2). I have given you something good, Hashem says – do not forsake My Torah. If you want to pursue the good, you will find it only in the Torah.

It's interesting that in each episode, the *pasuk* by David Hamelech is amplified by a *pasuk* by his son, Shlomo Hamelech.

The mouth is a powerful tool, for good or, God forbid, for bad. Our power of speech distinguishes us from every species in creation. Man can raise himself up to be the highest of the high, or *Rachmana litzlan*, the lowest of the low, even as his range of potential for *tumah* or *taharah* is the greatest of all things on earth. We are not helpless in this. True, we are affected by how we are raised. Ultimately, it is up to us. Controlling what we say is one of the great challenges in life; we are completely surrounded by a human culture that militates the direct opposite. *Lashon hara* must be a terrible sin, because for so many, it is not only so easy, but so much fun.

We are blessed to have among us so many excellent people who are constantly on guard against this grievous sin. Like them, we can buy life for ourselves by being so, so careful not to slip into forbidden – deadly – territory. My grandfather, Shloime Nussbaum, *a"h*, was a *shaskan*, a laconic person who had great presence but generally refrained from saying too much. Part of that is a person's nature. Part of that is a conscious decision, an avoidance tactic against this grievous sin. It is no accident that *lashon hara* is associated with *tzaraas*, not actually leprosy as we medically know it, but a concept that evokes horror, a frankly disgusting malady that disfigures from without to reflect the disfigurement within that caused it.

A kosher phone is only as kosher as you make it.

God hates the awful sin of *lashon hara*. Want to buy life? Just ask the Chofetz Chaim. No one has taught us more about guarding the tongue.

*Parashas Metzora 5782, Yerushalayim Ir Hakodesh*

# Acharei Mos-Kedoshim

## Haughty

When I first saw them, I was somewhat startled by my instinctive reaction: there was something somehow off-putting that I did not quite understand. Perhaps it was because it was against my natural inclination to conclude that what I sensed in the two yeshiva fellows – who attended a different, more prestigious institution of higher learning and whose hats were set at precisely the correct angle – who stopped in to daven in our local shul/yeshiva and stood there looking around at their perceived "lessers" was their haughtiness. It's not fair, of course, to judge someone in just the blink of an eye, and that instant judgment may not be correct. But we also know that it may be quite correct after all and very often is.

Not long ago, I saw a young man I had not seen for a while, a young Talmudic scholar from a well-known family of Talmudic scholars and leaders in the yeshiva world. I know his family personally, and, along with others, have played my own modest role in sustaining the institution that has made his life as a growing Torah scholar possible. I know he knows who I am. But knowing who I am was apparently insufficient reason for even a minimal greeting, perhaps a *"chag kasher v'sameach,"* maybe a hello or even a slight nod of the head, as he briefly looked at me and then, with an utter lack of interest, immediately turned his gaze past me. He wasn't preoccupied. His body language clearly did not project shyness. Read: *haughty.* Maybe I'm mistaken, but…I fear I am not.

I hasten to note that this kind of thing is quite rare. The true princes of Torah – the dedicated scholars of the holy Torah who spend their lives absorbing its holy lessons – most commonly do reflect its exalted values. They are warm and friendly, their essential goodness and their empathetic decency central to their character, obvious in their actions and written on their faces.

And let's be careful here. There are all kinds of personalities. Not everyone is naturally warm and friendly (although they should work on it!), and that reserve may be mistaken for hostility or indifference. Some people are awkward in this way, or just never learned appropriate social norms. But even with this in mind, haughtiness stands recognizably apart not as an inadvertence, but as a chosen stance.

During Pesach, there are many people who, following a longstanding honorable tradition, are so careful about what they eat, for love of the mitzvah so intent on getting everything for Pesach so stringently right, that they do not "mix" with their friends and neighbors, in that they do not eat outside their own homes, even if they do so otherwise all year. That is well and good and respectable, a laudable stringency. But even those who do so make a point of lessening these restrictions on the eighth day, which is *d'rabbanan*, in order to demonstrate and practice *achdus* and mutual love and respect in Klal Yisrael.

The *parashah* that follows immediately after Pesach most years is Shemini. While it continues the story of the initial inauguration of the Mishkan, the outstanding and striking feature of Shemini is the sudden and horrific death by fire of Aharon's two sons Nadav and Avihu for introducing *esh zarah*, an alien or unauthorized fire, into the Mikdash. There is much discussion in the *mesorah* as to what that might mean, ranging from less than complimentary (even though they were tzaddikim) to most laudatory. These deaths and their attendant mystery, with Aharon's dignified, faith-filled response of silence, with Moshe's sudden grasping of the unfathomable concept of "*b'krovai akadesh*," stand out in the spiritual foundation of our faith system, as we fixate upon it throughout the generations. Such deaths, the inexplicable, are, for reasons known only to God, part of our national legacy. How interesting – and how telling – that we read about this incident in the Torah portion immediately after Pesach, the joyous holiday of our freedom.

This year is a leap year, with Pesach celebrated a month later than usual. And yet the *parashah* that follows immediately after Pesach is Acharei Mos, meaning literally "After the Death," which opens with a recounting of the death of Aharon's two sons, Nadav and Avihu!

The period after Pesach is known as the Sefirah, when we count the days until Shavuos. In our minds, however, the first reaction to the word *sefirah* is the mourning period after Pesach during which we do not marry, listen to music, or even take a haircut, because we are mourning the deaths of the twenty-four thousand students of Rabbi Akiva, who met an untimely mass death during that time.

What is all this about?

*Yevamos* 62b recounts the death of the students and mentions only cryptically that they died because they did not treat each other with proper respect. What does that mean? What did they do? Were they haughty? I don't know. How did they die? The Gemara says they died a cruel and difficult death, of *askerah*. *Askerah* is understood to refer to a restrictive disease of the throat, perhaps diphtheria or some other asphyxiating illness. Why that specifically? Because, the *meforshim* (Maharal and others) say, it affects the uniquely human power of speech, a gift they "abused" by their behavior, in belittling their fellows. The Maharsha spells out that they were not respectful of each other's Torah knowledge.

If, as we believe, Torah is for us life itself (*"ki hu chayecha v'orech yamecha"* [Devarim 30:20]), they thus used their very God-given powers of communication to belittle the value of their colleagues' lives. And they were punished specifically at this time of the year because this is the very time of the year, between Pesach and Shavuos, that the healing powers of the relevant medications and treatments should have been the most effective (see *Shabbos* 147b), and for them they were not.

It is interesting to note that Rav Sherira Gaon, in his *Iggeres* to the community of Kairouan, refers to the death of Rabbi Akiva's students as resulting from *shmad*. Perhaps he is saying that they were murdered by the Romans during the Hadrianic persecutions, as was their rebbe, Rabbi Akiva, and the use of the term *askerah* is a deliberately oblique reference, chosen for reasons unknown to us. But their offense, such as it is, remains the same.

In either event, this tragedy, and our mourning it, follows hard on the joyous holiday of Pesach, when we should be in purely celebratory mode, especially as we begin the countdown to Shavuos and Matan Torah. How many blood libels and other depredations have we been subjected to during this period that should have been purely joyful? One cannot help but come to the conclusion that this juxtaposition is intentional.

We have been conditioned, from our earliest history, even from the very day that God came to rest His Presence in our midst in the Mishkan, that we cannot take our joy for granted. Being God's special nation is the most privileged position in the world to be in. But like *tumah* and *taharah*, in which the greatest potential for *taharah* carries with it, inherently, the greatest potential for *tumah*, exalted status before God also carries with it enhanced responsibility, obligation for perfection, and potential to fall.

God hates haughtiness. It is a not-uncommon human trait that exposes an ugly *middah*, one that opens the door to that terrible malady which is a physical manifestation of a spiritual illness, *tzaraas*, *lo aleinu*. We don't see *tzaraas* today, but haughtiness hasn't gone anywhere. And haughtiness on the part of those who should know better is all the more offensive.

Champions know that upon winning their championships, their training and conditioning begins all over again, or they will fall behind and lose what they have so painfully gained. All of us Jews – and that includes yeshiva princelings – who have been chosen to be *mamleches kohanim v'goy kadosh*, who relive each year at this time that moment when God Himself plucked us from the depths of bitter bondage and placed us on the very top of the world, do well to remember that at this dizzying height, we must beware the slippery slope that threatens on every side, the pitfalls that are obvious and those that are not apparent at all but that beckon to the unheeding and the unmindful, even as the *esh zarah* brought down fire on the holy sons of Aharon Hakohen, even as for the students of Rabbi Akiva, the heady heights of intellectual Torah achievement somehow obscured, *lo aleinu*, key aspects of what real Torah achievement is all about.

*Parashas Acharei Mos 5779*

# Snatched Away, God Forbid

Lest you lose your chance: One of the cruel realities of life is that you can plan and expect, even most reasonably, but in the end you never know. Who – what normal person – would have imagined, much less expected, the devastating losses from COVID-19? How many widows, widowers, orphans so numerous, are suddenly bereft, often even without the chance to say "goodbye," or "I love you." Boatloads of tragedy. May Hashem protect us. It's bad enough when people who love each other don't bother to express it as they should – one of the greatest gifts a human being can confer. It's bad enough when people who love each other go to sleep at night angry or sulking – something they should not do. What happens when lost opportunities for the most important things in life are, *lo aleinu*, suddenly and irretrievably lost forever?

I am haunted by the story I heard some years ago about a family in New York, told to me by my relative, who knows them. In normal hectic life, families often don't all get together at the same time except at the Shabbos meals. And, given human nature, that's when "fights" sometimes break out – a situation that has been homiletically warned against with the admonition *"lo sevaaru esh b'chol moshvoseichem"* (Shemos 35:3), do not light a "fire" in your homes on Shabbos.

In this true story, an argument flared between father and teenaged daughter. Words were said that should not have been. Terribly upset, the father rose from the table and stalked off, to let his anger cool down. When he failed to return, he was found dead, apparently of a heart attack, in another room. The last angry words that father heard from his daughter could never be taken back, nor his to her. Their effect was irrevocable.

We should never wait – we should never defer expressing the love and appreciation we have for others. It's too important and too precious. And because, as life sometimes teaches in hard lessons, *lo aleinu*, you never know.

*Parashas Acharei Mos-Kedoshim 5780*

# Temporary Insanity

We all know them. They do self-destructive things while well aware, at least intellectually, that those acts are self-destructive. They are the sick diabetics – retinopathy, nephropathy, and neuropathy notwithstanding – who continue to eat every bad thing. They are the smokers – heart disease and lung disease notwithstanding – who continue to light up. They are those who sometimes do and sometimes say things they should not, and they know they should not.

If they know, why do they do it?

They know that they are harming their beloved children with their self-destructive acts. They are not bad people, or indifferent. They do care, and they do know. But they do it.

They are the sinners who may not be essentially sinful people, who believe, and who know the score, yet they do it anyway. They don't want to break up their families, ruin and scar those they love, but in the heat of the moment, even knowing what's at stake, they do it anyway.

We know them because they are everywhere. We know them because, to a greater or lesser degree, they are us. Most of us, at least sometimes, do really foolish things, things that if we were to stop and think clearly, we would not do. But sometimes we do them anyway, not because we are actually stupid, or necessarily evil, but because at that critical moment, we are temporarily insane.

We know what we are doing, but we rationalize and allow our judgment to be clouded. Much of the struggle of the moral and religious life is about fighting off those insane impulses. They have to be insane moments, because doing those acts makes no sense at all.

Chazal teach us that *ein adam choteh ela im ken nichnas bo ruach shtus*. A man would not sin if he were not taken over, at least for that moment, by a spirit of foolishness. Call it a form of temporary insanity. The downside to his sinful or foolish action is too great for a rational person to do it; if he did it anyway, we must conclude that his rational judgment has clouded over. He was temporarily insane.

It does not exculpate him in any way – he's not really crazy; he has just allowed himself not to act rationally.

This "insanity" can be finely nuanced and is not limited to actual sin or obviously self-destructive behavior. It might even *pose* as meritorious behavior (the Devil is such a devil!). But the result can be self-destructive. The level of risk that a man with a dependent family subjects himself to, when he can help it, is not and should not be the same as someone in that same circumstance who has no one at all dependent upon him. He owes that to them, and he should be aware of that obligation at all times.

But in life, we don't always see risk even when it is there before us. We don't think of it, sometimes, when we should, even when what we choose to do may be a good thing, an innocent thing, but dangerous. In our moment of "temporary insanity," in a moment of passion, even for a good end, we may not think of it. But we have to. Too much is at stake. Or we may be, at that moment, so committed that we think we must follow through, no matter what. Most people with families, with responsibilities, do think of those responsibilities, and that holds them back. They are, simply put, less likely to go skydiving on a lark than a young kid with no responsibilities at all. (That getting killed jumping out of an airplane for no reason at all would also kill their parents, they seem not to think about.)

Nadav and Avihu, the older sons of Aharon, died on the day the Mishkan was inaugurated for the trespass of *esh zarah*, an unauthorized, inappropriate flame. Exactly what that means is not made clear. Their motive is not made clear. Whether they were, at that time, altogether good or not so altogether good is also not made clear, although the preponderance of opinion is that they were holy indeed: *b'krovai akadesh*. Chazal take us through the various scenarios regarding their behavior, positive and negative.

Only later is it mentioned that they had no children. It is apparent that this too played a role in what happened to them. Some hold that without children, lacking the *zechus* of great or worthy descendants in whose merit they might have been spared, they perished.

But there is another way to think about that.

Hashem spoke to Moshe *acharei mos*, after the death of Aharon's sons, *b'korvasam lifnei Hashem va'yamusu*. They died when they brought an unauthorized *ketores korban*. And so one would naturally take *b'korvasam* to refer to their bringing a *korban*. In understanding what happened here, the Lubavitcher Rebbe cites the Ohr Hachaim's remarkable insight into the text that goes to the very nature of Hashem's holiness and how the very greatest among us might strive to come close to that holiness, and to the limits and boundaries that even the very greatest and most pure must adhere to. For the Ribbono shel Olam, even in His Revelation to us, even in the relative closeness He permitted to that unique generation, is still *esh ochlah*, a consuming flame.

He may approach us to the degree He chooses. We, however, may make no assumptions. No matter how pure our motives, no matter how ardent our desire to be close to Him – and there is much we can and should do to be close to Him – even for Moshe and Aharon and Aharon's holy sons, there is a limit.

In the initial description of the tragedy, in Parashas Shemini, the Torah tells us that Nadav and Avihu each took his *machtah*, his firepan, placed fire in it, put *ketores*, the holy incense, on the fire, and *va'yakrivu*, they brought that as an offering, albeit one that was not authorized. And for that trespass, they were, sadly and tragically, consumed by Godly fire. In Acharei Mos, the word *va'yakrivu*, they *brought* near, is replaced with *b'korvasam*, they *came* near, elucidating what they were apparently up to, what they were trying to do.

*B'korvasam* – in their ardent passion to be *close* to Him, they came *too* close. They threw caution to the wind and grasped where they should not have. They thought it was worth it, come what may. God kissed them – but they tried, in their zeal, in their passion, to kiss God. And they were burned. It was too much for any mortal. The Ohr Hachaim suggests that if it were Moshe himself, the result would have been the same. *B'krovai akadesh.* Only those close to Hashem, as were Nadav and Avihu, could aspire to such a thing. But it was beyond what was possible for a human being. They reached for a level of holiness that was incompatible with earthly, mortal life. And perhaps because they had no inhibiting circumstances – *u'vanim lo hayu lahem*, because they had no children that they felt responsible for, that they had to live for – they allowed themselves to go too far, even knowing that they should not, perhaps even that they *could not*. They did it anyway, and they paid the price.

Moshe, Aharon, and Miriam famously passed from this world in the gentlest and holiest way possible, *b'neshikas Hashem*, a celestial "kiss" with which Hakadosh Baruch Hu lovingly takes back the tzaddik's holy *neshamah* from the earthly vessel that had contained it. From time to time, we encounter this phenomenon, apparently, even today. It is always Hashem Who bestows this "kiss"; the tzaddik is the recipient. As the Lubavitcher Rebbe describes it, Nadav and Avihu were so impassioned with their love and devotion to Hashem, so taken with, so drawn to His divine holiness that, perhaps impulsively, they could not hold back. In the heat of the moment, their judgment failed them. They attempted to penetrate a level, an awareness of God that was so supremely holy that, in their attempt to "kiss" Him, they absorbed with that kiss *esh ochlah*. Though their physical bodies remained intact, the living human spirit within them was consumed by heavenly fire.

It's exalted, but that's literally no way to live. The Rebbe quotes Yeshayahu Hanavi on the way the Creator expects us to function in the world He created: "For thus says the Lord that created the heavens, He is God; that formed the earth and made it, He established it, He created it not a waste, He formed it to be inhabited: I am the Lord, and there is none else" (Yeshayahu 45:18).

*I did not create the world*, says Hashem, *to be empty* – לֹא־תֹהוּ בְרָאָהּ לָשֶׁבֶת יְצָרָהּ – *but to be lived in by human beings living human lives, pursuing human pursuits*. Be spiritual, by all means, but be human.

The Gemara (*Shabbos* 33b) tells us the story of Rabbi Shimon bar Yochai, whose yahrzeit falls on Lag b'Omer, and his son Rabbi Elazar, who had to hide in a cave for twelve years while the Romans sought to kill them, living on carobs and water that were miraculously provided. All twelve years they were deeply immersed in Torah, shedding virtually every human mundane concern as they became more and more purified, to the point of becoming otherworldly. When word reached them (also miraculously) that the edict on their lives was nullified, they emerged from the cave to find the world proceeding in its mundane way. They spied a man tending his field. How could he be wasting his life on such a trivial pursuit, when he could and should be busy with *chayei olam*, enduring matters of the spirit? They had achieved, in the cave, such an exalted level of purity and holiness that the normal, mundane functions of the world were intolerable to them. The intensity of their holy intolerance of the mundane was enough to cause whatever they looked at in disapproval to be burned up on the spot.

*Enough!* a heavenly voice proclaimed. *Do you seek to destroy the world I have created? Return to your cave!*

And they did, for another twelve months. Finally, they mellowed enough to allow for, to be tolerant of, what the rest of us would consider normal human function. It's interesting that thereafter, it was the older, more mature, more seasoned Rabbi Shimon whose role it was to mitigate the zeal of the younger, more zealous, more difficult to reconcile with mundane life Rabbi Elazar.

*I did not create the world*, says Hashem, *to be empty, but to be lived in by human beings living human lives, pursuing human pursuits. Be spiritual, by all means, but be human.*

We must strive for holiness, but not in a way that burns us up or destroys those near to us, that leaves them bereft. We must be careful with our lives, physical and spiritual. We can respect the ordinary, admire the extraordinary, aspire to be extraordinary, to be as great as we have the capacity to be. To be as close to the Ribbono shel Olam as we can be, by channeling our lives and our actions toward holiness and away from the abundant foolishness of this world. To take those moments of high passion, when we are blessed enough to have them, not consuming ourselves in the flames but harnessing that light and energy and power to illuminate all the otherwise mundane moments in our lives. To be, however exalted, of this world God has presented us with, perfecting it as we pass through it, as is our mandate, all the while never losing sight of our responsibilities within the world, never forgetting as we toil to be exceptional, no matter how high we reach, that we also have a mandate to be normal, to be human.

לֹא־תֹהוּ בְרָאָהּ לָשֶׁבֶת יְצָרָהּ

*Parashas Acharei Mos 5782*

# Je t'aime

*Je t'aime.* I love you.

You probably recognize this as French, and if you do, you probably also recognize that it is in the more intimate grammatical form, the contracted *je te aime*, rather than the more formal *je vous aime*. The two phrases say the same thing, but they actually don't.

Like many languages, French has two forms for the second person. These languages (Yiddish included) have separate words for the singular and plural forms of the word we in contemporary English would render as "you," using the same word for the second person singular as well as plural. English used to have separate forms, but *thou* has disappeared, giving way to *you* for both.

But the difference is not just in singular and plural. It has to do with respect and with intimacy, with familiarity. *I love you* uttered to an intimate is not the same as *I love you* said to, say, a favored politician or performer. In the languages that differentiate the second-person pronoun, someone we are not intimately connected with is addressed, as a form of respect, in the plural form (*vous*) rather than in the singular (*tu*), even though one is addressing one person.

*Je t'aime* is reserved for one who is intimately near and dear.

We see the analog in our own Jewish world when, out of reverence and respect, a *talmid* addresses his rebbe in the third person (*Would Rebbe like a cup of tea?*). This is a holdover from a more formal past, when this was actually a common form of addressing one's "betters" – his lordship, his majesty, his honor the judge, etc. (I have patients – always *frum* Yidden – who address me this way. I appreciate the gesture, but it always makes me cringe: *I know the truth about myself.*)

And so the old joke: Why in the Aseres Hadibros does it say *Lo signov*, second person singular, while in Parashas Kedoshim, it says *Lo signovu*, the more respectful second person plural? My old friend Mr. Engel, *a"h*, a master of cynical realism, used to explain: the more respectful form of the commandment not to steal is reserved for *de bessere menschen*, the more important, highfalutin' people.

Actually, if you look at the commandments in Parashas Kedoshim Tihyu, enjoining us to observe these mitzvos and to be holy, like *lo signovu*, they are nearly all couched in the grammatical plural form. And then there's a sudden switch to the singular: *lo saashok, lo sigzol, lo salin pe'ulas sochir.* These are about not oppressing those who are under our control and who are dependent upon us.

What's the difference between a *ganav* and a *gazlan*? The classic explanation is that a *ganav* steals in secret and a *gazlan* steals openly. Thus, the *ganav* is seen as worse than the *gazlan*, because while the brazen *gazlan* is not afraid of man or of God, the *ganav* is not afraid of God but steals in secret because he *is* afraid of man.

The context here, however, changes the equation somewhat. People often do what everybody else does. This can serve as an excuse, of sorts, for bad or subpar behavior. People let things slide along with "everybody else" and, looking around, don't feel particularly guilty about it. It is thus addressed in the plural form. But there are categories in life one cannot make any excuses about, because they are simply too important. They are not as much about what we should be doing as long as we are here, but they go to the essence of *why* we are here. They are about goodness and justice and kindness and *chesed*. They are essential to the very purpose of creation, and they are the reason Hashem put us on this earth.

And so the outstanding exception to the list of plural-worded mitzvos that begin the *parashah* is about feeding the poor. All these mitzvos that relate to tzedakah and *chesed* and justice, about not oppressing those who depend upon us for their livelihood, are couched in the singular.

I had a very scary teacher in the seventh grade who would single out a student and ask a question; the student would have to rise and give the answer. If the poor victim looked around, presumably in the hope of catching a clue from a classmate as to what the answer was, the teacher would sharply say, "Don't roll your eyes around like a kewpie doll! Look at me and tell me the answer!" That student, at that moment, was absolutely alone, facing his judge. (My insides are roiling now even as I think about it all these years later.)

*L'havdil*, the Torah is telling us here, I suggest, with this shift from plural to singular, that for some categories of behavior, we can't look around us for support or excuses; we cannot point to community standards to hide behind. It's completely up to us. The Torah is an all-encompassing guide for life, in all its varied facets.

We are a communal people, and in many spheres, we act out our lives as part of a larger whole. But not in everything. There is a reason each individual is here in this world, and it is the duty of that individual to perform. Looking around for support from communal "norms" that don't measure up is like rolling your eyes around like a kewpie doll and will get you no further than it got those poor students who withered and wilted and collapsed into their seats in embarrassed – indeed, humiliated – failure.

Sometimes, use of the plural may be addressing the singular or the plural – the individual, the group, or both. But use of the singular is very specific. It means you. It means me. It means the Torah is telling us, where it really counts, when it comes to goodness and fairness and kindness and tzedakah and *chesed*, each of us stands before and answers to our Creator, alone with our choices, alone with our actions.

*Kedoshim tihyu.* It's what Hashem requires of us because He loves us. Because He wants us to be as good, as perfect as we can be. Because, in His closeness and intimacy with us, he declares, *"Je t'aime."*

*Parashas Kedoshim Tihyu 5782, Yerushalayim Ir Hakodesh*

# Emor

## Tosefes Kedushah

Yechezkel Hanavi lived in a time of great turmoil, upheaval, and downfall. The people were beset by fear, confusion, and hopelessness. He told us there will still be life, there will still be Judaism, the nation of Israel will survive and thrive, even as normal national life as they knew it was in utter disarray. And he offered us a formula to help us get there.

Parashas Emor describes the enhanced state of *kedushah* of the Kohanim and the special regulations that apply to them. A Kohen cannot become *tamei l'meis*, unless it is for one of the closest of relatives. He may not destroy his beard, he may not marry a divorced woman; Kohanim must maintain an enhanced state of *kedushah*.

Yechezkel, in the *haftarah*, restates some of these laws. Chazal were hard pressed to reconcile some of his statements with the laws as written in the Torah, which is a broader discussion, beyond the scope of this essay. But why Yechezkel says that a Kohen should not marry a widow, when the Torah says he can, is, for us today, right on message.

There are those who explain that statement as referring to the Kohen Gadol, who indeed may not marry a widow. But the straightforward language certainly seems to refer to *any* Kohen. And the reason, Radak tells us, is that when we've fallen and need to stand up again, when we need to rise above terrible circumstances, *tosefes kedushah* is called for. Enhanced holiness. To help us rise above where we are.

During COVID-19 lockdowns, at a time when we could not say Kaddish or Kedushah, acting in our daily mundane lives with *tosefes kedushah* offered us hope and a way. God did not take out advertisements in the newspapers telling us exactly and specifically what to do to change our circumstances, but He has told us plainly, *kedoshim tihyu*. A healthy dose of *tosefes kedushah* can go a long way.

How we talk. The language we use. The things we read and the things we look at. The things we think about. *The things we talk about.* How we spend our time. How we look upon others. How we treat others. How we *talk about* others. How we treat those near to us, as well as the stranger. How we judge others. How we regard the dedicated pious among us. What we think and do about how we dress and present ourselves to the world, about modesty, about care regarding the beard and *peyos*. About learning Torah. About how we *daven*. About doing what we can to effect *tosefes kedushah* in our personal lives, even as we wait hopefully for the time when we can come together again, in loving community, and proclaim, *"Kadosh! Kadosh! Kadosh!"* declaring before all, *"Yisgadal v'yiskadash Shmei Rabbah!"*

*Parashas Emor 5780*


# Armed

The entrance courtyard to her home is striking in its profound messiness. It is full of junk, but a closer look tells you that there is some order to the junk. And it may not be altogether junk to everyone: one man's junk is another man's treasure. *Och and vey* to such treasure: it is objectively old and junky, but there are those in this world – too many – to whom an old, worn coat is blessed, welcome relief from the cold and damp that he would otherwise not have.

People deposit here old, used stuff that is still too usable to throw out when there are poor people with families who cannot afford to buy such things for themselves. And here in Jerusalem, there are, sadly, many such poor families.

The hard-luck stories are endless. The poverty, in this time of plenty, is profound. And, in sections of this town, there is plenty of it.

She is no youngster, but she is fully occupied, as she has always been, with tzedakah and *chesed*. She raises money for the desperate. There are, of course, others, but she is a primary address for those in dire need. It has always been so with her, as it was with her late husband, *a"h*. She herself does not have money, but she is immeasurably wealthy.

There is a photo on the wall of her apartment that she showed us. It has about two hundred people in it, all her descendants, *kinnehora*. What's especially striking about that is that she was the lone survivor of her family, every member of which was cruelly murdered by the Germans, may their accursed memory be blotted out. Somehow, as a baby, she was successfully hidden and later brought to America, where she grew up, married, and eventually *went up* to Eretz Yisrael, involved constantly in Torah and *chesed*. May God grant her many more healthy years doing His work.

Imagine if the six million had not been murdered. If that large, beautiful family is the result of one saved soul, what would there have been thriving today? The loss is not just the unimaginable six million. It is the unimaginably unimaginable loss of each of those souls multiplied by the hundreds and thousands.

This is a backdrop to a parallel story – I believe a closely related one – that I experienced the same day.

That very morning, my local rabbi, a gentle, soft-spoken and sweet-tempered *talmid chacham*, walked into shul with a pistol strapped to his hip. He teaches Torah in a yeshiva, the road to which renders him vulnerable, God forbid, to deadly attack by the latter-day successors to the Germans, those who would kill us all, God forbid, if they could.

We know that everything is from Heaven. And we also know that Heaven requires of us that we do *hishtadlus* for ourselves even as we look to God to protect us. And so a *rav* in Yerushalayim must pack a pistol to protect himself and his family while he goes to teach Torah. There has been a rash of terrible attacks and murders, mutilations and attempted mutilations, leaving a tragic army of grieving widows and orphans. All while the nations of the world do their best, when they even bother to *cluck cluck* about it, to keep the Jews from defending themselves. And, while they are at it, being very *understanding* of the "desperation" that drives those murderers to do their evil mayhem, "by any means necessary."

We have a complex belief system, in which we have faith in God, we trust Him, we place our hope in Him. But the specifics of what we hope for, what we pray for, are not necessarily what we get. For that, we need trust and faith, sometimes a great deal of it, sometimes a nearly unbearable amount of it. God has His own *cheshbonos*, a bigger picture than we can possibly perceive. May we not be tested, please God; some of us are so tested, *lo aleinu*. We pray, always, that Hashem's blessing be obvious, not requiring reservoirs of faith to perceive it as blessing.

There is a midrash on Tehillim 119 that Klal Yisrael complain to the Ribbono shel Olam. David Hamelech, for all his greatness, was beset by critics and detractors his whole life. They even tried to delegitimize him as a Jew. They have dug many pits, he says (Tehillim 119:85), trying to make me fall in, that I be lost. Ribbono shel Olam! they cry, You have commanded us (Vayikra 22:28) not to slaughter an animal and its child on the same day. That would be cruel. And yet You have permitted our enemies to dig so many pits to engulf us that, as described in Hoshea 10:14, mothers and children are slaughtered, not just on the same day, but all together.

Oh, how bitterly we have come to learn, *Rachmana litzlan*, how often exactly that has been our tragic fate in this world. A millionfold! And yet, *b'emunah shleimah*, challenged as it may be, we cling to Him.

The latter part of Parashas Emor presents the various *yamim tovim*, and the latter part of that segment presents the *yom tov* of Sukkos. It commemorates our forefathers' exodus from Egypt and Hashem's protecting them in the desert with His *anenei hakavod* hovering protectively over them for the forty years of their journey.

We step outside the comfort of our homes and move into the *schach*-covered, ramshackle, temporary abode. As we enter, especially on the first night, we pray that Hashem accept our service of moving into the sukkah to fulfill His mitzvah, that He accept our placing our faith in Him, and that we be blessed, as were our forefathers in the wilderness, with His protection. We seek His protection, not only from the usual and unusual dangers of this life, but in the life after this life, from the fiery *zerem u'matar* that awaits the sinners and the wicked.

But life and history have taught us that the feared *zerem u'matar* are not only manifestations of that other world; they have so painfully and tragically marked the lives of so many, *lo aleinu*, in this world, in nearly every generation, spectacularly in some. For those of faith, it is part of the deep unknowable.

That wonderful woman's spectacular family, which arose from the ashes that engulfed her, is a sign. That pistol-packing *rav*, whose bravery and whose efforts – along with those of his fellows who face danger and loss every day – rebuild this holy land and Torah in it, is a sign. The message in the Torah is a sign.

We have a mandate to live our lives as God has commanded us. Torah, mitzvos, *maasim tovim*. *Chesed*. Dedication. Prayer and faith. To place our faith in God for the big picture and also for the little picture, the here and now.

To arm ourselves with Torah, mitzvos, and *maasim tovim*, with *chesed* and with *rachamim*. And to arm ourselves, when necessary, with the pistol or with whatever else is necessary, for such is life, sometimes, and we are commanded to hold our lives precious and dear.

Learn Torah and live it. Achieve holiness by whatever means we are able. Cling to life and propagate it, support it, wherever we can. Do justice and place our reliance on our Father in Heaven to spread His Succah of protection over us all, in this life and the next.

*Parashas Emor 5782, Yerushalayim Ir Hakodesh*

## Polin

My brother, who is four and a half years older than me, was haunted by a dream he remembered, in which he saw our father, in severe distress, opening his mouth to scream, but with no sound coming out.

One day, he told our father about it. My father told him that it was no dream. It actually happened, in 1945, while he held my brother in his arms.

A group of surviving Jews was sheltering in a building in a Polish city, organized by a Jewish rescue agency. A mob of Poles, their fellow citizens, was attacking the building, trying to break in and murder the survivors, my parents and brother included. They retreated to the roof, from which they frantically called out for the police to rescue them. They screamed and screamed, my father and mother among them. With my brother in his arms, my father screamed until there was no voice left. He opened his mouth to scream but no sound came out. This is what my brother, then aged two or three, saw, what seared itself into his memory and his psyche, which in later years he thought must have been a bad dream.

Who could believe it was actually true? Who would imagine that after a Holocaust, there would be those, who themselves had suffered in their way, who sought to perpetuate that Holocaust?

At Yad Vashem, the moving and deeply disturbing memorial in Jerusalem to the millions of victims of the Holocaust, there is also a special area to honor the Righteous Among the Nations, *chassidei umos ha'olam* (חסידי אומות העולם), who risked and often gave their lives and those of their families to shelter and rescue Jews, out of selfless heroism.

By far, the largest group of these gallant and righteous people is Polish, over sixty-eight hundred of them, about one in thirty-seven hundred ethnic Poles then alive in Poland. There are people listed from many nations, in smaller numbers, including even Germany and Austria. With the greatest concentration of Jews in Europe, Poland was also the site of the greatest mass murder and thus provided the greatest opportunity for heroism. But that leaves 3,699 out of every thirty-seven hundred who are not listed. May we never be tested – and most people don't have the courage, especially when terrorized, to be such heroes – but Poland is Poland.

When the Germans were driven out, the few surviving Jews who emerged from their hiding places or who came from the camps or other places often returned to their original homes to see if they could find any relatives still alive. They were at great risk for murderous attack by their neighbors, who found the survival of those pesky Jews annoying, as they were often already living in those Jews' homes, wearing their clothes, and eating off their dishes and resented the prospect of possibly having to give it all back. Even Jews who were quick to inform them that they were not interested in property but were only hoping to find living relatives were at times murdered "just in case," or just out of hatred.

And often Jews were attacked, as were my parents and brother, not because they were poking about their stolen property, but because they had the temerity to be alive. The attackers sought to "rectify" that.

In August 1939, there were about fifteen hundred Jews living in Jedwabne, Poland, out of a total population of about twenty-two hundred. With the entry of the Germans, the killings began. On July 10, 1941, hundreds of Jewish men, women, and children were locked into the town shul, which was then set on fire, immolating them all, their screams filling the night. Poles described how the Germans perpetrated this ghastly mass murder. The event they were describing was true, but tied to a big lie. The Germans were actually *not* involved. It was their Polish neighbors who burned those Jews alive.

In May 2019, there was a major demonstration in Warsaw, protesting diplomatic initiatives to help Jews claim prewar property stolen from them by Poles. Placards were angrily raised high, denying any need for such arrangements. And there were placards that read, "I will not apologize for Jedwabne!" Another said, "This is Poland, not Polin!"

Polin is the way Poland is rendered in traditional Jewish writing. It actually suggests something positive, a place to rest. Jews fled to Poland many years earlier from persecutions in western Europe and found respite there.

This past week was the one hundredth reading of Parashas Emor since my father read it at his bar mitzvah in Reishe (Rzeszow), Poland, in 1919. Things were done somewhat differently in those days. Boys were called up for the *maftir*. The recitation of the *haftarah* was done quietly, by the entire congregation (Chassidic style), except for the last two verses, which were read out loud by the bar mitzvah. And then after davening, *lekach und bronfen* (cake and schnapps). That was it. No big party. No catering hall. No sushi bar. Rich and poor alike.

There was another difference in that time and place. They had only recently ventured out into the open. When my father first put on his tefillin a few weeks earlier, it was done in an underground bunker. Upstairs, Poland was "breaking out," like a war (or an epidemic).

In newly independent Poland, many of the citizens celebrated their newly formed republic with pogroms, all over the country. Many Jews were killed or otherwise hurt in every terrible way. Poland was being Poland.

Polin. *Poh lin*: *"Rest here."* Jews migrated to Poland at a time when life was becoming almost impossible in western Europe, with burnings and massacres and expulsions and oppression of every kind. They found a haven. God tells us not to hate the Egyptians despite what they did to us because they were a haven for us when we needed them.

But why do we need safe havens in the first place? Why have we not been in our own land, safe and secure?

Because we sinned against the God Who gave us the land, so grievously that it did just as He said it would if we rebelled: it vomited us out. As usual, we, as a nation, brought it upon ourselves.

There are many kinds of misdeeds that the Torah tells us might bring this about. Parashas Behar opens with a discussion of some of those principles that are so basic to who we are and how we became who we are, how we come to have what we have. Just as keeping Shabbos serves as a testament that it is God Almighty Who created the world, keeping Shemittah and Yovel and the justice with which we treat those in our society who, due to their misfortune, look to us for safety and sustenance bear testimony as to Who really owns the things we "own." Keep these laws, the Torah says (25:18), and you will sit safely and securely in your own land. It will produce sustenance for you aplenty, and you will be satiated, even when others are hungry.

We are told that the Babylonian exile came about at least in part as payment for the many times Shemittah was not observed when our forefathers were in the land. When a Jew knowingly does not keep Shabbos, does not keep Shemittah, does not give tzedakah, and deals harshly with those under his control, he is denying God. We have paid a long, long time for those sins.

Obviously, the many generations of pious, God-fearing Jews who are kindly and loving and *gomlei chesed* have not been enough to bring us home. Not yet, at least. Surely it will count in the big picture. There have been and still are too many who just don't get it. Today, most of those were just raised that way. In the past, there were those who just walked away. And tragically, there were so many who were torn away.

It is time for us, all of us, to return. To our God and to our land. It is time for *poh lin* to refer not to a place in exile that is temporarily less hostile than others, but to our own God-given place. It is time for us to arrive *el hamenuchah v'el hanachalah asher Hashem Elokecha nosen lecha*, a place where a bar mitzvah boy need not don his tefillin for the first time in an underground bunker while hateful, murderous thugs rampage above in the streets; a place where we sit, by the grace of our loving God, in safety and security and tranquility, amidst the bountiful blessings of the land, a beautiful, magical, wonderful place, a holy and hallowed place, blessed by God and sanctified by our own righteous lives, the Land of Israel.

*Parashas Behar 5779*

# Bechukosai

## A Healthy Nation

Being very patriotic Americans, our family observed Memorial Day weekend with not one but *two* barbecues. And being *especially* patriotic, we had a great deal – an excess – of yummy, smoky food. And we all had some. After all, we are truly, seriously, devotedly patriotic Americans.

And because we are also devoted Jews, fervently Orthodox, the day before being Shabbos, we honored the holy day with three major, religiously inspired, belly-filling, mind-numbing feasts, in addition to a Kiddush and Melaveh Malkah.

Properly *frum* and properly patriotic.

A few years ago, we attended a baseball game between the Hatzalah and the New York Police Department teams. How disturbingly fascinating it was to note the generally slim NYPD players and the big *chulent* bellies common on the Hatzalah team. How ironic, it seemed, that some of the very fellows who devotedly spend their days and nights rushing their *chulent*-bellied, chest-clutching compadres to the emergency department, *lo aleinu*, don't seem to make the connection with themselves. Most of us are quite the same. It would be funny if it weren't so unfunny. (Oh – not every NYPD player was slim; there were a couple of *frum* cops there too.)

Parashas Bechukosai opens with the promise that if we hold up our end of the bargain, our agreement with God, He will bless us with peace, prosperity, and security. It describes the good things that will be ours if we are faithful to God. We will have secure sustenance, food aplenty. The nurturing rains will fall; the land and the trees will yield so much produce that the harvesters will still be busy collecting the abundance of this year's crop when the sowers of the next crop begin their work (see the beautiful parallel prophecy in Amos 9:13). We will have to consume the older produce to make room for the abundance of the new. "You will eat your bread to satiety" (Vayikra 26:5).

Here and in Parashas Behar (25:19), the concept of satiety is presented quite clearly in the Midrash as a notion other than what we apparently have in mind (or in action) when we have at it at that Kiddush, or at the Shabbos table, or at the barbecue. "*Sova*," here referring to satiety, does not necessarily refer to overeating or even to eating one's physical fill. Rather, it refers to our eating not much at all, *kimah*, a bit, but that which we do eat will be so blessed within us that it will satisfy us while it keeps us healthy. That is the true blessing.

Throughout the history of mankind, in most of the world, for most people, getting enough to eat has been a major challenge of survival. Many in my own generation, children of refugees and survivors, were pushed by their elders to eat out of habitual fear that there may not be enough tomorrow (not me; I have only myself to blame). We live, thank God, in a time and a place in which food is plentiful and available to virtually everyone. That's a great thing. But like most everything else in life, too much, and without *seichel*, is also no good. Eating, for the Jew, requires prayer. A valuable lesson for life, implicit in the *pesukim*, is that it also requires the intellect.

And so, with *seichel*, and the intellect, we segue into another aspect of the lesson and the mandate of *Im b'chukosai telechu v'es mitzvosai tishmeru v'asisem osam* (26:3). Chazal teach that this means not just that we perform the commandments, but that we be ardently and energetically diligent – *amelim* – in the *study* of Torah as well as in its fulfillment. Indeed, intensive study – *laboring at it* – is part of that fulfillment. But while we must engage it with all the powers of our intellect, at whatever level of capability we possess, it is not, in fact, about the intellect but about knowing how to serve God.

Historically, we have been plagued at different times by those who lose sight of what it's really about, and, divorced from the spirit, disconnected from learning as a means of serving God, they are capable of, to use the classic extreme example (which has been known to happen), studying complex and sophisticated Talmudic issues while smoking on Shabbos. The driving force of *amelim* is not just intellectual, but to know the will of God *for the sake of serving Him*.

Certainly not every Jew is an intellectual, but we are a people thoroughly bound up with the intellect. It is a tool for learning as well as for understanding the rest of the world. But it can be a slippery slope. Even here, too much, in the wrong way, is also no good.

As a people, we have certain predilections. In the *haftarah* for Bechukosai, Yirmiyahu Hanavi bemoans the fact that in his time, the Jews had a terrible inclination for *avodah zarah*, seemingly built in, part of their makeup, etched on their hearts. It was a built-in lead weight that had to be thrown off. In more modern times, a different kind of *avodah zarah* plagues the Jews: the misdirected intellect. Jews have been in the forefront of nearly every bad intellectually driven movement and ism that distances them from their Father in Heaven. It is the latter-day equivalent of the *avodah zarah* that the *navi* decries.

God calls upon us to follow His ways. *Im b'chukosai telechu*, if we follow that path, with energy, with intellect, with diligence, with loyalty, with *seichel*, if we labor at it for the sake of being close to Him, He will bless us in every way. The earth and the trees will produce their plenty, we will live at peace and without fear, our enemies will fear us, we will be satiated physically and spiritually, and we will, individually and as a nation, in every way, be *healthy*.

*Parashas Bechukosai 5779*

# Ask Me, Just Ask Me

After the miraculous victory in 1967, we were all swept up in the heady excitement of the remarkable, clearly heaven-sent victory in Eretz Yisrael. Just days before that conflict, we were all so frightened, so aware that our people and our Holy Land were so vulnerable, as vicious, blood-thirsty enemies literally rattled their sabers and openly declared before all their intention to murder the Jews of Israel (*as a starting point*). Thousands of graves were already being prepared in the parks of Israel, in case…

More than seven hundred young Israelis died in that war, a terribly high price for such a small country to pay, but also a price other nations described as a relatively small price to pay for such a great victory.

That aside, we were all deliriously happy. The whole deliverance was so miraculous, and, it seemed to us, so complete. Even the hard-core secularists in Israel were, for the moment, on some level, believers. How could they not be?

Many of us also naively thought that here in America, where society was normal, with normal values, people generally rejoiced with us. We had seen startling hatred at the UN during all this. The more Israel triumphed, the more frantically and the more hatefully many nations behaved, including some European nations. Soviet Russia was among the worst, threatening to intercede militarily. It reached fever pitch during the Golan campaign against Syria. These nations liked it fine when the Syrians rained down fire on Jewish towns and farms from the heights Syria occupied. When Israel, at great cost, went up those hills to seize the heights from the enemy, diplomatic frenzy broke loose at the UN, with demands to stop immediately. The hatred, the hateful language that reverberated in the UN, were deeply unnerving. But we thought that here at home, our friends and neighbors sympathized with us. Many, in fact, did.

That summer, I worked at the mayor's office in City Hall along with other college students. We were a friendly and compatible group. Once, as we were sitting having lunch, a new fellow came in, a Jew, who joined us late because he had been away until then. He said he had been someplace very remote, but had just learned that there had been a war in the Middle East. He asked what happened. I told him, with obvious excitement in my voice, of the miraculous great victory over our would-be destroyers.

It was while I was talking that I noticed something chilling. My "friends" and coworkers, Eithne and Brian, had less than happy or sympathetic faces as I recounted the recent events, and a couple of others had faces of stone. I don't know whom they rooted for in that war, but once the Jews won, like many in their world, they didn't like hearing about it. They were neither Muslims nor Arabs. I suddenly understood that we have neighbors who share our society whom we automatically wish well as our neighbors who do not reciprocate those feelings as a default position. We were all quite young; this was an attitude learned at home. Certainly not all the non-Jews reacted that way. But the fact that there were some was a disconcerting discovery.

Christianity in general, and Roman Catholicism in particular, had a serious theological problem with the very existence of Israel. According to their theology, it is, actually, an impossibility. The only way they could explain the inexplicable rejection by the Jews of the Christian deity, who arose from the Jews, is stubborn, evil perfidy, for which the Jews were condemned to wander and suffer in eternal exile. Now how could there arise an independent Jewish state in the Land of Israel, exile from which was their punishment? The Vatican did not get around to extending formal diplomatic recognition of Israel until 1993, when they essentially had to.

After the Six-Day War, Arabs everywhere in the Land of Israel were afraid of the Jews. We who visited in those years went everywhere without concern. We could wander the streets of Shechem (Nablus) and feel entirely safe. It was only later that *we taught the Arabs* that we could be afraid of them, thus empowering them.

Sadly, it was, it seemed to me, an opportunity squandered. God so clearly handed us a miraculous victory. *She'al Mimeni*, ask it of Me, says Hashem, *v'etna goyim nachalasecha*, and I will hand the nations over to you (Tehillim 2:8). God will do it – but it requires *she'al Mimeni*, we must ask it of Him. We must believe and we must pray.

How long did it take for the old patterns to reassert themselves, for the forces of secularism, the deniers of God and His hand in the world, to shake off their initial awe and realization of His Providence, and to reinterpret what they had witnessed, what we all witnessed, as the result of purely military genius, of *kochi v'otzem yadi*, of *anything-but-God*? And that's how we have wound up in the difficult situation we are in today.

*Im b'chukosai telechu*. If you follow My Torah, God says, He will bless us in every way. The land and its people will prosper. *V'nasati shalom ba'aretz*, I will send peace to the land, *u'shechavtem v'ein macharid*, you will rest tranquil with no one to frighten you. You will chase away your enemies, who will fall before you. *V'radfu mikem chamishah me'ah u'me'ah mikem revavah yirdofu* (26:8); five of you will suffice to defeat a hundred of the enemy, and one hundred of you will repel ten thousand, who will fall in battle before you. *This is exactly what happened in that war*. My Face will be turned to you, and you will be plentiful in the land.

But if, *chalilah*, not, if you turn away from the Torah, you will be so consumed with fear that you will flee the enemy even if no one is chasing you. A falling leaf will frighten you.

Oy. God forbid. But it's right there. How to win, and, *Rachmana litzlan*, how to lose. It's too frightening to contemplate, but we must. The curses, the dire punishments, listed here and in the second *tochachah* in Ki Savo are too terrible to bear. With so many of Klal Yisrael so far removed from Torah, *nebech*, how will we survive?

That said, with so many so far removed from Torah, how could we have had such a victory in 1967? How could we have won in 1948? Obviously, there is much more to the story. The Ribbono shel Olam does not spell out for us the specifics of His plan. But clearly, with all the ups and the downs, He is moving history around us and for us. We have already, in our long and tortuous history, suffered all the agonies outlined in the *tochachah* and then some (and then a lot). God sees our suffering. By this time, we can argue, Jews falling away from Yiddishkeit is the result not so much of deciding to be bad, but of a kind of madness that is the result of our suffering, and for which we are, hopefully, not quite fully responsible.

It's enough. It's time for our bitter *galus* and our suffering in that *galus* and in Eretz Yisrael to be over. We can point to excuses, but that alone does not suffice. We need, as a nation, to turn to the Ribbono shel Olam. Those frightening and then glorious days in 1967 show that we can, at least in some measure. Ask it of Me, Hashem says. Live the life I have created you for. Turn to Me. Return to Me.

*She'al Mimeni*, Hashem says, *v'etna goyim nachalasecha*.

And so may it be, please God, speedily and in our day, before our very eyes.

*Parashas Bechukosai 5782*

# ספר במדבר

# Bamidbar

## Bamidbar – In the Sandy Wilderness

It is no accident that the Torah was given to us not only in the *midbar*, the empty wilderness, but also intentionally outside the Land of Israel. Many reasons and lessons are associated with that; a discussion would fill a large essay. Shavuos, the holiday that commemorates that world-changing event, Matan Torah, is always preceded by the reading of Parashas Bamidbar.

Rashi explains the census that comprises much of the *parashah* as an act of God's love to mark the establishment of the Mishkan, and with it, the Divine Presence coming to rest among Klal Yisrael.

Chazal have taught us the remarkable dictum *Am Yisrael v'Oraysa v'Kudsha Brich Hu chad hu*: Israel, the Torah, and the Ribbono shel Olam are *one*. They are, as a gift of God, inseparably intertwined. The Torah is the world's most precious gift, but it's not exactly a free gift. We need to continue to work to deserve it.

The *haftarah* for Bamidbar, with its enumeration of the numbers of Israelites, is in Hoshea 2, which begins with a reference to great numbers of Jews at a future time: *And the numbers of the children of Israel will be very great, like the sand of the seashore.* This is good; it is part of a kind of consolation, but it is connected to an associated declaration that is actually quite harsh.

Hoshea comes to chastise Israel upon its wicked ways, in the waning days of the sinful northern kingdom of Israel just prior to its destruction and exile. He is instructed by God, as a living symbol of his troubled prophecy, to marry an unreliable woman, whose children's names will be symbolic of the *separation* of God from Israel because of their persistent rebellion against Him.

The first is named Yizrael, alluding to their impending exile and dispersion, *zeruin ba'aratzos*. The second is Lo Ruchamah, indicating that God will no longer have *rachamim* upon them, and they will get what they deserve. And the third child is named Lo Ami, *for in your sinful ways*, God says to Israel, *you are no longer My nation, and I am no longer yours.* Very harsh, but sadly deserved.

Hoshea is terribly upset at this, and he begs God for mercy for Klal Yisrael. And the next prophecy indeed reveals how in the end, the numbers of Israel will be so great that they will be virtually uncountable. Instead of being considered *Lo* Ami, they will be known as Ami, My nation, *bnei Kel Chai*, children of the Living God. Instead of being dispersed and utterly lost among the nations, Yizrael, Yehudah, and Yisrael will reunite, and Yizrael will be understood in another sense, a gathering together, on that great day, of what had been dispersed. And the sister will be known not as *Lo Ruchamah*, but as Ruchamah, evocative of God's mercy.

In the desert, in His great love and mercy, the Ribbono shel Olam bestowed His presence upon us and within us. Yisrael, Oraysa, and Kudsha Brich Hu – *chad hu.* How priceless a gift! We squandered it in the past; we should learn the lesson and never do so again. The price has been so terribly high. And for what?

Chazal teach in *Midrash Rabbah* (Bamidbar 6) that the Torah was given *ba'esh, ba'mayim, u'va'midbar.* With fire, water, and wilderness. Chazal teach further that the lesson is that all these entities are freely available to all. It is within everyone's reach, if one only reaches out for it. So too is the Torah.

And then they teach another, profound lesson, and it is about Bamidbar, the desert. A person cannot be a proper repository of the Torah unless he also possesses the humility to make himself as *hefker*, as plain, as simple, as approachable, as utterly lacking in haughtiness as the sandy desert. For haughtiness and Torah are altogether incompatible. And indeed, our greatest Torah leaders have always also been exemplars of humility, sensitivity, and refinement. It is an absolute requirement.

If this is true for someone who otherwise might indeed have something to be haughty about (his attainment of much Torah), how much more is that true for the rest of us plain folks, whose accomplishments, such as they are, are so much more mundane?

*Chag sameach*, and an *emmese kabbalas haTorah!*

*Parashas Bamidbar 5778*


# Kevorkian Begone

Remember Dr. Kevorkian?

Back in the 1990s, Jack Kevorkian, an MD who thought his degree was a license to kill – as long as the patient, or perhaps the family, welcomed that death – gained notoriety as "Dr. Death." He pioneered physician-assisted suicide in the United

States at a time when this country had not yet lost its moral compass. He admitted to sending off 130 people who he said wanted to die, arrogating to himself the power of life and death that American society still believed belonged only to God. He was convicted of murder and was sent to prison. He himself died in 2011 while seeking medical help for himself.

Europe was "way ahead" of the United States in such things. Historically, Europeans committed mass murder in the name of God. More recently, that same society, having thrown off God, or their notion of God, commit mass murder that they call humanism, post-Christian *Christian charity*, which they consider fine, even commendable, as long as the patient doesn't mind and the murderers are called "doctor."

A relative of mine, a child survivor with lifelong physical maladies along with a difficult personal life, decided, some years ago, that she had had enough and signed up with the medical establishment in Amsterdam to be put to death. I know this because she called to say goodbye. She could not be dissuaded. She had no terminal or life-threatening illness. She was just tired. And so the humane doctors of that fine, humane country killed her.

For a while, we were safe here in the United States, as the people of this country, clinging to more traditional values, would not allow such a thing. Canada, however, is far more "enlightened"; death teams roam the hospital corridors looking for victims. The mother of a friend in Canada was ill with a deadly disease but was far from ready to die. Her daughter was badgered regularly to stop being so selfish and to let them kill her beloved mother, who herself would have had to be convinced. They would wait until the patient was having a bad day and when her children were absent to converge on her bedside and make their case for ending it all. She resisted their deathly enticements, went home, and had a good, loving, and life-affirming half year or more with her beloved children.

I fear for this country. Something has changed as the political winds have been blowing moral and ethical rot in our faces. Abnormal and immoral is now, in many places, held to be a virtue. God, in that mindset, has been deposed. Thank God, this is not everywhere, but the nefarious influence of that mindset has affected nearly every sphere of society. Sad to say, even in medicine, a realm where it should be the furthest away from actual practice. Where God is removed from the equation, anything goes. Especially in matters of life and death.

The man in my exam chair last week was a beautiful Jew. A gentle, *eidel talmid chacham*, a *marbitz Torah*, he was in general good health. A few months before, however, he had been in a desperate struggle for life as he lay prone in a hospital bed for weeks, intubated, on a respirator. A COVID-19 victim with a family. After some time – apparently a predetermined set time established by hospital protocol – the wife was informed that it was time to pull the plug and say goodbye. The wife, herself in the medical field, had to struggle mightily to fight them off. In the face of her fierce defense of her husband, they relented for a few days, during which he woke up. He is fine now, working, teaching, *living* – conducting life.

It's true that those were desperate, overwhelming times, but it is simply not a doctor's or a hospital's role to play God. Perhaps they felt pressured beyond pressure to triage, to prioritize resources for those they considered salvageable. The dedication and the heroism of the frontline health care workers, doctors and nurses and aides, respiratory therapists, clerks and workers of every description who braved a horrible, terrifying disease, who were exposed constantly, in order to help others is indescribable. Every one of us is in their debt. Even so, there are moral parameters, lines that should not be crossed. The moral framework of society, the objective truth of right and wrong, must never be lost, lest civilization itself be lost.

The wife says that the hospital he was in was somewhat better than some others in responsiveness to a family's refusal to give up. There are choices to be made, moral ones, that can be made and that must be made.

The same week, another patient, a middle-aged woman, sat in the same exam chair in my office and told me almost the same story. The husband had to fight hard to keep them from pulling the plug. She's entirely fine now. Quite healthy, in fact.

Parashas Bamidbar begins with yet another census, a counting of Bnei Yisrael. It was the third time in about one year that they had been counted. The reason, Rashi tells us, is *mi'toch chibasan milfanav*, because Hashem loved them so much. Even though the count would not differ much, each one, each individual, was so precious to Him, each one was counted and loved, all over again.

The prophet Hoshea was commanded to take a wife who was a harlot and to have children with her. In castigating Israel for its sinful ways while imploring it to return to God, such a wife and her children of doubtful origin – who might be repulsive and who might also be precious and beloved, never to be exchanged – serve as a metaphor for Israel's behavior and hoped-for return. In the *haftarah* for Bamidbar, God says to Hoshea that even when Bnei Yisrael are as numerous as the sands of the sea, which can neither be measured nor counted, it will not be said of them, even in the place of remote exile, *even in the most extreme circumstance*, that they are no longer God's people, *lo ami atem*, you no longer count to be among God's people, *you are no longer among the children of God*. It will rather be said of them and to them, *bnei Kel Chai*, you are children of the Living God. Declare of your brothers – all of them – *ami*, you are my (My) nation, and of your sisters, *ruchamah*, compassion.

All of them. Each one. Though they be as numerous as the sands of the sea, which cannot be measured or counted. Each precious one is *ami*, each is *ruchamah*. Even those who had been the most remote, the most far gone. No one is extra, no one is expendable, no one is not wanted. Precious. Beloved.

In life, there are people who appear to be lost or remote. Or different. Who don't operate according to our usual expectations. In our busy lives, it's easy to pay them little mind, to write them off from serious consideration. To turn them off. To pull the plug, so to speak.

But we dare not. We dare not, we may not say of them *lo ami atem*, you don't count anymore. The same God, the same Creator Who gave us our lives also gave them theirs. They are *bnei Kel Chai*, children of the Living God.

Whether desperately sick and on a respirator, whether ill of the spirit, whether otherwise damaged or irregular or even offbeat in any way, they are not extra, they are not expendable, they are not to be written off or ignored. They are *tzelem Elokim*. They are to be loved, as we would be loved. Each precious one is *ami*, each is *ruchamah*.

Like us, children of the Living God.

*Parashas Bamidbar 5781*

# Naso

## Counting Gershon

How do you say "divorce" in Hebrew, or in Aramaic? *Gerushin*. It's not just "sent away." It means "chased away." Forced out. Expelled. As in Adam and Eve, who were thrown out of Paradise. The expulsion of the Jews from Spain, with its attendant horrors, is known as Gerush Sefarad.

In the previous *parashah*, God lovingly has Bnei Yisrael counted, not for the first time.

The Levites were excluded from that census, and now God instructs Moshe to "also count Gershon" (Bamidbar 4:22).

Imagine you're trying to make it in business, or socially, or perhaps politically. You're at an important event where you might be able to make advantageous and useful contacts. You want to meet the important people who might be useful to you. But there are also *shleppers* present. They say hello to you, and you might politely say hello back, but if you are a certain type (which of course you are not), you will look right past them, searching for someone who counts. The *shlepper* who is trying to say hello and chat you up is of no use to you, and if you are that type (which you are not), you only want to get away from him. He is of no account. And unless he is utterly clueless (which many, but certainly not all *shleppers* are), he is acutely aware, as you abruptly disengage, of what was just done to him. Again.

Consider the people who appear to have no *mazal* in this world. You've seen them, wondered how they get by, wondered how bad luck and failure seem to follow them in life, wondered at how they seem to keep trying, wondered if they were even aware that they had no *mazal*.

Take a closer look at the apparent *lo yitzlach*s in this world. There may be more there than meets the eye.

The Rebbe Rav Shlomo of Radomsk asks us to look at "Bnei Gershon" here as a *remez*, a hint, alluding to those in this world, in particular the tzaddikim, who seem to be *megorashim*, divorced from, excluded from, what we normally take, justifiably, as the goodness in life. They can't seem to catch a break. Everything is hard for them. Things don't seem to work out for them. They have more than their share of suffering. We look at them and, as much as we sympathize, we're quietly grateful that it's them and not us.

You know exactly what I mean.

And yet among them are tzaddikim who suffer quietly and yet accept it, in their *temimus*, as *yissurim shel ahavah*. They don't know the meaning of a good day the way most people would, and yet they are as close to God as one can get.

Hashem is telling us here, now that you've counted the regular people, the good and the less good, the *mazaldig* and the less *mazaldig*, the more successful and the less successful, the always robust and the not always robust – *the everyday people* – now look at these special people, the people who may not, at first glance, seem to count, *and count them*.

These are the people who bear the heavy burden for the rest of us. No one gets a free ride in life, but there are those who bear, for reasons known only to God, more than their share of the suffering that is apportioned to the world.

These are the "Bnei Gershon" whose assignment is *"la'avod u'l'masa,"* to work and to bear the burden (*Zos avodas mishpachos haGershuni la'avod u'l'masa* [4:24]). *Avodah* is serving God. *Masa*, literally "bear the burden," alludes to the ability, the predilection, indeed the choice, even the patience, to bear that burden, and to do so with love and faith. *V'es kol asher ye'aseh lahem*, whatever happens to them, *v'avadu*, they will continue to serve God faithfully (4:26).

In Krias Shema, our personal and national primal declaration of faith, we declare, *v'ahavta es Hashem Elokecha b'chol levavcha u'v'chol nafshecha u'v'chol me'odecha*: you shall love Hashem no matter what befalls you – with all your heart, even if, in His judgment, He takes all your possessions from you, even if He takes your very life from you. For that is faith, and that is – may we not be tested – what God asks of us.

A Jewish *neshamah* wants to serve God. That is built in. But in life, there are all manner of circumstances that can stand in the way. The history of mankind and the history of our people amply demonstrate that. Things happen, *lo aleinu*, that can deflect us from that goal and that desire. But God is telling us that He wants us to serve Him, if need be, even under those difficult or even terrible circumstances.

We cannot understand the ways of God, or His judgment. We pray that we not be among those who are so sorely tested. But when we see those who are, *lo aleinu*, when we look at them, we should see before us not *shleppers* and *lo yitzlachs*, not "useless" people you look past but not really at, not those who don't count, but those who God says are the people who *really* count, the pure souls who bear the burden for the rest of us, the unseen and unappreciated heroes who may appear to the rest of the world as losers, but of whom it is written *"v'at alit al kulanah,"* the precious downtrodden who in the end will be sitting on top of the world.

*Parashas Naso 5778*

# Phineas T. Bluster, aka "Mr. Bluster"

We all know a Mr. Bluster, although he comes in various forms, shapes, and sizes. But you recognize the type: he blusters and bullies his way through life. He's awful. He may mask it sometimes, but being who he is, it always emerges. Sometimes it rubs off on those who associate with him, but perhaps that's why they choose to associate with him in the first place.

Phineas T. Bluster, for those who are not old enough to remember, was a puppet character on a children's program who personified some of those qualities. "Mr. Bluster" is a metaphor for such a person.

Often the blustering works. Some years ago, there was a popular book I did not read, *Winning through Intimidation*, which I suspect was for Mr. Bluster wannabees. But really, I think, it is as much part of the nature of the person as it is a calculated tactic.

True story: Two couples walked into a lawyer's office to sign a contract for the sale of a house from one couple to the other. The four were friends and neighbors. There was complete agreement and understanding, as well as good will, with regard to terms and conditions of the sale. What they did not know, as they walked in, was that sitting behind the lawyer's desk was Mr. Bluster himself.

This is not about lawyers. This incident involved a particular lawyer, who probably became a lawyer because it's a great outlet for blustering if one is so disposed. But there are infinite opportunities for blusterers in all walks of life. It took this guy about five minutes to get the two couples to look at each other, get up, and go home. The transaction was successfully and peacefully concluded shortly thereafter in another venue with another lawyer – a normal, decent person. I don't know if that version of Mr. Bluster has a normal family life or not. I suppose it's possible that some of these guys (it's more often men, but not necessarily) switch it off at the front door to their homes, but I suspect that most don't.

And so we come to the tragic, anguished case of the *sotah*. A wife misbehaves in a serious way, secluding herself, even after being warned, with a man not her husband. She may or may not be guilty of the ultimate betrayal, but the husband suspects she is. She is brought before the Temple authorities and must undergo the *sotah* test. If the husband himself is a good person and the wife is bad, the test works: if she persists in denying her guilt, she will die. If he is good and she did not sin, peace will be restored to their newly repaired relationship, and they will have a child together. If, however, he himself is a bad guy, a sinner, the test will not work.

By all accounts, while the wife definitely misbehaved in secluding herself with another man, even if she did not actually sin, the husband in such a case is looked upon suspiciously as possibly an instigator. He might be Mr. Bluster.

Remember the tragic story of Pilegesh b'Givah (Shoftim 19)? It resulted in the deaths of many tens of thousands of Jews and the near-total eradication of the tribe of Binyamin. It started, says the Gemara (*Gittin* 6b) with the man, apparently a creep, who was too harshly strict with his woman. He was a blusterer who kept her in an oppressive state of intimidation until she ran off and misbehaved, leading to a cascade of national catastrophe. *Amar Rav Chisda: L'olam, always, a man should not cast excessive intimidation upon his household* (I suppose a little is OK), as the consequences can be catastrophic; that excessive fear he induces can lead to every cardinal sin (the *meforshim* there spell out how).

Things come up in any relationship, especially in a home. Most people react normally. Others think that the way to assert their manhood is to intimidate, dominate, and crush the spirit of those around them, those who should look to that bully as their loving, safe, and secure place in the world and instead find Mr. Bluster. *Gittin* 90a describes how Papus ben Yehudah, a rich and powerful big shot, so dominated and controlled his wife that he used to lock her in the house every time he went out (*Shabbos* 104a). Chazal say she was so driven to hate him that she rebelled and punished him by making of him a cuckold.

*Ish ish ki sisteh ishto*: a man (*ish*) who foolishly tries to prove or assert his manliness (*ish*) by dominating with fear may well *foolishly* (implicit in "*sisteh*") provoke his wife to foolish behavior, she finding the entire fault for her own bad behavior with *him*: *maalah bo maal*, all bad things she does are *his* fault, and she takes license from that.

*Ki sisteh*: Reish Lakish (*Sotah* 3a) declares that a person does not sin unless he or she is taken over by foolishness (*ruach shtus*). Any rational Jew understands that sinfulness is never worth it. And yet people sin, because, like the diabetic who eats rich sweets even though he knows how self-damaging it is, they are overcome with a moment of utter foolishness, a kind of temporary insanity.

Many terrible and foolish factors go into the making of a *sotah* situation. But like every bad thing, every sin, every abuse of power in any relationship, the slide begins with bad thinking, sometimes driven by the simple momentary desire for some pleasure, sometimes driven by the arrogant character flaw that disregards the humanity of others, the sensitivities and the rights of others, that callous indifference to other people we recognize in Mr. Bluster.

*Parashas Naso 5780*

# Behaaloscha

## Why Do You Wear That Thing on Your Head?

Having had virtually all my schooling in a *frum* setting, I first sustained intense exposure to others in a school setting in medical school. Everyone, of course, on some level knew that religious Jewish men typically wear a yarmulke, although probably no one really understood why. It was, after all, a Jewish medical school (Albert Einstein College of Medicine of Yeshiva University), a highly respected top medical school where, for medical students, Shabbos and *kashrus* were protected. But it was open to all, admission based on merit. We had a nice cadre of *frum* students, male and female, and everyone got along fine. It was only from an alienated Jew, however, that I heard us referred to as *"yommie boppers."* There was no mistaking the disdain.

To nearly all of my classmates, it was a non-issue, but apparently not to all. His behavior, from a Jewish perspective, was rather egregious all around. And there is a difference between ignorance – the spiritual malady, the emptiness of being raised in a manner that is utterly bereft of Yiddishkeit by parents who robbed their children of the lifeline that is their heritage – and actual contempt, a worse disease that usually, but not always, like bigotry, is typically learned behavior (*"Lukas! Lukas!"* See *Sukkah* 56b: *Shuta d'yanuka b'shuka o da'avua o d'imeia* [שׁוּתָא דְיָנוֹקָא בְּשׁוּקָא אוֹ דַאֲבוּהּ אוֹ דְאִימֵיהּ], What a child utters in the street is learned at home.)

And so I am reminded of a comment my father made when I was a young boy, that President John Kennedy single-handedly ruined the hat business. He was this "cool," sophisticated figure who, unlike his predecessors and really all of society until then, virtually never wore a hat. Look at old films up to about 1961, and you will see that men in the street typically wore hats. Kennedy's style, emulated by many, did away with that. Except in *frum* enclaves, the men's hat business nearly disappeared.

What other effect on society, if any, might have been a spinoff from that? It didn't take long for society in general to begin the process of throwing off heretofore normative societal restraints, the idea that there is objective right and wrong, the progressive, incremental abandonment of moral restraint in virtually all spheres of life, leading us into the morass, the moral vacuum, we are now confronted with.

Is it possible that the concept and the role of the yarmulke for Jews, *yirei Malka*, fear of Heaven, the ongoing consciousness and awareness that God is above us, on our heads, so to speak, has some sort of analogue in the non-Jewish world, in some way applicable to all humans? Certainly, nasty gentiles throughout the ages, *with* hats on their heads, engaged in the most terrible behavior. But at least they paid lip service, however hypocritically, to a basic morality. We are being told now, defiantly, that the threads of morality and decency that bound all civilized people are now dissolved, not just irrelevant but noxiously *repressive*. Oh, and racist and sexist. White male supremacist (you know, as mathematics is now portrayed in the woke world, *with a straight face.*)

*Why do you wear that thing on your head?* It used to be, frequently, an innocent question. It can also be a defiant challenge, depending upon who is asking it and how it is asked, like the *rasha*'s seemingly innocuous question at the Pesach seder, which in tone and intent is evil and defiant.

How do people get that way? Some are actively indoctrinated. Most are ignorant. And some are, I believe, carrying out an ingrained, almost preprogrammed function: yes, they have free choice, they are responsible for their actions, but on some spiritual level, they don't belong among us, and by their actions, they rail against their fate to be one of us, to be where they don't want to be. There have been such Jews throughout our history, Jews who are startlingly out of sync with the heart of the nation. They may even go through the motions of normative Jewish life, but something inside is out of place. They may even be "rabbis." Or they may sit in the United States Senate, as point men for hatred of everything we hold dear.

There is a profound lesson to be learned from the fact that this painful and seemingly eternal thorn in our side was the result of a well-intentioned but flawed decision made by the greatest Jew of all time, one who cared about and loved Klal Yisrael, who sacrificed everything for them, who was dedicated beyond dedication, Moshe Rabbeinu, *a"h*.

The great tragedy in Moshe's life was that having delivered the nation from bondage, through forty difficult years, up to the borders of the land, he himself did not merit to enter the holy Land of Israel, despite all his travail, all his yearning, all his pleas and prayers. *Rav lach*, Hashem told him, you can stop pleading. *Al tosef daber Eilai od ba'davar hazeh* (Devarim 3:26). Sorry, the answer is *no*.

The well-known reason is *mei merivah*, Moshe hit the rock rather than speak to it, as God had commanded. Seems somewhat strict, but Moshe was held to a higher standard, especially where *kavod Shamayim* was concerned.

But there may be more to the story.

In Behaaloscha, we are told of an unhappy group of complaining malcontents, referred to as *ha'asafsuf* (Bamidbar 11:4). A gathered rabble. *Ha'asafsuf asher b'kirbo*, the gathered rabble clinging to Israel's coattails upon their glorious exodus from Egypt, a "mixed multitude" insinuated into the midst of Klal Yisrael. The Erev Rav, who were the instigators of every bad act the Jews in the *midbar* did. It was Moshe's choice to let them come along. A bad idea, an attempt to do a good and noble thing, for which Israel as a nation, and Moshe personally, paid very dearly. *Rav lach, meforshim* tell us, is a reference to the Erev Rav: *lach*, Moshe. They are "yours." They are on *you*. You undertook to bring them along. It will cost you. *Al tosef daber Eilai od ba'davar hazeh.* You will not enter the land.

There's a great midrash (*Lekach Tov*) that identifies the *asafsuf* as ignorant and ill-intentioned outsider hangers-on. It then goes on to offer quite the opposite view, based on associative language clues, that they are *zekeinim, rabbonim*, and leaders (!) – and if *they* can do this, it concludes, how much more so ordinary people.

They complained about the *mon*, that wondrous food that fell from the heavens and tasted like anything and everything the eater wanted – except garlic, cucumbers, leeks, and watermelon. "No good!" they cried. "No good! We want garlic and leeks and cucumbers and watermelon! *The whole thing is no good!*"

They wanted, *they demanded*, bowel movements. The holy *mon* was absorbed completely and was not degraded into body waste. But there was other food available from local sellers of produce in various locations of their travels. That was, of course, subject to the normal rules of nature, and they could have, if they wished, bowel movements galore. For that reason, there was a mitzvah to maintain sanitary facilities outside the camp (*v'yased tihyeh lecha al azenecha* [Devarim 23:14]). "No good!" they cried. "No good! We want bowel movements from the *mon*! *The whole thing is no good!*"

They tasted anything delicious they wanted (OK, not garlic) when they ate *mon*. But they only *tasted* rib steak. They even enjoyed the mouth feel of it. But they didn't *see* rib steaks on their plates. They wanted to *see* rib steak! They wanted to *see* barbecued franks with mustard and sauerkraut, not just taste it. "*No good! No good! The whole thing is no good!*"

And they wanted to "eat flesh." *Mi yaachilenu basar. Midrash Tanchuma* tells us that they had a different kind of "flesh" in mind. They wanted unfettered and uninhibited license to couple with anyone they chose, even the closest family members, a practice common in Egypt. As for today's libertines – in this regard, at least – there is no such thing as objective right and wrong; in their godless world, rules are arbitrary and repressive. Anything goes as long as "no one gets hurt," and, as they used to say in the sixties, when today's mess started, "If ya dig it, do it."

*Why do you wear that thing on your head?* We wear it because we are so blessed that our God places Himself *k'v'yachol* among us. He is, in a manner of speaking, *wherever we let him in*. We wear that thing on our heads because we place Him, and the holiness that He has taught us, above us. Because we are aware, always, of His Presence.

The Erev Rav of every generation, in whatever guise they take, try always to break that connection. They are not just a historical bit mentioned briefly in the Torah. The Torah tells us nothing of what happened to them after the forty-year trek in the wilderness was over. They didn't go away; they didn't disappear. They are the bad Jews of every generation who, subtly or overtly, in whatever guise they take, holy-roller fakers or outright radicals, try to destroy the bond between us and our Father in Heaven.

But they will not. Klal Yisrael at its core remains loyal to the Ribbono shel Olam. Individuals, even large segments, may be seduced away; hopefully, they will return, and many do. But we will not forget. We will always be aware of Him; we will always feel Him with us and upon us, because, literally and figuratively, we wear that thing that reminds us always of Him upon our heads.

*Parashas Behaaloscha 5781*

# Shelach

## Black Lives Matter

Most of us have, at some time, done it. We labor to set up something good, perhaps with a spouse. It's going well, and then, with a foolish word or thoughtless act, we ruin it. That's what people do – some more than others, sometimes trivial, sometimes catastrophic, sometimes benign, sometimes not.

I once came across a group of teenagers davening Minchah. I was impressed at how beautifully they davened. It then occurred to me that, given their particular orientation, they might "ruin it" at the end of davening with a pointed chanting declaration most of us would object to. Led by their counselors, they did. Okay, you can argue the point in this case. You can contend, with justification, that if *that* is how young Jews "ruin" things, *ashreinu* indeed. May there be many such more in Israel.

Real ruination, and especially broader societal ruination, is bad indeed. Our loving God wrought miracle after miracle and brought us out of slavery in Egypt, and led us to the Promised Land, where all would be wonderful. Inconceivably, time and again, we, our ancestors, ruined it. We ruined it before we got there, and later we ruined it time and again after we got there.

The *meraglim* were prominent men – leaders, not slackers. They were, up to that point, not sinners. They were chosen to prepare the way to the Promised Land – they were in such an enviable position, and yet they ruined it. And then the people ruined it.

They should have known better. All of them, not just the leaders. The *amcha Yidden*. Every Jew had *yichus*. He knew who he was, from where and from whom he derived. He understood where he should be headed. He was *somebody*, and he knew it. He had identity not just as an individual, but beyond just his own existence. He had purpose. And in their failure, they failed their purpose as well.

In our long journey in this world, a source, in human terms, of our strength is our sense of identity and of purpose. Where that lapses, tragically, in segments of Jewish society where that is allowed to be lost, we disappear, *Rachmana litzlan*.

Because we are so secure in our sense of self, individually and as a people, we can lose sight of the reality in this rough world that not everyone has that benefit.

In my youth, during the civil rights struggle, I remember clearly being struck and deeply moved by a slogan that was being taught to young black people: "*I am somebody!*" and "*I am a man!*" It had not occurred to me that anyone needed to be taught to think of himself that way. And at the same time, it was clear that there was a reason – quite apparent to any thinking person who then cared to look – that it was indeed necessary for very many people in America, whose experience in society, whether from outside or even from inside, made little of the fact that they were, in fact, someone who mattered and had value, part of a societal group who mattered and had value. Part of the crime foisted upon them, historically, is that they did not, as we thankfully do, have four thousand years of high-minded tradition as the engine that drove them, to give them a healthy sense of identity and purpose.

Thank God, things have changed so much for the better in America. The mindset in white America is *not* what it was generations ago. Most people are fair minded and happy to let society move on in an open and fair way. That is the norm in the public sphere, despite all the loud pronouncements to the contrary. Racists, for the most part, are viewed as primitives, as morons. And then there are the preeners and the posturers who have hijacked the good fight and have ruined it for their own gain and political advantage. Not only have the insane taken over the asylum, they have declared the sane to be insane.

Blame for societal failures is placed where an agenda-driven political mindset *wants it to be*, rather than where it really belongs. Goals are what that political mindset insists they be, rather than focused where normalcy, decency, and consensus would have them be. Entirely extraneous issues, driven by extraneous agendas, are tied to the effort, gratuitously infusing it with hatred and antisemitism. A now prominent organization with a laudable name ruins, with its outrageousness, the very laudability it purports to represent. Thuggery and bigotry are explained away, even praised, or, incredibly, even encouraged. The "soft bigotry" of low expectations of people, part of the very problem keeping them down, parades as the highest social virtue. And don't you dare complain about it, or even point it out. Sanctimonious hypocrisy abounds. The stupidest, most outrageous ideas are presented with a straight face and then parroted by others, as if any normal person would agree, along with utterly false narratives that it is blasphemy to deny. The ruiners are having their day. What a tragedy.

Which brings us back to the *meraglim* and the terrible sin of that time. Even thirty-three hundred years ago, our ancestors had a glorious and, to them, well-known tradition behind them, which they should have respected and heeded.

They may have been slaves, but they knew who they were. They retained very strongly their *yichus*, their distinct traditional language and dress, their identity as the children of Avraham, Yitzchak, and Yaakov, of the Imahos, of the *shevatim*. They had organized, traditional societal structure. They had the God of their fathers, even if they had lapsed here and there. They did not need anyone to tell them that they were "somebody." Their sin was terrible and "unforgivable," even as our merciful God responded to Moshe Rabbeinu's urgent pleas on their behalf, "*Salachti ki'dvarecha*," I will forgive them as you have requested.

Since then, we have an additional thirty-three hundred years of tradition, of unbroken *mesorah*. It makes no sense at all to violate that. But people do, very many have, and it has cost us very dearly. We may try to find excuses, but we know the guilt of our sins, the fruit of the ruiners. We should know better.

And like the rich person who doesn't know the feeling of hunger but who must, as a moral and practical imperative, nevertheless sympathize, even empathize with and support those who do, we must also look past the terrible, even disgusting noise that sadly surrounds today's social upheaval – noise that is often fomented and whipped up, violent and sometimes gratuitously hateful noise that is fueled by lies and distortions and exaggerations, noise that risks "ruining" a laudable goal, even as it is also driven by a painful, undeniable underlying truth – to acknowledge that whatever the failings in certain segments of society that play a serious role in perpetuating these problems, even their own problems, the first order of business, for black as well as for white, is that every human being is created *b'tzelem Elokim*, that each person on God's earth *is somebody*, that every human life is sacred, that the *cri de coeur* at the core of all this is something every one of us must take to heart, that black lives matter.

*Parashas Shelach 5780*

# Holding On, by a String

I knew him to be a *shomer Shabbos*. I didn't know much else about his personal life. The doctor worked bareheaded, but that was quite common years ago when he came of age in medicine. With rare exceptions, even very *frum* doctors in the generations before mine did so, a kind of *derech eretz* that was the commonly accepted "norm" in the public sphere, in business and especially in medicine. Mine was the first generation that had the comfort and the confidence, the self-assuredness as Americans, to present ourselves as we are.

It was a disappointing shock to me to notice, as he changed back into his regular clothing in the locker room of the OR, that he wore no tzitzis. I could not know for sure, but I preferred to think that on non-surgical days, when no one saw him, he did wear tzitzis, and that he went without on OR days for the same reason he wore no yarmulke. I felt bad and embarrassed for him. Years his junior, I wore both.

Well, we know that not every garment requires tzitzis, just a four-cornered one. And therefore it is theoretically not a required garment at all, as long as one doesn't wear a four-cornered garment. And yet no God-fearing Jew would dream of going without tzitzis, so we intentionally wear such a garment, either over our shirts or underneath, according to custom, and with the tzitzis strings visible or tucked away, according to custom. We are, in any event, (hopefully) conscious of their presence upon us at all times. For this garment reminds us, at all times, of who we are, what is expected of us, and above all, before Whom we stand and live out our daily lives. All the time, always.

That doctor, a good man and a good Jew, whom I later came to know well and to admire, was stuck in what has become, thank God, an outmoded mold, fear of too much obvious exposure in an unkind, even hostile world. We no longer feel the need to be invisible. We are, proudly and boldly, who we are. And the tzitzis are too important a tool and a gift to let go of, even in a public professional locker room. It is just too central to how we hope to navigate our way through this world.

*U're'isem oso*, you shall see it, *u'zechartem es kol mitzvos Hashem*, you will remember all of God's mitzvos, *v'asisem osam*, and you will perform them; *v'lo sasuru*: you will not be seduced away after your hearts and your eyes, that you lust after them. The eyes see, then the heart desires, then the body chases after the forbidden. The tzitzis short-circuit that disastrous cascade. They can supersede those baser impulses; they remind us of who we are; they save our very lives.

Seeing something stirs us to action. It can be for the good, and it can be, God forbid, for the bad. *Menachos* 43b on *u're'isem u'zechartem* says that seeing brings the mind to dwell on something, and thinking about it brings one to doing something.

It is our choice to do good or to do bad. To surround ourselves with good or with bad, with the likely outcomes to follow. The tests in this life are endless and are not by appointment. They spring upon us. The same God Who created us knows human nature, and in His infinite lovingkindness, He gave us, His children, this precious mitzvah that keeps us anchored, that helps us fight off the sometimes overpowering forces that seek to drag us away from Him.

No one is immune to the *yetzer hara*. Enveloped in this precious mitzvah, wrapped up in it, we are bolstered in that eternal fight the Jew must wage against the very devils that are within each person, to reach up, cling to, envelop ourselves with our loving God, the Most High.

*Parashas Shelach 5781*

# Korach

## Of the Insane, the Nearly Insane, and the Formerly Insane

Most of us have encountered crazy people who are, *nebech*, truly crazy. Most of us have encountered people whose behavior is crazy, but who are, in actuality, not clinically crazy. Life has taught us that one can be crazy and not crazy.

Indeed, many of us have, at some point, been that person, driven by some difficult circumstance in life. How would you characterize someone who is not, in fact, clinically crazy, but does crazy things because there is something wrong with his character? Or because he is pathetically morally weak?

In my medical practice, I encounter people all the time who are not crazy but who act medically crazy. They are out-of-control diabetics who eat every bad thing, or desperately sick people who don't take their life- or sight-saving medication and do every other foolish thing you can think of. They're not crazy, but they're acting crazy.

I see it as a kind of temporary insanity. We've all been there. Wisdom and good judgment fly out the window for that moment. That they will be mighty regretful later does not stop them now. Know what I mean? Of course you do.

Chazal tell us that *ein adam choteh ela im ken nichnas bo ruach shtus:* a person would not sin but for a spirit of idiocy seizing hold of him for that moment. Considering the high stakes, and the fact that the sinner knows that the momentary pleasure he thinks he's getting is just not worth it, it takes a moment of craziness to do that sin. And so we are all, at least sometimes, at least a little crazy.

Think of the diabetic (I see this too often) whose vision is going, whose kidneys don't work, whose feet are falling off, who wants to be well, but who just can't help himself – he cheats, often in a big way. He's not a bad person. It's his "insanity."

And then there are people, otherwise sane, who are driven by all manner of motivations that are far less honorable than a piece of chocolate cake. It may make sense to them, but we know it makes no sense for people to act that way. It's fool-ish and self-centered and destructive. Think of Korach.

Korach was driven by a bad spirit. He cleverly got others to join him in his campaign, thus masking, somewhat, his self-centered motivation, but the driving force was his mean-spirited ego and ambition and jealousy – and that of his wife. And so Moshe, confronted by this unjust and sinful rebellion, falls to his face in prayer and beseeches *Kel Elokei Haruchos l'chol basar,* God of the *ruach,* the spirit of all flesh, who knows what spirit, what *ruach,* motivates each person, including – and especially – when they sin. Korach was not looking for a piece of chocolate cake. The *ruach* of a Jew is typically what saves him. Korach's *ruach* destroyed him and brought down the rest of his party with him.

Korach's sons did not die. Although they were initially part of the rebellion, at the last moment they had *hirhurei teshuvah,* thoughts of *teshuvah.* A *ruach* or spirit of *teshuvah* came upon them. And thus, Shmuel Hanavi was among their descendants.

Korach should have learned from the *ruach,* the spirit that saved Calev from the fate of the other *meraglim,* the spies Moshe sent to Canaan, whose treachery wrought such lasting tragedy for the Jewish People. Yehoshua was protected from their influence by Moshe's *berachah,* but Calev was not. Feeling the pull of their arguments, and fearing he might succumb, he ran to Hevron and poured out his heart in prayer at Me'aras Hamachpelah, invoking the merit of the Avos and draw-ing spiritual sustenance from them to hold firm. And so, later, God blesses him and praises him for all time: *V'avdi Calev ekev haisah ruach acheres imo va'yemaleh acharai,* Calev who had within him *a different spirit, ruach acheres,* will inherit the land, as will his descendants.

The *ruach acheres* that Calev found within himself gave him the fortitude to remain sane when the others around him were fomenting a craziness that appar-ently made perfect sense to them.

And so I offer you a latter-day story about *ruach acheres* and the flight from an insanity that appeared, on the surface, to many people, to make perfect sense. In the context of that time and place, insanity was normal.

No one, not any survivor, could escape the Holocaust unscathed. All suffered, but of course, depending on place and circumstances, to sometimes vastly dif-fering degrees. Some had a most terrible time for a few terrible months. Others endured the worst for nearly six years. Some people were, as a result of their suf-fering, crazier than others. It was unusual not to be. What that craziness consisted of varied, of course, from person to person. For no one was life as they had known it normal again.

The teenage boy, a Polish Jew who had somehow remained alive during the nearly six years of terror that consumed nearly everyone he knew and his entire family, was living in a DP camp in Germany with hundreds of other survivors, waiting for a visa to go *somewhere*, to somehow get on with life. Hungry, he stopped in the kitchen to get a sandwich. A *treif* sandwich from a *treif* kitchen.

He'd been raised in a Chassidic home, but that former life was so far away and so long ago, with so much craziness filling the intervening years, that such concerns no longer occupied his conscious mind at all. As far as he could tell, that former life, however rich and spiritual, played no role at all in anyone's survival, and he felt no need for or interest in it now. The camp had a kosher kitchen too for those still interested.

Sitting on a crate, he dug into the sandwich. For years, he could only dream of eating a nice, tasty, belly-filling sandwich whenever he wanted. He became aware of a shadow nearby, and there stood a young fellow he knew casually from the camp, a Hungarian Jewish boy whose parents and siblings had perished in Auschwitz in its final months of operation.

"Berel!" (Not his real name). "Enough of this craziness! What do you need that *tarfus* for? Do you want the Germans to have taken *everything* from you? Don't let them! Throw it away!"

At that moment, Berel understood that the magnitude of his loss was even greater than he had realized. Like Calev at Me'aras Hamachpelah, he connected with his parents and holy forebears in a way that gave him the insight and strength to remember who he was and from whence his very spirit derived. Like Calev, he latched on to a *ruach acheres*, a different spirit, which saved his life and restored his sanity.

Berel threw that *treif* sandwich away and never looked back, except to the *ruach* that guided his parents and grandparents before them. And like Calev, he merited great people, great Jews to follow in his generations. Today, Berel's family is filled with *doros* of Torah and *chesed*. And each new generation is taught the life-giving lesson that it is indeed possible, even in the depths of loss and despair, to find that *ruach acheres* that can rescue a Jewish *neshamah* from spiritual insanity.

Berel's story, and that of untold numbers of others like him, those who recovered their sanity and those who, *nebech*, never did, is one of goodness within that is overwhelmed and smothered by evil from without. Korach was surrounded by goodness and greatness, with wealth and privilege and hope and glory, but those weren't enough for him; that goodness he overwhelmed and smothered with the evil and the rot that was within. His craziness was not imposed upon him by a tough life, was not a mental illness he could not do anything about, but the product of bad character, a fatal flaw of the spirit, a self-inflicted squelching of the *ruach* of goodness he could have chosen, rather than the *ruach hara* that he made his own, which brought him down together with all those he brought down with him.

Korach reminds us that while there is much in life that can make us crazy in one way or another, may Hashem protect us, we must be ever so careful not to let our own baser instincts seduce us into needless acts of "craziness" that are destructive to ourselves and to those around us. And we pray that when the challenges and the vicissitudes of life fall upon us, we have the strength to remain sane and true. And if, God forbid, those circumstances that are overwhelming and beyond our control ever do drive us to the point of "insanity," we pray that we find and latch on to the *ruach acheres* that saved Calev, that saved Berel, that saved countless brave and noble and dedicated Jews throughout our long and difficult journey in this world.

*Parashas Korach 5779*

*July 4, the holiday of American Independence, when God Almighty blessed mankind with the birth of a country whose strength and principles and goodness are matched nowhere else on Earth, which, despite the many human flaws that have marked its development, is, in human terms, the great hope of mankind, for which our people must be eternally grateful*

# Chukas

## Death by Proboscis

The murder weapon was less than two inches long and less than an inch wide. While its primary function, by design, is to transmit air and to detect smell, it can be used as well to express anger, disdain, and derisive dismissal, as well as haughtiness.

A nose can kill.

Yaakov Avinu famously criticized Shimon and Levi for what he considered their rash slaughter of the people who abducted and abused their sister. *Ki b'apam hargu ish* (Bereishis 49:6) – in their anger, they killed. *Apam*, literally their noses, is an allusion to their great anger, as in *charon af*, as if air is blown and huffed through the nose in great anger. Homiletically, it has been said that this language reminds us as well that one can "kill" someone with a public nasal twitch of derision.

A companion murder weapon, also small and soft, without an actual sharp edge at all, but which can also be fatally sharp and most deadly, is the *lingua homicidam*: the homicidal tongue. Aside from the many unkindnesses the human tongue is capable of, its primary purpose in creation can be perverted to being the destructive medium of *lashon hara*.

Purity and propriety of speech (and of nasal expression) are hallmarks of Judaism. One who is legalistically ritually pure but impure in these areas can hardly be considered actually pure.

Parashas Chukas opens with the classic *chok* regarding purity, with all its mystery and apparent internal contradictions. Much has been said about the role of accepting and fulfilling a *chok* that we understand not at all, as a function of our faith and subservience to God. But we do not have to understand this mystery to understand that its very existence is a flag that signals to us its importance and highlights the very issue that is at its core: purity.

Purity of speech – avoidance, even, whenever possible, of language that evokes the concept of impurity – is demonstrated to us as a high ideal very early in the Torah. Noach is instructed to bring all species of animals into the ark: of animals

240

that are *tahor*, seven pair; of those that are *tamei*, one pair. But it doesn't say *tamei*. The language of the Torah *goes out of its way*, so to speak, to avoid the word *tamei* here, saying instead *animals that are not tahor*, to teach the lesson of avoiding where possible even innocent reference to *tumah*, and all the more so language that is base or that serves a base purpose.

Thus, regarding *Zos chukas haTorah*, the *Midrash Rabbah* (Bamidbar 19:2) quotes Tehillim (12:7), *Imros Hashem tehoros*, the words of God are holy and pure, and cites the above example from the Flood story.

Further, in enumerating the signs of kosher animals (Vayikra 11:4), the Torah mentions several species of unkosher animals by citing first their characteristics that might make them kosher, only afterwards specifying what they are lacking in order to actually qualify as kosher. It comes to teach us not only which animals are kosher, but how a kosher person speaks.

And then the Midrash relates something astounding.

In King David's time, the learning of Torah was so strong that even little children were experts in every detail of the complex *halachos* of *tumah* and *taharah*. Even the soldiers in the army were accomplished *talmidei chachamim*. David prayed that such a repository of Torah should be preserved and protected for all time. And yet, in those Torah-filled days, many soldiers fell in battle, apparently unprotected by their learning. And that was because *lashon hara* and bad speech were, paradoxically, rife at the same time, and there were among them informers.

The Midrash contrasts that with the soldiers in the army of the wicked king Achav, many years later. They were a generation and a society that was rife with *avodah zarah*, idol worship, and abandoning God, yet they routinely overwhelmingly won their wars, protected by the saving grace that they lived well with each other and did *not* speak *lashon hara* about each other, nor were they informers.

A parallel exists in comparing the fate of the generation that was wiped out in the Flood and the generation of the dispersal, *dor hapalagah*.

Both generations were bad. The generation of the Flood was destroyed completely because, essentially, they were mean to each other. The generation of the dispersal, who actually set out to make war on God Himself, who built their tower in order to wave a sword at Him, was spared because they treated each other nicely, with kindness and consideration. Wow.

*Lashon hara* kills three: the speaker, the listener, and the subject of the *lashon hara*. God, it seems, is more likely to tolerate rebellion against Himself than people's sinfulness against each other. He gave us our bodies and our spirits, our noses and our tongues and all our senses and all our powers of life, to do good in this world, to show our devotion to Him through our goodness and devotion to each other.

*Parashas Chukas 5778*

# Paradox

Sometimes the paradox derives from the story. And sometimes the paradox *is* the story itself, or key to the story.

Sometimes the obvious is the story. And sometimes the story must be analyzed and dissected until the obscure becomes the obvious.

The wondrous greatness of creation is readily obvious in the mountains and the seas, the sky and the earth, the flora and the fauna. And sometimes that greatness is ever more wondrous in obscurity, hidden, until it is revealed, as in a single mitochondrion in a single nucleus of a single cell, a thing vastly, infinitely more complex and more wondrous than any device man has ever devised.

No species in the world has to struggle with paradox, except the human, for whom paradox is that distressingly common, disturbing reality of life that is part of what sets us apart from all of creation. And so the paradoxes in life, burdensome and vexing as they may be and often are, are to the discerning also a gift.

We, people of faith, also understand that this apparent state of contradiction, the paradoxes that may serve to mystify and obfuscate, are not paradoxes at all, but built-in, intentional limits to our understanding that serve the purposes of our Creator in giving us this challenge, to help us understand that life is not simple or monotonal, that we are given the capacity to choose to soar so high or to sink so low, that the challenges in life – physical, spiritual, intellectual – are the very rungs in the ladder God has provided us, in the opportunity to climb toward Him that we call life.

*Zos chukas haTorah*. The mysterious ritual, the paradoxical outcomes – the *chok* – is not an isolated rule but *chukas haTorah*. It sheds light and perspective on the rest of the Torah, in why and how we follow its dictates and its lessons, in what it does to us and for us, in what we make of it. The Parah Adumah is *metaher temei'im and metamei tehorim*; the unclean become clean, while the clean become unclean. But, the sages have taught us, the same can be said of the Torah in general: *zachah*, if he (who studies it) merits it, *naasah lo sam chaim*, it is for him an elixir for life; *lo zachah*, if he is undeserving, if he perverts its purpose, *naasah lo sam misah*, it becomes for him a deadly poison (see *Yoma* 72b).

There is the classic and apparently sadly true story of the *maskil*, the yeshiva student turned cold-hearted to Judaism, to faith, to God Himself, who continues to study, even intently, for the intellectual satisfaction he derives from it, who is seen deeply immersed in a Talmudic/halachic analysis, an intricate, erudite *Ketzos*, on Shabbos, while smoking a cigarette.

*Metaher teme'im u'metamei tehorim.* The sincere yeshiva student, in this endeavor, reaches the greatest heights. He who perverts the Torah in this way would have been better off doing something else while being *mechalel Shabbos*.

The case in the Gemara applies to someone as well who gains mastery in Torah for the sake of gaining mastery over others, for power and position, and not for the sake of Heaven. The concept of doing something even *mi'toch she'lo lishmah*, in the hope that it will ultimately lead to *lishmah* doesn't apply here, where the motive is an evil one.

But *metaher teme'im u'metamei tehorim* can be more subtle and more insidious than that. We pray every day, at Maariv, that God remove the Satan from *before* us and from *behind* us: *v'haser satan milfaneinu u'me'acharenu.* The classic understanding is that the Satan tries to get us not to do the right thing, or actively to do the wrong thing. To sin. If he fails, he then tries, through his unceasing wiles, to get us to regret having done the right thing.

Imagine Avraham Avinu's reaction when he heard God telling him to take his promised, long-awaited, deeply beloved and miraculously born son and kill him upon a sacrificial altar. Impossible! God *hates* the human sacrifice that was rampant in that time, and Avraham knew it. *Impossible! Did he actually hear God telling him to do that, or did he just think he heard it?* Maybe he was delusional and now was about to kill his son on that basis! The greater a person is, the greater is his *yetzer hara*. The Satan must have been working overtime on Avraham.

Of course, the Satan failed. But he wasn't through. With the death of Sarah Imenu upon hearing of the Akeidah – when, not knowing that Yitzchak was actually *not* killed, she expired in anguish – the Satan tried to make Avraham and Yitzchak regret what they did.

But the Satan is such a subtle devil. He is even more devious than that. There is a midrash ascribed to Rabbi Meir (מרגניתא דר' מאיר) that the Satan will try his hardest to dissuade someone from doing a mitzvah (*what's all this mumbo jumbo with the hyssop branch and the Red Heifer that makes the* tamei tahor *and the* tahor tamei? *An illogical paradox!*). He will apply this to any mitzvah he can. And when he fails, and the Yid does the mitzvah (resisting the Satan's blandishments, *metaher teme'im*), if he can't make him regret it, the Satan pats him on the back: *Wow! What a great person you are! What a great Jew! How pious!* The pride, the swollen head, at least diminishes the mitzvah. *Metamei tehorim.*

Rashi spells it out. *Zos chukas haTorah*: This is the statute, the *chok*, of the Torah. The Satan will try to dissuade you by making you think that your logic is greater than God's. Analyze it all you will, you cannot master the reasoning behind it. The nations of the world will ridicule you, and if you try to explain it in any rational way, they've got you, because you can't. Rather, blow off the Satan and the scoffing nations of the world with the *real* reason you do this. You don't keep kosher because it's healthier. You don't wave a lulav because it's the fall harvest festival. You do all these things, all God's bidding, because He is our loving father and we His loving children; He is our absolute ruler, and we are, gratefully, His utterly obedient servants. When He says do it because *gezerah hi milfanai*, it is a decree from before Me, *ein lecha reshus l'harher achareha*, you are not to analyze or question it.

There are many mitzvos we can understand. We perform them not because we understand them, but because our God wants it of us. And that we demonstrate by performing just as fervently and enthusiastically those we do not. A lesson of *metaher temei'im u'metamei tehorim* is that God's mandate of *kivshuha*, conquer, dominate, master the wondrous, beautiful world He has given us, like the capacity of the human intellect itself, is not unlimited. There are things that are beyond our ken. God does want us to strive – and to strive mightily. But our role in this world is to be *metaher temei'im*. Those who, in their arrogance – and today there are many – set up their own intelligence as the final arbiter of truth fall frightfully into the pit of *metamei tehorim, Rachmana litzlan.*

*Parashas Chukas 5781*

# Balak

## Bloodlust

As the Red Army rampaged through Germany in 1945, no German female between the ages of eight and eighty was safe. And even those age parameters were stretched. It was about angry payback for the unspeakable cruelties and barbarism of the German occupation of the Soviet lands; it was, as in armies since time immemorial, about utter dominance, humiliation of the enemy, and the soldier's mindset that he is entitled. It was about bloodlust, the age-old companion of war.

Armies have behaved thus since the beginning of time, although in the frenzied activities of Soviet soldiers at that time, they acted not so much individually as in packs; perhaps the mindset of collectivism, inculcated by the Soviet system, played a role in a "collective" of dozens of men occupied with each victim.

The Germans, when it had been their turn, were, in effect (if not by regulation), free to do as they wished. With regard to Jewish women, it was OK to torture, torment, mutilate, and murder; rape, however, was forbidden, as it was beneath their racial dignity to be sullied by such contact with a Jew. Any other debased activity, including the rape of non-Jewish women, was their Teutonic right as conquerors of inferior races.

The Japanese were notorious in this regard, wherever they conquered. So it has always been in the world – some worse than others, but depressingly commonplace.

In modern, contemporary armies of the Western world, such activities are, of course, strictly forbidden and punished, *if* investigation is pursued. But historically, it has always been this way, this ugly aftermath part of the war strategy itself, breaking and demoralizing the defeated enemy, and a kind of reward to the victorious troops. This behavior, this cruelty, is expected. It was itself an instrument of war.

But it's not expected, or tolerated, of everyone. Klal Yisrael at war, even when intensely destructive, may not lose sight of its moral imperatives both at war and upon return home. *V'nasan lecha rachamim v'richamcha* (Devarim 13:18): Jews, being who they are, fear that war will make them cruel, and so God promises them that He will shield them from the moral degeneration and cruelty that such war tends to generate in its participants.

245

The Ohr Hachaim cites murderous Ishmaelites who have told him that they take great delight in killing and maiming, especially when they believe they are doing so in fulfillment of their leaders' command. Sound familiar? In fact, they expect a reward of seventy dark-eyed virgins if they die in the process, and plenty of loot and satisfied bloodlust if they survive. In 1948 and 1949, Muslim rioters ran wild in Jewish neighborhoods throughout the Arab world, looting and much, much worse, calling out, in Arabic, "Robbing Jews is [legally] permitted!" Their religious leadership had declared it so. And a lot worse than robbing.

Our enemies never fail to accuse us of all manner of atrocity, oppression, and cruelty. They are, of course, projecting their own cruel character traits onto us. The armies of Israel, since ancient times, have been remarkably restrained, even kindly. The Tanach relates how enemy soldiers facing starvation turned themselves in to the Israelites, knowing them to be a kindly people, a nation of *chesed*, who would feed them and not abuse them. And think back, in our own time, when the Kingdom of Jordan, in 1970, turned on the PLO, which was trying to overthrow it, and butchered the PLO terrorists wherever they found them. The terrorists fled to Israel, the very people they were dedicated to killing, and begged the Jews to save them – which they did, as the terrorists knew they would.

On that most joyous holiday of Pesach, when we celebrate our redemption from bitter bondage in Egypt, we of course sing Hallel, at the Seder and during davening. On the seventh day of Pesach, when the great miracle at Yam Suf occurred, where not only were we saved but our relentless pursuers, the great, mighty army of Egypt, was utterly destroyed before our very eyes, we should say double Hallel. Instead, we reduce the Hallel of the first day to "half Hallel," because while we rejoice for being saved, total deadly tragedy befell the Egyptians, good for us but still a somber reality that gives us pause. God Himself put the brakes on the *malachim* singing Hallel in Heaven, with the famous reproof, *Maaseh Yadai tov'im ba'yam, v'atem omrim shirah?* (*Sanhedrin* 39b, *Megillah* 10b): Those that I have created, that I fashioned, are drowning in the sea; at such suffering and loss of life, (even of bad guys), you want to sing?

Bnei Yisrael approached Eretz Yisrael from the east, having circumnavigated Edom because the Edomites refused them permission to pass through their lands, avoiding Moav because they were not permitted to come into conflict with them. Israel was not a threat to them at all. And yet they so seethed with fear and loathing that they tried what they could, entirely gratuitously, to undo, to destroy Israel. Step one was to hire the evil prophet Bilaam, whose curses were known to be effective, to curse them into destruction.

So why was there even such a thing as an evil prophet among the *goyim* who was, in fact, an actual prophet? Chazal tell us that it was to counteract the argument, the defense, that would otherwise be put forth, that they failed because unlike Israel they had no prophets. Rather, they did have prophets, but the evils of that society spawned "prophets" who chose to do evil.

Enter Bilaam. He was, *Midrash Tanchuma* tells us, so capable of prophecy that like Moshe, he was able to communicate with God whenever he wished. But what did Moshe and the prophets of Israel do, and what did Bilaam and the prophets of the nations do? The Jewish prophets exhorted their people to do good and to be holy. Bilaam advised Balak to destroy Israel through the holiness-destroying, seductive wiles of the daughters of Moav.

This cruel person, and those like him, sought to destroy our people, and for no good reason. Just gratuitous hatred. It seems as if nothing much has changed in this regard right up to the present day. And so, ultimately, God removed the power of prophecy from the nations, as they utilized it only with cruelty.

Now let's look at the prophets of Israel, who prophesied not just about Israel but about the other nations as well. We are accustomed to seeing, in their prophecy, sometimes harsh criticism of Israel gone astray, with dire consequences, usually followed by some consolation. And when they prophesied harshly about the downfall of our enemies, those who harmed us cruelly, that too was tempered by the pain of their human suffering. Hence, Yeshayahu says (16:11), *Al ken*, therefore, *me'ai l'Moav ka'kinor yehemu*, my insides moan like a harp for Moav, *for their suffering*. And in the impending destruction of Tyre, Yechezkel (27:2) cries: *Sa al Tzor kinah*, take up for Tyre a lamentation.

And so, *Tanchuma* informs us, the Torah tells us of the evil machinations of Bilaam not just because it is a narrative we must know, but to explain why Hashem took *ruach hakodesh* away from the nations, for Bilaam was the greatest prophet of them all, and look what he did.

Bloodlust, all too often in history central to the strategy of war for the nations of the world, free rein, license, to put every moral restraint known to man entirely aside, is, for us, in every possible application of the word and the concept, no way at all. Struggle we must, war we must, but even in the heat of that struggle, in whatever context, we may never lose sight of the higher purpose to which our God calls us. And the more our enemies accuse and vilify us, as has recently been so amply illustrated, the more we know that we have remained true to our calling.

*Hashem oz l'amo yiten, Hashem yevarech es amo ba'shalom.*

*Parashas Balak 5781*

# Pinchas

## Pinye

The world is divided into two groups of people: those who, in putting away their *tefillin shel yad*, wrap the straps all on one side, to avoid the *yud*-shaped knot on the other side, and those, a much smaller group, who wrap the straps evenly on both sides, placing the *retzuos* right over the *yud*.

The word *yud* (as in the Hebrew letter *yud*) is pronounced "*yud*" by most people, but others pronounce it "*yid*" (rhymes with *deed*). The Yiddish word for Jew, "*Yid*" (rhymes with *deed*), *is pronounced "Yud*" by others. In a sense, as used, the same word seems to cross over in meaning between representing a Jew, the tenth letter in the Hebrew alphabet, and, if you look at how God's name is often represented in printed Jewish religious texts, the very name of God. A *yud*.

When my brother, older than me by four years, started putting on tefillin, I remember the *rav* of our shul asked him why one doesn't wrap the *retzuos* over the *yud*-shaped knot. The reason, he quipped, is that one should never put anything over on a Yid.

Think about how important that little letter *yud* is. Its presence can make all the difference between the most sacred and the most profane. Consider prayer, תפילה. The little *yud* in that word, which in addition to being a letter, also represents the Jew *and* represents God, makes the difference between *tefillah*, prayer, encountering God, and *tiflah*, folly, pointless behavior, superstition. What a profound impact one *yud/yid* can make.

So how do you spell Pinchas? You will see it spelled both ways, with and without the *yud*. In this *parashah*, it is spelled פינחס. I suggest that the *yud* is there to bear testimony that Pinchas's brave and rash act – which, had he asked permission, he would have been told *not* to do – was, in fact, the right thing for him to do, and therefore, God put his stamp on it by spelling Pinchas's name *with* the *yud*.

And so, may Hashem avenge my Uncle Pinye's blood and that of his wife and children.

Pinchas Nussbaum, my mother's brother, was born in Kolbesov. Early in life, he gained renown as a *talmid chacham* and a *yerei Shamayim*. Like his father, he was a dedicated Dzhikover Chassid. When my grandfather, who did survive the war, passed away in New York at age ninety, the Kolbesover Rov, in his eulogy, said that he came to give *kavod* to the father of his rebbe, my Uncle Pinye. He was known as an uncommonly fine person, kind, considerate, charitable, highly spiritual but highly capable as well in the necessary skills required in *this* world, and *very* smart.

When I was young, my mother would sometimes look at my face and burst into tears, calling out "Pinye!" She said I looked just like him. Years later, we acquired a photo that survived the war because it had been sent to relatives in America sometime in the 1930s. Today, it sits in my study. Except for minor differences (the lips are different), it looks very much like me – or like I did when I was in my thirties. A bearded young man in Chassidic garb (with a necktie), with a fine face and obviously intelligent eyes. I am considerably older today than Pinye was when he and his family were martyred for the sake of Heaven.

Pinchas married a young woman of the Weiss family and moved to Stryj, where her family lived. His son Baruch, named for the same great-grandfather that I was, by age seven was regarded as an *iluy*, accomplished in Gemara with Rashi and Tosafos. It was in Stryj, to the best of our knowledge, that the entire family was murdered, along with all the rest of that accursed town's Jews, with the collusion of the local gentiles.

Pinchas ben Elazar ben Aharon Hakohen stood up for God. He survived his crisis and the danger he was in. He received God's blessing and great spiritual reward. He eventually became the Kohen Gadol, in which office he served for many years. Today, his descendants are everywhere Jews are to be found, still carrying the badge of *kehunah* bestowed upon him. Every year, we read a *parashah* in the Torah that bears his name and tells his glorious story.

Pinchas Nussbaum, of blessed memory, also stood up for God in everything he did, in the way he lived, in the way he treated other human beings. But he has, today, no living descendants. Together with millions like him, he was utterly erased from the world – except for the legacy of goodness, piety, and dedication that we can recall, not because we knew him, but because those qualities were such that others spoke of them long after he was gone.

Pinchas ben Elazar the Kohen and Pinchas Nussbaum the martyr were each פינחס with a prominent and pronounced *yud*, absolutely loyal and dedicated Jews, bound up with God Himself through that *yud*, through the way they lived their lives, through their faith and the strength of their resolve, through their undying legacy of standing up for God.

ברגז רחם תזכור
ברגז עקדה תזכור
ברגז תמימות תזכור

*Pinchas Nussbaum, of blessed memory*

*Parashas Pinchas 5778*

# Vus Ligt oyf'n Ling

A popular and high-quality Jewish interest publication asked one of its star writers, one who investigates thoroughly and writes captivatingly, to consider writing a major piece sure to arouse a great deal of interest: the propagation from generation to generation of child abuse in the families of Holocaust survivors, a direct outgrowth of the traumatization by the Holocaust and its lingering effects generations later.

Sound like a good thing to write about? Assuming that the premise is even true (and I will say right here, as a child of survivors, who grew up amid many such survivors, that I never saw it even once; parents showered love and healthy devotion on their precious children), why would they want to write about it and bandy it about? Haven't those poor people been battered enough? One wonders if the publication would similarly undertake to write an expose about the sad, secret lives of the children of abusive *roshei yeshiva* (imagine it, for the purpose of this discussion), who go on to be *roshei yeshiva* themselves and then also secretly abuse their own children. *Never in a million years would they publish such a thing, even if it were true!* Nor should they – about either subject.

You don't *have* to say everything that it's possible to say, even if it's true. There is a Yiddish expression about someone who blurts out whatever is on his mind, even if it would be wiser and far less harmful just to keep quiet: *Vus ligt ihm oyf'n ling, ligt ihm oyf'n tsing.* What is in his heart (on his chest) is promptly on his tongue (he blurts it out). It is the foolish trait of someone who is missing a critical social filter.

Sometimes, however, it's far more complicated than that. There are times when on one level something needs to be said, or to be done, but there is no one individual who should be the one to say it or do it. It's not prudent, it's radical, it's too much, even while it's true. Society will correctly say, *"you're right, but don't say that; you're right, but don't do that."* And sometimes, there is a fine line between the one who does so act and emerges an imprudent and unreasoned zealot and the one who turns out a hero, admired by all. Which brings us to Pinchas.

Pinchas was, of course, quite right to do what he did, although no one, including Moshe, would have explicitly told him to do it. In fact, had he asked first, he would have been told not to do it. But in doing it, he saved the day. And there was no one else to do it, even as the leadership stood there, apparently helplessly crying in the face of the sinful and destructive tragedy unfolding all around them. He opened himself up to harsh retribution, which thankfully never came. Instead, for his violent act, he was rewarded with *brisi shalom*, God's covenant of peace. And a *parashah* in the Torah was named in his honor.

Pinchas is, in Jewish lore, closely bound up with another zealot, one who spoke out and suffered for it, who acted for the sake of Heaven and had to flee for his life, Eliyahu Hanavi. There is even a tradition that they were, somehow, the same person. But by way of introduction to this concept, let us take a brief look at another of our all-time great prophets, Yeshayahu.

Yeshayahu's call to prophecy is described in chapter 6, in which he becomes prophetically aware of God sitting on His lofty throne, surrounded by fiery *serafim* who call out *"Kadosh, kadosh, kadosh Hashem*, Lord of hosts; the entire world is filled with His glory." The scene is so awesome that Yeshayahu concludes that having witnessed it, he will now surely die. "Woe is me! I am doomed, for I am a man of impure lips [*temei sefasayim*], dwelling among a nation of impure lips [*am temei sefasayim*], for my eyes have seen the King, Lord of hosts!" (Yeshayahu 6:5).

Yeshayahu was saying that he was unworthy to have witnessed what was revealed to him. But what was the point of declaring, as well, that the entire nation of Israel was unworthy? That was extraneous, really, to this occasion. It was unnecessary and uncalled for, *even if true*. Yevamos 49b tells us that years later, Yeshayahu suffers a fatal trauma to his mouth, symbolically a punishment for besmirching the name of Klal Yisrael, even if they deserved it. Some of the most beautiful and lyrical expressions of love and consolation for Israel are to be found in Sefer Yeshayahu. And Israel is also harshly criticized many times in Yeshayahu's prophecy, always appropriately, always for a reason, always at God's direction. There was, sadly, plenty to criticize Israel for. Here, it was not necessary, it was not prophecy, and it was wrong to say it. Not everything that *can* be said needs to be said.

The idea of Eliyahu Hanavi in Jewish lore is a powerful one. We lovingly and longingly anticipate that it is Eliyahu who will herald the arrival of Mashiach (speedily, please God!), and especially moving is his perceived role in rescuing individual Jews and Klal Yisrael in tough situations throughout history, in mysterious ways. But the text of the Navi (I Melachim) portrays him as something of a fierce character, defending Judaism from the overpowering assaults upon it by the wicked King Achav and his even more wicked non-Jewish wife Jezebel, who fostered idolatry and its related abominations, and who persecuted and killed the true prophets of Hashem. He is fierce and unrelenting. He calls upon God to withhold the rain and bring about a famine in the land until Achav and his followers repent, which brings great suffering. He seeks confrontation.

When Eliyahu shows up the false prophets of the Baal at Mount Carmel, killing 450 of them, Jezebel tries to kill him. He flees and winds up on Har Sinai, taking refuge in the very cave or cleft in the rock that Moshe stood in during his own Revelation. God asks him, *Mah lecha poh, Eliyahu?* Why are you here?

Eliyahu replies, "*Kano kineisi la'Hashem*, I acted with great zealotry on behalf of God, for the Children of Israel abandoned their covenant with You, Hashem. They destroyed Your altars, killed Your prophets; I alone remain as Your public advocate, and now they seek to kill me" (I Melachim 19:10).

God tells him to exit the cave, stand on the side of the mountain, and to behold: as He passes (*k'v'yachol*), a great and powerful wind smashes mountains and pulverizes rocks, but God is *not* in the wind. After the wind comes a powerful earthquake, but God is not in the earthquake. And after the earthquake comes a great conflagration, but God is not in the fire.

And then, after all the noise and the terror, comes a small, still sound. And when he hears the "thin voice," Eliyahu understands that he is in the Presence, He wraps himself in his prophet's cloak, and he hears the voice ask him, yet again, *mah lecha poh Eliyahu*, Eliyahu, why are you here? *What are you doing here? How did it come about that you are here? Eliyahu, what are you doing?*

Eliyahu answers yet again the same way, *kano kineisi la'Hashem*, I acted with great zealotry on Your behalf, Hashem, for the Children of Israel have abandoned their covenant with You. They destroyed Your altars, murdered Your prophets; I alone remain as Your public advocate, and now they seek to kill me (I Melachim 19:14).

Eliyahu was standing at exactly the spot where Moshe pleaded with God to have mercy for His children and to forgive them their sins. Eliyahu, in that spot, in his zealotry, condemned them not once but twice.

God had just shown Eliyahu that His power and presence were not in the wind or the earthquake or the fire, but in the small, still sound that is His essence. The rest, the noise and the turmoil, are just His servants. They have their place, but that is not where God chooses to manifest Himself in this regard. *Eliyahu, what are you doing? Even after I showed you, you persist in harshly criticizing and blaming My children, which displeases Me.*

*Mah lecha poh, Eliyahu? What are you doing? Here, of all places, where Moshe pleaded for and tried to excuse the Children of Israel, a place of* rachamim! *Here, you castigate and blame them!*

Eliyahu is immediately instructed by God to find and appoint his own successor, Elisha ben Shafat – as if to say, *I don't want your prophecy anymore, Eliyahu! You are too much of a zealot! This is not how I want it done. Your mission is closing down. You will be leaving.*

Zealotry is a tricky thing. Sometimes it works out just right, as it did for Pinchas. More often, however, even for Yeshayahu and for Eliyahu, two of the greatest prophets of all time, it is too much. God can manifest Himself in the wind, in the earthquake, in the fire, and sometimes He does. But the way He wants us to think about and talk about our fellow Jews is *nur mit gitten*, as my mother used to advise me in parenting, only through goodness, gently, with love, with the gentle, refined voice, with the small, still sound, the *kol demamah dakah*, that in its gentleness holds such power that it reverberates still, from Sinai itself, from the very core of God, *k'v'yachol*, reaching every one of us in all the generations of our existence.

*Parashas Pinchas 5779*

# Throwing Out the Baby

Pinchas is immortalized for his brave and zealous defense of the honor of God and of *kedushah*.

Midian is punished for its attempt to destroy Israel through immorality.

Another census of God's beloved Klal Yisrael, about to enter the Land of Israel.

How to apportion the Land of Israel among the people.

The great and wise daughters of Tzelafchad.

The designation of Yehoshua as Moshe's successor.

These are the themes in Parashas Pinchas, until *chamishi*. From there till the end, an exhaustive listing and description of the communal *korbonos* to be brought by Klal Yisrael all through the year, the source of Torah readings on Rosh Chodesh and holidays throughout the year. How appropriate, as we enter the Three Weeks and the period culminating in Tisha b'Av, of intense mourning for the loss of these rituals, to recall these *korbonos* and the Mikdash at which they were offered, *korbonos* that were, for our nation, a very lifeline, an avenue to God Himself, through which to please Him and to earn His blessing. To this day, thousands of years later, we remain in misery and mourning for this inestimable loss.

We are at a loss. The passage of the centuries has made some people lose sensitivity to it, but that too is part of the tragedy. What recourse do we have, other than Torah and *chesed*, powerful as they are, to try to mitigate this loss? Hoshea (14:3) tells us, *unshalmah parim sefaseinu*, we will offer the *korbonos* with our lips: *in prayer*.

A great *chesed* of the Ribbono shel Olam is that He lets us, on at least some level, fulfill what we cannot do, offer actual *korbonos*, with *virtual* ones: we recite, in our davening, the order of the *korbonos*, asking Hashem to accept our recitation as if we had brought the actual *korbonos* themselves.

Each morning, and for many each afternoon before Minchah, we devotedly recite the order of the *korbonos* accompanied by a supplication for each one: *Oh, Ribbono shel Olam! May it be Your Will that our devoted recitation of each* korban *that we can only wish we could bring, that we so yearn to one day be able to bring, be accepted by You as if we had brought the actual* korban! The *tamid*. The *olah*. The *chatas*. The *ketores*. The Shabbos and Rosh Chodesh *korbonos*.

What a precious and invaluable opportunity in our hopes to earn God's favor!

And so, I am really at a loss to understand why it is routinely skipped in some shuls. At Minchah? *Fuhgeddaboudit*. Among Ashkenazim, only the Chassidim do that. At Shacharis on weekday mornings? *Mekadesh Shemo ba'rabim* – zip! to Rabbi *Yishmael omer*. Okay, gotta get to work, right? What about on Shabbos? Gotta get to Kiddush? Sunday? Gotta get to the lox and bagels?

I've looked very carefully at the siddur, the organized order of prayer established by our Chachamim, which details what we are supposed to say at davening. I've searched in many different editions, and I have not found even once where Chazal included in the instructions a note about Korbonos that says, *Heh heh, we don't really mean it. We put this here to look good, maybe for someone who is into it, but you can forget about it.*

Did you ever climb Masada? In the summer heat, it would be nearly suicidal for most people. Now there's a cable car. When I first got there as a student, there was none. There was only the winding, steep, and treacherous "snake path." And you couldn't climb in the daytime. At the youth hostel at the foot of the mountain, they would wake us up at 2 a.m., and we would climb in the cool of night, backpacks over our shoulders, reaching the top just as dawn broke rosy over the mountains of Transjordan. People would then divide into groups to daven Shacharis.

We placed our tefillin bags on the ancient rocky formations, donned our tefillin, faced Yerushalayim, and in this place made holy by our zealous, martyred forebears, began to daven. In my group of youths, made up of a few friends and other boys we didn't know, there was a young fellow who volunteered to be the chazan. In short order, Berachos, straight to Baruch She'amar, Ashrei, Yishtabach, Shema, Shemoneh Esreh. Nothing in between. All skipped. *Whoa! What are you doing?*

He looked at us in confusion. "What are you talking about?" he replied. *"Nobody* says the other stuff!" He was actually a very sincere young man. That's how they daven at the Conservative congregation he belongs to, he explained. That's how he was taught. He thought everybody did it that way.

Somehow, I can't help thinking of this when I contemplate the skipping of Korbonos in shul, especially when there is no good reason to.

There must be something lacking in my education or my *frum* bona fides, because I just don't get why it's so often done. Ask someone who should know, and you might get a subtle but discernible condescending look (but no answer). It's the same look one got from some *frum* people, back in the bad early days of the COVID-19 pandemic, as to why they were not wearing a mask or taking any precautions: *Yeah, yeah,* a half shrug, and a look that said *you just don't really get it, you clueless outsider.*

So, can someone explain this to me? I must be, at least in this, a clueless outsider.

*Parashas Pinchas 5781*

# Mattos-Masei

## Tribal

Why do we have twelve tribes? Why did it start with Yaakov's sons (twelve tribes) and not his grandsons (which would make it fifty-one tribes) or with Yaakov himself (one tribe!)? Why have tribes altogether? Is "tribalism" a good thing or a bad thing? One unified nation, without distinctions, sounds good, right?

Sometimes, as in this *parashah*, the tribes are referred to as *mattos* (plural of *mateh*) and other times as *shevatim* (plural of *shevet*). Why is that? Interestingly, each of those words, which we use in this context to refer to a tribe of people, has as its primary meaning a stick, or a slim tree branch. They are more or less the same thing, but one (*shevet*) is said to describe the characteristics of a slim branch still attached to the tree, so it is more soft and flexible, while a *mateh* is detached from the source, so it tends to be drier and thus more rigid and strong. Much has been written about how this distinction may apply to Klal Yisrael in different times and to different aspects of its character and experience.

Okay, but why do we need tribes altogether, and why twelve of them? Well, if we need tribes, one is too few, and fifty-one is too many. And we need different tribes within the nation, I submit, because we cannot be, and clearly God does not want us to be, monolithic automatons who need to be absolutely uniform in our thoughts, words, deeds, and style. Within the framework of His Torah as a mandated guide to life, there is much room for the individual to express himself as an individual. That is a great strength. Perhaps that's why we don't all look or think alike.

There are multiple faces to Judaism. Each of the *shevatim*, in fact, had its own personality and style. And so today, and throughout our history, we have and we have had all the various *nuschaos* of davening, the various traditions, the Litvaks and the Yekkes and the Galitzianers, the Sephardim and the Yemenites, the Italian and the Greek, and everything else, all good, all kosher, all legitimate, all *l'shem Shamayim*.

The God Who designed life also ordained that the differences between people and between tribes, harnessed to work together for the common good, make the world go round.

Authoritarian humans in positions of leadership – in any context – who try to force people to think and act absolutely alike are despotic tyrants. They crush the creative human spirit with which the Creator has endowed us.

The Creator, however, made us *shevatim, mattos,* branches of one tree, all connected to each other, all derived from one source, all nourished from the same roots. But we are not, nor should we be, nor does He want us to be, absolutely identical. How boring and listless, how uninteresting, how uncreative that would be.

Every one of us has unique gifts to offer. And so he made us twelve tribes, *a bunch*: a lot more than one, but *not* fifty-one, or a hundred one, not chaotic – for along with our individuality, for all the variations, branches of the same tree, we are also, as a nation, *one.*

*Parashas Mattos-Masei 5778*

# Systemic Palestinism

The shul was having a hard time paying its rabbi. The budget included $147,000 that had to go to pay the state-mandated and appointed diversity officer, whose Jewish credential (nice to have but not necessary) was that her cousin had briefly been married to someone who'd had a bat mitzvah. (It had been a blast, with a hip-hop theme.) With a fairly small membership, the shul's resources were limited, and money was tight. They could have a rabbi if they wanted, the government bureaucrat in charge of such things said, but the diversity officer was mandatory.

The shul was plagued by systemic racism, a fact determined not only ipso facto by default, but also by its 100 percent white membership. Two off-white members, darkly complected folks of Yemenite ancestry, were deemed white anyway, because they were Jews, and everybody knows that Jews are white. These people routinely failed to check their white privilege, persisting arrogantly and stubbornly in living their lives as usual, working, attending classes and worship, nearly all of them with two parents in the home, the children all in school. In their arrogance, they claimed not to understand what they were doing wrong. They claimed to be just living quiet, normal lives, not bothering anyone, dealing honestly, cheerfully, and faithfully with everyone. They claimed that they got along openly, easily, and with friendliness toward everyone, all clear proof of their systemic racism, a rotten malady that affected all of society.

To make matters worse, they all favored Israel. How could any decent person favor a society made up entirely of invaders who had no ties to the land, who arrived in droves "from Europe" to uproot those indigenous, innocent, and virtuous "brown" people, the Palestinians (no matter how white they may actually be), the rightful inhabitants, who had, since time immemorial, peacefully and benignly lived their national Palestinian life there. The "enlightened" critics know, actually, nothing at all about the subject, but of this, in their hatred, in their arrogance, even the nominal Jews among them, they are utterly convinced. Colonialism, racism, white supremacy, ethnic cleansing, genocide. These people, these shul-goers, need some lessons in diversity and ethnic sensitivity. They are systemic racists. People who live in such a society, who benefit from their constant white privilege, are not even "woke" enough to realize, much less admit, that they live off the enforced misery of the darker races. They will now, along with the rest of the systemically racist and white supremacist society, be forced to make that journey.

This is a scenario that I would have believed, a few short years ago, to be impossible. A journey indeed. Our people have made innumerable journeys in our long years of wandering. This is a journey that America was not supposed to make. Its unique journey, since its founding, has been a difficult, often traumatic, but progressive society-wide march toward universalizing the attainment of the lofty moral civil principles upon which it was founded. In this it has been doing very well indeed. But it is now, frighteningly, at risk. Stupidity, insanity, utter ignorance, and cynical evil are the loudest voices today, voices that viciously tolerate no other voice to counter them. Poseurs who think nothing of ruining people because they think it makes them look virtuous and enlightened, because they *can*, even as their behavior places them as far from virtue as one can imagine. Crime is perversely portrayed as righteous, and those who seek protection from that crime are charged as bigoted criminals.

That vicious racism and bigotry are "systemic" in America, as we now hear ceaselessly from every corner, from the race hucksters, the poseurs, the cynical opportunists and their useful idiots – a racism that is so pervasive that it "colors" every encounter, a contempt that is always there, always by whites against blacks and never in the opposite direction – is, of course, a damnable lie and a cynical political invention.

The notion that the "Palestinians," a recent political invention as a nation, are the age-old true natives of the Land (of Israel!) since time immemorial, and that the nation of Israel are the cruel, bigoted white interlopers (thank you, Reverend

Al, for that colorful term) is itself a "systemic" invention that is the product of a "systemic" hatred. We are all too familiar with that hatred, and with its sometimes – indeed ofttimes – terrible consequences. Call this aspect of it Systemic Palestinism.

The Torah, in Parashas Masei, enumerates the many stops our forefathers made in their forty-year eventful trek to the Land of Israel all those thousands of years ago. Of those forty-two stops, many were associated with strife, even horrible strife. In the end, however, they entered the land that became our eternal, God-given inheritance.

The *meforshim* say that there is a great lesson here, that people, as well as nations, must sometimes pass through very difficult stages, with ups and downs, with triumphs and with tragedies, with losses and with gains, as we journey through life. The road we must travel, we individuals, we Jews, we Americans, people of all backgrounds and places, can have many stops and stages that appear to be bad, hurtful, dangerous. The quest for the larger, greater goals may be fraught. If we persevere, if we hold fast to our faith and our principles, to the truth, and *b'chasdei Hashem* we do achieve our goals, we can then look back, from the perspective of our spiritual achievement, and see that the challenges and difficulties we had to deal with were also opportunities to grow and to earn merit, as painful and as trying as the process may have been.

The pitfalls, in retrospect, become rungs in the ladder.

May it be the will of our Father in Heaven, in these difficult times, that the terrible challenges we face, we Jews, we Americans, our brothers and sisters in the holy Land of Israel – in this fraught time of frightful disease, strife, economic distress, social and political hatred and upheaval, war and threats of war, brazen and cynical evil, power in the hands of the mindless as well as the mindfully corrupt, attempts to tear down our civilization, in this earnest and historically dangerous time of *bein hametzarim* – be revealed very soon, as we look back, as stepping stones, however painful, to peace, prosperity, respect, love, and Redemption.

*Parashas Mattos-Masei 5780*

# The Arduous Journey

Tante Liebe, my mother's sister, was, like many of her generation, an ardent Zionist. As a very young woman in Poland, she won the lottery: a rare and much-sought visa to Palestine. The British occupiers did everything they could to keep

Jewish immigration as close to zero as possible, so this was a great and rare opportunity. It was 1932.

Her parents very much did not want her to go. Devout Dzhikover Chassidim, they feared the likely and common outcome for such cases, in terms of the ongoing religiosity for such young people alone in Palestine. There was plenty of precedent for them to be worried. It was a big problem indeed, for the families, for the nation, and for the Land of Israel.

She went. In Tel Aviv, she met a nice young man from a good family who lived not far from my grandparents. The families met and agreed to the *shidduch*. The young couple married and started a life together. Uncle Tzvi was a very hardworking and capable man, but life was very difficult in those years. There were very lean times, with not enough to eat. And then children came along.

Tzvi's brother was cruelly killed by Arabs during the War of Independence. In that fierce war, about 1 percent of the Jewish population was killed – that's the equivalent of losing a staggering *three million* people for the United States today.

Postwar, the family settled on a moshav just created, hard on the hostile border. Everything, everything was difficult. Living conditions were poor and primitive. My uncle had to build his family's home with his own hands. I remember my parents, survivor immigrants themselves in the United States, sending packages to them on a regular basis, with commodities they needed and could not get or could sell to live off the proceeds. Aside from farming, my uncle sat day and night sewing work gloves for the army and, I suppose, sanitation crews, to help make ends meet. Tante Liebe's siblings in New York pooled their resources to buy her a refrigerator, which she did not have. They worked and they persevered. Life was hard, but they were building up Eretz Yisrael.

My cousins told me that in the hot summer nights, there was no relief from the heat, the humidity, or the mosquitos. But here is where the story turns. Those same cousins, the three sons, each received a fine engineering education at the Technion, and today *baruch Hashem* live comfortable lives, with all the air conditioning and other comforts they want.

We are told by many sources that acquiring Eretz Yisrael is difficult, and, *lo aleinu*, often involves *yissurim*. Even our original entry into the land in Yehoshua's time and after was difficult and prolonged. The Torah tells us it will be a gradual process. How difficult, it appears, depends on when and how. In Yehoshua's time, it was clearly less difficult, but still dependent upon our good behavior, which we are notoriously slack on. And that cost us. The original return to Zion, after Galus Bavel, was very difficult indeed. And our return today is so slow, so hard, so painful, so costly, so bloody, and so amazing.

There were several thousand Jews altogether in the Land of Israel in the early 1800s. The dedicated pioneers suffered terribly, but when Tante Liebe arrived, there were about 175,000. At the time of the War of Independence, there were 630,000. Today there are, *ken yirbu*, about seven million. A miracle before our eyes. Aside from other sources and avenues, Nefesh B'Nefesh is in its twentieth year of organizing, facilitating, and transporting flights of Jews from North America making their ascent, their aliyah, to Eretz Yisrael.

The problems, the challenges, are very great – but far less difficult overall, it appears, with each generation. Just a generation ago, people often arrived with nothing, and some spent years in *maabarot*, tent slums, under terrible conditions. But that is long past.

Ah, but the political, the political! And the disheartening loss of religion by so many. There is, sadly, tragically, a segment in this country that, denying the very God Who bestowed this Holy Land upon them as their birthright and their legacy, don't really know by what right they are here. And so, to them, Israel is guilty of every crime. To them, the Jews are wrong, and the Arabs are right (except perhaps about the artsy cafés of north Tel Aviv). Failure to achieve peace is, in their view, virtually always Israel's fault. Prominent in the media and the public sphere, whatever their numbers, their voices are very loud. They too are part of the difficulty foretold.

To them, and to the faint of heart of every segment of the population, God says to Israel, in Parashas Masei, chronicling the arduous journeys of Bnei Yisrael (then and predictively for all time to come), *When you cross the River Jordan and you arrive in the land of Canaan, V'horashtem es kol yoshvei ha'aretz mi'pneichem* (Bamidbar 33:52). You will "disinherit," displace, those who are there. Says the Gemara (*Sotah* 34:1): displacing those who are there (and creating your unique, holy civilization in this Holy Land) is a *condition* of your crossing the Jordan into the land.

*V'horashtem es ha'aretz vi'shavtem bah, ki lachem nasati es ha'aretz lareshes osah* (33:53). You will take over the inheritance of the land, and you will dwell there. Says Rashi: *If you displace the people who are there, you will be able to exist there; if you do not, you will not be able to exist there.*

Wow. This concept is laid out in other *pesukim* as well. You cannot allow them to influence you, and unless you are determined, they will. No good will come of it. Shake off as well alien philosophies from other nations that de-Judaize your own.

And do not be afraid.

The beautiful growth and flowering of this country, for all its problems, for all its internal dissensions, for all its blustering enemies, within and without, is a miracle before our eyes. The courageous, struggling early *chalutzim*, the utterly determined, sacrificing Tante Liebes and Uncle Tzvis, the latter-day arrivals from lands of plenty who are drawn like magnets to Zion, those who bravely live on the dangerous frontiers under constant threat, are, with God's help and direction, builders of this dream. We cannot know, of course, but we pray that it indeed be *reishis tzmichus geulasenu.* The struggle continues to be very great. But our nation must persevere. Masei Bnei Yisrael, the fraught, arduous journeys of Bnei Yisrael, have brought us to this point.

And now, please God, our loving and merciful Father in Heaven, bring that frightful journey to its happy end. Bring us Home.

*Parashas Eleh Masei Bnei Yisrael 5782, Yerushalayim Ir Hakodesh*

# ספר דברים

# Devarim

## Is Anything OK?

Everybody knows the joke about the waiter who asks the diners if everything's OK, but based on experience, he asks Jewish diners if *anything* is OK.

Why should that be? What's with these people? Why are we not surprised by the joke? *Why do we get it?* Why do we so get it that we aren't even really offended by it?

How did we – or at least enough of us to create this impression – get this way?

I don't know, but it started a long time ago. Like in Egypt. It is most evident, from way back then, in the behavior of the Israelites in the *midbar*. They complained about everything. It wasn't enough to complain about the hardships; they complained as well about the wonderful and miraculous things that were done for them (things done free of charge, by the way).

They complained about the holy hero who came to rescue them and wrought miracles beyond number. They accused him, utterly without cause, of all manner of malfeasance.

See Rashi and the *midrashim*: If they saw Moshe go out early, they would say, "Look at Ben Amram!" Calling him Ben Amram is like calling Rabbi Goldberg "Goldberg." You know why he's leaving his tent so early? He's got wife trouble! No *shalom bayis*! He's escaping! If they saw him go out late, they would say, "That Ben Amram has been busy at home plotting against us!"

If they saw Moshe go out early, they would say, "Look at that Ben Amram, sneaking out early to collect the best of the *mon*!" If they saw him go out late, they would say, "Look at that Ben Amram! He eats and drinks his fill and then sleeps late!" If they saw him walking in the middle of the street, they would say, "Look at that Ben Amram! He struts about *in mit'n derinen* so that everybody has to stand up to greet and honor him!" If he walked on the side path, avoiding the crowds, they would complain, "Look at that Ben Amram! We have an easy mitzvah to perform, standing up for the Torah leader, but he denies us the opportunity by slinking about on the sides!"

And at one point, they even suspected him of dallying with their wives.

And these were the *good* 20 percent of the Jews in Mitzrayim who actually got out. The same 20 percent that included Dasan and Aviram. What a tough crowd.

Is *anything* OK?

Moshe was so exasperated with them that at one point, he begged God to kill him so that he wouldn't have to put up with them anymore. But being who he was, the incredibly loyal and protective shepherd of this unruly and errant flock, he never failed to come to their defense, and he saved them time and again.

So now, as Sefer Devarim opens with Moshe's farewell address and admonition to the difficult people he has led through the wilderness for forty years, he chooses his words and his approach carefully, that they hear him and heed him, that they take his words to heart so that they might survive when he is no longer there to protect them and to shield them from God's anger, as he has done for all those years.

He scolds them; he gives them *mussar*. But there is *mussar* and there is *mussar*. There is a method to *mussar*. *Mussar* is good only if it is likely to accomplish anything. Ask any effective parent or teacher.

Much has been written on Moshe's strategy here and the lessons to be learned from it. Let me, as a parent, concentrate on one.

The Torah spells out – and the Torah uses no extra words – that Moshe admonished the people *after* he defeated the mighty kings and nations blocking their path of entry into the Promised Land, Sichon king of the Emori and the frightful Og king of Bashan.

In fact, these conquered lands, while still east of the River Jordan, became a peripheral part of Israel. The people now understood that their entry to the land had begun, that the promises were being kept, that Moshe was still struggling and still producing on their behalf.

Rashi says that Moshe understood that if he admonished them before that, those ingrates would likely complain that *there he goes again, criticizing and criticizing*, probably to cover up his own inadequacies and inability to get them into the land. *He's complaining about us*, they would say, *because he can't deliver. What's he done for us lately?* And so he waited until he conquered the two mighty nations and presented their lands and their rich resources to the people *as a bonus*, a precursor to the big prize they now knew was surely coming, the Land of Israel itself.

If you want your *mussar* and *tochachah* to be heard, if you want it to be effective, you have to offer more than just pontification or preaching or tough love. You need to offer more than just *mussar* and *tochachah*. You need a credential: when your heart and your soul and your self-sacrifice are evident, you have at least a chance to be heard and heeded.

As we read Parashas Devarim, we stand on the cusp of the annual observance of the date associated with all the many tragedies in our history, the Ninth of Av. It didn't have to be this way. For all the goodness and the greatness in Klal Yisrael – and there is much of that, so much that despite our many failings, our loving God continues to love us unfailingly – as a nation we have brought, with the stubborn recalcitrance we are familiarly known for, all this tragedy upon ourselves.

It didn't have to be this way. But this is how it has been. And yet the same God Who has visited these many punishments upon us – which we have to believe was, in some way we cannot fathom, somehow necessary for us – also somehow continues to love us, to keep this stubborn and complaining nation alive, to send us His servants in every generation, who are so loyal and so loving and so protective that they struggle with God Himself on our behalf, even as we often fail to appreciate them in the way they need to be appreciated. And if they do also offer us criticism as part of their teaching, they have more than earned that right.

Perhaps that is one of the keys to the puzzle of our getting out from under this perennial morass. We know from many examples that God seems to be more demanding in how we honor each other than in how we honor Him. His preferred way for us to honor Him is for us to honor and respect each other, especially those who, by word and deed, teach us His word.

We live in a time when the society around us is actively trying to banish God from public consciousness, when *anything goes*, where *everything is OK*, no matter how base, no matter how perverse, the further from Godliness the better.

Our mandate, it would seem, personally and collectively, perhaps the antidote to Tisha b'Av itself, is to look at that *anything* and that *everything*, to stand up and to *put things right*, the way God has mandated, the way our revered teachers, Moshe Rabbeinu and his successors, have always taught us, continue to teach us, and always will.

And to stand up for them as well.

*Parashas Devarim 5778, Shabbos Kodesh, 9 Av*

# Va'eschanan

## Rat-tat-tat-tat-tat-tat-tat

When I was a little kid, we never had comic books at home. Too junky and not worth the precious dime they cost. I never challenged my mother's judgment on this. I did get to "read" them, before I learned how to read, at the corner barber shop.

Angelo, with his neatly trimmed pencil-thin black mustache, in his blue barber's shirt, had a supply of Superman and, in those post–WW II years, with the Korean War raging, GI Joe comics. It was a real old-time barber shop, with a striped barber pole out front, brass spittoons, and sometimes colorful characters. Before it was my turn, when Angelo would place a special padded plank across the armrests of the barber chair for me to sit on a kind of elevated throne (so he shouldn't have to bend over too much while cutting my golden red locks), I would look at the comics and follow the story line based on the pictures. It wasn't too hard; I suppose that was the point of the comics.

It was early on that I learned to read one of my first printed "words": *RAT-TAT-TAT-TAT-TAT-TAT-TAT!!* It always accompanied a picture of a grimacing soldier, American or enemy, mowing down his enemies with a rapid-fire machine gun. No thought; just shooting. *RAT-TAT-TAT-TAT-TAT-TAT-TAT!!* The word depiction of a sound to create an image, which I later on learned was called onomatopoeia, must have made quite an impression on me: I think of it sometimes when I come to Parashas Va'eschanan.

*Va'eschanan.* I appealed. I implored. I begged. I entreated. I prayed for God's graciousness. For His compassion. His *chanunim*. There are ten *leshonos*, ten word types of prayer, says the Midrash, but Moshe specifically appealed for *tachanunim*. Rabbi Yochanan teaches that we learn from this that no one, not even Moshe, has any claim on God. We may, in fact, have *zechuyos* before Him, but that is His judgment, not currency that we can ask to collect on. Moshe appealed for *tachanunim* – as should we when we pray – a free gift from God, purely a function of His mercy. *V'chanosi es asher achon, v'richamti es asher arachem.*

Especially in the most desperate of prayers, it is the most powerful Godly attribute to appeal to. It is the one Hashem taught us to appeal to.

*Chanunim* – compassion, mercy, kindness – is so powerful, whether vested in the Divine or in an individual, that it can move worlds.

A gift, if you please, to anyone named Chana: My mother, of blessed memory, a woman of great compassion and empathy, was named Chana. She was quite friendly with Chana Kaminetsky, wife of the great Rav Yaakov Kaminetsky. Rav Yaakov would sometimes get on the phone to wish my mother a good Shabbos or good *yom tov*. One time he said to her a great truth: *Mrs. Reich, ihr zult vissen* (Mrs. Reich, you should know): *s'nisht du kein shlechte Chana*. There are no bad Chanas. The power of *chanunim* is so great that the very name already says a great deal about the person.

Moshe's situation was desperate. God had already decreed that he would not enter the land, but that he would die in the desert, and Yehoshua would lead the nation into the Promised Land. It was, it would appear, too late. The decree was already enshrined in the Torah. How would Moshe think that he might still change it?

Actually, he did have the power to effect such change. Way back at the *chet ha'egel*, Hashem said to Moshe, *heref Mimeni v'ashmidem*, let go of Me (*release Me!*), and I will destroy them. *Release Me?* Did Moshe have some kind of hold on the Ribbono shel Olam? The Sifri (3:24) says *yes*. God vested such power in prayer that such things are possible.

Here Moshe says, *Ribbono shel Olam, You opened a door for me then when You declared, "Release Me." I seized that opportunity and prayed. You listened and forgave them. I thought, in my current predicament, that they were with me now in my prayers, as I was with them then. If my individual prayer for them then was effective, then surely the entire community's prayer now on my behalf should be effective.* And Moshe was right. It would have been. But it didn't happen, because the people did not join Moshe in his entreaty. They failed him.

Moshe's error was hitting the rock rather than speaking to it, as God had commanded. That failure in *kiddush Hashem*, whatever the reason it happened, was the basis for Moshe's punishment. The people had clamored for water, but hitting the rock was Moshe's mistake, not theirs. And yet here, Moshe says *va'yisaber Hashem bi l'maanchem*, Hashem was angry with me because of you. How so?

Here Rav Soloveitchik hits us right between the eyes. Moshe's complaint to the people, he says, starts with the very first word: *Va'eschanan. I* entreated. *I* prayed. *I* begged for God's *chesed*.

"I." Not "we." *I prayed alone. You did not pray for me. My solo prayer did not have the power to reverse the gezerah. But if you had prayed for me as well, it would have worked.* Such is the power of communal prayer. Such is the power of praying on someone else's behalf.

*When you all sinned, grievously, when by your actions you brought yourselves to the brink of destruction, I prayed, I begged, I entreated, and you were saved. Time and again. I was always there for you. Why were you not there for me?*

*Va'yisaber Hashem bi l'maanchem. Hashem's decree against me stands* because of you, *because of your failure to stand up for me. L'maanchem.*

It was bad enough for Moshe that he could not enter the Promised Land, his great dream. How heartbreaking it must have been for him that his beloved nation, for whom he struggled and suffered so much, to whom he dedicated his life, whom he had, by his strenuous efforts, rescued from Hashem's wrath time and again, just let him down. They could have saved him, had they tried. They didn't get it.

Chazal teach that had Moshe entered the land, all of history would have been different. We would never have been expelled. Our endless suffering would have been avoided altogether. What a terrible waste. What a tragedy for every one of us. What a loss. What a lesson in what we could accomplish, if we have the wisdom and the heart to do so.

One of the *leshonos* of prayer is *liz'ok.* It is a crying out, the Rav says, but that cry is not only to God, but to all of Klal Yisrael to cry out together. It is a summons to prayer as well as an expression of prayer, gathering the power of the many in our supplication before Him, a many that exponentially potentiates the power of that prayer.

And so the prayers that we utter even for individuals virtually always include the many. When we pray for a sick person, we also pray for all the sick. When we comfort the mourner, we also include all who mourn. When we ask for sustenance for ourselves, we also pray for that of all who need it. And therein, in the prayers on behalf of others as well as ourselves, lies the true power of our prayers.

When we recite Tachanun, begging for Hashem's *tachanunim* as Moshe did when he declared *Va'eschanan,* we do so *b'nefilas apayim,* falling on our faces in abject supplication, calling upon God's mercy as a free gift, claiming no merits other than the hope that all of us, praying for each other even as we pray for ourselves, will move God to show us His mercy.

This is serious, serious business. It is truly life and death for each of us and all of us. Our entreaties, our supplication, our heartfelt begging for our lives, for those of our children, for each other's lives which are as precious as our own, must come from the deepest and most sincere core within us. Prayer must be about others as well as ourselves. Our prayers must be...*prayerful, tachanunim,* and *never* mindless rat-tat-tat-tat-tat-tat-tat.

*Parashas Va'eschanan 5782*

# Ekev

## He Has Brought Me into His Innermost Chamber

The earlier generation of "cardiac Jews" contributed to Jewish causes as an expression of their Jewishness. Along with attending Kol Nidre services (and perhaps more) and throwing bar mitzvah parties, donating money to Jewish hospitals, the United Jewish Appeal (UJA), Israel Bonds, and their temples was, in their estimation, their fulfillment of the Judaism they inherited from their forebears.

They were often generous, and their hearts were very likely in the right place, even as their perspective was rather skewed. They were trying to be Jewish in a way that was comfortable and easy for them, a way that was, for the modern Jew, all he needed to do to remain a good Jew. Shabbos, tefillin? Of course not. Kosher? Perhaps nominally, at home.

Their "rabbis" had taught them that what really counts is what's in the heart. And what Judaism is really about – what the prophets railed about, they were taught – is social justice. And so, while they still cared about being Jewish, they gave to the UJA and voted Democratic. They worshiped FDR as a demigod who could do no wrong. That was also a way to be Jewish.

There were also those who still had more of a connection, who came to shul from time to time, but whose observance was certainly not in accordance with the Torah as we know it. They felt some guilt, and they assuaged that guilt with donations. That made it, in their minds, OK.

The children of these "cardiac Jews" (a great term I heard from our old friend and neighbor Rabbi David Rubin, *a"h*) in general had a worse heart condition than their parents. And so the watering down of what was left of their Jewishness has resulted in the utter alienation of so many, *nebech*. They may still contribute – but more often now to museums and hospitals and universities, monies that do nothing for Klal Yisrael. They think, however, that they are being Jewish in doing so. Well, in a way they are, as the motivation comes from a good place. But they are clueless about how it should be expressed. They are, after all, in their view, giving tzedakah, and giving tzedakah is what, in their view, Judaism is about. Unlike the residual fanatics, the primitives, to them God, as we "understand" Him, has little to do with it, and certainly not the Torah, of which they know pitifully little.

Oy, oy, oy. It is their children who are the troops, the useful idiots, of Jewish Voice for Peace, BDS, and other hate groups against Israel, all in the cause of "social justice."

The idea of tzedakah is so powerful among Jews that some do think it alone is a sufficient and legitimate path to God. Parashas Ekev tells us otherwise.

*Al tomar bilvavcha b'hadof Hashem Elokecha osam milfanecha leimor, b'tzidkasi heviani Hashem lareshes es ha'aretz hazos* (Devarim 9:4). Don't tell yourself that God is chasing away the nations and giving you the land because you are so righteous. It is not *b'tzidkascha*.

On *heviani*, "God has brought me," Ateres Yeshuah cites the three places in Tanach where this word appears: here and twice in Shir Hashirim. *Heviani el beis hayayin* (Shir Hashirim 2:4), the repository of wine, is an allegorical allusion to Sinai, to Torah, and refers to the study of Torah and most certainly adherence to its mandates. *Heviani haMelech chadarav* (Shir Hashirim 1:4), God has brought me to His inner chambers, alludes to *tefillah*, to intimate connection with Him. This is the intimacy with God that can only be achieved through *tefillah*, also identified as *avodah*.

To those Jews who think they fulfill their obligations as Jews just by charitable giving, God is saying, *very nice, but that alone doesn't do it. Lo b'tzidkascha u'v'yosher levavcha ata ba lareshes es artzam* (Devarim 9:5).

Why is the law of the jungle – eat or be eaten, kill or be killed, survival of the fittest – not the way of civilization? Because while that exists everywhere else in nature, for human beings, and particularly for Jews, there is a moral overlay imposed by the Creator that we are different, and that we were, in fact, created for the purpose of being different.

Tzedakah and *chesed* are a function of that difference – its highest expression. And the same divine source of justice, kindness, tzedakah, and *chesed* is also the source, for the Jew, of the mandates of Torah and prayer. The three do not exist independently for us. They are one package, all dependent on each other, each validated by the others. The same God Who wants us to give tzedakah requires us also to keep all the mitzvos of the Torah and to connect with Him through prayer.

In turn, we connect with Him through all three. On these three pillars the world stands: on Torah, on *avodah* (prayer), on *gemilas chasadim*. They may exist independently for others, but for us they are one. We can affirm that we are doing His will when we give tzedakah by doing His will with Torah and *avodah* as well.

Otherwise, it may be a good deed, but it is not in His service, at least not in the way He requires of us.

*Rachmana liba ba'i.* God wants our hearts. The cold, ritualistic practice of Judaism without the warmth of heart is anathema. But Judaism is, in fact, a religion of laws; the heart alone – vague, feel-good sentiment – is also not enough. Our Father in Heaven has invited us into His inner chamber – *heviani haMelech chadarav.* To enter, we must work, to present ourselves with our lives, completely His: with Torah, with *avodah*, with *gemilus chasadim.*

*Parashas Ekev 5782*

# Re'eh

## The Frontier Thesis

Barack Obama was the first American president, as far as I know, to publicly deny that America is exceptional. To deny that, especially for a president of the United States, so flies in the face of historical truth as to be absolutely stunning, not just in its intentional, ideologically driven untruth, but in its obvious intent to denigrate exactly what makes America great – and different from virtually every nation in history.

The fact that America is great, that it is historically exceptional among the nations of the world, does not mean that everything about America was or is great or good. The sordid history of violence, bigotry, slavery, the willful destruction of the Native Americans (the American Indians) as if they were of no account at all, antisemitism and other racial and religious biases all weigh heavily upon America's past. But nasty as that history is, it is not a function of the *idea* of America, but a distortion and a failure to live up to that idea. Those blots notwithstanding, America has been evolving into America. It is painful that there has arisen a subculture of those who wish to deny and to destroy the greatness of that idea and that ideal.

The Frontier Thesis, as stated by Frederick Jackson Turner in the 1890s – which builds upon observations made over the years by others, such as Alexis de Tocqueville in his 1835 treatise *Democracy in America* – posits that the nature and character of America were heavily influenced and even formed by the fact that for most of its history, there was at its edge a vast frontier where Americans ventured, largely unencumbered by the Old World's civilizational and cultural restraints on the individual and his freedoms or by intrusive government. This created an ethic of personal freedom, individuality, equality, courage, and self-reliance, in a setting of unlimited horizons and opportunities where any individual could strive and achieve to the limits of his ability and good fortune. For the first time in most of history, land was plentiful and available to all who had the ability, the courage, the perseverance, and the gumption to tame it. The burden and the restrictions of class, of a landed aristocracy, of Church establishment, were left far behind; personal achievement is what counted. The remarkable product of these factors is the most successful nation the world has ever seen.

I would add to this that even on the East Coast, in the original colonies, which bore the heaviest burden of old-world cultural restraints, the settlers from that old world were transformed by this new land. I have long been grateful for the founding of the thirteen colonies by the English, as I do not think the nation that subsequently arose on this continent could have arisen from any other culture. But even then, it required their presence here for 150 years in order to evolve, in this new land, into the people who could break away from the old world, with its restraints on the individual in worshipful obeisance to an all-powerful state, and conceive and create a societal system with the freedom and the opportunities for the individual that have been, historically, peculiar to America and the key to its success.

These *parashiyos* in Devarim are Moshe's charge to the people as they are on the brink of a totally new phase in their existence, poised at the frontier of the new, promised land. There would be no king (except for Yehoshua's initial leadership). There would be no central government. Each person would become a landowner, equal to all others, free to manage his affairs as he wished. The God Who bestowed the rich and beautiful land upon them also promised to keep His eye upon it and to bless it all the year long. And that is where the parallel ends.

The unfettered and uncontrolled freedom in the American frontier produced, along with all the good, a dark side of violence and lawlessness. A Wild West, governed by six-shooters. A place where high ideals came into conflict with self-centered cruelty.

God tells Israel that He is bringing them into a rich and good land where they will have everything. But don't test God, they are warned. Don't forget that it became yours not by the strength of your arms, but because He gifted it to you, because it was He Who swept your enemies away. And to acknowledge that, you must live by the terms of the covenant you made with Him, do what is good and just, and remain true to Him and His Torah. It is for that purpose that He chose you to be His special, treasured nation. It is to fulfill that purpose that He gave you the land. If you do so, you will always win, you will be healthy, you and your children will thrive.

What does God ask of you? To fear Him and to love Him and to live your lives walking His path, with all your heart. *Re'eh*, God says, *look, I am placing before you the choice, blessing or curse. Choose blessing, choose life.* Live, and thrive, with God. With His Law.

Chazal have taught that there is no one as free as one who has taken upon himself the yoke of halachah. He can live a full, free, but *directed* life, with the strength of moral and spiritual rectitude liberating him from the real yoke – that of his baser instincts.

Government, in fact, has no business and no moral right to intrude into our private lives, to legislate every aspect of our personal business, as the old, regimented order did in the old world, and as some now want to do here, to ruin and to stifle the very America that sets the world free. America achieved that exceptionalism through the unparalleled freedom in which it grew up, shaping a society that valued the individual and gave him room to become everything he can be. And the unbound, unchained human being can achieve so much. The aggregate of that is this great and special nation.

But when people – or segments of society, or even most of society – believe or act as if the high ideals of freedom and opportunity apply only to them and not to others whom they look down upon, those high ideals are cruelly betrayed. And when, in the course of pursuing opportunity, that pursuit is unlinked from morality and awareness of God Above, destructive excess and cruelty abound.

Israel's glorious and triumphant entry into the Promised Land, the rich and beautiful frontier that lay before them, opened a world of infinite possibility and the potential for eternal, unending blessing. And yet, it did not take long for things to go wrong. It's crazy, but that's human nature. We see the dispiriting evidence of that nature all around us.

Without freedom, without feeling free of the shackles of impositional state authority, man cannot thrive. Without the self-restraint borne of God's moral order, the chaos of disorder and evil prevails.

As our forefathers stood, poised at the frontier of the Land of Israel, with Moshe Rabbeinu's heartfelt pleas that they do good and live ringing in their ears, their potential for eternal success was unlimited and in their hands, theirs for the having. Well, it didn't quite work out that way. They didn't hold up their end of the bargain, and our long and troubled history bears that out.

We do not know God's plan, but we do know that His promised Redemption is waiting somewhere in the wings. Perhaps, hopefully, it is somewhere on the frontier of where we are right now. We live in a time of unparalleled personal freedom, in a wonderful land of golden opportunity. So many Jews have lost touch, seemingly lost on the fringe. Without the Torah, they are not truly free, even if they imagine, falsely, that their estrangement from it is some kind of freedom. We pray that God will gather them up, that they will "find" each other.

It is for us, who have the opportunity, the freedom, and, hopefully, the spiritual clarity, to do what we can, to help our battered nation finally cross that frontier into the Promised Land.

It is for *us* to do that. Who else is there?

*Parashas Re'eh 5778*

# The Early Bird Catches the Worm…Maybe

I once saw a cartoon poster in a doctor's office that was, to me, highly inspirational. It showed a large, long-necked bird of prey in the process of devouring its victim, a smaller animal. The victim's head, neck, and much of the torso were already down the raptor's throat, with the forelegs still outside, in position to follow. That victim, however, succeeded in wrapping its "hands" around the bird's throat, and was in the process of choking it to death. The bird looked surprised. The title: "Never Give Up."

My summers as a kid in a bungalow colony years ago were not like today. We were utterly free, our time unstructured. Yes, today's *mechanchim* would be horrified. No day camp; just freedom, morning till night. It was hot and humid in New York. For $250 (not so cheap as it now seems, in those days), we got a one-bedroom bungalow with paper thin walls (of course, we paid no attention to what the neighbors were saying) in Swan Lake. Mom had one bed, my brother and I the other. My father, minding the store (literally) in Brooklyn, came up for one or two weekends. We had no car.

It was wonderful. Pure freedom. Except for six weeks in sleepaway camp one summer, we did this every summer from my early childhood until I was about eleven. Yes, no one does that today, and we understand why, but I think it was also psychologically extremely healthy for me and had a positive effect on the formation of my character and happy psychological makeup.

If we felt like going fishing, we went fishing. We would find an appropriately sized and shaped branch to break off, tie some strong thread to the end, attach a fishing hook, and go find some worms. We knew just where to look: a shady area where, when you turned over the earth a bit, you could count on a rich haul of worms. These we put in a jar, and off we traipsed to the lake. We caught fish, usually unkosher catfish, which we promptly unhooked and threw back in. I sometimes wondered if I was catching the same catfish I had thrown back in, the critter being too stupid to recognize the same wriggling worm I had tantalized him with minutes before.

And so we come to the joint moral of these two stories.

On a recent early morning, while walking to shul, I encountered a bird and a worm doing nature's dance. We all have seen films of papa bird flying to the nest with a worm in its mouth to feed the nestlings. That is the way of the world. Here before me was a bird. Yeshiva-boy city guy that I am, I have no idea what type of bird it was. Its breast was dull, dark orange and the rest of it sort of muddy black. It was pecking at a wriggling earthworm about three inches long, at the edge of my neighbor's lawn. The bird's beak looked strong, long, and sharp, perfect for worm catching. The worm, a small fraction the size of the bird, was not cooperating in its own demise. The degree to which it could wriggle and jump was startling. After multiple failed attempts to grab it in its beak, the bird gave up and hopped away. The worm slithered into the lawn, where it disappeared. I thought immediately of that poster (and, nostalgically, of my childhood summers of freedom). The bird *was* early, the worm *was* in its grasp, but in the end, it did not get the worm. The worm never gave up.

In these *parashiyos* after Tisha b'Av, Moshe recounts for Bnei Yisrael the troubles and travails the Jews brought upon themselves with their stubborn penchant for rebellious behavior toward God. God tells Moshe that He will destroy them and start all over again with Moshe. But Moshe doesn't let go. He does not, *k'v'yachol*, let God do it.

"*Heref Mimeni*," Hashem says (Devarim 9:14). "I will destroy them and erase their name." What an astounding statement. *Heref Mimeni* means "let go of Me," or "don't hold Me back," "don't stop Me." *Don't stop Me?* Can a man, even Moshe, stop God from doing what He wants to do?

Apparently, yes. A closer look at that word *heref* may help us understand this better. The word *rafeh* means "weak." *Heref* may be taken to mean "weaken your grip upon Me" so that I can do what I want.

What controlling grip does man have on God? The grip that God *gave* to man, to empower his prayers. The Ribbono shel Olam, *k'v'yachol*, puts Himself, in a manner of speaking, in this limited way, in our "control," in that He listens to our prayers and allows Himself to be "persuaded" by their power and sincerity. That is what He wants.

Even when all appears lost, when the *gezerah* is set, *lo aleinu*, when we think it's over, all is lost, it may, in fact, not be. Because God is waiting for our prayers; for through those prayers, we have a "grip" on Him that He welcomes, that He encourages us to exercise, and, using the same word in a different but related context, *yeshuas Hashem k'heref ayin*, God's salvation can come instantly, like the blink of an eye.

I live my life, I do my work, I have raised my children, and they raise their children, by the grace of God, and by the God-given power of audacious determination. There are people who, as an expression of piety, think that man has no power at all to affect the world. They don't vote, for example, because, they say, it makes no difference. God rules the world, so whatever we do makes no difference. *L'aniyus daati*, it seems to me that God did not put us here to be powerless puppets in a show, whose individual actions are meaningless. God leads us through life, as He leads the world. And He built into creation a system whereby we, by our choices and by our actions, *k'v'yachol*, lead Him. *Hakol bi'ydei Shamayim chutz mi'yiras Shamayim. B'derech she'adam rotzeh leilech bah molichin oso*, for good as well as for bad. The power of audacity, of determination, is very great, for good as well as for bad. The Creator has empowered human beings, through their choices and their actions, to be His partners in creation. What we do matters, and how we do it matters. Everything we do matters, everything we don't do matters, and we can never know what will emerge from either.

Only God knows.

The early bird does usually catch the worm. But sometimes the determined and feisty worm can manage to wriggle out of the bird's hungry beak. Sometimes the apparently doomed prey, even in the gullet of the predator, can wring the neck of that predator and set itself free.

This is a powerful lesson my parents, of blessed memory, taught me from the strength of their faith, their character, and their steely determination. We certainly cannot control everything in life, but more often than one might think, there is more power within us than we might think, and certainly more than meets the eye. That is how the Creator, Who governs all of life, made us, and that is how, it appears, He empowers us to live.

*Parashas Re'eh 5781, Erev Rosh Chodesh Elul*

# Shoftim

## *Tzedek* by Means of *Tzedek*

My cousin came by to warn me. He was making a bar mitzvah in a few weeks, and he thought it best to let me know what to expect: "It's going to be over the top."

This cousin is a nice fellow who lives in a well-off suburban society, where over the top is de rigueur. That's how they do things, making sure that everybody else sees what they can do in the over-the-top department.

He said that he *has to*, or his friends and neighbors will conclude either that he is cheap, that he is a jerk, or that his business is failing. He can't have that and risk his standing in that *kehillah*. It's bad enough that he drives or owns *not even one* German car, unlike virtually all his neighbors, who apparently have more loyalty to the image of the expensive and sleek German car in the driveway than to the honor and memory of the countless Jewish victims of the Germans, and they feel no shame about it. Their *importance* makes them exempt.

(For the record, I didn't make it to the bar mitzvah, so I can't tell you what transpired there. I'm sure that a grand, lavish time was had by all, and my cousin's reputation kept safe.)

And so this story reminds me of another Jewish family, as real in the history of it as they are apocryphal in the telling, that lived long ago in the Land of Israel.

Yaakov and Leah were a hardworking couple with children, who just eked out a living by the sweat of their brows. And then Leah's elderly mother, who lived with them, died. That very fine and pious lady, who recited a whole section of Tehillim every day and was an exemplary mother, deserved to be put to rest in the most honorable way. The problem was the commonly accepted standard for an honorable funeral in those days.

The mode of the day was an expensive, lavish funeral, with luxurious robes for the deceased and other pricey accoutrements, perhaps a really convincing group of wailing professional mourners. Anything less was considered a *bizayon*, a shameful mistreatment of the departed, and socially unacceptable. Not to conform was to be shamed.

And so, utterly unable to provide such a funeral, and too ashamed not to, Yaakov and Leah did what an increasing number of people in that desperate situation did. The Gemara (*Kesubos* 8b and *Moed Katan* 27b) tells us that apparently keeping quiet about it, they carried the body off a ways and then abandoned it by the side of the road. Now a *meis mitzvah*, the body was eventually interred by the local community where it was found.

Rabban Gamliel, the *nasi*, as rich and powerful as he was learned and pious, addressed the problem with a definitive solution that has lasted and remains the norm throughout the entire nation of Israel until this day. He commanded that upon his own death, he should be buried in the simplest of shrouds, in the simplest and least expensive way, and he insisted that everyone else do the same. And so it has been. No competition, no keeping up with the (Jewish) Joneses, no over-the-top as the deceased is brought down under. No exceptions. Problem solved.

Fast-forward to contemporary weddings. Everyone is aware of the often unsustainable strain of making an expensive wedding that conforms to community "standards," lest the family be socially shamed and lose their standing, lest tongues wag, lest they find it harder to marry off the next children.

Some years ago, there was a laudable effort to set up community-wide guidelines mandating simplicity and limits, to bring the situation into rational control. By and large, it failed. People looked over their shoulders and, seeing that most people ignored it, they ignored it too, even if they desperately needed it. Lately, there has been talk again about these *takanos*, and indeed it has become more widely practiced, although still in a small minority of weddings.

In the public discourse on this subject lately, there has been a rather stark lack of candor about what went wrong initially, although it was rather obvious to most people, when the original *takanos* were publicized, that the effort would fail, as it did, and why.

I remember it well. Ads were placed in Jewish media laying out the measures designed to curb excess. It was great. The problem was the disclaimer placed at the bottom of the notices, which said, in effect, that if you are a big shot, important, a *gvir*, a big rabbi, someone who really counts, well, all this doesn't really apply to you. Your *importance* makes you exempt. If, however, you are just a *shmendrik*, a regular nobody, nothing special, then you must follow the rules and identify before all that you are, in fact, a *shmendrik*, a no-account *shmegeggy*. Sorry, but it was laughable – and obvious – to just about everybody that this would not work. It was utterly contrary to human nature and to how people in our society think and operate.

We are commanded, in Parashas Shoftim, to appoint leaders who will mete out justice and judgment absolutely fairly, showing no favoritism. They must not be blinded by wealth and power. We are also instructed, in another context (Bamidbar 16:17), that *Torah achas u'mishpat echad yihyeh lachem*, there is one Torah, one teaching, for all.

The *pasuk*, in our parashah, commands, "*Tzedek tzedek tirdof*" (Devarim 16:20). Of the many explanations offered for the meaning of this mandate to pursue justice, a particularly appealing one addresses the repetition of the word *tzedek*. Pursue justice only *through* justice, only by just means, only with fairness.

My own inclination – as someone who values the freedom of the individual to act, within the law, as he sees fit, including how he spends his own honestly acquired resources – is that the actions of the individual must also at times be tempered by the needs and the well-being of the larger society. Thus our *chachamim* have made many *takanos* of various kinds over the millennia. For the sake of the greater good, we conform. Theoretically, *all of us*.

We do need to get our societal heads straight about excess, because it makes sense; because it is right; because social pressure is a foolish but remarkably potent instigator in overspending and its ensuing stress, even for those who cannot afford it; because modesty, *hatznea leches*, demands it; because *others*, those who surround us, look upon us with resentment; because there are more important and productive ways to spend our resources; because we have to help and protect those who cannot spend so much.

And there is no room, I submit, in such an important initiative to save so many people so much heartache and anguish, to make *takanos* that differentiate based on class or perceived class, or ego, or *kavod*, to set aside notions of justice and fairness in applying the rules, to forget that *tzedek* must be achieved *through tzedek*.

And so the leadership, lay and rabbinical, the rich and powerful, the showoffs, the VIPs, the big shots, whom the first *takanos* exempted, if they do not learn the timeless lesson of Rabban Gamliel, if they do not assume the mantle of moral leadership in this issue and lead by example, will bear a measure of responsibility for any failure in this current worthwhile initiative.

We, the people, the Nation of Israel, as we have always done, look to our Torah leadership for the wisdom, the moral vision, and the *tzedek* to guide us in living our lives as would please our Creator, as it would our fellow man.

*Parashas Shoftim 5779*

# Ki Setzei

## U'b'tzeisi Likrascha, Likrasi Metzasicha

How Moshe Rabbeinu loved us! He knew better than anyone how difficult we could be, and he let us know it. And he knew how exalted this nation could be, and he let us know that as well. Dedicated shepherd, loving parent, teacher and guide, that man whose greatness was unparalleled in all of human existence, tried with all his heart and all his might to get us to follow the right path, frustrated that despite its obvious truth, despite that truth being so clear to him, despite the life-altering high stakes, the utter obviousness of it was somehow not so obvious to others, and the price paid by those so clueless, in his generation and in all generations to follow, is so painfully high and so foolishly needless.

What to make of that human capacity for so many to not see what should be so clear? It is perhaps the oldest spiritual story in human existence. That's how God made us. And, with the power of free choice, that's also how we make ourselves. It's quite obvious that we do not all have the same capacity to see matters of the spirit clearly. But it's also obvious that we each have the mandate to seek to do so, at whatever level we can, and that potential level, for any normal person, is quite high. Some will always have the potential to attain more than others, and some will find the struggle harder than others, but virtually everyone can achieve what is appropriate for him or her. And yet so many people don't bother very much and don't see much of a reason to try. They just don't get it. How terribly sad for them. And how terribly sad for us, who love them and care about them.

Moshe tells us that part of being a human being of flesh and blood, preoccupied with making our way through this difficult and challenging world, is that we have been created with a *klippah*, a kind of shell or covering attached to our hearts, which it is our job to "circumcise," to cut away, in order to liberate our hearts and souls and to connect with God. But what does it take? Can we just wish it away? Think good thoughts? How about if we pray and sway?

Well, yes, in a way, but not quite. If thinking good thoughts and praying and swaying includes doing good by your fellow man, by being kind and just and charitable, then that praying and swaying works too. It helps. If it includes whole-hearted faith in the One Above, *temimus*, then that certainly works. If it includes scrupulous adherence to the Law, and making every effort to learn the Law, to fulfill it properly as well as to know God through it, then that works. If it includes following prescribed ritual as a means of approaching God, alongside *bein adam l'chavero*, in fulfilling His will, then that works. If it includes being as careful with *mitzvah kallah k'v'chamurah*, then that helps. And if it includes being as careful with *mitzvah chamurah k'v'kallah* (think about that one), then I think that really helps too.

It is in the nature of the human being that there is an internal war within. That war can be barely discernible, smoldering, or raging, depending on the human factors at play.

There are people who give not a thought to goodness and are quite content – even at peace – with their sinful ways. That does not normally apply to a Jew, even the most remote, unless there is something wrong with him. For the Jew who knows who he is and has an understanding of what his life, spiritually speaking, should be like, well, we all have our internal demons. It is our mission, each one of us, every individual in the Nation of Israel, to cut away that *klippah* and to connect to God, in thought, word, and deed, manifested in punctilious *bein adam la'Makom* and *bein adam l'chavero* (which is, of course, one of God's devices in measuring our *bein adam la'Makom*).

And so, we go out to war. At whatever level we are, there is, for the normal person, a struggle of some kind, which we must go out and initiate.

We always read Parashas Ki Setzei during the month of Elul. "When you go out to war on your enemy" (Devarim 20:1). The Chasam Sofer, in *Toras Moshe*, notes that it would have been simpler and less wordy for the Torah to write "*Ki silachem*," when you fight. And a reason for stating "When you go out" is that this is the time, before Rosh Hashanah, when the Jew undertakes to *go out to war* with his enemy, the *yetzer hara*, with that inner demon that makes him want to do the wrong thing or tries to keep him from doing the right thing, or that tries to interfere with his connection to the Ribbono shel Olam, to make him not see it, to make him not feel it. It is a difficult war, even for the best of us. It is said that the greater the Jew, the more powerful his *yetzer hara* is (sort of a fairer fight). But in this season of the Yamim Noraim, we have a special *siyata di'Shemaya*, help from Heaven, in that fight, as long as *we* initiate it and make our most sincere and strenuous efforts.

An interesting observation about that *klippah*: "Circumcising" it away is referred to first as *u'maltem es orlas levavchem*, you shall cut away that *klippah* that interposes between you and God. The next reference to it says *u'mal Hashem es orlas levavchem*, God Himself will cut that *klippah* away – He will help you with it, once you have set out to actually do so. But you must set out first. He will be there, waiting for you. Lovingly, reaching out to you as you reach out to Him.

I was at a wedding recently where the *mesader kiddushin* mentioned a beautiful and moving poem by Rabbi Yehudah Halevi, the great religious romantic who lived and wrote with such love for God and for Eretz Yisrael. It made me think of this very struggle, of this *parashah*, of this concept, of this effort, of this loving encounter with God, of the certainty of His loving embrace.

Let me quote from this beautiful and powerfully moving poem.

מְקוֹמְךָ נַעֲלָה וְנֶעְלָם!    יָ-הּ, אָנָה אֶמְצָאֲךָ?
כְּבוֹדְךָ מָלֵא עוֹלָם!    וְאָנָה לֹא אֶמְצָאֲךָ?
בְּכָל-לִבִּי קְרָאתִיךָ    דָּרַשְׁתִּי קִרְבָתְךָ
לִקְרָאתִי מְצָאתִיךָ!    וּבְצֵאתִי לִקְרָאתְךָ
בַּקֹּדֶשׁ חֲזִיתִיךָ    וּבְפִלְאֵי גְבוּרָתְךָ
הֵן שָׁמַיִם וְחֵילָם    מִי יֹאמַר לֹא רָאֲךָ?
בְּלִי נִשְׁמַע קוֹלָם!    יַגִּידוּ מוֹרָאֲךָ

Ribbono shel Olam – where will I find you?
Your place is so lofty and beyond my sight!
And where will I not find you?
Your Presence fills the World!
I sought Your closeness.
With all my heart I called out to You
and as I went out toward You,
I encountered You right there, approaching me!

In the wonders of Your greatness,
I perceived You in Your holiness.
Who can say they don't see You?
The very heavens and the earth
proclaim Your awesome Presence

without even making a sound.
As I went out toward You
I encountered You right there, approaching me!

וּבְצֵאתִי לִקְרָאתְךָ    לִקְרָאתִי מְצָאתִיךָ!

*U'b'tzeisi likrascha, likrasi metzasicha.* I went out seeking You, I reached out to You, and I found that You were already right there, waiting for me, waiting to embrace me.

I am safe in Your embrace. I must engage in that struggle, I must tear away that *klippah*, I must reach out, even go out to war if that is how it must be, but I know that You are already right there before me, waiting for me, especially in this month of *ani l'Dodi v'Dodi li*, waiting to make me Yours as I reach out to make You mine.

*Parashas Ki Setzei la'Milchamah al Oyvecha 5778, Yerushalayim Ir Hakodesh*

# Ki Savo

## The Darkness

There is no shortage of dark places in this bright world.

Joseph Conrad famously wrote of the heart of darkness. The story of human existence, and certainly of Jewish existence, has been the struggle to drive the darkness from the heart and to dispel the darkness from the world.

At the Kotel, just as Shacharis was over, a young man – perhaps in his early forties – approached the Yid standing next to me, a pious regular at the Kotel, and told him, in softly spoken Hebrew, that he wished to don tefillin. My neighbor started to refer him to a nearby tefillin stand, but the fellow asked, nicely, if he could use that man's own tefillin. *Of course*, he replied, and proceeded to help him with them.

There's nothing unusual about that scene. It was when he came to reciting Shema Yisrael, and he placed his fingers over his eyes, Sephardi style, that I saw a story in his face.

We cover our eyes when we recite Shema so that nothing should distract us while we are declaring our faith. Not seeing anything extraneous is not at all about darkness. But it seemed to me, as I observed this fellow, as I looked at his face and his habitus, that in covering his eyes, he exposed a sad darkness within.

I saw him a while later sitting alone at a little table in the Old City, staring into space. In front of him were three telltale items, which together often serve as companions to the forlorn: coffee, Coca Cola, and a pack of cigarettes.

Who can know his story? There are so many stories in this world. And Jerusalem, it seems, is a place where many come to seek spiritual solace. We pray that the world brightens for them, that they can exorcize the devils that bedevil them, whether internal or external. Darkness of the spirit is a terrible affliction, *lo aleinu*.

Much in Parashas Ki Savo is about darkness, and, on a national level, how to prevent it. We are told of all the goodness and the light that Hashem will send our way if we live according to His Torah. We are taught to appreciate God's blessings, and praying for them is part of our mandate as well. The world will be ours, we are assured; we will be prosperous and well, if, as a nation, we remain loyal to God.

And then the Torah describes the terrible things in store if *chalilah* we turn away from Him. The picture is so horrible, so utterly dark, that *yirei Shamayim* over the generations have been known to faint upon hearing it read in shul, especially during those dark periods in our history when the horrors foretold were the horrors they were actually living.

The choice is so starkly clear that it defies the imagination how our nation could have allowed itself to fail so badly so many times, to pay the price and to continue or to repeat its intransigence. And that is, I submit, because by design, God is not obviously sitting on our shoulders and whispering instructions in our ears as we go about life, unless we actively invite Him there. And even then, that whisper is really our own conscience based on our faith.

As obvious as it should be, if it were *really* that obvious to us all the time, how would we ever earn merit before God? A monkey quickly learns not to stick its finger into an electrical socket, and not because it is so smart or so virtuous. The socket that the wayward Jew is sticking his finger into when he turns away from God is a delayed-reaction one, and for the most part, such Jews lose sight of the fact that they are damaging themselves and their future generations and bringing down the rest of the nation with them.

The rewards for remaining true to God are very great, and they are spelled out. And as punishment for rebelling against God, the list of miseries is long – seemingly endless. Many bad things happen, the specifics spelled out in that portion of the *parashah* known as the *tochachah*, the admonition. But then they are capped in a terrible final common pathway: the descent into the darkness.

*God will disperse you among all the nations, from one end of the world to the other. You will be lost there, and you will serve strange gods, unknown to you, made of wood and stone.*

*Your spirit and your body will find no peace. Your heart will be always agitated and angry, your eyes will feel exhausted, and your spirits will be anguished.*

*Your lives will be utterly insecure. You will be fearful night and day; you will have no confidence in your very lives.*

*From the fear in your hearts and the bleakness of your vision, in the mornings you will wish it were night, and in the night you will wish it were morning. You will be utterly depressed; you will never feel that things are well.*

A striking irony is that we are told that these bad things could befall us for not serving God with joy and a glad heart when we could have and should have. When we had everything, we should have appreciated everything, we should have understood and acknowledged where all the goodness in life came from. And, spoiled by all the good, taking all the good for granted, for rejecting happiness and lightness of heart, we may have to endure, God forbid, the very heart of darkness. And then, whatever else may be happening in life – even the good, even, by objective standards, the *very* good – darkness of the spirit renders everything dim, tasteless, and ruined. Happiness is destroyed and replaced by constant fear.

May God protect us. And by our actions and the choices we make in life, may we protect ourselves. There are no guarantees in life for any of us individually. We cannot know God's accounting. But we do know the *cheshbon* He keeps with Klal Yisrael as a whole, for He has clearly spelled it out. We just have to put aside the arrogance of disbelief and take heed.

We read Parashas Ki Savo as a prelude to Rosh Hashanah, the ultimate annual time of reckoning. And while this period is known as the Days of Awe, when, it is said, even the fish in the waters tremble for fear of the Lord and the Day of Judgment, it is a common misperception that Rosh Hashanah and Yom Kippur are sad days. They are solemn and serious, awe inspiring and frightening, in that they are the days of judgment, but they are also *yamim tovim*, holidays, a time set aside for God to bless us according to His best judgment.

He asks of us that we be loyal to Him. He has chosen us to be His special, treasured nation, His Am Segulah. We should live up to that exalted status. There is much that our people have done wrong over the years, and much that we have paid for it. But in perhaps the most remarkable civilizational miracle in all of history, for all that has gone wrong, for all that we have strayed, no one can deny that we are, as a nation, at least at our core, after all these years, all these generations, all these dispersions, all these persecutions, all these internal dissensions, all the dropouts, *all this darkness*, incredibly, steadfastly, lovingly if sometimes argumentatively, loyal to Him.

And so may He bless all of Klal Yisrael, all His children, with a *kesivah v'chasimah tovah*, a year of life and health and prosperity and of *nachas*, a year of joy and lightness of spirit, a year in which the brooding darkness is finally banished from this world, and we are blessed, all of us, with *light*.

*Parashas Ki Savo 5778, Yerushalayim Ir Hakodesh*

## Samachti v'Simachti

The morning breeze carried the lilting sound before it, as the procession paraded – indeed, danced – into the town. Farmers from all over the district were carrying beautiful, adorned baskets with their first fruits, designated in the fields while still growing, with a festive ribbon and the declaration that these fruits were *bikkurim*, holy and dedicated to God.

In the town, people slept outside that night, excitedly awaiting their arrival. *Arise!* they cried out. *Let us go up to Zion, to the House of our God!* They joined the procession, singing praises of God, Tehillim sung to the accompaniment of flutes. An ox went before them, its horns overlaid with gold and a crown of olive branches on its head.

As they approached Jerusalem, delegations of notables went out to greet them and bid them shalom. Townspeople lined the streets, offering them a warm welcome. The flutes continued to play until they arrived on the Temple Mount, where the farmers placed their fruit-filled baskets on their shoulders, and, entering the inner precincts, as the Leviim sang Psalms, they carried out the ancient ritual, prescribed in Parashas Ki Savo, reciting the words of praise for God, Who had redeemed them from their oppressors, brought them to this blessed land, and blessed them with a bountiful crop.

*V'samachta b'chol hatov asher nasan lecha Hashem* is not just a prediction; it is a commandment that we *rejoice*, fully, in the bounty God has bestowed upon us, and in the *fact* that He has chosen us for this. The joy of this mitzvah was very great indeed. And part of that joy lay in *understanding* to thank God for this opportunity to thank Him. Indeed, one of the purposes of creation, as described in *Midrash Rabbah* (Bereishis 1) is that man have the moral and spiritual accomplishment of thanking as well as worshipping his Creator. The Midrash includes the related mitzvos of *terumos*, *maasros*, and taking challah in this concept as well.

Shabbos too, and Yovel, and tzedakah all reflect a related idea. When we observe Shabbos, when we set all else aside and live it as a day of rest, we are, in effect, testifying that it was Hashem Who created the world and "rested" on Shabbos as a model for our future behavior. When we observe Shemittah, we are, in effect, testifying that Hashem created the world, and it is He Who bestowed the land upon us. And in giving tzedakah, we are, in effect, testifying that what we have comes from Hashem, and we are sharing it with the less fortunate, as that is a principal reason that Hashem put that money in our possession in the first place. It allows us to have; it allows us to acknowledge where it came from, how it came to us, that we appreciate it and understand what our obligation is regarding it, and, in sharing, to manifest the goodness that is a human being's primary purpose in life – and indeed a purpose of creation.

And so Ki Savo continues with *maaser oni*, the tithe for the poor. Joyfully, the donor declares, in a remarkably moving passage, that he has faithfully fulfilled God's will. *Asisi k'chol asher tzivisani:* I have given the Levite his due portion (*maaser rishon*), I have shared with the poor proselyte, the orphan, the widow. Look down upon us kindly, Hashem, from Your holy abode, and bless us, bless Your Nation of Israel, and the land, flowing with milk and honey, that You promised to our forefathers and have given to us.

And this sharing is a *joyful* act. But it has another dimension, a critical one. It makes others happy as well, which is exactly what we want it to do, and indeed what God wants it to do, specifically with us as His agents in accomplishing this.

There is a remarkable midrash (*Sifri*) on *asisi k'chol asher tzivisani*, I have done all as You have commanded me: *Samachti v'simachti*. I have rejoiced and have caused others to rejoice.

The joy, the *simchah* in fulfilling a mitzvah is very great, if you understand what you are accomplishing by fulfilling it. The joy of fulfilling those mitzvos that in particular the Ribbono shel Olam has designated as defining our unique relationship with Him is great beyond measure.

We are commanded to rejoice on Sukkos, *v'hayisa ach sameach*, amidst the plenty of God's blessing. *V'samachta b'chagecha*, rejoice on your holiday, *you, your son, your daughter, your male and female servants, the Levite, the proselyte, the orphan, the widow*. And we are commanded to rejoice on Shavuos, *V'samachta lifnei Hashem Elokecha*, *you, your son and your daughter, your male and female servants, the Levite, the proselyte, the orphan, and the widow*.

God is telling us, says the Midrash, *if you make My four* (the Levite, the proselyte, the orphan, the widow) *happy, if you look after them, as they have only you to look to for their sustenance, then I will make your four* (your son, your daughter, your male household, your female household) *happy as well*. Quid pro quo. Tzedakah.

In the dreaded *tochachah*, later in the *parashah*, enumerating all the terrible punishments that lie in store if Israel veers from its God-given path, it is summed up that this happens *tachas asher lo avadeta es Hashem Elokecha* b'simchah u'v'tuv levav, me'rov kol. When you had everything, when God provided you with everything, you failed to appreciate that it was He Who gave it to you, you did not rejoice in His being your God, you did not rejoice or revel in the very act of thanking Him, as you should have, *and you did not use the blessings that God gave you to make* others *happy*. And in this, for this, you have lost everything.

God does not want us to be dour. He wants to bless us. He wants us to rejoice in His blessing. That is part of why He created the world. Israel's mandate is to acknowledge and to appreciate that blessing *and to share it with the less fortunate*. One hinges on the other. *Samachti v'simachti*.

*Samachti* cannot be sustained without *simachti*. I have rejoiced, and I have caused *others* to rejoice.

And then may the full measure of Hashem's blessing be upon us.

*Parashas Ki Savo 5779*

# Nitzavim-Vayelech

## Standing Today, All of You, before God

This story is as timely as it is true.

A busy, hardworking doctor was pressed for space in his office. He needed to expand, but the neighboring offices in the building on both sides were occupied. One belonged to the landlord, who was not going anywhere. He asked the neighbor on the other side, a health-care professional in a small office, if she had any thoughts of moving, as then he would know how to plan. She told him that she had no such plans, but if he would pay her $100,000, she would move.

He told her he would not do so. Two or three weeks later, she vacated her space and moved into her newly renovated office in a nearby neighborhood, a long-planned move. Yikes.

Some of us are naturally cynical and suspicious, while others are naturally too trusting. It is said that Ulysses S. Grant got himself taken advantage of many times because, as good a general as he was, he tended to trust people more than he should have. The doctor in our story is somewhat like that. It's a good thing that scoundrel asked for a lot of money – for a more manageable amount, he might have agreed and been taken for a ride.

The point is, of course, that it shouldn't be that way. That's not how a mensch behaves. That woman, a Jew by birth, acted like a scoundrel when God tells us quite stringently not to. I don't know if she was in any way otherwise observant (pretty sure not), but we have all heard stories of people *who should know better, who have been educated to know better*, who have the business ethics of a scoundrel, and they somehow think that in business, it's OK.

*Atem nitzavim hayom.* We are standing today before God, all of us, the high and the low, the mighty and the meek, the rich and the poor, the men and the women, the adults and the children, the clergy and the lay folk, the leaders and the led, people with every variety of innate nature, but with the knowledge and the God-given ability to govern that nature, if they are normal, whatever it may be. We are

293

standing before God the Judge as Yom Hadin approaches. And the first step in negotiating that reality is understanding, to the extent that we are capable, that this is, in fact, the reality: our lives, the lives of our families, our health, our livelihood, our freedom, our freedom from fear, our freedom from disease, our peace, our peace of mind and spirit; everything and anything about our lives, our people, our country, our Holy Land, our world, is in the balance.

And it's not a remote or abstract thing. It's about *us*. It is, in large measure, about what we do and how we do it. It's about how we stand when we stand before God. It's about the *peckel* on our shoulders, the baggage we bring with us, *that follows us*, when we stand before Him.

It's about how we relate to God in ritual, prayer, and Torah, for that delineates the seriousness with which we approach Him, but even more so, as He has taught us so clearly, it's about how we relate to God through how we relate to our fellow human beings, His children, for that *defines* the seriousness with which we approach Him and *validates* all the ritual and prayer and Torah.

Make no mistake: the ritual, the commandments, the prayer, *the Law*, loyalty to God, pursuit of Torah, are key and an absolute necessity. That is God's mandate and His requirement, as those are what makes a Jew a Jew; they are the God-given path for a Jew to come close to his God and to fulfill his role in creation. It's not optional. Those who undertook to "reform" Judaism by dropping all that and redefining Judaism as a kind of social-justice mandate alone have destroyed generations of Jews, tragically sending them off to be lost, not just among the nations indifferent to us and our God, but, as we see tragically, even into the arms of those who are hostile to us.

But God also places a kind of screen door in the pathway; if one does not open that as well, opening the "solid" door of ritual still doesn't get one into the palace. One and the same as the rest of the laws, those between *adam la'Makom*, between an individual and the Ribbono shel Olam, are the laws He mandated on how we behave with our fellow man, *bein adam l'chavero*.

In fact, there really is no difference between the two categories. How we behave to our fellow man is exactly how God sees us as we relate to Him.

The final nail in the coffin of our freedom and national life in the commonwealth created when God led us into the Promised Land, that which finally sealed the fated exile and destruction of the Beis Hamikdash, the place of holiness and miracles built by Shlomo Hamelech, even in the face of all their other cardinal sins, was high-handed cruelty to poor Jewish servants of the ruling class (see Yirmiyahu 34).

We don't mess up other people. We are not indifferent to them. We don't fool them, and we don't take advantage of them. We are kind to them, and giving, and caring and charitable, not only with our money, but with our judgment of them and their actions. Their lives and their well-being matter to us in a serious way. We care, and we act upon that caring. We feel for them. We love them.

We are generous with them, both spiritually and economically. Tzedakah buys us life.

The Baal Shem Tov famously taught, on *Hashem tzilcha* (Tehillim 121), which in its basic explanation means that Hashem will protect you like shade (*tzel* [צֵל]) from the sun, that He *shadows* you: as you treat others, so He will be inclined to treat you.

*See! I have placed before you today es hachaim v'es hatov – life and the good, death and the evil (you have free will!)...to love Hashem your God, to walk in His ways, to observe His mitzvos...then you will live and you will multiply and God will bless you... Choose life! Listen to Him! Cling to Him!* Choose wisely, and be blessed.

We also know that what is obvious to God, in the big picture, is utterly beyond our own understanding. And so we do the best we can and place our faith and trust in Him. As Rosh Hashanah approaches, we all try to be more scrupulous in our observances. That is great, and it no doubt pleases Hashem greatly. But, I submit, and He has let us know this, "proof" of our sincerity and our seriousness in serving Him as we now come to stand *before* Him is how we stand *with*, how we regard and treat other people. How we love them, even as we ask our God to love us.

*Parashas Nitzavim-Vayelech 5780*

# Staying Alive

I have written elsewhere (*Heaven and Earth*, vol. 1, Vayechi) about the passage of power and authority, but really life force (let's call it *chayim* and *chiyus*), when the time of one generation has come to pass its power to the next. We see this if we look realistically around us. And the *mesorah* gives us famous examples. Yaakov and the *shevatim*, Moshe and Yehoshua, Aharon and Elazar, David and Shlomo. In each case, the waning of the former, a giant, is apparent as soon as the time of the ascension of the latter has arrived.

Koheles 8:8: *Ein adam shalit ba'ruach lichlo es haruach, v'ein shilton b'yom hamaves* (אֵין אָדָם שַׁלִּיט בָּרוּחַ לִכְלוֹא אֶת-הָרוּחַ וְאֵין שִׁלְטוֹן בְּיוֹם הַמָּוֶת). There is no man that has power over the wind to retain the wind, nor power over the day of death.

Moshe famously retained, until the very end, all of his strength, his vigor, his senses. *Lo kahasa eino v'lo nas leicho* (Devarim 34:7). There is an abundance of *midrashim* that describe how Moshe, *who knew he was going to a very good place,* still did not want to die. He wanted to hold on; he wanted to serve God; he wanted, above all, to enter the Promised Land and fulfill its special mitzvos. When Hashem tells him the decree that he will not enter is irrevocable, he asks if he can remain outside the land, even as everyone else crosses over. *Impossible,* Hashem says. How will you be *oleh regel* if you cannot, and how will it appear to all if they must, and you, who gave them that very law, do not? You would be undoing the Torah. It's Yehoshua's time. *Let Yehoshua lead them over there, and I'll just stay here by myself and continue to serve You here! Yehoshua will be the Rebbe, and I will be the* talmid, *hidden in the tent!* And do you think the people will stay with Yehoshua, when Yehoshua's great rebbe is alive? No, Moshe. Yehoshua's time has arrived. It is time for you to join your ancestors.

We see this elsewhere: David starts I Melachim as David Hamelech and abruptly becomes simply David, as his majesty has already passed to Shlomo; the dying Yaakov appeals to Yosef not to bury him in Egypt in the language of a powerless petitioner. Despite Moshe's *lo nas leicho,* there is already a subtle sign of Moshe's waning as his end approaches and Yehoshua's time begins. Moshe announces to the people that he is now 120 years old, and *lo uchal od latzeis v'lavo.* Literally, I will be unable to come and go before you. *Amar Rabbi Shmuel bar Nachmani, amar Rabbi Yonasan (Sotah 13b): She'nistamimu mi'menu shaarei chochmah.* The gates of wisdom in Torah were cut off from him. Rashi amplifies: the depths, the wellsprings of Torah wisdom were closed off to him. Tragic for Moshe, but it was now Yehoshua's time. *Dabar echad,* in the language of the Midrash, one speaker of the Law shall there be, not two. And now that *dabar* is Yehoshua.

No one escapes this reality. It is our mission to impact the world the way we need to while we can. To accomplish what we ought to accomplish while we are still able to accomplish. While it is our time.

But then, can we always know what our time is? And so a story. It is a true story, and I am witness.

It was back in President Reagan's administration, I believe at the American Gathering of Jewish Holocaust Survivors in Washington in 1983. It was a very big deal, with many dignitaries, headed by President and Mrs. Reagan, on the dais. The president spoke. My parents, *a"h,* my brother and his son, and I attended. A reporter noticed the three generations and wrote about it.

One aspect of that meeting struck me so deeply that I will never – can never – forget it.

One of the speakers was Rabbi Herschel Schacter, a respected communal *rav* in the Bronx who had been a chaplain in the US Army in World War II. He described, upon the military's liberation of the infamous Buchenwald concentration camp, finding a little Jewish boy survivor, as improbable as that was. He described the child's debilitated state. So many of those survivors were so sick that they did not survive liberation and continued to die in significant numbers. But that little boy didn't die, he said. His time had not yet come. In fact, he said, that little boy was there in the room that evening! And then he introduced Yisrael Meir Lau, Chief Rabbi of Israel. The effect was overwhelming.

Then Rabbi Lau spoke. He remembered the kindly American soldier (Rabbi Schacter) who picked him up and helped him. He told of the horrors, of his older brother caring for him, protecting him, trying to keep him alive in that factory of death. There were constant selections for death. Those selected had no future. No escape. Only death. One day, his brother told him that he had been selected and would die. He could not get out of it. He could not hide. He could no longer protect his little brother, he could no longer scavenge a bit of food for him to keep him alive. And then his brother told him, as a parting *tzavaah: I am done, but if you survive, if you somehow manage to live through this hell, know that there is a place called Eretz Yisrael. It is our God-given Holy Land and now the only place in the world for a Jew. Do not agree to go anywhere else. Nowhere else! Only to Eretz Yisrael!* And with that, his brother was gone.

Rabbi Lau paused and said that life and death are in God's hands. Somehow, he said, his brother was not murdered that day. Somehow, he too remained alive. And in fact, his brother was at that moment in the audience of this very room. And then he introduced Naphtali Lavi, Consul-General of Israel to New York.

It was utterly overwhelming. Stunning. One could see Nancy Reagan, on the dais in her signature red dress, deeply moved. To this day, I am moved to tears at the very thought of this story, which is an amazing, light-noted subscript to the superstory, the millions upon millions who did not live, whose lives were extinguished in every cruel way by the evil Germans and their eager helpers of various nations.

Life and death are, indeed, in God's hands. We don't know what will be. But we must certainly make the most of the opportunities we have, for they do not come back to us.

Moshe Rabbeinu impacted the world as no one else ever did. He was able, *k'v'yachol*, to "make" God do things. Such was his power. But in the end, when it was his time, when his successor's star rose, such is life, Moshe's star in this life had to set. And the world went on.

No man has power over the wind to retain the wind, nor power over the day of death. It is for us to do what we can when we can to make our lives as meaningful and as productive as we can, to bring goodness into the world. Time, life, and opportunity are too precious to waste. Yes, "miracles" may occur, but only God knows our time, and we do not. Ours is to do. Build for tomorrow today. It is the one way to somehow stay "alive."

*Parashas Vayelech 5782, Yerushalayim Ir Hakodesh*

# Haazinu-V'zos Haberachah

## Murphy's Gift

Congregation Chovevei Torah, a grand edifice, sits high on Eastern Parkway, itself at the crest of a high hill in central Brooklyn. It is more than a hundred feet above sea level; on some street corners, you can see all the way to Manhattan. Next door, more modestly housed, was the Yeshiva Ramailes Netzach Yisroel, resurrected from the Holocaust (and now beautifully revived on Rechov Ramban in Jerusalem). Two blocks from where we lived, Chovevei Torah was not where we davened on Shabbos, and so I had only a brief acquaintance with the main sanctuary, which was indeed grand. I remember my parents going there once to hear Rav Schwadron, the famed Maggid of Jerusalem, speak.

Today, long after its heyday and with the old congregation long gone, as with many of the old shuls in Crown Heights, it continues to function as a Lubavitcher outpost.

People used to refer to it, oddly, as Murphy's Shul. Many people still do, but they have no idea why. So I'll tell you: it stands where Murphy's Bar and Grill used to.

Many of us were more frequent visitors to the downstairs *beis midrash*, which was, in Crown Heights' heyday, what we call today a minyan factory. It was a beautiful thing. And herein is the story.

My *zeide*, Reb Shloime Nussbaum, *a"h*, a Holocaust survivor who lost many children and grandchildren to the German murderers, widowered, lived with us in our walk-up apartment on Eastern Parkway. Each morning, this Dzhikover Chassid left home early to attend the first minyan and did not return home until many hours later, after the last. He spent the morning learning, but he had another agenda as well. As he explained to my mother, he spent all morning, minyan after minyan, answering amen to every *berachah*, and *amen, yehei Shemei rabbah mevorach* to every Kaddish. How could he pass up such an opportunity?

299

I thought of this often during COVID, when I did not attend shul for so long. When I did return, the thrill and the privilege of responding *amen, yehei Shemei rabbah mevorach* was overpowering, but it was accompanied by pangs of guilt: Why wasn't it *always* overpowering, *as it should be*?

Moshe Rabbeinu taught us: *Ki Shem Hashem ekra, havu godel l'Elokeinu* (Devarim 32:3): When the Name of God is heard, praise of God is required in response. Thus, *amen, yehei Shemei rabbah mevorach*; thus, *baruch Hu u'varuch Shemo*; thus, in the Beis Hamikdash on Yom Kippur, *achas ba'shanah*, when the Kohen Gadol utters the ineffable Name, the whole nation who hear it fall to their knees and call out, *Baruch Shem kevod malchuso l'olam va'ed*, which we recapitulate in some measure in our Yom Kippur davening.

And thus as well, the *berachos* we make when we are called up to the Torah (*Berachos* 21a and Yerushalmi 87:5). The Torah Temimah raises the question, why do we make a *berachah* before reading from the Torah, and before learning (Mishnah, Gemara), but we only make an after-*berachah* by *krias haTorah*, but not after learning? Because, he says, there is a defined time to read from the *sefer Torah* in shul. But our requirement to learn is always – *yomam va'lailah*. There is never an after-*berachah*, even if we do stop for the day. The time and the obligation for learning is still there, whether we have stopped for the day or not.

The importance of answering *amen, yehei Shemei rabbah mevorach* is very great. It's a fulfillment of a *mitzvah d'Oraysa*. Its power is very great. Its *zechus* on behalf of each of us and our families is very great. And it's *b'yadcha*; it is right there for you. You just have to be in shul, to think about it and to do it. To pay attention. To concentrate. You don't have to be a *talmid chacham*. You just have to be an *oved Hashem*, to bless His holy Name when given the opportunity. And for shul goers, the opportunity is there. Sometimes its absence, as during Covid, as during a Holocaust, *Rachmana litzlan*, reminds us of how precious each opportunity is.

It's a gift. At that stage of his life, when my *zeide* had thought that he might never have it again, he made sure to take full advantage of that gift. I'm sure he didn't think of it as Murphy's gift, but the minyan factory in Murphy's Shul just two blocks away was a great gift indeed. It is a gift each of us should think of anew and take full advantage of. Because our time here is finite, our opportunity is finite, while our obligation to Him – and what we can accomplish with its fulfillment – is infinite.

*Parashas Haazinu 5782, Yerushalayim Ir Hakodesh*

# Legacy

God chose us because he wants us to serve Him in a particular way. Yes, each of us individually, but also each of us as part of the family we are – or are supposed to be. And so, davening as a minyan is much more important and more potent than the sum of its individual parts.

There is a beautiful midrash that describes how each day the Ribbono shel Olam sends His *malach* all around the world, to all the shuls and minyanim, to bring Him their *tefillos*, with which He makes for Himself a beautiful garland crown, *k'v'yachol*, and says, *Look how My children gather together to serve Me!*

Why do you suppose Hashem wants it this way?

Moshe's parting *berachah* includes the verse every Jewish child is taught early on in life: *Torah tziva lanu morashah Kehillas Yaakov.* As Rashi explains it, it is an admonition that the Torah that Moshe commanded us *is the legacy* of the children of Yaakov; we shall grab hold of it and never let it go. It is our communal inheritance. It is what we have. We have it individually and we have it in common, each with its own perspective.

And so the Gemara says (*Sukkah* 42a): when a small child learns to speak, his father begins to teach him Torah. What does he begin with? Says Rav Hamnuna, this *pasuk* and this concept: Torah *tziva lanu Moshe morashah Kehillas Yaakov.* This is who you are, child, this is who we are; this is what you possess, child, this is what we possess. This concept is a *yesod*, says the Torah Temimah, a foundational principle underpinning our existence as a people, faithfully and reliably transmitted from generation to generation, without interruption, back to Moshe Rabbeinu and *kabbalas haTorah*, an eternal legacy. This is further bolstered by the Yerushalmi's dictum, the Torah Temimah says, teaching the child the *pasuk* in Mishlei, *Shema beni mussar avicha v'al titosh Toras imecha* (Mishlei 1:8).

I remember as a child the wonderment of discovery and recognition when I encountered that *pasuk*. I learned much from my father, but he worked long, hard hours; my first rebbe was clearly my mother.

Well and good for a Jewish child. The unbroken chain, the legacy. But we are also a nation whose mission has included gathering in the *nitzotzos hakodesh*, the holy sparks that are everywhere in creation, and allowing them, welcoming them, into the fold. There have been many *gerim* over the generations of our existence. What foundational principle, other than the belief in One God, is offered them?

Hillel famously taught it to the gentile who wanted to convert in a hurry: *What is hateful to you, do not do to others.*

And this brings us back to the I/We duality of our arrangement with God, in which the I cannot exist without the We, nor the We without the I.

What Hillel told the potential convert was essentially a central message emphasized over and over in Navi, based on the Torah: *You must serve Me,* Hashem says, *and no other. You cannot distinguish between mitzvos; all derive from me. The requirements of the Torah do not apply just to rabbis and scholars. They apply to all. And so you must be fastidious in your observance of the mitzvos. But you cannot possibly observe the mitzvos, or the Torah, you cannot possibly serve Me, unless, in a very real way, you serve each other. With goodness and kindness. With love and concern. With sharing and with caring. With mutual support. With justice. With charity. The path to Me,* says Hashem, *is through your fellow Jew and your fellow human being.*

And so, there is a required dimension to the practice of Judaism, Kehillas Yaakov. The Congregation of Jacob. You need to be able to get together and work together to practice and foster your *avodas Hashem.* And you need also to see all the different *kehillos* of Jacob, from all around the world, of every background, as really the same as you.

We have a lot of history. We've been all over the world, and everywhere we settle, things tend to be done somewhat differently. That's human nature. But it's also human nature, sometimes, to look down at others, *including others like us who are not quite like us.* Litvaks might scoff at Galitzianers. Galitzianers might scoff at Yekkes. Everybody might scoff at Hungarians. Hungarians might scoff at everybody. The Ashkenazim might scoff at the Sephardim, who might scoff at the Ashkenazim and the Persians; the Syrians might scoff at the Moroccans, the Halabis might scoff at the Shamis, etc., etc., ad infinitum and ad nauseum. Those who are more stringent might scoff at those who are stringent enough, but not quite as stringent. Those who use one particular type of Hebrew pronunciation might scoff at those who use another. The basic underlying *ahavas Yisrael* is no doubt there, but much is allowed, attitudinally, to get in the way of feeling like one unified *kehillah,* vitiating the concept of Kehillas Yaakov.

We look at certain traits commonly exhibited by people from the different backgrounds that rub us the wrong way. We might hold it against them. It might even be somewhat justifiable. Well, what do you think that is, other than the *galus* rubbing off differently upon different Jews, depending upon where that *galus* has flung them? It's not the fault of the precious Jews! It's the Germans! It's the Russians! It's the Persians! It's the Arabs! It's whatever local society inevitably rubbed off on them in the long, grinding, and oh, so difficult *galus.* Just love them and be one with them.

*Torah tziva lanu Moshe morashah Kehillas Yaakov. Toras Moshe* is the legacy of each of us and of all of us. It does not belong exclusively to any one group. Local *minhagim* are important and may generally govern but do not define Torah and Judaism, especially elsewhere. Matters of style may be important in creating a sense of common purpose, of identification, but do not define identity to the point of exclusion of others. It is only conformity to the divine Torah, Written and Oral, to halachah, that does. For that is the legacy that binds us all together, that makes us one.

On this *pasuk*, on this enduring principle that binds all of Israel together, Kesav Sofer and others teach that it is not possible for any one Jew to keep each and every mitzvah of the Torah. There are many mitzvos that do not apply to everybody. It is only possible if every individual and every group band together, pooling our spiritual effort as one, as Kehillas Yaakov, with loving devotion to one another, with common purpose, so that we can fully acquire this eternal legacy, this *morashah*, this Torah that *tziva lanu Moshe*, that our loving Father in Heaven has bestowed upon us all.

*V'zos Haberachah 5782, Yerushalayim Ir Hakodesh*

# חגים

# Pesach

## Cherus

In a few days, when you're propped on a pillow and leaning way over to the left while you're drinking the four cups of wine at your Seder, be careful not to spill any on your clothes or on the rug. Red wine is such a stain maker. And be careful not to let any dribble down your chin, making you look ridiculous while you're trying to exhibit *cherus* (liberty, freedom), a mandated posture for the Seder.

People who are truly free don't really need prescribed forms to demonstrate how free they are. They are free, and they feel it, and they look it. One might even think that a person who is free is free to drink his four cups of wine in any position that's comfortable for him. In their wisdom, however, Chazal ordained otherwise.

How free are we? Well, obviously that varies according to time and place. The generation that left Egypt was certainly free. But one wonders, as they left, did they all actually feel free? Utterly and carelessly happy? No worries? The insecurity they felt and expressed at having left behind the known situation they were used to and, difficult as it was, could live with did not take long to manifest itself.

Furthermore, who was left behind? According to those who say that ultimately up to 80 percent of the Israelites in Egypt were lost there and never left, having assimilated completely, how did that play out? Was it whole families that were lost and other whole families that were saved? Or were families divided, with some members lost and others remaining Jewish?

Look at pictures of European Jewish families from a hundred years ago. Typically, there's the old father and mother, obviously pious and identifiable Jews, and then the next generation is divided into those who follow the parents and those who have obviously followed another path altogether. So what about the Israelites in Egypt? Who knows?

It's certainly clear that by the time the Israelites saw their pursuers washed up dead by the shores of the Yam Suf, they finally understood and felt that they were truly *free*. And then the rest of Jewish history could begin.

And we have, in our long history, had periods when we were quite free, periods when we were not at all free, and everything in between. So we have to remember the freedom we had at that first Pesach, when we marched out of Egypt *b'yad ramah*, and dream of and pray for that future freedom when Moshiach will finally arrive to free us once again. We resort to symbols at the Seder to remind us of the freedom we once had and the freedom we hope to have, while we cope and do the best with what we do have.

We, in this time and place, are among the most blessed in history in this regard. Just a generation or two ago, it could not have been worse. And sometimes just an arbitrary line, a border, or some geography separates freedom from the nightmare of its absence.

We who are so blessedly free in this blessed country cannot always grasp what it means not to be free. Thank God for that. Last year, in Cartagena, Colombia, I suddenly came face to face with an image that so depicted the opposite of freedom that it shook me to the core and reminded me of how blessed we are here.

Moments before, in the old seaside town, I came upon an imposing building with a sign identifying it as the "Office of the Holy Inquisition." It utterly spooked me out, and I would not join the other tourists who went in to take a look at what was to them just a historical curiosity. In that place, until not really all that long ago, our people who sought escape in the New World from the terrors of the Church in Europe were hunted down, tortured, and burned.

But that was only a backdrop to the Pesach aspect of that short visit to Cartagena. About a hundred yards away, in the old town square, in front of a church, there was a sculpture that I could only stand and stare at as my emotions roiled within me.

It is a bronze statue of an African slave, naked from the waist up. His look of despair, hopelessness, and utter helplessness virtually shouts at the observer. It was captured with dramatic but understated power by the sculptor. A second figure, apparently offering him some moral support, is that of a priest, Pedro Claver, who dedicated his life to succoring the many slaves who were brought to Colombia, and in so doing incurred the enmity of the cruel Spanish overlords.

One look at that slave reminds any but the most insensitive what it means to be free. And it drives home that we – all of us Jews – are the children of such slaves in Egypt, and but for the miracle of the Exodus on Pesach, we would still be there, helpless, hopeless, and in despair, without even a Pedro Claver to soften that misery. But by God's great deliverance, we were set free, a freedom that through thick and thin, through harder times and better times, set us on the path to eternal *cherus* in the future. And so, in this iffy world we live in, we have symbols and forms that Chazal ordained to help us remember.

And speaking of latter-day slaves, if we go back a bit to those same tormentors, the accursed Spanish, let me tell a bit about some other slaves and *cherus*, or the lack of it.

If you ever travel to the island of Malta in the Mediterranean, I suggest you arrive by ship, approaching the old port of Valetta in the early morning. The old battlements there are designed to frighten off invaders, and even those who arrive today for a holiday visit will find it dark, brooding, and forbidding – exactly as intended. Malta has a long and complex history, with many invasions and ethnic input from various sources. It is intensely Roman Catholic; its language is a form of Arabic, written in Latin letters.

Although official Church doctrine teaches that baptisms should not be forced, forced baptism has been the terrible lot of large segments of our people through history. Terrible religious riots broke out in Spain in 1392, with mobs rampaging through Jewish neighborhoods, going house to house to force Jews to be baptized at the edge of the sword. Anyone refusing was butchered. Many were baptized this way, to stay alive, but as soon as things settled down, they renounced those baptisms as fraudulent and illegitimate.

The authorities would have none of it. Forced or not, there was no going back. Judaizers – those still practicing Jewish rites – were liable to be burned. When, a hundred years later, the Jews were finally expelled from Spain, it was the hundreds of thousands who refused to give up the faith of their fathers who, under terrible conditions, suffered the horrible exodus of Gerush Sepharad. Jews set out to wherever they could to escape the scourge of baptism.

Two shiploads (who knows? perhaps more) of such dedicated Jews were captured at sea by pirates and were brought to Malta and sold as slaves. They were immediately forcibly baptized. And there, in Malta, their descendants still exist, totally lost into the general population.

In the one day I spent there, I met a local woman who, as a tour guide, was wearing a name tag. This small, swarthy woman, with a large cross around her neck, had a name that made me suspect that she was descended from those Jewish slaves. I actually asked her. She didn't really want to talk about it, but her response indicated to me that she in fact was.

*Cherus* is a precious commodity indeed, not to be taken for granted.

And so another *cherus* story, one that highlights how subtle and nuanced *cherus* can be and how precious even a bit of *cherus* is.

Years ago, a man with a long grey beard appeared in shul on Friday night who davened with great fervor. Quite thin, with an otherworldly, even haunted look about him, he was alone. I approached him and invited him to our Shabbos table. He accepted.

The man spoke some English, with a heavy Russian accent. He recited Kiddush, made all the *berachos*, and bentshed after the meal, reciting each word carefully and with obvious *kavanah*, entirely in the Russian language. He had with him an old, well-used and well-worn small siddur from which he prayed, which contained no Hebrew. It looked homemade and was obviously very precious to him. He told us that he had never been able to learn Hebrew at all, not even to read, but he had managed to piece together, in Russian, the various blessings and prayers that a Jew needs to live a Jewish life, and they were compiled in that *siddur*.

I'm sorry to say that I lost touch with him. He seemed utterly alone. He did not tell us his story. That Shabbos, as I watched him devotedly pray from that precious *siddur*, I came to understand another kind of enslavement and another kind of *cherus*. And, in the face of that cruel subjugation, I'm not sure, as he huddled over those holy words in Russian, that I have ever seen someone who embodied freedom, the triumph of *cherus* over spiritual enslavement, more than that holy Jew.

*Pesach, Zeman Cherusenu, 5778*

# Oh, Freedom!

Oh, freedom! Oh, freedom!
Oh, freedom over me!
And before I'd be a slave,
I'll be buried in my grave
and go home to my Lord and be free!

She was uninspiring and kind of cranky. All these many decades, when I thought back to elementary school, I was really annoyed at the school for subjecting us to her "teaching" my class not just for one awful year, but for several. It was as if she was stalking us, with the help of the school. What a waste!

And yet somehow, in recent times, when we are being overwhelmed with increasingly outlandish attacks on the principles of civics that we grew up with and that have served as the basis for how we view our personal and communal freedoms and how it is possible for people with differing points of view to live together in society with mutual respect and consideration, all the while those attacks being presented as if they were rational and actually *sane*, I find myself thinking of that teacher more and more.

I have, I believe, a well-developed sense of how American freedom works, a loving appreciation of it, and a profound gratitude for it. It hurts me and frightens me to hear the ever more strident demand that our traditional freedoms be shut down, suborned to a kind of mad radical orthodoxy that grows madder by the day and demands that all deviation from the insanity of the day be punished and utterly suppressed.

It wasn't my math teachers who set me to thinking about our American freedoms. It was, I have come to realize, that very teacher that I always thought taught me nothing. I was wrong, and I apologize. This she had right. As I recall, she didn't always practice it in the classroom, but I suppose that wasn't really expected. We did come to understand that out in civil society, everyone is entitled not only to have an opinion, but to express it, without fear of shunning or destructive ad hominem attack for having that opinion, or for living a principled life that may not conform to the current fashion.

Freedom, to some, is an odd thing. They see their rights to it – and to their opinions – as requiring others not just to agree with those opinions but to actively validate them, even if that means that those others have thereby lost their own rights. Those who disagree, in this view, are painted as haters, violent by virtue of their disagreement and therefore undeserving of the same rights.

A look at what appears to be driving this awful phenomenon sheds some light, I think, on its nature and is most relevant for us on our own festival of freedom, Chag Hapesach.

Historically, and still today among some in the world (*Shh! Don't spell it out, lest you be branded Blankophobic!*), this absolutism was often driven by religion, typically resulting in the cruelest behavior, directly opposite to the more kindly principles of faith unctuously referred to but rarely practiced. Today it is also about God – not about life with Him, but *without* Him. It is driven by the desire to do away with Him altogether, never needing to answer to Him for one's actions, that there be no brake whatsoever on the pursuit of unbridled libertine pleasure, which they take to be freedom.

It's interesting that in Yiddish, one who has thrown off the constraints of Yiddishkeit is referred to as a *freier*, someone who fancies that he is now "free."

The development of oral contraceptives about fifty years ago, "the pill," for whatever medical and societal benefits it has – and it does – was also driven by and itself serves as a driving force for utterly unfettered libertine amorality with no price to pay for behavior that throughout the history of civilization was utterly unacceptable. With God out of the picture, there is no one to answer to.

There is an obvious, direct line from the throwing off of these restraints to the neonatal infanticide that is now being foisted on society as the new "normal." *And don't you dare speak up against it, you hater!*

Why would brilliant physicists, using scientific logic and observation, arrive at a "Big Bang" but absolutely "refuse to think about" (I am quoting here) Who put that in motion, however obvious that might be? Because if God did it, they, and the rest of mankind, must answer for their actions, and that they refuse to do. They imagine that in this, they find their freedom. And for this, they stridently shun those scientists who do not deny God, who see the obvious Hand of a Creator.

The very voices that demand for themselves that unfettered libertine freedom would also deny, as a condition of their own license, the rights of others to disagree or even, "God forbid (!)," disapprove.

Pesach teaches us that they could not be more wrong. They have no idea what freedom is. Pesach teaches us that real freedom requires also a freedom of the spirit, which finds its freedom and its definition and its fulfillment in binding itself to its very Source, infusing that freedom with dignity and purpose and holiness. There is no greater, more meaningful, or more lasting freedom than the bond with our Creator, Who, in setting us free, also made us His. Making us chosen to be His servants also made us, in a very real sense, the most empowered and the freest people on earth.

The ballad above, an anthem of the newly freed slaves in the American South, speaks so movingly of the dignity and strength of the human desire to be free and every human being's inherent right to freedom of the person, of the mind, and of the spirit. We are all God's children, created equally by His holy Hand. Let no man, ever again, in any form, enslave another.

For us, for our particular people, there is a particular aspect to freedom. All human beings find their greatest expression of freedom not in libertine abandon, but in serving the Creator's purpose in this world by living a moral life. We, whom our Heavenly Father plucked from bitter bondage in Egypt to be His special people, have been given the opportunity to achieve the greatest freedom of all, by becoming one with Him: *Am Yisrael v'Oraysa, v'Kudsha Brich Hu chad hu.*

*Chag kasher v'sameach!*

*Shabbos Hagadol 5779*

# In It for Our Lives

Given the danger of the moment, I was afraid to step outside the door. I couldn't take the chance, even though I had things to do and people to see. It was Shabbos afternoon, quiet, but we all knew that something terrible could God forbid befall us.

Growing up almost always feeling safe, I knew that at that moment, none of us was safe. I could not risk going outside, not because the danger there was any greater, but because I feared, with justification, that at any moment, catastrophe might strike, and if I was away from home, I would not be able to get back to my parents when they needed me. We all knew, on that Shabbos afternoon, that the fate of the world hung in the balance; nuclear Armageddon threatened as the Cuban missile crisis raged about us. It was October 1962, and we half expected a nuclear attack at any moment.

Well, thank God, that turned out OK. Throughout the years of my growing up, coming of age, and living my life with my family, I don't remember any other time, outside the occasional mugging or perhaps an illness, when we felt especially threatened. Life was, in general, blissfully safe. (Vietnam, a world away, was another matter.)

I knew very well that one generation before, in my parents' own lives, millions lived through unrelenting threat, fear, and mortal danger hour after hour, day after day, month after month, year after year. Of the relative few who survived, it is hard to understand not only how they survived, but how those who emerged with their sanity intact in fact did so. And yet there were many who did, my parents included.

And so, on these blessed shores, I grew up feeling safe. It was my legacy as an American, and the loving way my parents raised me.

Our lives, for most of us (and God bless those who, *nebech*, have had troubled and unsafe lives), have been blessed with a fortunate degree of personal and societal safety. Suddenly that is gone. We are overwhelmed, frightened, hopeful about the long-term prospects but threatened terribly by the shorter term realities and how they may harm those prospects.

And we have our faith. We know that trials and tribulations, *Rachmana litzlan*, are, for God's reasons, part of this life. And we know that when we come out on the other side, when the danger passes, even as we are still shaking, even as we struggle to clean up the mess, even as some are so badly hurt or damaged, as much as some have lost, as so many mourn their tragic losses, how we act and how we respond when the dust settles counts. And the dust will, please God, eventually settle, even if it leaves us, God forbid, dustier than we ever thought possible.

*With loving blessings to all for life and health, for peace and prosperity*
*Parashas Tzav, Shabbos Hagadol 5780*

# Tisha b'Av

## Whose War Is It?

How many books have been written trying to explain the age-old plague of antisemitism? About as many theories as you can think of have been proposed. Jews and gentiles alike, for different reasons, often come up with some reason to blame the Jews for the world's hatred of them, based on bad behavior. The Israeli left, and now the American Jewish left, see "clearly" that "cruel and oppressive" Israeli policies (and everybody "knows" that this is so) cause everyone to hate Israel and all Jews.

Historically, the secular Zionists, the socialists, and other such ideologically driven groups believed that if only the Jews would stop being different, and more like everybody else, antisemitism would disappear.

They were quite wrong, of course. And at the same time, they were, in a perverse way, sort of right.

In acquiring the Torah, to which we are bound for all time, we also acquired, at Sinai, for all time, the enmity of the world. I wonder if our ancestors realized this when they proclaimed *naaseh v'nishma*. The Gemara (*Shabbos* 89a) discusses symbolic meanings of the name "Sinai." Most striking is the parallel between Sinai and *sin'ah*, hatred. An implacable hatred was born at Sinai.

The seven nations who occupied the Promised Land had reason to fear and hate the Jews; they were threatened. Many of the hateful encounters related in the Torah, however, in which the refugee Israelites were set upon in some way, were with nations that had no reason to fear or resent the Jew. Amalek. In the Bilaam story, Moav and Midian team up to destroy Israel. The latter two nations sent their daughters in to perform harlotry in order to defile the Jewish People and thus bring them down.

God tells Moshe, afterward, to conscript an army and go to war, to exact *"Israel's revenge"* from the Midianites. Moshe does so and sends them off to exact *"God's* revenge." There has been much commentary on Moshe's switch in language. *Midrash Tanchuma* (Mattos 3) quotes Moshe:

> Ribbono shel Olam, if we were uncircumcised, or idol worshipers, or rejecters of the mitzvos, they (the gentiles) would not hate us, nor would they persecute us. They would have nothing against us. It is only because of the Torah that YOU gave us. Therefore this vengeance is Yours, "God's revenge." It is about You.

Whose war is it? Ours or God's?

Both perspectives are correct. Israel stands up for God's honor, and God stands up for Israel's. Israel brought the concept and the Name of God into the consciousness of humanity, and God elevated Israel to its high station of specialness, the sole receivers of His Torah and solely responsible for its manifestation in the world.

God, being God, cannot be touched. But Israel, being human, is vulnerable. And being chosen for its special role makes Israel a target.

On one level, God uses the nations of the world as a stick to punish us for our bad behavior. Our sins bring on the punishments. But, it seems to me, it goes beyond that. It's not just when we are bad that the others come to hurt us. It's just because of who we are that they come to hurt us. They hurt us when God allows. They want to hurt us because of our relationship with God, whether we are behaving well or not. The default position is that they resent us and want to hurt us. When we are good, we hope, God keeps them away. But, it seems, He doesn't even have to actively send them our way, *chalilah*, for us to get hurt. All he has to do is, *Rachmana litzlan*, to look the other way. *Hester panim*, God forbid, allows them to get past His protective barrier, which must otherwise be up always and at all times.

What a price our privilege has, worth it as it is. And what a privilege we earn with that high price.

Tisha b'Av reminds us of our tenuous balance in this world. The choice to do good should be so obvious to us all, and yet it obviously is not. That's how we fall, *chalilah*, and that's how we earn merit. Entities that can reach the highest form of *kedushah* are the very ones that can fall to the lowest level of *tumah*, very much analogous to this.

But we can and should take heart from the very fact that we have been placed in such a vulnerable position. It tells us that we are also in the most enviable and exalted position on Earth. Tisha b'Av does not have to remain the terrible day it is. One day it will not be, and we pray that the Ribbono shel Olam, in His wisdom and mercy, will bless us with that miracle. He is ready, in His good time, and may that time come speedily and in our day. Meanwhile, He is watching us to see what signals we choose to send Him.

May He never again stand aside and allow those who hate us just because we are His to hurt us. Rather, may He envelop us in His warm and protective embrace as we, He and we, become one.

*Am Yisrael v'Oraysa v'Kudsha Brich Hu chad hu.*

*Tisha b'Av 5779*

# Hearing Eichah

I had a happy, normal, and psychologically healthy childhood. It is one of the amazing miracles of human nature that Holocaust survivors could live normal lives and raise normal children. The demons my parents and others like them had to contend with, lurking somewhere beneath the surface, affected our lives and our psyches, of course, but in an essentially normal and entirely functional way.

I know there were those who were even more scarred. There were those who suffered even more terribly. But I also believe of survivors that the inner strength that allowed them to live a normal life after the Holocaust was, in human terms, part of what made their survival possible.

I was born some years after the war; life was peaceful, and I never felt unsafe from war, although, especially with the Korean War in the news, I did think that war was always raging somewhere. But I knew that we in America were safe.

That said, and I remember this clearly, if I was ever alone in a room (and I had no problem being alone in a room), I often thought that if I were to turn around, there would be a German soldier, Schmeisser machine gun at the ready, standing menacingly behind me. Intellectually, I knew he wasn't there. But I would not have been entirely surprised if he were.

This phenomenon has not entirely left me, but it has morphed. These days, when I go downstairs, often before dawn, to get some exercise, when I turn on the light in the basement, I half expect to be greeted by a raccoon or a possum, standing menacingly, beady eyes fixed on mine. Intellectually, of course, I know (*I hope!*) I won't. But, knowing that it's not impossible, I would not be entirely surprised if one were.

I do believe that the sensitization that became part of my makeup as a child – which we all receive as children – colors the way we see the world in every way. We're lucky if it doesn't make us too crazy, or cruel or cold and indifferent, or bigoted, or stingy, overly timid, or any of a million other objectionable things. And how blessed we are when that sensitization results in the goodness, the kindness, the empathy, *the sensitivity* that is the ideal good people aspire to, and that eases, for us, the pathway to Godliness that we Jews aspire to.

I also believe that the metaphysical world we are surrounded by affects us to a greater or lesser degree based on our own sensitivities, the same thing affecting some people profoundly and others apparently not at all.

And so we are lucky, blessed, if our spirits are attuned to the things they should be attuned to. As Jews, we are preprogrammed, as part our spiritual heritage, implanted in our spiritual DNA, to be sensitive to all the right things. But our *klippos*, those hard shells covering our hearts that it is our duty to tear away, are not all the same, nor are the circumstances of our upbringing. For some, the life of the spirit comes much more easily than for others. But regardless of any individual's starting point, our essential obligations are the same, even as different people's struggles vary wildly. And only Hashem Yisborach, Who knows the content of every human heart and the circumstances of every life, can judge, as only He truly understands.

And so, it is our duty, and our opportunity, if we are smart enough to understand it, to look everywhere in life for the clues that are all around us that God sends us, to hear the messages, however inadvertently they appear to be sent, to wake us up and to teach us. If we will only listen.

The first time I remember hearing Eichah read was when I was nine years old, in Bunk ה in Camp Yeshiva in Swan Lake, New York. I'm sure I'd heard it before, but I have no memory of it. But the memory of hearing it that night in camp has never left me, and I am so grateful for it.

An older boy read it. He might have been nineteen or twenty years old. That means that unlike me, born after the Holocaust but certainly aware of it in a profound way, he grew up during the Holocaust, and although he'd been safe in America, its horrors had to have affected him deeply.

When that young fellow read Eichah, he made me feel the Churban and every subsequent *churban* our people have experienced. I remember his clear voice, enunciating the words in the perfectly chanted, mournful Eichah *trop*, a melody that, if done right, itself conveys meaning as much as do the words themselves. I don't remember if my Hebrew was good enough then to understand all the words (for the most part I did), but I do know that I got the message. Clearly. And I was also aware that not everyone did.

It was, for me, a formative moment. It helped me realize, sensitized as I already was, not just what Tisha b'Av is about, as profound as that is, but also that there are messengers out there, God's emissaries to each of us who aren't even aware of this particular role they are playing in our lives, to wake us up, to help us tear away those *klippos* from our hearts, to build on the sensitivities we do have and to develop ones that we need, so that in our limited sojourn in this world, we may not only fulfill the roles we were born for but also realize that part of that role, for each of us, is that our impact on our fellow Jews and on our fellow human beings, can, in fact, be limitless.

*Tisha b'Av 5781*

# Yamim Noraim: Days of Awe

## Machar Yihyeh Ha'os Hazeh

When there was prophecy in Israel, there was also prophecy in the other nations as well. Thus, we are told, they could have no excuse that they were unfairly disadvantaged relative to the Jews in doing God's will, or in knowing right from wrong. Famously, Bilaam was a real prophet, but he chose an evil path, and his followers chose with him.

Thus, while the prophets of Israel had, on occasion, messages for the nations of the world, their designated mission was always Israel. God had other messengers for the other nations. This applies to Yonah as well, even though his most known prophecy, with all the drama surrounding it, was to the people of Nineveh.

Yonah, apparently of the tribe of Zevulun, preached, along with his colleagues in prophecy, to the northern kingdom of the ten tribes of Israel. They might have repented and been spared the destruction and disappearance that befell them, but in their recalcitrance, they would not, and disappear they tragically did.

The hammer poised to smash them was centered in Nineveh. That was their historic mission. But the measure of Nineveh's own sinfulness was such that if they did not reform, their own time would be up – *before* they could come and destroy Israel. And so they needed to repent in order to survive and punish the unrepentant Kingdom of Israel. How ironic. And Yonah didn't like that one bit.

As much as he was exasperated by the recalcitrant Hebrews, he also loved them dearly, as did all the other holy prophets God sent to try to get them to return to Him. Even though he surely knew that God has many messengers, and some other nation could have presumably taken Ashur's place as the conquering destroyer of Israel, at that time it was Nineveh that had to be staved off. And so rather than go to Nineveh as God wanted, and get them to repent, Yonah fled.

It's interesting that when Yonah's ship was tossing and foundering, as everyone else was on deck trying to save themselves, Yonah went down to the depths of the ship, the first place that was likely to fill up with water, and lay down to sleep,

320

expecting to drown and thus escape what to him was a fate worse than death, the destruction of his beloved Israel. He offered his life for ours.

Yonah was sent to Nineveh with a specific mission to the Assyrians, *but it was really about us*, the everlasting message was to us, about the desperate need for and the incredible power of *teshuvah*. And thus, the critical place of the Yonah story in the annual, ongoing life of our people, on its most solemn day, the Day of Atonement. If Yonah could survive three days in the belly of the sea beast, because that was God's will, if wicked Nineveh could save itself from destruction through *teshuvah*, then surely we, by following God's will, can be saved, for He has told us quite clearly that that is what it takes, that He wants us to be blessed and to be His. That is His will.

And so, freighted with all the heavy history of our people, we turn to God on this day and beseech Him. And, as we have been taught by our champions over the ages, God allows us to put up something of an argument before Him. A classic is the powerful *selichah* we recite on the third day of Aseres Yemei Teshuvah: Eich Uchal Lavo Adecha (איך אוכל לבא עדיך).

How can I return to You, oh God, when those who worship other gods prevent me? They seek constantly to separate us, but I continue to cling to Your mitzvos!

How I have been exiled and flung about the world by idol worshipers who rule the world, while I have been kept low and unable to return to You!

How rivers of tears flow from me, as I have been dominated by evildoers who, together with their children, shoot me with their arrows as a calf brought to slaughter!

How I have no notion of when I might be redeemed, as they strut about thinking they are so much wiser than me, and they rule the world!

How the kingdom of Your special nation has been destroyed, while the reign of the evildoers goes on and on, and they sit in security and joy!

How I drink the cup of bitterness, as they mock me, and I have no response!

How God has struck me, and the wound does not heal, as the oppressors are fat and content!

How those who hate all things pure and holy have ruled over Zion! How can it be His will that they should sit in wealth and power while I am so poor and powerless!

How can they occupy the holy precincts of the Beis Hamikdash while I sit without! On this day of judgment and atonement, remember us with Your Redemption, and *b'rov chasdecha*, in the greatness of Your *chesed*, return us to Your House, return us to You!

And so comes the awesome day. We pray for our individual salvation as well as the national. We fast before God, and we pray, as we do all through the Aseres Yemei Teshuvah, that He accept our fasting and prayer and consider it as a holy *korban* on His altar. We pray that the rivers of blood we have spilled for His sake be as precious and as redemptive before Him as they have been unspeakably painful for us. As the *pasuk* for which this *selichah* is named promises us, *L'machar yihyeh ha'os hazeh* (למחר יהיה האות הזה [Shemos 8:19]), tomorrow this sign will come about.

**מחר יהיה האות הזה**
Tomorrow:

Accept our prayers and our fast, and seal us for life.

Cloak Yourself in righteous charity and raise up Your downtrodden people.

Have mercy on Your people, who believe in You. Put away our sins and consider only our merits.

Come close and hear our prayers as we beseech You. Open Your gates for us.

We are powerless and undeserving. We have no *korbonos* and no Mikdash and no Kohen Gadol. *We have You.*

Your dispersed children come now to shelter under Your protection. Remember the merits of their holy forebears. We put aside our own internal squabbles and we stand before You in loving brotherhood, as You desire, praying for a *G'mar chasimah tovah.*

**מחר יהיה האות הזה**

*Erev Yom Kippur 5779*

# Ahavas Yisrael, No Strings Attached

After a visit to a shul in another area, some years ago, I felt compelled to write the rabbi a letter. You will find it below. But let me first put it in context.

The rabbi in question was a rising star in his world. Everybody said so. Learned, erudite, well spoken, highly personable, indeed charismatic, he was headed for great success in his community. In his presence, I saw and felt that. And so my distress at what unfolded was all the greater. Following is my letter. See what you think.

Dear Rabbi X,

I very much enjoyed – except for what will be referred to below – my recent visit to your shul, as I always do. I have an appreciation of the special *ruach* of the shul, its style, and, in particular, its *rav*. As you gear up for the exciting expansion and growth that's planned, I wish you and your congregation every success.

You will likely remember a brief conversation we had during my visit. It was clearly uncomfortable for you, as it was for me.

The shul said a *tefillah* on behalf of the United States, which was, for me, very gratifying. The prayer for the American soldiers who are fighting and dying in faraway lands was especially appropriate, and laudable [American forces were at that time fighting in Afghanistan and Iraq]. The well-being of the *medinah shel chesed* in which we live is, of course, extremely important to us, and we pray, appropriately, for its success and the safety of its soldiers, our fellow Americans, who are fighting – and dying – on our behalf. To do less would be insensitive at best, and foolishly, *kofeh tovah*. Sadly, not enough shuls, especially what we might think of as *frum* shuls, bother with it, or, presumably, think much about it. But they should. And thank you for doing so.

I then asked you: Do the Jewish soldiers in Eretz Yisrael, fighting, dying, placing themselves in constant danger on our behalf, deserve our prayers less than the gentile soldiers in the US Army? If you take the trouble to daven for American boys (and girls) at war, why would you not care enough to do the same for the Jewish boys who place their lives on the line daily so that Jews in Eretz Yisrael can live? The Israel Defense Forces have been taking casualties, suffering grievous losses, nearly every day. There is a beautiful *tefillah*, calling on Hashem to protect them. You could have said that prayer as well, or any other of your choosing. But you did not. Was it an oversight?

My question left you visibly uncomfortable, and your response left me deeply upset. You fumbled and mumbled something about "politics" and suddenly had to race off far across the room (the fastest I had ever seen you move) – away from me and my uncomfortable question.

This is not about politics. This is not about political Zionism, secularism, or religious political camps. This is not about positioning yourself or your shul in some advantageous position on the *frum* political spectrum. I have no interest in those issues, and I am not afraid to state the obvious: *this is about decency*. This is about the religious obligation of *ahavas Yisrael*. This is about doing the right thing, without the need or compulsion to look over your shoulder.

Do you ever travel to Eretz Yisrael?

Who do you think stands between you and the Arab cutthroats who would indeed be happy to cut your throat, and those of your children, *chas v'chalilah*, if given the opportunity? Certainly, *hamaves v'hachaim b'yad Hashem*, and the Ribbono shel Olam determines who will live and who will die. But we also know that there is a *mashchis* out and about, targeting Jews, *Rachmana litzlan*, and we do not know where it will strike, except that the Jewish soldiers are in its path – *for the sake of the rest of us, they place themselves in its path* – they are susceptible to its evil powers, and they, along with the rest of all Yisrael, need our prayers. But they especially need them and deserve them.

Rabbi, I cannot help but think of a colleague of yours, also a *rav*, whose name is eerily similar to yours. Not long ago, his oldest son, a *yeshiva bachur* serving in the Israel Defense Forces, was gunned down and killed by the terrorist murderers he was trying to find and immobilize before they could plant another bomb in a bus or a supermarket or in front of a yeshiva or a shul. He was trying to save your life and that of your immediate and extended family, and he gave his life for you. *For you. For your children.*

This boy, this pure *neshamah*, this *yeshiva bachur*, could have used our prayers. He could have used your prayers and those of your *frum* congregation. How frightened he must have been! I hope he did not realize, as he lay dying, that only some Jews bothered to pray for him, while others thought it was politically incorrect, that it was somehow less *frum*, to do so. I hope he never did realize, as he lay dying, the sad reality that there are some Jews who perversely believe, apparently, that not praying for him and his colleagues at risk for their very lives somehow brings them, those who refuse to pray for *chayalei Tzahal*, closer to God, more beloved by Him, more esteemed by Him. That that's part of how they define their refined *frumkeit*. I hope, as he lay there, his life ebbing away, that he did not sense that the *ahavas Yisrael* that some Jews piously and lovingly preach has these perverse *frum* PC strings attached.

There. I've gotten it off my chest.

Please do not misunderstand. I am not, *chas v'chalilah*, characterizing you or your *kehillah* in this negative way. I know that you and your congregants care very much indeed about all Jews, and, I am sure, the *chayalim*. I hold you in the greatest respect. And for this reason, I have taken the time and the trouble to express myself in this way, to share these thoughts with you. I believe they need to be shared with you. I also doubt that I am the only one to react in this way. I am not simple, nor am I unsophisticated in the intricacies of contemporary Jewish politics. I do not involve myself in such politics. I am also not in the somewhat vulnerable position a rabbi is in. But I do believe very strongly that there are issues that are too important to hide from, that one morally cannot hide from, and the "simple" mitzvos of *ahavas Yisrael* and *V'ahavta l'reacha ka'mocha* are things one need never be shy about or afraid of, except, *chas v'shalom*, in the breach.

Extending you my best wishes, with all sincerity, friendship, and respect,
Yerucham Reich

So here I will tell you about a shul in Israel that has a policy that the *shaliach tzibbur* must daven with Israeli-style pronunciation. I suppose they were trying to instill – to impose, really – a sense of Israeliness. When I was asked to be the *chazan*, I told them that I am perfectly capable of putting on a fake Israeli accent, but that I would not. I can converse very well in modern Israeli Hebrew. But the way I daven, the way I commune with God, the way I talk to Him, was determined by my forebears, I said, not by Ben-Gurion and his *chevra*. It's entirely appropriate for one's politics to be informed by one's religion. But it's hardly religion if it is informed by one's politics. Oy, they didn't like that at all. Of course, I was never asked again.

Politics should play no role in *ahavas Yisrael* either. Certainly not for a *yerei Shamayim.*

Under the British occupation, it was those who had thrown off their Yiddishkeit who informed on, imprisoned, beat and tortured, even handed over to the British hangman their fellow Jews who more actively resisted the British, the generally more traditional Jews who were not subservient to the dominant secularist socialist power structure in Jewish Palestine and its relatively passive, "respectable" acceptance of the British yoke, the "important" Jews, the "Establishment" Jews. It was never the other way around.

It was the same British "hangman" who deliberately kept the gates of Eretz Yisrael closed to the millions of Jews seeking refuge, with nowhere else to run, condemning them to be murdered by the accursed Germans and their happy helpers in Ukraine, Poland, Latvia, Lithuania, and other such lands, the same British "hangman" whose policy it was – and this is, almost unbelievably, quite true – that there be but a *minimal number of Jewish survivors*, in order to minimize the number of pesky Jews who might eventually try to reach the Land of Israel.

Some years ago, when I was on a *shivah* call, a woman I had known for many years told me, rather cluelessly, I think, that her late husband, whom I also had known, was one of those who fired on and sank the Irgun ship *Altalena* in 1948, killing numerous Jews, upon the orders of the ruling secularist socialists who hated and feared Menachem Begin and his like-minded, "more Jewish" Jews. This despite the agreement in place to offload the desperately needed weapons it was carrying and turn virtually all of it over to the Establishment's Haganah, with the also agreed-upon proviso that some would be sent to the beleaguered forces in Jerusalem where an Irgun detachment, out of ammunition, was barely holding on. Well, when the Haganah (in essence, the provisional government) agreed to this, they "forgot" to mention that in sending the arms to Jerusalem, they would *not* send them to any Irgun soldiers, come what may, no matter how desperate their situation – only to Haganah units.

In the end, they decided to sink the ship and tried to kill Begin and the many soldiers on board who had come from abroad to help. They were of the wrong political persuasion. The excuse they gave was the false accusation – the blood libel – that they were plotting a violent coup d'état. Hard to believe, isn't it? But that's what partisan hatred can do. Begin and his people resolutely refused to fire back; they would not shoot at fellow Jews, even to defend their own lives. *Ahavas Yisrael.*

The woman told me that her husband, himself a Holocaust survivor, had always felt bad about participating in that travesty. "But what could he do?" she said. *"He was only obeying orders!"*

It took all of my willpower not to spit those words back at her in a German accent. Given where we were, I said nothing.

Now I'll tell you what happened with my letter.

I had pity on the fellow, as I thought his mistake, weighty as it is, was not really ill-intentioned, just ill-considered. But I also really, *really* wanted to send it. I felt I had to, I had to express myself, and that he really needed to hear it – *he deserved to hear it* – for his own sake as much as for mine. So I did something somewhat uncharacteristic for me. I showed it to a wise friend, a learned man with good judgment. I asked him what he thought I should do.

His reply was nuanced. He thought I *should* send it. But if you do, he said, "you'll kill him." *If you don't want to kill him, don't send it.* The more a mensch the recipient is, the more likely you'll kill him. And so he appealed to me not to. (No surprise, he was a rabbi too.)

I did not send it. That too is *ahavas Yisrael.*

Instead, I filed it away, keeping it as something to brood over, saving it for you to consider.

So, what do *you* think?

*Tishrei 5783*

# Sukkos

## Malach Habris

הושע נא מרוטת לחי!

הושע נא נתונה למכים!...

הושע נא שואגים הושע נא!

Is the pillar of salt that used to be Mrs. Lot *metamei b'ohel*, or even by contact?

Is the wife of Eliyahu Hanavi, after his living ascent into the heavens in a whirlwind, upon a chariot of fire, an *eishes ish*?

No and no. (See Tosafos to *Yevamos* 61a; *Even Ha'ezer* 17; *Darkei Moshe* 5.)

And yet we have been taught that Eliyahu does, in fact, become manifest in the world from time to time, in some manner, corporeally or incorporeally, as the Ribbono shel Olam sees fit, as a *malach*, a messenger of God, whether to herald the redemption (*bimherah v'yameinu!*), on rare known occasions to communicate with *yechidei segulah*, such as *chachmei haTalmud*, or, in Jewish tradition and lore, to step in on behalf of a Jew in a dire situation. It was Eliyahu (while still of this world) who saved the starving widow and her son, and we are told this for a reason.

Eliyahu as the world might experience him now is not perceived as the imposing figure with big hair and a leather belt. He is a *malach*, who may assume any shape or form needed for the situation he has come to affect, or no shape or form at all. Thus, he is *malach habris* at every bris milah, and he attends every Pesach Seder. We understand that this is so, in some manner, even as we understand that none of these things is one of Rambam's Thirteen Principles of Faith.

Thus, we are told, as well, of Eliyahu's experience of God during his own time of hiding in the cave in the desert. "Why are you here, Eliyahu?" And God shows him that He manifests Himself not in the wind, and not in the earthquake, and not in the fire. For Eliyahu, God is manifest in *kol demamah dakah*, the small, still sound. And it is in that small, still voice that Eliyahu will, as a *malach*, until the great day of the Redemption, manifest himself in the life of the Jewish People. Not as the fierce prophet who publicly confronts the powerful king, but as the sometimes barely noticeable but utterly indispensable agent whose intervention is God's designated small, still sound made manifest for His people in their need, at such times as He might see fit.

That agent of salvation, whoever he might be, who utterly inexplicably appears and acts, even if otherwise a natural being, is, at that moment, Eliyahu Hanavi. And sometimes his presence simply cannot be explained naturally. *Cannot.* And that is, for the purposes of our understanding, also Eliyahu Hanavi. That distinction, such as there is, is up to God.

There are those who, by disposition or by choice hyperrational (*hyperlitvik Litvaks!*), choose to apply that hyperrationality to the subject of Eliyahu Hanavi and dismissively "*mach avek*" any post–Talmudic stories about him, complete with an eye roll. That is their privilege. They can understand Eliyahu in any way they wish. But they have, in all likelihood, themselves never experienced him, in the whirlwinds of life, nor have those close to them. But mockingly dismissing out of hand those who have – credible people in incredible difficulty – is somewhat reminiscent of the well-known story, apocryphal or not, of the non-*frum* Israeli taxi driver whose non-*frum* friend was saved in war, clearly by the extraordinary intervention of the Hand of God, whose life was thereby transformed and who became a *yerei Shamayim*. The driver, who witnessed it and testified to it, was himself oddly not transformed by it. "It didn't happen to me."

You don't have to believe that Eliyahu Hanavi roams the earth as, *l'havdil*, a deus ex machina, waiting to jump out of a box to save the day. That is not what it is about. God has many messengers. The "small, still sound" of God's interventional presence in our lives, His Hand clearly reaching out to us in some natural yet miraculous way, when there is no other source of salvation but when salvation is God's will, perhaps delivered via Eliyahu Hanavi, or what we can *understand* as Eliyahu Hanavi, is very much what this is about.

When we know, with utter clarity and certainty, that God has, in His lovingkindness, sent a messenger from out of nowhere to pull us from the abyss and give us life, we can only proclaim, as did Elisha when Eliyahu ascended in the whirlwind, *Avi, avi, rechev Yisrael u'farashav* (II Melachim 2:12)!

**אבי אבי רכב ישראל ופרשיו!**

*Chol Hamo'ed Sukkos 5779, Hoshanah Om Ani Chomah*